*Economics of Corporation Law
and Securities Regulation*

D1525376

Economics of Corporation Law and Securities Regulation

Richard A. Posner

Lee and Brena Freeman
Professor of Law, University of Chicago

Kenneth E. Scott

Professor of Law, Stanford University

Little, Brown and Company   Boston and Toronto

ALP

Published simultaneously in Canada
by Little, Brown & Company (Canada) Limited

Printed in the United States of America

Fourth Printing

Contents

v

Preface

This book, the sixth in a series of readers* published by Little, Brown, affords supplementary materials for law school courses in corporation law, securities regulation, and corporate reorganization. Like most of the others, it focuses on economic readings. This focus is virtually dictated, in the present instance, by the sheer volume of the relevant economic literature. The literature on corporations and corporation law in economics and finance[†] is very large and growing rapidly, and it would be impossible to give the reader an adequate view of this literature if we were at the same time trying to convey noneconomic perspectives on the subject.

The volume and variety of the literature have persuaded us to modify the format of the previous readers in this series in two ways. First, we have limited our selections to the recent literature. Hence classics such as Berle and Means' The Modern Corporation and Private Property[‡] are omitted. The older standard works are described or excerpted in most of the corporations casebooks, and their views are summarized and analyzed in the modern literature reprinted in our selections. For similar reasons we have omitted the influential noneconomic writings on the economics of corporation and securities law by Cary, Nader, and others; that literature, too, is excerpted in the corporations casebooks or reflected in the selections in this volume.

Second, we have been ruthless in editing down many of the articles selected for inclusion — perhaps our procedure is better described as excerpting than as editing. We have done this not because

---

*The other readers in the series are Economic Foundations of Property Law (Bruce A. Ackerman ed. 1975); Perspectives on Tort Law (Robert L. Rabin ed. 1976); The Economics of Contract Law (Anthony T. Kronman & Richard A. Posner eds. 1979); Perspectives on the Administrative Process (Robert L. Rabin ed. 1979); The Economics of Antitrust Law (Terry Calvani & John Siegfried eds. 1979).

[†]"Finance" is the branch of economics that studies the private financing of economic activity — i.e., the capital markets. Finance has become virtually a separate field, in much the same way that statistics is now a separate field from mathematics.

[‡]Adolf A. Berle, Jr. & Gardiner C. Means, The Modern Corporation and Private Property (1932).

we think the articles are prolix and can be drastically shortened without loss of meaning, but because we thought we could give the reader a better sense of the issues and approaches in the economic literature on corporation law by including many rather than few selections. Likewise, the exigencies of space have led us to eliminate most footnotes, article subheadings, tables of data and authors' acknowledgements of the work or comments of others; such deletions are generally not marked by ellipses. We have also largely, though not entirely, dropped the mathematical expression or derivation of the propositions in many of the articles, in the hope that the basic reasoning will remain both intelligible and accessible to those who find formal mathematics intimidating. Any reader wishing to pursue further an interest in the economics of corporation and securities law will be well advised to read the selections in their original, unedited form, for much that we have edited out for practical or pedagogical reasons is germane to the authors' arguments.

The large number of selections has led us to include at the beginning of each chapter a brief introduction to the selections in that chapter. Read seriatim, these introductions constitute a general introduction to the book and allow us to dispense with a separate introductory chapter. Those desiring such an overall introduction may want to consult Richard A. Posner, Economic Analysis of Law chs. 14–15 (2d ed. 1977).

June 30, 1980

Richard A. Posner
Kenneth E. Scott

*Economics of Corporation Law
and Securities Regulation*

Part I

The Economic Function of the Modern Corporation

Chapter 1

The Theory of the Firm

The subject of this book is the economics of corporation and securities law. But the corporation is simply one type of firm, and the legal regulation of the corporation deals with the characteristics that the corporation shares with other types of firm as well as the characteristics that distinguish it from other types of firm.* It is appropriate therefore to begin our consideration of the economics of corporation law with a glance at the economic theory of the firm.

As explained in the reading in this chapter, which is excerpted from an article by Ronald Coase, the "firm" in economics refers to the coordination of production by fiat within an organization — by the employer telling his employees how much to produce of each component, of what quality, etc. — rather than by contracts among independent contractors specifying the price, quantity, and quality of the inputs into the finished product. (Even assembly — for example of the parts of an automobile — could be a service purchased, like the parts themselves, from independent contractors.) The substitution of firm (fiat, hierarchy, bureaucracy) for contract as the method of organizing production has benefits in reducing transaction costs but it also imposes costs, including loss of information. As we shall see in the next chapter, an important function of the corporate form and of corporation law is to minimize the costs of using the firm to organize production.

A fundamental issue in the economic theory of the firm is the nature, function, and allocation of profit. "Profit" in economics usually refers to the excess, if any, of total revenues over total costs, including the opportunity costs of equity capital (i.e., the return necessary to attract that capital from alternative uses). In contrast, the accountant treats the opportunity costs of equity capital as a part of profit. Profit in economics is thus a surplus over *all* costs, since

*See Richard A. Posner, Economic Analysis of Law 289–292 (2d ed. 1977).

the economist will have included a normal return to the equity owners as a part of those costs. What are the functions of profit in the economic sense? One function is to signal areas of the economy where additional investment is socially desirable. Another is to ration certain scarce goods, such as entrepreneurial skill. When a good is scarce relative to demand, and its supply cannot be readily increased, it will command a price in excess of its cost. The difference between price and cost is known as economic rent and is illustrated by the high prices that land having locational advantages commands or the high wages that opera singers and professional athletes — and superb lawyers — command. If entrepreneurship is one of these inherently scarce and valuable skills, it will command a rent which will be profit to the firm to the extent that the firm is the entrepreneur. Finally, some firms will obtain rents in the form of monopoly profits from creating an artificial scarcity of their product.

The big question in analyzing profit in relation to the firm is the distribution of profit within the firm. Who gets it? The management, on the theory that it corresponds to the entrepreneur of classical economic theory (which treats the firm as if it were an individual)? The shareholders? But why should they receive a return over and above the opportunity costs of the equity capital that they supply to the firm, costs that are *not* part of the economic concept of profit? These questions are addressed in an excerpt from the writings of the late Frank H. Knight, professor of economics at the University of Chicago, which appears in the Notes and Questions at the end of this chapter.

The Nature of the Firm*

Ronald H. Coase

    . . . [I]n economic theory we find that the allocation of factors of production between different uses is determined by the price mechanism. The price of factor A becomes higher in X than in Y. As a result, A moves from Y to X until the difference between the prices in X and Y, except in so far as it compensates for other differential advantages, disappears. Yet in the real world, we find that there are many areas where this does not apply. If a workman moves from department Y to department X, he does not go because of a change

Source: 4 Economica (n.s.) 386–405 (1937), reprinted with permission. Ronald H. Coase is Musser Professor of Economics Emeritus at the University of Chicago Law School.

in relative prices, but because he is ordered to do so. . . . Outside the firm, price movements direct production, which is co-ordinated through a series of exchange transactions on the market. Within a firm, these market transactions are eliminated and in place of the complicated market structure with exchange transactions is substituted the entrepreneur-co-ordinator, who directs production. It is clear that these are alternative methods of co-ordinating production. Yet, having regard to the fact that if production is regulated by price movements, production could be carried on without any organisation at all, well might we ask, why is there any organisation? . . .

. . . The purpose of this paper is to bridge what appears to be a gap in economic theory between the assumption (made for some purposes) that resources are allocated by means of the price mechanism and the assumption (made for other purposes) that this allocation is dependent on the entrepreneur-co-ordinator. We have to explain the basis on which, in practice, this choice between alternatives is effected. . . .

The main reason why it is profitable to establish a firm would seem to be that there is a cost of using the price mechanism. The most obvious cost of "organising" production through the price mechanism is that of discovering what the relevant prices are. This cost may be reduced but it will not be eliminated by the emergence of specialists who will sell this information. The costs of negotiating and concluding a separate contract for each exchange transaction which takes place on a market must also be taken into account. Again, in certain markets, e.g., produce exchanges, a technique is devised for minimising these contract costs; but they are not eliminated. It is true that contracts are not eliminated when there is a firm but they are greatly reduced. A factor of production (or the owner thereof) does not have to make a series of contracts with the factors with whom he is co-operating within the firm, as would be necessary, of course, if this co-operation were as a direct result of the working of the price mechanism. For this series of contracts is substituted one. At this stage, it is important to note the character of the contract into which a factor enters that is employed within a firm. The contract is one whereby the factor, for a certain remuneration (which may be fixed or fluctuating), agrees to obey the directions of an entrepreneur *within certain limits*. The essence of the contract is that it should only state the limits to the powers of the entrepreneur. Within these limits, he can therefore direct the other factors of production.

There are, however, other disadvantages—or costs—of using the price mechanism. It may be desired to make a long-term contract for the supply of some article or service. This may be due to the fact that if one contract is made for a longer period, instead of several shorter ones, then certain costs of making each contract will be avoided. Or, owing to the risk attitude of the people concerned, they may prefer to make a long rather than a short-term contract. Now, owing to the difficulty of forecasting, the longer the period of the contract is for the supply of the commodity or service, the less possible, and indeed, the less desirable it is for the person purchasing to specify what the other contracting party is expected to do. It may well be a matter of indifference to the person supplying the service or commodity which of several courses of action is taken, but not to the purchaser of that service or commodity. But the purchaser will not know which of these several courses he will want the supplier to take. Therefore, the service which is being provided is expressed in general terms, the exact details being left until a later date. All that is stated in the contract is the limits to what the person supplying the commodity or service is expected to do. The details of what the supplier is expected to do is not stated in the contract but is decided later by the purchaser. When the direction of resources (within the limits of the contract) becomes dependent on the buyer in this way, that relationship which I term a "firm" may be obtained. A firm is likely therefore to emerge in those cases where a very short term contract would be unsatisfactory. It is obviously of more importance in the case of services — labour — than it is in the case of the buying of commodities. In the case of commodities, the main items can be stated in advance and the details which will be decided later will be of minor significance. . . .

The question of uncertainty is one which is often considered to be very relevant to the study of the equilibrium of the firm. It seems improbable that a firm would emerge without the existence of uncertainty. But those, for instance, Professor Knight,* who make the *mode of payment* the distinguishing mark of the firm — fixed incomes being guaranteed to some of those engaged in production by a person who takes the residual, and fluctuating, income — would appear to be introducing a point which is irrelevant to the problem we are considering. One entrepreneur may sell his services to another for a certain sum of money, while the payment to his employees may be mainly or wholly a share in profits. The significant question would appear to be why the allocation of resources is not done directly by the price mechanism. . . .

The approach which has just been sketched would appear to offer an advantage in that it is possible to give a scientific meaning to what is meant by saying that a firm gets larger or smaller. A firm

*[See Note 1 in the Notes and Questions at the end of this chapter — Eds.]

becomes larger as additional transactions (which could be exchange transactions co-ordinated through the price mechanism) are organised by the entrepreneur and becomes smaller as he abandons the organisation of such transactions. The question which arises is whether it is possible to study the forces which determine the size of the firm. Why does the entrepreneur not organise one less transaction or one more? . . . Why is not all production carried on by one big firm? There would appear to be certain possible explanations.

First, as a firm gets larger, there may be decreasing returns to the entrepreneur function, that is, the costs of organising additional transactions within the firm may rise. Naturally, a point must be reached where the costs of organising an extra transaction within the firm are equal to the costs involved in carrying out the transaction in the open market, or, to the costs of organising by another entrepreneur. Secondly, it may be that as the transactions which are organised increase, the entrepreneur fails to place the factors of production in the uses where their value is greatest, that is, fails to make the best use of the factors of production. Again, a point must be reached where the loss through the waste of resources is equal to the marketing costs of the exchange transaction in the open market or to the loss if the transaction was organised by another entrepreneur. Finally, the supply price of one or more of the factors of production may rise, because the "other advantages" of a small firm are greater than those of a large firm. Of course, the actual point where the expansion of the firm ceases might be determined by a combination of the factors mentioned above. The first two reasons given most probably correspond to the economists' phrase of "diminishing returns to management." . . .

Other things being equal, therefore, a firm will tend to be larger:
(a) the less the costs of organising and the slower these costs rise with an increase in the transactions organised.
(b) the less likely the entrepreneur is to make mistakes and the smaller the increase in mistakes with an increase in the transactions organised.
(c) the greater the lowering (or the less the rise) in the supply price of factors of production to firms of larger size.

Apart from variations in the supply price of factors of production to firms of different sizes, it would appear that the costs of organising and the losses through mistakes will increase with an increase in the spatial distribution of the transactions organised, in the dissimilarity of the transactions, and in the probability of changes in the relevant prices. As more transactions are organised by an entrepreneur, it would appear that the transactions would tend to be either different in kind or in different places. This furnishes an additional reason why efficiency will tend to decrease as the firm gets larger. Inventions which tend to bring factors of production nearer together, by lessening spatial distribution, tend to increase the size of the firm. Changes like the telephone and the telegraph which tend to reduce the cost of organising spatially will tend to increase the size of the firm. All changes which improve managerial technique will tend to increase the size of the firm. . . .

Only one task now remains; and that is, to see whether the concept of a firm which has been developed fits in with that existing in the real world. We can best approach the question of what constitutes a firm in practice by considering the legal relationship normally called that of "master and servant" or "employer and employee." The essentials of this relationship have been given as follows:

> (1) the servant must be under the duty of rendering personal services to the master or to others on behalf of the master, otherwise the contract is a contract for sale of goods or the like.
>
> (2) The master must have the right to control the servant's work, either personally or by another servant or agent. It is this right of control or interference, of being entitled to tell the servant when to work (within the hours of service) and when not to work, and what work to do and how to do it (within the terms of such service) which is the dominant characteristic in this relation and marks off the servant from an independent contractor, or from one employed merely to give to his employer the fruits of his labour. In the latter case, the contractor or performer is not under the employer's control in doing the work or effecting the service; he has to shape and manage his work so as to give the result he has contracted to effect.

We thus see that it is the fact of direction which is the essence of the legal concept of "employer and employee," just as it was in the economic concept which was developed above. It is interesting to note that Professor Batt says further:

> That which distinguishes an agent from a servant is not the absence or presence of a fixed wage or the payment only of commission on business done, but rather the freedom with which an agent may carry out his employment.

We can therefore conclude that the definition we have given is one which approximates closely to the firm as it is considered in the real world.

NOTES AND QUESTIONS

1. What is the nature of the disagreement between Coase and Knight mentioned in Coase's article?

Frank Knight's theory of profit has been influential. He defined it:

> as what is or would be left ("residual") after deducting wages and/or interest at the "going rates" for the entrepreneur's own services. This is often distinguished as "pure profit."
>
> . . . [Pure profit] would be absent under the conditions of equilibrium with "perfect competition," (which may be defined in more than one way). The "tendency" of the competitive processes of buying and selling and the control of production is to impute the whole product to the productive agencies which create it, leaving nothing for entrepreneurship as a distinct function.*

Knight relates pure profit in his sense to the role of the entrepreneur. The entrepreneur's

> first and primary function, in a progressive society, is that of leadership or economic pioneering; it is to initiate useful changes or innovations. The incentive to new departures is profit in the corresponding sense, just suggested; it is a temporary gain, of the nature of monopoly revenue, beyond the value of resources in other uses, during a period while the innovation is being imitated and is spreading through the economy as standard practice. The innovation itself may have various forms, and usually involves some change in the character of products, combined with some improvement in methods of production—though the function of the entrepreneur must be distinguished from those of the inventor and of the research scientist. It goes without saying that making innovations usually involves substantial cost, and that the innovator himself cannot predict the results in advance, or even be sure that the innovation will not be a failure, and consequently the activity is connected with "risk-taking."
>
> Entrepreneurship also includes two other more or less distinct functions, connected with corresponding meanings of profit. Any established business, especially in a progressive society, is affected by various changes in conditions, some due to innovations or attempted innovations by other entrepreneurs, and some which simply occur in consequence of natural or social processes. Consequently, any business which is to remain successful, or even continue to exist, must be constantly adapting itself to and attempting to "forecast" such changes. Thus, successful adaptation is different from innovations in degree and in detail rather than in principle. Adaptive change is to be added to innovation as a second function of the entrepreneur. In this connection, it is necessary to recognize a distinction between entrepreneurship and management. Here again no clear line can be drawn. But in general, entrepreneurship is the more "dynamic" activity, connected with the major or more important changes, in contrast with management, which is closer to the routine activities which can be classed as "labor."
>
> In the third place and finally, business operations are affected by various contingencies which are inherently unpredictable, of which no

*Frank H. Knight, Profit and Entrepreneurial Functions, 2 J. Econ. Hist. 126 (December 1942), with permission.

one would think of trying to predict, and to which no real adaptation can be made or is attempted. It is necessary simply to take their consequences, for good or ill, as the case may be. The entrepreneur as owner of any enterprise places himself in the position to take the consequences of such changes, (wholly or up to a point) relieving those from whom he hires productive agents of this uncertainty and insecurity. In this regard, the entrepreneur is simply a specialist in risk-taking or uncertainty bearing, apart from any constructive action. But entrepreneurial risks should not include such hazards as damage by fire and storm, or burglary and embezzlement, which can be covered by insurance.*

For discussion and extension of Knight's theory of profit, see Martin Bronfenbrenner, A Reformulation of Naive Profit Theory, 26 S. Econ. J. 300 (1960).

In what circumstances might a competitive firm yield no profit in the economic sense to its owners?

2. Does Coase's article tell the reader when to expect production to be organized through the firm and when through the market?

Another name for the firm is "vertical integration." Vertical integration refers to the situation where a firm produces some input into its final output (the input might be a raw material, or a service such as typing or legal counseling, or some aspect of distribution such as warehousing or even retail outlets) rather than purchasing the input from another firm. The decision to make rather than buy is simply the decision to organize production through firm rather than through contract. The literature on vertical integration is vast. Most of it is oriented to antitrust problems and is hence outside the scope of this book. For an analysis of vertical integration that is indebted to Coase's theory of the firm, see Oliver E. Williamson, Markets and Hierarchies: Analysis and Antitrust Implications (1975), especially Chapters 5–7.

*Id.

Chapter 2

The Economics of the Corporate Firm

The selections in this chapter extend the theory of the firm discussed in the last chapter to the corporation itself. The piece by Armen Alchian and Harold Demsetz provides an appropriate bridge from the last chapter to this one. Their article begins by refining the theory of the firm proposed by Coase, and moves from there to the particular type of firm that is the subject of this book, i.e., the corporation. There is an argument for placing the last two selections in the chapter, by Michael Jensen and William Meckling and by Eugene Fama, right after Alchian and Demsetz's piece rather than at the end of the chapter, because they are further developments of the theory of the firm first announced in Coase's paper and then refined and applied to the corporation in Alchian and Demsetz's. But to run all three papers together in this fashion would obscure the Berle-Means tradition to which the papers may be viewed as a criticism and response. The other three papers are included in the chapter to give the reader a sharper sense of that important tradition.

Adolf A. Berle and Gardiner C. Means, in their famous book The Modern Corporation and Private Property (1932), observed the increasing diffusion of stock ownership and inferred from it that corporate management was becoming less and less subject to the effective control of the corporate shareholders — the nominal owners of the corporation — and more and more free to manage the corporation in the managers' own self-interest. This was the "separation of ownership and control" thesis that has since loomed so large in debates over public policy toward the corporation.*

To evaluate the Berle-Means thesis requires addressing two fun-

*See also the discussion in Carl Kaysen, Another View of Corporate Capitalism, 79 Q.J. Econ. 41 (1965).

damental questions. The first is whether diffusion of stock ownership really leaves managers so autonomous as Berle and Means
thought, given the constraints supplied by competition in both the
corporation's product markets and its capital markets (and perhaps
also, as argued by Fama, in the market for corporate managers). We
cannot in this book consider the degree to which the many markets
in which American corporations sell their products are effectively
competitive; that question is the subject of courses in industrial organization in economics departments and business schools, and of
antitrust courses in law schools. The competitiveness of the capital
markets is, however, an important theme of this book.* Both the
Alchian and Demsetz and the Jensen and Meckling papers consider
how managers are constrained by the capital markets.

The second question that must be answered in evaluating the
Berle-Means thesis, the question which is the focus of the paper by
Oliver E. Williamson, is: what will managers maximize if they have
discretion to pursue their own ends rather than the ends of the shareholders? Perhaps their self-interest will coincide with that of the
shareholders after all; Fama's paper offers one theory of why it might.

The correctness of the Berle-Means thesis is not a question that
need be left solely to the plane of theoretical dispute. It is in principle an empirical question, and as the selections by Louis De Alessi
and Miron Stano indicate, the empirical evidence regarding the thesis is mixed and inconclusive.† Certainly, then, the Berle-Means thesis cannot be regarded as established fact, as lawyers writing on
corporation law perhaps tend to regard it.

Notice when you come to the Jensen and Meckling piece how
they attempt to shift the debate from the normative question of
whether shareholders have too little control over managers to a positive inquiry into the devices by which the market maximizes shareholder welfare. They emphasize that the diffusion of shareholdings
comes about because shareholders dislike risk and are thereby led to
hold diversified portfolios rather than concentrate their wealth in one
or a few corporations. They then note the institutional arrangements
that have arisen to prevent managers from exploiting the diffusion of
shareholdings to transfer wealth from shareholders to themselves.‡

---

*For a witty and concise treatment of the question see also George J. Stigler,
"Imperfections in the Capital Market," in his book The Organization of Industry 113
(1968).
†For another recent contribution to the empirical literature see J.Y. Kamin &
J. Ronen, The Effects of Corporate Control on Apparent Profit Performance, 45 S.
Econ. J. 181 (1978).
‡For similar approaches see Fischer Black, Merton H. Miller & Richard A.
Posner, An Approach to the Regulation of Bank Holding Companies, 51 J. Bus. 379
(1978); Richard A. Posner, Economic Analysis of Law 289-314 (2d ed. 1977).

In a sense, this entire chapter is simply an introduction to Part II of this book, where we examine how corporation law and capital markets protect shareholders from managers. There we examine in detail the workings of the market in corporate control and other devices by which capital-market discipline is brought to bear on managers in an effort to make the firm behave like the profit maximizer of classical economic theory.

Production, Information Costs, and Economic Organization*

Armen A. Alchian and Harold Demsetz

It is common to see the firm characterized by the power to settle issues by fiat, by authority, or by disciplinary action superior to that available in the conventional market. This is delusion. The firm does not own all its inputs. It has no power of fiat, no authority, no disciplinary action any different in the slightest degree from ordinary market contracting between any two people. I can "punish" you only by withholding future business or by seeking redress in the courts for any failure to honor our exchange agreement. That is exactly all that any employer can do. . . . What then is the content of the presumed power to manage and assign workers to various tasks? Exactly the same as one little consumer's power to manage and assign his grocer to various tasks. The single consumer can assign his grocer to the task of obtaining whatever the customer can induce the grocer to provide at a price acceptable to both parties. That is precisely all that an employer can do to an employee. To speak of managing, directing, or assigning workers to various tasks is a deceptive way of noting that the employer continually is involved in renegotiation of contracts on terms that must be acceptable to both parties. Telling an employee to type this letter rather than to file that document is like my telling a grocer to sell me this brand of tuna rather than that brand of bread. I have no contract to continue to purchase from the grocer and neither the employer nor the employee is bound by any contractual obligations to continue their relationship. Long-term contracts between employer and employee are not the essence of the organization we call a firm. . . .

Wherein then is the relationship between a grocer and his em-

*Source: 62 Am. Econ. Rev. 777-795 (1972), reprinted with permission. Armen A. Alchian and Harold Demsetz are professors of economics at the University of California, Los Angeles.

ployee different from that between a grocer and his customers? It is in a *team* use of inputs and a centralized position of some party in the contractual arrangements of *all* other inputs. It is the *centralized contractual agent in a team productive process* — not some superior authoritarian directive or disciplinary power. . . .

I. The Metering Problem

The economic organization through which input owners cooperate will make better use of their comparative advantages to the extent that it facilitates the payment of rewards in accord with productivity. If rewards were random, and without regard to productive effort, no incentive to productive effort would be provided by the organization; and if rewards were negatively correlated with productivity the organization would be subject to sabotage. Two key demands are placed on an economic organization — metering input productivity and metering rewards.

Metering problems sometimes can be resolved well through the exchange of products across competitive markets, because in many situations markets yield a high correlation between rewards and productivity. If a farmer increases his output of wheat by 10 percent at the prevailing market price, his receipts also increase by 10 percent. This method of organizing economic activity meters the *output directly*, reveals the marginal product and apportions the *rewards* to resource owners in accord with that direct measurement of their outputs. The success of this decentralized, market exchange in promoting productive specialization requires that changes in market rewards fall on those responsible for changes in *output.*

The classic relationship in economics that runs from marginal productivity to the distribution of income implicitly *assumes* the existence of an organization, be it the market or the firm, that allocates rewards to resources in accord with their productivity. The problem of economic organization, the economical means of metering productivity and rewards, is not confronted directly in the classical analysis of production and distribution. Instead, that analysis tends to assume sufficiently economic — or zero cost — means, as if productivity automatically created its reward. We conjecture the direction of causation is the reverse — the specific system of rewarding which is relied upon stimulates a particular productivity response. If the economic organization meters poorly, with rewards and productivity only loosely correlated, then productivity will be smaller; but if the economic organization meters well productivity will be greater. What makes metering difficult and hence induces means of economizing on metering costs?

II. Team Production

Two men jointly lift heavy cargo into trucks. Solely by observing the total weight loaded per day, it is impossible to determine each person's marginal productivity. With team production it is difficult, solely by observing total output, to either define or determine *each* individual's contribution to this output of the cooperating inputs. The output is yielded by a team, by definition, and it is not a *sum* of separable outputs of each of its members. . . .

How can the members of a team be rewarded and induced to work efficiently? In team production, marginal products of cooperative team members are not so directly and separably (i.e., cheaply) observable. What a team offers to the market can be taken as the marginal product of the team but not of the team members. The costs of metering or ascertaining the marginal products of the team's members is what calls forth new organizations and procedures. Clues to each input's productivity can be secured by observing *behavior* of individual inputs. When lifting cargo into the truck, how rapidly does a man move to the next piece to be loaded, how many cigarette breaks does he take, does the item being lifted tilt downward toward his side?

If detecting such behavior were costless, neither party would have an incentive to shirk, because neither could impose the cost of his shirking on the other (if their cooperation was agreed to voluntarily). But since costs must be incurred to monitor each other, each input owner will have more incentive to shirk when he works as part of a team, than if his performance could be monitored easily or if he did not work as a team. If there is a net increase in productivity available by team production, net of the metering cost associated with disciplining the team, then team production will be relied upon rather than a multitude of bilateral exchange of separable individual outputs. . . .

What forms of organizing team production will lower the cost of detecting "performance" (i.e., marginal productivity) and bring personally realized rates of substitution closer to true rates of substitution? Market competition, in principle, could monitor some team production. (It already *organizes* teams.) Input owners who are not team members can offer, in return for a smaller share of the team's rewards, to replace excessively (i.e., overpaid) shirking members. Market competition among potential team members would determine team membership and individual rewards. There would be no team leader, manager, organizer, owner, or employer. For such decentralized organizational control to work, outsiders, possibly after observing each team's total output, can speculate about their capabilities as team members and, by a market competitive process, revised teams with greater productive ability will be formed and sustained. Incumbent members will be constrained by threats of replacement by outsiders offering services for lower reward shares or offering greater rewards to the other members of the team. Any team member who shirked in the expectation that the reduced output effect would not be attributed to him will be displaced if his activity is detected. Teams of productive inputs, like business units, would evolve in apparent spontaneity in the market — without any central organizing agent, team manager, or boss.

But completely effective control cannot be expected from individualized market competition for two reasons. First, for this competition to be completely effective, new challengers for team membership must know where, and to what extent, shirking is a serious problem, i.e., know they can increase net output as compared with the inputs they replace. To the extent that this is true it is probably possible for existing fellow team members to recognize the shirking. But, by definition, the detection of shirking by observing team output is costly for team production. Secondly, assume the presence of detection costs, and assume that in order to secure a place on the team a new input owner must accept a smaller share of rewards (or a promise to produce more). Then his incentive to shirk would still be at least as great as the incentives of the inputs replaced, because he still bears less than the entire reduction in team output for which he is responsible.

III. The Classical Firm

One method of reducing shirking is for someone to specialize as a monitor to check the input performance of team members. But who will monitor the monitor? One constraint on the monitor is the aforesaid market competition offered by other monitors, but for reasons already given, that is not perfectly effective. Another constraint can be imposed on the monitor: give him title to the net earnings of the team, net of payments to other inputs. If owners of cooperating inputs agree with the monitor that he is to receive any residual product above prescribed amounts (hopefully, the marginal value products of the other inputs), the monitor will have an added incentive not to shirk as a monitor. Specialization in monitoring plus reliance on a residual claimant status will reduce shirking; but additional links are needed to forge the firm of classical economic theory. How will the residual claimant monitor the other inputs?

We use the term monitor to connote several activities in addition to its disciplinary connotation. It connotes measuring output performance, apportioning rewards, observing the input behavior of inputs as means of detecting or estimating their marginal productivity and giving assignments or instructions in what to do and how to do it. (It also includes, as we shall show later, authority to terminate or revise contracts.) . . . All these tasks are, in principle, negotiable across markets, but we are presuming that such market measurement of marginal productivities and job reassignments are not so cheaply performed for team production. And in particular our analysis suggests that it is not so much the costs of spontaneously negotiating contracts in the markets among groups for team production as it is the detection of the performance of individual members of the team that calls for the organization noted here.

The specialist *who receives the residual rewards* will be the monitor of the members of the team (i.e., will manage the use of cooperative inputs). The monitor earns his residual through the reduction in shirking that he brings about, not only by the prices that he agrees to pay the owners of the inputs, but also by observing and directing the actions or uses of these inputs. *Managing or examining the ways to which inputs are used in team production is a method of metering the marginal productivity of individual inputs to the team's output.*

To discipline team members and reduce shirking, the residual claimant must have power to revise the contract terms and incentives of *individual* members without having to terminate or alter every other input's contract. Hence, team members who seek to increase their productivity will assign to the monitor not only the residual claimant right but also the right to alter individual membership and performance on the team. Each team member, of course, can terminate his own membership (i.e., quit the team), but only the monitor may unilaterally terminate the membership of any of the other members without necessarily terminating the team itself or his association with the team; and he alone can expand or reduce membership, alter the mix of membership, or sell the right to be the residual claimant-monitor of the team. It is this entire bundle of rights: 1) to be a residual claimant; 2) to observe input behavior; 3) to be the central party common to all contracts with inputs; 4) to alter the membership of the team; and 5) to sell these rights, that defines the *ownership* (or the employer) of the *classical* (capitalist, free-enterprise) firm. The coalescing of these rights has arisen, our analysis asserts, because it resolves the shirking-information problem of team production better than does the noncentralized contractual arrangement.

The relationship of each team member to the *owner* of the firm (i.e., the party common to all input contracts *and* the residual claimant) is simply a "quid pro quo" contract. Each makes a purchase and sale. The employee "orders" the owner of the team to pay him money in the same sense that the employer directs the team member to perform certain acts. The employee can terminate the contract as readily as can the employer, and long-term contracts, therefore, are not an essential attribute of the firm. Nor are "authoritarian," "dictational," or "fiat" attributes relevant to the conception of the firm or its efficiency. . . . .

The Corporation

All firms must initially acquire command over some resources. The corporation does so primarily by selling promises of future returns to those who (as creditors or owners) provide financial capital. In some situations resources can be acquired in advance from consumers by promises of future delivery (for example, advance sale of a proposed book). Or where the firm is a few artistic or professional persons, each can "chip in" with time and talent until the sale of services brings in revenues. For the most part, capital can be acquired more cheaply if many (risk-averse) investors contribute small portions to a large investment. The economies of raising large sums of equity capital in this way suggest that modifications in the relationship among corporate inputs are required to cope with the shirking problem that arises with profit sharing among large numbers of corporate stockholders. One modification is limited liability, especially for firms that are large relative to a stockholder's wealth. It serves to protect stockholders from large losses no matter how they are caused.

If every stock owner participated in each decision in a corporation, not only would large bureaucratic costs be incurred, but many would shirk the task of becoming well informed on the issue to be decided, since the losses associated with unexpectedly bad decisions will be borne in large part by the many other corporate shareholders. More effective control of corporate activity is achieved for most purposes by transferring decision authority to a smaller group, whose main function is to negotiate with and manage (renegotiate with) the other inputs of the team. The corporate stockholders retain the authority to revise the membership of the management group and over major decisions that affect the structure of the corporation or its dissolution.

As a result a new modification of partnerships is induced — the right to sale of corporate shares without approval of any other stockholders. Any shareholder can remove his wealth from control by those with whom he has differences of opinion. Rather than try to control the decisions of the management, which is harder to do with many stockholders than with only a few, unrestricted salability provides a more acceptable escape to each stockholder from continued policies with which he disagrees.

Indeed, the policing of managerial shirking relies on across-market competition from new groups of would-be managers as well as competition from members within the firm who seek to displace existing management. In addition to competition from outside and inside managers, control is facilitated by the temporary congealing of share votes into voting blocs owned by one or a few contenders. Proxy battles or stock-purchases concentrate the votes required to displace the existing management or modify managerial policies. But it is more than a change in policy that is sought by the newly formed financial interests, whether of new stockholders or not. It is the capitalization of expected future benefits into stock prices that concentrates on the innovators the wealth gains of their actions if they own large numbers of shares. Without capitalization of future benefits, there would be less incentive to incur the costs required to exert informed decisive influence on the corporation's policies and managing personnel. Temporarily, the structure of ownership is reformed, moving away from diffused ownership into decisive power blocs, and this is a transient resurgence of the classical firm with power again concentrated in those who have title to the residual. . . . [14]

14. Instead of thinking of shareholders as joint *owners*, we can think of them as investors, like bondholders, except that the stockholders are more optimistic than bondholders about the enterprise prospects. Instead of buying bonds in the corporation, thus enjoying smaller risks, shareholders prefer to invest funds with a greater realizable return if the firm prospers as expected, but with smaller (possibly negative) returns if the firm performs in a manner closer to that expected by the more pessimistic investors. The pessimistic investors, in turn, regard only the bonds as likely to pay off.

If the entrepreneur-organizer is to raise capital on the best terms to him, it is to his advantage, as well as that of prospective investors, to recognize these differences in expectations. The residual claim on earnings enjoyed by shareholders does not serve the function of enhancing their efficiency as monitors in the general situation. The stockholders are "merely" the less risk-averse or the more optimistic member of the group that finances the firm. Being more optimistic than the average and seeing a higher mean value future return, they are willing to pay more for a certificate that allows them to realize gain on their expectations. One method of doing so is to buy claims to the distribution of returns that "they see" while bondholders, who are more pessimistic, purchase a claim to the distribution that they see as more likely to emerge. Stockholders are then comparable to warrant holders. They care not about the voting rights (usually not attached to warrants); they are in the same position in so far as voting rights are concerned as are bondholders. The only difference is in the probability distribution of rewards and the terms on which they can place their bets.

If we treat bondholders, preferred and convertible preferred stockholders, and common stockholders and warrant holders as simply different classes of investors—differing not only in their risk averseness but in their beliefs about the probability distribution of the firm's future earnings, why should stockholders be regarded as

VII. Firms as a Specialized Market Institution for Collecting, Collating, and Selling Input Information

The firm serves as a highly specialized surrogate market. Any person contemplating a joint-input activity must search and detect the qualities of available joint inputs. He could contact an employment agency, but that agency in a small town would have little advantage over a large firm with many inputs. The employer, by virtue of monitoring many inputs, acquires special superior information about their productive talents. This aids his *directive* (i.e., market hiring) efficiency. He "sells" his information to employee-inputs as he aids them in ascertaining good input combinations for team activity. Those who work as employees or who rent services to him are using him to discern superior combinations of inputs. Not only does the director-employer "decide" what each input will produce, he also estimates which heterogeneous inputs will work together jointly more efficiently, and he does this in the context of a privately owned market for forming teams. The department store is a firm and is a superior private market. People who shop and work in one town can as well shop and work in a privately owned firm.

This marketing function is obscured in the theoretical literature by the assumption of homogeneous factors. Or it is tacitly left for individuals to do themselves via personal market search, much as if a person had to search without benefit of specialist retailers. Whether or not the firm arose because of this efficient information service, it gives the director-employer more knowledge about the productive talents of the team's inputs, and a basis for superior decisions about efficient or profitable combinations of those heterogeneous resources.

In other words, opportunities for profitable team production by inputs already within the firm may be ascertained more economically and accurately than for resources outside the firm. Superior combinations of inputs can be more economically identified and formed from resources already used in the organization than by obtaining new resources (and knowledge of them) from the outside. Promotion and revision of employee assignments (contracts) will be preferred by a firm to the hiring of new inputs. To the extent that

---

"owners" in any sense distinct from the other financial investors? The entrepreneur-organizer, who let us assume is the chief operating officer and sole repository of control of the corporation, does not find his authority residing in common stockholders (except in the case of a take over). Does this type of control make any difference in the way the firm is conducted? Would it make any difference in the kinds of behavior that would be tolerated by competing managers and investors (and we here deliberately refrain from thinking of them as owner-stockholders in the traditional sense)?

this occurs there is reason to expect the firm to be able to operate as a conglomerate rather than persist in producing a single product. Efficient production with heterogeneous resources is a result not of having *better* resources but in *knowing more accurately* the relative productive performances of those resources. Poorer resources can be paid less in accord with their inferiority; greater accuracy of knowledge of the potential and actual productive actions of inputs rather than having high productivity resources makes a firm (or an assignment of inputs) profitable.

Managerial Discretion and Business Behavior*

Oliver E. Williamson

. . . The essential notion that we propose in order to connect motives with behavior is that of *expense preference*. That is, the management does not have a neutral attitude towards costs. Directly or indirectly, certain classes of expenditure have positive values associated with them. In particular, staff, expense, expenditures for emoluments, and funds available for discretionary investment have value additional to that which derives from their productivity.

Expansion of staff is an activity that offers positive rewards, the benefits of which can be enjoyed quite generally. Indeed, since promotional opportunities within a fixed-size firm are limited, while increased jurisdiction has the same general effect as promotion but simultaneously produces the chance of advance for all, the incentive to expand staff may be difficult to resist. Not only is it an indirect means to the attainment of salary, but it is a source of security, power, status, prestige, and professional achievement as well.[4]

*Source: 53 Am. Econ. Rev. 1032-1057 (1963), reprinted with permission. Oliver E. Williamson is Day Professor of Economics and Social Science at the University of Pennsylvania.

4. As has been observed among organization theorists, "the modern organization is a prolific generator of anxiety and insecurity." This insecurity is partly due to uncertainty with respect to the survival of the organization as a whole and, more important (and more immediately relevant to its individual members), of the parts with which the individuals identify. Attempts to reduce this condition can be expected; indeed, the direction these efforts will take can be anticipated. If the surest guarantee of the survival of the individual parts appear to be size, efforts to expand the separate staff functions can safely be predicted.

That staff contributes to power, status, and prestige should be self-evident. This is true within the organization as well as in the manager's business and social relationships outside the firm. The vast influence that executives in large industrial organizations enjoy arises much more from the perceived control over resources that they possess than from the personal wealth which they have attained.

The "professional" inducement to expand staff arises from the typical view that a progressive staff is one that is continuously providing more and better service. An

We use the term "emoluments" in a somewhat special sense. They refer to that fraction of managerial salaries and perquisites that are discretionary. That is, emoluments represent rewards which, if removed, would not cause the managers to seek other employment. They are economic rents and have associated with them zero productivities. Thus they are not a return to entrepreneurial capacity but rather result from the strategic advantage that the management possesses in the distribution of the returns to monopoly power. Being a source of material satisfaction and an indirect source of status and prestige, they are desirable as a means for satisfying goals in each of these respects.

The management would normally prefer to take these emoluments as salary rather than as perquisites of office since, taken as salary, there are no restrictions on the way in which they are spent, while, if withdrawn as corporate personal consumption (such as expense accounts, executive services, office suites, etc.), there are specific limitations on the ways these can be enjoyed. However, there are two considerations that make perquisites attractive. First, for tax purposes it may be advantageous to withdraw some part of discretionary funds as perquisites rather than salary. Second, perquisites are much less visible rewards to the management than salary and hence are less likely to provoke stockholder or labor dissatisfaction. Hence a division of emoluments between salary and perquisites is to be expected. . . .

The existence of satisfactory profits is necessary to assure the interference-free operation of the firm to the management. Precisely what this level will be involves a complicated interaction of the relative performance of rivals, the historical performance of the firm, and special current conditions that affect the firm's performance. Management, however, will find it desirable to earn profits that exceed the acceptable level. For one thing, managers derive satisfaction from self-fulfillment and organizational achievement, and profits are one measure of this success. In addition, profits are a source of discretion (indeed, we define "discretionary profits" as the difference between actual profits and minimum profits demanded). Discretionary profits represent a source of funds whose allocation may be importantly determined by managerial, in addition to economic,

---

aggressive staff will therefore be looking for ways to expand. Although in choosing directions for expansion the relative contribution to productivity will be considered, the absolute effect on profits may be neglected. As long as the organization is able to satisfy its performance requirements, there is a predisposition to extend programs beyond the point where marginal costs equal marginal benefits. The incentive to increase staff, having both natural and legitimate elements, is exceptionally difficult to resist.

considerations. As with the expansion of staff, the expansion of physical plant and equipment provides general opportunities for managerial satisfaction and for much the same reasons. . . .

. . . Thus, the utility-maximizing theory is based on the proposition that opportunities for discretion and managerial tastes will have a decided impact on the expenditures of the firm. More precisely, those expenditures that promote managerial satisfactions should show a positive correlation with opportunities for discretion and tastes. The profit-maximizing theory is somewhat ambiguous on this question. Interpreted as a theory which attends entirely to the stockholders' best interests, it clearly implies that expenditures which, under the utility-maximizing hypohtesis, will be positively correlated with measures of discretion and tastes, will instead be uncorrelated with these relationships. Interpreted somewhat more loosely, closer agreement with the utility-maximizing hypothesis can be obtained. Thus, it is possible that the management first selects that physical combination of factors that maximizes profits and then absorbs some amount of actual profits as cost. These absorptions may be correlated with the same measures of discretion and taste as would be expected under the utility-maximizing theory. Hence, evidence that managers respond to opportunities for discretion is not inconsistent with the profit-maximizing theory, but neither is evidence to the contrary; the theory is simply silent on this question. However, the failure of firms to respond to opportunities for discretion constitutes a contradiction of the utility-maximizing hypothesis, while observations that firms do display expense-preference behavior supports it.

The executive compensation and retained-earnings analyses reported in Section A are designed to test for the effects of discretion and taste in management expenditure decisions. The summary of the field studies in Section B is concerned with the question of physical magnitudes of adjustment to adversity and provides some indication of what criteria are involved in making expense adjustments as well as what effects a lump-sum tax has on business behavior.

A. Principal-Firm Analysis

If the firm is operated so as to attend to managerial interests, then the classes of expenditures for which expense preference was indicated should be expanded beyond the levels called for by strictly profit considerations. The amount by which such expansions occur should be positively related to the opportunity for discretion and the tastes of the management. . . .

Since it is in the large corporation that manifestations of discretionary behavior are alleged to be important, and as complete data are most readily available among larger industrial firms than their smaller counterparts, the tests are restricted to those firms that clearly qualified as "principal firms." Among the 26 industries included in the analysis, selection was limited to the two largest firms, ranked according to sales, in each. The tests performed are cross-section tests for the years 1953, 1957, and 1961.

1. *Executive Compensation.* George Stigler has observed that the estimation of the effect of monopoly on profit may be complicated by the absorption of some fraction of "true" monopoly profit as cost. In particular, "the magnitude of monopoly elements in wages, executive compensation, royalties, and rents is possibly quite large." Our interest here is limited to testing only a part of this hypothesis. Specifically, we examine the effect of discretion on compensating the top executive.

Focusing on a single representative of management might appear to restrict severely the relevance of our results. If the compensation of the rest of the management group were determined independently of that of the chief executive, this would certainly be the case. However, payments between executive levels are carefully scaled. . . . Hence, the factors that influence compensation to the top executive can be presumed to affect the level of staff compensation generally. . . .

. . . The concentration ratio* reflects the influence of realized interdependencies between rivals. Where concentration ratios are high, interdependencies will generally be intimate, and behavior between rivals will at least be circumspect and may involve explicit agreements. In either case, the influence of competition will be consciously controlled. Hence, an increase in the concentration ratio will tend to widen the opportunities for managerial discretion. Obviously, this measure is defective and there will be exceptions. However, we are content merely to account for average rather than exceptional behavior.

The barrier to entry measure . . . is explicitly designed to estimate the extent to which firms are insulated from the effects of competition. Although concentration and entry conditions are correlated, they are by no means identical. In combination they provide a particularly good measure of the opportunities for discretion. High concentration together with a high barrier to entry will tend to produce substantial discretion, for not only is potential competition lim-

---

*[A concentration ratio is the extent to which a market is dominated by a few large firms — Eds.]

ited, but existing rivals are few enough to appreciate their conditions of interdependence. Low values for each of these measures will tend to produce the reverse effect, while mixed values, presumably, give rise to mixed effects. . . .

A sharp measure of managerial tastes . . . is not available. However, the composition of the board may act as a proxy measure of the extent to which management desires to operate the firm free from outside interference. Although low proportional representation of the managment on the board of directors need not reflect a "taste" for active outside participation in the affairs of the firm, clearly a high internal representation does reflect the intent of the management to conduct the affaris of the firm free from such outside influence. We hypothesize that, as the management representation on the board increases, there tends to be a subordination of stockholder for managerial interests. In this sense, the composition of the board reflects management's attitude toward discretionary resource allocations and a voluntary change in composition reflects a change in these "tastes."

An estimate of stockholder diffusion . . . was not obtained. Such a measure would probably be correlated with the composition of the board variable. However the association may not be great. Where substantial concentration of ownership exists, there is frequently a tendency towards nepotism. This in turn may produce high internal representation rather than the high outside representation that would otherwise be predicted. . . .

The signs for each of the parameters in all three years are as predicted by the expense-preference hypothesis [Table 1]*. Moreover, with the exception of the composition of the board coefficient, which is significant at the 10 percent level only in 1957, all of the regression coefficients are highly significant — two-thirds being significant at the 2.5 per cent level. Whereas the relation of executive compensation to general administrative and selling expense (i.e., "staff") is almost certain to be positive and significant, there is no reason to believe that the measures of taste and discretion that we introduce should have the effects shown (unless one endorses the view that management responds to opportunities for discretion in the ways indicated). Since the compensation of the chief executive generalizes to the entire staff structure, these results have broad significance for the resource-allocation process within the business firm. Furthermore, we would expect that these same measures of discretion would produce similar effects over the entire range of expenditures on emoluments.

*[For an explanation of regression analysis, which Williamson uses to test the hypothesized relationships, see note 4 in the Notes and Questions at the end of this chapter — Eds.]

Table 1

**Regression of Executive Compensation on "Staff,"
Concentration Ratio, Composition of the Board,
and Barriers to Entry**

	Year		
	1953	1957	1961
"Staff"			
Coeff.	.228[a]	.240[a]	.218[a]
S.E.[c]	.061	.052	.054
Partial	(.564)	(.610)	(.614)
Concentration			
Coeff.	.503[a]	.513[a]	.423[b]
S.E.	.157	.143	.152
Partial	(.517)	(.517)	(.470)
Composition			
Coeff.	.137	.139	.053
S.E.	.118	.101	.120
Partial	(.213)	(.224)	(.084)
Entry Barriers			
Coeff.	.446[a]	.221[b]	.200
S.E.	.110	.114	.126
Partial	(.606)	(.307)	(.290)
Coeff. of Correl.			
(adjusted)	.786	.724	.687

[a]Significant at the 0.1 per cent level
[b]Significant at the 2.5 per cent level
[c][S.E. refers to standard error—Eds.]
Source: Williamson, Table 4.

Of course it could be argued that the concentration ratio and
entry-barrier variables have positive regression coefficients because
they are correlated with the profit rate—that this profitability effect
is responsible for the results obtained. But obviously the causality
runs from concentration and entry barriers to profits rather than the
reverse. Thus, by focusing on the market structure, the model directs attention to the ultimate determinants of discretionary behavior
(competition in the product market) rather than the apparent determinant (the profit rate). Although these market variables might not
perform as well as the profit rate among the smaller firms in the
industry, it does not seem inappropriate to use them for studying
the behavior of the two largest firms where the relationship between
market structure and behavior is probably reasonably direct. Indeed,
it is of interest to note that: (1) if the profit rate on the stockholders
equity is substituted for the concentration ratio and entry-barrier
variables, the coefficient of determination (R^2) falls to two-thirds of

the value obtained using these market variables in 1953 and 1961, and yields less than a ten per cent increase in R^2 in 1957; (2) if the profit rate, concentration ratio, and entry-barrier variables are all included, the profit rate is significant only in 1957 and has the wrong sign in 1961, while the concentration ratio and entry-barrier variables remain significant at the ten per cent level or better in every year. . . .

Some feeling for the responsiveness of salary to the independent variables in the regression equation can be obtained by taking the median of the estimates for each parameter and finding the effect on salary of increasing each individual independent variable by a factor of two. In some gross sense we can expect that executive salaries will possibly increase on the order of 17 per cent if the level of staff activity were to double, on the order of 41 per cent if the concentration ratio in the industry were to double, on the order of 10 per cent if the internal representation on the board were to double, and on the order of 25 per cent if the industry of which the firm was a part had a substantial or high barrier to entry rather than a low one. Thus, not only are the signs as predicted by the theory, but the magnitudes are sufficiently large to render somewhat doubtful the contention that discretionary effects are unimportant.

2. *Earnings Retention.* The composition of the board variable was used in the executive compensation model to reflect the "tastes" of the management for discretion. Internal representation on the board acts as a proxy for the attitude of the management towards outside influence. As the proportional representation of management on the board increases, it is assumed that stockholder interests tend to be subordinated to managerial objectives. This was manifested in the executive compensation regression by the positive regression coefficient associated with the composition of board variable.

A second test for this effect is to examine the relationship between composition of the board and earnings-retention policy. Consistency with our model requires that the earnings-retention ratio be directly related to the composition of the board. This follows since retained earnings are a source of discretion and a high internal representation provides the opportunity for management to shift the dividend policy to its advantage.

Alternative theories of the firm that regard managerial objectives as unimportant implicitly predict that there will be no association between the composition of the board and retention policy. Thus, our hypothesis of a direct association is tested against the null hypothesis of no association.

Earnings retention will, of course, be responsive to a number of considerations other than that of the composition of the board. Most important, investment opportunities will differ between industries and these could easily be overriding. If it can be assumed that the firms in the same industry have identical opportunities, however, these effects can be neutralized.

A paired-comparison technique was used to neutralize the industry effects. That is, between the two principal firms in each of the 26 industries we compare the composition of the board and earnings-retention ratio. The random variable can take on either of two values: 1 if the higher internal representation is paired with the higher earnings-retention ratio, and 0 otherwise. Hence it is distributed as a binomial. Under the hypothesis that no association exists, the expected number of times the positive association will occur, divided by the total number of observations, is one-half. Thus the null hypothesis is that the binomial parameter p is .50. Our model, however, predicts that the positive association will occur more than one-half of the time — i.e., that p exceeds .50.

The results for each of the three years as well as the pooled results for all three years are shown in Table [2]. The proposition that internal representation has no effect on the earnings-retention policy between pairs of firms in the same industry is unsupported by the data. In every year the proportion of positive observations exceeds .50. In 1953 and 1957 the probability that a value as high as that observed if the null hypothesis were true is .34 and .13 respectively, and in 1961 this drops to .02. Clearly we are inclined to reject the hypothesis in favor of the alternative suggested. That is, due to the discretion associated with the retention of earnings and the opportunity to influence the retention policy which arises from repre-

Table 2
Binomial Test for Association Between Composition of Board and Earnings Retention Policy

	1953	1957	1961	All Years
Number of observations	25	26	26	77
Expected number of positive occurrences under the null hypothesis	12.5 ($p = .50$)	13 ($p = .50$)	13 ($p = .50$)	38.5 ($p = .50$)
Actual number of positive occurrences	13.5 ($p = .54$)	16 ($p = .62$)	18 ($p = .69$)	47.5 ($p = .62$)
Probability that a value as high as observed would occur if the null hypothesis were true	.34	.13	.02	.02

Source: Williamson, Table 5.

sentation on the board, the relation that we suggested (namely, that between pairs of firms in the same industry, the higher the internal representation, the higher the earnings retention rate) is supported by the data. Although it is possible that the composition of the board is acting only as an intervening variable and that the real explanation for this association lies elsewhere, no simple connection suggests itself.

The strongest evidence in favor of our hypothesis is provided by the pooled results for all three years. Here the observed number of positive occurrences would appear by chance under the null hypothesis with a probability of only two times in a hundred. Before the pooling of the observations can be justified, however, it is first necessary to establish that the observations are independent and that the association observed in one period is simply not carried over to the following period. Since the composition of the board and earnings-retention decisions reflect policy considerations that exhibit continuation in consecutive years, lack of independence between consecutive years would be expected. On the other hand, our observations are separated by a period of four years. The association between consecutive years may well be eliminated over this interval. Since the issue can scarcely be resolved on a priori grounds, we submit the hypothesis that the observations are independent to test.

A chi-square test for association was used. A low value of χ is consistent with the hypothesis that the observations between successive four-year intervals are independent. The value of χ^2 between 1953 and 1957 is .0065, and between 1957 and 1961 is .62. Sampling randomly from independent populations, values as high or higher than this would occur 95 per cent and 45 per cent of the time respectively. Hence the hypothesis of independence is supported, the pooling of the observations is justified, and the best test for the composition of the board effect is that of all three years combined. Here the possibility that the positive association observed has occurred by chance is only .02. Indeed, among pairs of principal firms we can expect that the firm with the higher internal representation on the board of directors will have a higher earnings-retention ratio about three-fifths of the time. . . .

A tenuous connection between the composition of the board and the investment policy of the firm can be obtained by noting the results obtained by Gordon and Scott in their recent studies of investment financing. Gordon remarks that "The really surprising result is produced by return on investment. . . . In both industries there is a statistically significant tendency for the retention rate to fall as the corporation's rate of return increases. We must conclude that either [our estimate] is a poor measure of rate of return on investment or that corporations are not primarily influenced by the price of their stock in setting dividend rates." And Scott, in a somewhat more broadly based study of dividend policy, observes that the "negative correlation of −.30 between undistributed profits . . . and the subsequent growth of earnings . . . is somewhat surprising. It suggests that stockholders . . . might benefit from more generous dividend distributions." For a theory that makes the firm's objectives identical with those of the stockholders, such a result is somewhat disquieting. For an approach such as ours, however, which allows for the subordination of stockholder to managerial objectives, a possible explanation for these results based on the composition of the board analysis can be easily provided.

As was suggested above, high internal representation on the board of directors favors attention to managerial objectives, and this is manifested in a high earnings-retention rate. The funds thus provided are available to the management for the pursuit of expansionary objectives, and the resulting investment, being based on a combination of profit and expansionary goals, will exceed the amount dictated by profit considerations alone. As a result, the average rate of return in firms whose management is inclined to subordinate stockholder objectives can be expected to fall below that in firms where management interests are more nearly those of the stockholders. Thus the tastes of the management, as revealed originally in the composition of the board, make their influence felt through the earnings-retention policy and thence on the return on investment. Where these tastes favor expansion, there is an adverse effect on the rate of return on investment. This indirect implication of our theory is precisely the result that Gordon and Scott report. Although conjectural, it suggests the value of including a "taste" variable, of which the composition of the board is a somewhat imperfect proxy, in future studies of the investment decision.

B. The Evidence from the Field Studies . . .

1. In the face of a sharp drop in profitability, hierarchical expenses typically undergo extensive curtailment. One firm, after a long period of operating in a seller's market, responded to a sharp fall in profits with the following adjustments: (a) salaried employment over the entire organization was reduced by 32 per cent; (b) headquarters employment was reduced by 41 per cent; (c) the research and development staff was reduced from 165 personnel to 52 and much of its work was redirected to commercial R and D organizations; (d) the personnel and public relations staff was stream-

lined from 57 to 7; (e) a general reduction in emoluments of all kinds was realized. All this occurred with production unchanged. Return on investment over the interval was increased from the 4 per cent level to which it had fallen to 9 per cent. Further cutbacks in some areas are expected; additions are contingent on changes in volume and are tied to a new set of long-range plans.

Both the type and magnitude of these reductions suggest that the managers were operating the firm so as to attend to other than merely profitability goals in the period preceding the earnings decline. Invoking the notions of expense preference and discretionary spending makes it possible to provide an uncomplicated explanation for the adjustments observed.

2. The philosophy of management in instituting cutbacks is of particular interest. The chief budgeting officer in one organization made this observation:

> In any large organization, certain plants or departments will have found ways to habitually operate more efficiently than others. This may be due to *competitive pressure* which has historically been felt in some products to a greater extent than others. It may be due to differences in *individual management philosophy*. . . . It follows . . . that any approach toward an arbitrary management dictate for an across-the-board slash in all cost areas will inevitably damage necessary functions in some areas, and leave remaining inefficiencies in others.

As a result, cost reductions were tailored to the individual divisions — taking their competitive history and management philosophies into account. Whereas such behavior is consistent with the managerial model, it is less clear that it should occur in a profit-maximizing organization.

Private Property and Dispersion of Ownership in Large Corporations*

Louis De Alessi

Berle and Means long ago noted the increasing diffusion of ownership in large American corporations and concluded that control was shifting from the stockholders to the managers. Since then, the Berle-Means (B-M) thesis has been the subject of continuous and heated controversy both within and without the profession, and has provided a major rationale for the introduction and expansion of

*Source: 28 J. Fin. 839–851 (1973), with permission. Louis De Alessi is professor of economics at the Law and Economics Center, University of Miami School of Law.

government regulation of security transactions. It is therefore astonishing that, almost forty years after the publication of The Modern Corporation and Private Property, the empirical evidence produced on either side of the issue has been negligible. Until recently, the B-M thesis rested entirely on faith and on data reflecting increased diffusion of share ownership, with no empirical evidence regarding the validity of the consequences alleged to follow from such diffusion. This failure to pursue more rigorous testing seems due, at least in part, to a misunderstanding of the meaning and role of private property in decision-making. . . .

The B-M thesis asserts that the growing diffusion of ownership in the large, modern corporation increasingly vests control in the managers. Control, defined by B-M as " . . . direction over the activities of a corporation . . . " and identified for empirical purposes with " . . . the actual power to select the board of directors (or its majority) . . . ", presumably devolves to the managers of the diffused corporation via the proxy mechanism. Postponing some possible difficulties with the identification of the hypotheses at issue, consider the evidence provided by B-M.

B-M classified 200 of the largest U.S. corporations into five groups according to the highest percentage of voting stock held by a single economic unit, be it an individual, a family, or a group of business associates. The firms in the highest (80 per cent and above) percentage category were defined as "privately owned" and those in the lowest (somewhere just above 5 per cent and below) as "management controlled." The shift from minority to management control was considered to occur at about the 20 percentage level. B-M, and most subsequent writers on the subject, interpreted the observation that as many as 44 per cent of the firms in the sample fell into the management-controlled category as supporting the B-M thesis. . . .

. . . Larner attempted " . . . to measure systematically the extent to which management control actually exists among the 200 largest nonfinancial corporations in the first half of the 1960's." His evidence again related solely to the distribution of shares among stockholders. Larner classified firms pretty much as B-M had done (he chose a cut-off of 10 per cent instead of 20 per cent to identify minority-controlled corporations), and compared his findings for 1963 to those obtained by B-M for 1929. Having noted that ownership had indeed become more diffused (e.g., 84.5 per cent versus 44 per cent of the 200 largest corporations now fell into the management-control category), Larner observed that " . . . private ownership had *completely disappeared* among the 200 largest . . . " (italics in original). He concluded that the managerial revolution first noted by B-M now seemed almost complete. . . .

Whatever else these and similar studies may do, they provide no evidence whatsoever on management control for any non-trivial definition of the term. If a given profile of share distribution is to reflect management control, then the activities of the firm must differ in some observable way from the activities that would have occurred under an alternative profile, say one reflecting stockholders' control. Otherwise, different kinds of "control" are simply labels for different profiles of share distribution and have no ulterior information content. The hypothesis at issue must be that different profiles imply different outcomes of the firm's decision process, otherwise it is difficult to see what all the fuss has been about. And the literature does suggest a fairly precise statement of the behavioral hypothesis: Beyond some point, the greater is the dispersion of shares among owners the greater is the managers' opportunity to behave in ways inconsistent with the owners' welfare. Accordingly, the specific consequences implied by more dispersed ownership must be deduced (e.g., greater sales than would otherwise have been the case) and confronted with the evidence. . . .

To examine the problem in its proper context, it is important to recognize that the B-M thesis is supposed to be applicable only to large firms with some market power, that is, to firms facing a negatively sloped demand curve for their products. The rationale here seems to be that a purely competitive firm will either maximize profits or perish, whereas a monopolist will be able to survive even though it accepts a lower level of profits than it could have earned.

Such a dichotomy, however, cannot be deduced from the axioms of the standard (profit-maximizing) theory of the firm. In the case of open markets (i.e., no legal barriers to entry), profits, if any, are quickly reduced to zero by the entry or threat of entry of new firms. Symmetrically, losses induce resources to be shifted elsewhere, up to and including the demise of the firm. Since resource owners are hypothesized to respond frictionlessly to purely pecuniary incentives, these results occur whether the firms are price takers or monopolists. That is, an open market rules out monopoly rents. If monopoly rents are to occur, a necessary—but obviously not sufficient—condition is that legal barriers close the market to competitors. This applies whether the firms in the industry are price takers (e.g., tobacco farmers under an allotment system) or monopolists. Even then, classical theory implies that profits will be maximized: All rewards are pecuniary, and transferable resource rights will be acquired by those individuals who can use them most profitably.

The appearance of evidence seemingly inconsistent with the classical theory of the firm has elicited two major theoretical advances. First, the predictive content of the wealth-maximization hypothesis has been enhanced by explicitly taking into account adjustment, information, and transaction costs, where the last includes negotiation, contract, and police costs. Indeed, allowing these costs to be positive and rising at the margin has gone a long way toward the elimination of existing inconsistencies. For example, hierarchical control loss, which is positively related to the size and complexity of an organization, seems to explain at least some of the supposed inefficiencies of large firms. Second, some progress has been made in replacing wealth with the more general utility-maximization hypothesis. Under certain conditions non-pecuniary variables matter, and managers may not always make those choices intended to maximize the wealth of the owners.

Some of the points just raised, of course, are directly relevant to the consequences of share dispersion. More diffused ownership not only implies greater transaction costs, including greater costs of collecting and disseminating information regarding the efficiency of the managers' decisions, but also a smaller return to each stockholder from seeking to police inefficiencies. Among other results, the smaller would be the owners' incentive to police the managers' contractual obligations and the greater would be the latter's opportunity for utility-maximizing behavior. From these considerations it is tempting to deduce that more diffused ownership implies such things as larger staffs (as each manager seeks to increase his own apparent productivity and, therefore, his salary) and smaller wealth for the owners.

More diffused ownership, however, also permits greater specialization among stockholders. Thus, inefficient decisions by managers induce the better-informed owners to react sooner and more accurately, selling some or all of their shares and thereby lowering the stock's market price and the cost of taking over the firm. . . . Diffused ownership may also be offset by other factors. Stock options and other devices which tie managerial income and wealth more closely to owners' wealth certainly enhance managers' incentive to maximize profits. Competition among managers to attract better employment offers elsewhere also acts this way, though the incentives here need not be exclusively profit-oriented.

More concentrated ownership (e.g., a majority stockholder) admittedly lowers the cost of disseminating information regarding the efficiency of managerial choices and of organizing coalitions, and increases the benefits to the owner from policing managerial choices. In a world complicated by such things as progressive personal income tax rates and corporate income taxes, however, a majority stockholder may have the incentive and the opportunity to consume non-pecuniary sources of utility within the firm at the expense of his wealth, of the wealth of minority stockholders, and of the fisc. And the greater the tax rates, the lower the cost of non-pecuniary sources of income within the firm. Moreover, a majority stockholder — particularly one who has become so by inheritance — need not have the ability or the knowledge, even if he had the incentive, to encourage a profit-maximizing strategy by the firm's managers. Managers with the incentive to please a utility-maximizing majority stockholder may be expected to be less responsive to market signals. Thus, the utility maximization hypothesis does not imply that a large firm owned by a single individual will necessarily behave as a wealth maximizer. And this again seems to be independent of the degree of competition and of whether the market is open or closed. . . .

Beginning with B-M, much of the literature concerned with share dispersion has identified private ownership of a firm with the ownership by a single individual (or by a small group of associates) of enough voting stock to dominate the firm's affairs. As has already been suggested, such a definition is not very helpful for analytical purposes.

A priori, it is at least arguable that different degrees of dispersion reflect different distributions of control among owners rather than between owners and managers. Certainly an individual who owns nineteen of twenty voting shares outstanding is more likely to have his wishes implemented than if he were only one of twenty equal shareholders. On the other hand, ceteris paribus, any one of twenty equal shareholders is more likely to have his wishes implemented than if the other nineteen shares were held by a single individual. Moreover, granted that an individual has less control (than if he were sole owner) over the market value of the assets represented by his share in a firm owned jointly with others, he also has more control over the assets represented by the shares of the other stockholders. From this viewpoint, it is not clear why one distribution of shares is more "private" or more consistent with "owners' control" than any other distribution. Each individual stockholder has chosen voluntarily to allocate his resources in this way, and equally voluntarily, he has the option to revocate the committment simply by exchanging his shares in the market.

Increased dispersion of ownership (e.g., by increasing the numbers of equal shareholders) generally does imply a reduction in the ability of any given shareholder to revoke and to reassign the decision-making authority normally delegated to managers. But such a reduction is equally true of any individual who chooses to lease or to lend some of his assets to others. Surely one of the rights of an owner in a private property system must be to choose how much authority to delegate over the use of his resources.

Private property means that the right to make decisions regarding the uses (physical attributes) of a resource is vested exclusively in one individual and is transferable (voluntarily). The distinguishing characteristic of a private property system is the high positive correlation between the wealth of an individual and the consequences of his decisions on the value of resources. So long as the shareholders continue to bear the unpredicted changes in the value of a firm's goods and assets (i.e., bear the firm's profits and losses) and continue to have the right to exchange the firm's shares in the open market, they have the characteristics and the incentives of owners. They are the owners, and the fact that they have decided to allow their resources to be used as they have does not make them any less so. Dispersed ownership is just one particular kind of contractual arrangement possible under a private property system. To suggest otherwise simply confuses matters to no useful purpose. . . .

The empirical evidence currently available at best is weak. A widely quoted paper by Monsen, Chiu, and Cooley reported that, for the firms in their sample, the ratio of net income to net worth was higher for "owner-controlled" than for "management-controlled" firms. In view of their apparent use of accounting data to measure net income and net worth, however, their conclusion that " . . . large management controlled firms tend to be less profitable than comparable owner controlled ones" is open to criticism. Thus, for example, under reasonable conditions firms which favor the issue of new equity stock relative to debt and to retained earnings would show *both* an increase in management control (major stockholders need not be able even if they were willing to maintain constant the proportion of their holdings) *and* a decrease in the ratio of net income to book value of equity (the greater the proportion of new equity capital in financing any given additional investment with a positive payoff, the greater is the increase in book equity relative to the increase in accounting profits). In the case just noted, the test results would simply reflect differences in financial strategies — which may or may not be dispersion-related. Although the economic profitability of the two groups of firms may well differ, stronger evidence is necessary.

Kamerschen, using Larner's firms and classifications, also examined the B-M thesis. Taking the average rate of return after tax on year-end equity (1959–64, as reported in *Fortune*) to measure the profit rate, he regressed it on ten variables including "dummies" for type of control and for change in control. The regression coefficients that he reports for type of control are statistically significant at about the 4 per cent level (one tail) and support the B-M thesis. Kamerschen's surprising conclusion that " . . . type of control and change in size—do not appear to 'explain' very much of the variation in profit rates . . . " apparently rests upon using a two-tailed test, which seems inappropriate in view of the directional prediction of the B-M thesis, and upon regarding levels of significance greater than 5 per cent (two-tail) as not statistically significant. Kamerschen's findings, which also rely on accounting values, on the whole do not seem to be inconsistent with those reported by Monsen *et al.*

Hindley reasoned that if the market for corporate control were "ineffective," then the managers of corporations with a more dispersed ownership would have a greater opportunity to divert owners' resources and would exhibit a lower ratio (R) of potential to actual value. Hindley first examined the effectiveness of the market, concluding that it allowed managers some latitude. Next, he compared the relative change in the price of common stock for a group of firms classified in three dispersion and two industrial categories. The results suggested that owners' wealth was independent of stock dispersion. Since the differences in the returns to equity due to dispersion could have been capitalized prior to the period of observation, Hindley ran some additional tests. These culminated in the separate regression of two alternative definitions of R on the percentage of common stock held by the 20 largest stockholders and on several dummy variables reflecting industry. Although none of the six regression coefficients were statistically significant at the 5 per cent level (one tail), some were close to it and all had the sign predicted. Accordingly, these results could be interpreted as providing weak support for the B-M thesis.

. . . In addition to Hindley's work, some recent empirical studies suggesting the existence of managerial discretion deserve particular notice. Baumol, Heim, Malkiel, and Quandt found that the yield on ploughback, though positive, was sufficiently small (between 3 and 4.2 per cent) relative to the yield on new debt (from 4.2 to 14 per cent) and to the yield on new equity (from 14.5 to 20.8 per cent depending on the lag involved) to suggest that some managers' use of retained earnings may not have been in the best interest of the stockholders. Grabowsky and Mueller examined the determinants of firm expenditures on capital investment, on research and development, and on dividends, and reported some evidence inconsistent with a pure stockholders' welfare model. Since none of these tests took dispersion of ownership directly into account, one obvious line of investigation would be to introduce it explicitly into the analysis.

According to the analysis presented earlier, discretionary behavior would encourage internal control forces designed to curb it. Lewellen's studies of the composition of executive compensation indicate that, at least for the kinds of firms considered by B-M and others, a significant portion (over two-thirds) of the income and wealth of top management now arises from the ownership of shares in the firms they manage. These rewards would considerably enhance managers' incentive to maximize owners' wealth, and some empirical evidence bears this out. Larner observed that profits and the profit rate (as distinguished from assets, revenue, and their respective rates of growth) were the major variables in explaining the level of executive monetary rewards, and concluded that managers' incentives ". . . have effectively been harnessed to the diligence of managers in pursuing the interests and welfare of stockholders." Although Larner used accounting data, his results are not inconsistent with those reported by Masson in an independent study using market values. Masson, having found that the compensation of the top executives of the firms in his sample depended primarily upon stock market returns, carried the statistical analysis further and observed that the stronger the relationship the better did the firms perform in the stock market. These findings suggest that, if increased dispersion temporarily increases a manager's opportunity set, internal control forces operate to grind it down. Various tests of this hypothesis would be feasible and desirable. In particular, the relationship between degree of dispersion and the extent to which executive compensation is tied to owners' wealth could usefully be examined.

With some exceptions much of the empirical work to date has made extensive use of accounting data, some of which (e.g., profits) must be regarded as suspect. Moreover, again with some exceptions, a positive relationship between accounting profits and executive monetary rewards has been interpreted to imply that managers have the incentive to behave consistently with owners' welfare. This implication, however, is not warranted. The accounting periods relevant to a manager's wealth would roughly be limited to those occurring during his tenure in office, and this time horizon would necessarily be shorter than a shareholder's to whom *all* future accounting periods matter. It follows that a manager would have the incentive to increase current accounting profits and the length of his tenure at the expense of the owners' wealth (market value of equity). In testing some of these and associated hypotheses, it would obviously be desirable to control not only for such things as size, but also for attenuation of private property rights due to government regulation.

The empirical evidence available so far does not provide a definitive test of the hypothesis that different degrees of dispersion imply different outcomes to the firm's decision process. Testing has just begun, however. Should additional evidence eventually lead to rejection of the hypothesis, then the distinction among different degrees of dispersion would become pointless for economic purposes. Should the evidence lead to acceptance of the hypothesis, then degree of dispersion would seem sufficiently self-explanatory.

Executive Ownership Interests and Corporate Performance*

Miron Stano

This paper tests the hypothesis that the profit performance of the firm is directly correlated with the financial rewards arising from executive ownership interests. A widely used model of the determinants of profitability is extended to include average executive stockholdings as a measure of managerial profit motivation. . . .

Turning to the objectives of this paper, first, it is estimated that management-controlled firms have by 0.8 percent a lesser rate of return than nonmanagement-controlled firms. However, with a t-ratio of 1.49 no definite conclusion can be reached at this time.[†] Also, with only 8 of 46 firms classified as owner-controlled, any generalization of the results will be impossible.

Average executive stockholdings turns out to be a highly significant and important determinant of profitability. The relationship, as expected, is positive. An increase in average stockholdings from $100,000 to $1 million raises the firm's rate of return by 1.7 percent with a further increase of 0.5 percent if stockholdings rise to $2 million. When observations for firms with data for less than three executives are removed, the coefficient of the logarithm of average stockholdings remains highly significant, although its value diminishes somewhat. . . .

An unmistakable positive relationship between profit rates among the largest U.S. corporations and executive stock interests has emerged. For example, . . . an increase in executive stockholdings from $100,000 to $2 million will increase firm profitability by a sizeable 2.2 percentage points.

Differences in management ownership interests account for a substantial part of the higher rate of return for the nonmanagement-controlled firms . . . The mean rate of return for this group of firms is 12.8 percent with average executive stockholdings of $3,330,000.

*Source: 42 S. Econ. J. 272–278 (1975), with permission. Miron Stano is associate professor of economics and management at Oakland University.
    [†][A t-ratio is a measure of statistical significance. A t-ratio less than 2 indicates a correlation is not statistically significant — Eds.]

The corresponding figures for the management-controlled firms are 11.1 percent and $1,251,000 respectively. The substantially larger executive ownership holdings for the former group of firms account for 0.9 percent of their 1.7 percent greater profitability. Nonmanagement-controlled corporations are also $141 million larger, on the average, than their management-controlled counterparts. But, this accounts for less than 0.1 percent of the profitability difference. There is some evidence that the remainder of the difference is attributable to the nature of corporate control, though, the significance of the management-control dummy could not be clearly confirmed in this study.

Theory of the Firm: Managerial Behavior, Agency Costs and Ownership Structure*

Michael C. Jensen and William H. Meckling

In this paper we draw on recent progress in the theory of (1) property rights (2) agency, and (3) finance to develop a theory of ownership structure for the firm. . . .

We define an agency relationship as a contract under which one or more persons (the principal(s)) engage another person (the agent) to perform some service on their behalf which involves delegating some decision making authority to the agent. If both parties to the relationship are utility maximizers there is good reason to believe that the agent will not always act in the best interests of the principal. The *principal* can limit divergences from his interest by establishing appropriate incentives for the agent and by incurring monitoring costs designed to limit the aberrant activities of the agent. In addition in some situations it will pay the *agent* to expend resources (bonding costs) to guarantee that he will not take certain actions which would harm the principal or to ensure that the principal will be compensated if he does take such actions. However, it is generally impossible for the principal or the agent at zero cost to ensure that the agent will make optimal decisions from the principal's viewpoint. In most agency relationships the principal and the agent will incur positive monitoring and bonding costs (non-pecuniary as well as pecuniary), and in addition there will be some divergence be-

*Source: Excerpted with permission from 3 J. Fin. Econ. 305–360 (1976). Michael C. Jensen is Director of the Managerial Economics Research Center and William H. Meckling is Dean of the Graduate School of Management, both at the University of Rochester.

tween the agent's decisions and those decisions which would maximize the welfare of the principal. The dollar equivalent of the reduction in welfare experienced by the principal due to this divergence is also a cost of the agency relationship, and we refer to this latter cost as the "residual loss". We define *agency costs* as the sum of:

(1) the monitoring expenditures by the principal,
(2) the bonding expenditures by the agent,
(3) the residual loss. . . .

Our approach to the agency problem here differs fundamentally from most of the existing literature. That literature focuses almost exclusively on the normative aspects of the agency relationship; that is how to structure the contractual relation (including compensation incentives) between the principal and agent to provide appropriate incentives for the agent to make choices which will maximize the principal's welfare given that uncertainty and imperfect monitoring exist. We focus almost entirely on the positive aspects of the theory. That is, we assume individuals solve these normative problems and given that only stocks and bonds can be issued as claims, we investigate the incentives faced by each of the parties and the elements entering into the determination of the equilibrium contractual form characterizing the relationship between the manager (i.e., agent) of the firm and the outside equity and debt holders (i.e., principals).

Ronald Coase in his seminal paper on "The Nature of the Firm" pointed out that economics had no positive theory to determine the bounds of the firm. He characterized the bounds of the firm as that range of exchanges over which the market system was suppressed and resource allocation was accomplished instead by authority and direction. He focused on the cost of using markets to effect contracts and exchanges and argued that activities would be included within the firm whenever the costs of using markets were greater than the costs of using direct authority. Alchian and Demsetz object to the notion that activities within the firm are governed by authority, and correctly emphasize the role of contracts as a vehicle for voluntary exchange. They emphasize the role of monitoring in situations in which there is joint input or team production. We sympathize with the importance they attach to monitoring, but we believe the emphasis which Alchian-Demsetz place on joint input production is too narrow and therefore misleading. Contractual relations are the essence of the firm, not only with employees but with suppliers, customers, creditors, etc. The problem of agency costs and monitoring exists for all of these contracts, independent of whether there is joint production in their sense; i.e., joint production can explain only a small fraction of the behavior of individuals associated with a firm. . . .

The private corporation or firm is simply one form of *legal fiction which serves as a nexus for contracting relationships and which is also characterized by the existence of divisible residual claims on the assets and cash flows of the organization which can generally be sold without permission of the other contracting individuals.* While this definition of the firm has little substantive content, emphasizing the essential contractual nature of firms and other organizations focuses attention on a crucial set of questions — why particular sets of contractual relations arise for various types of organizations, what the consequences of these contractual relations are and how they are affected by changes exogenous to the organization. Viewed this way, it makes little or no sense to try to distinguish those things which are "inside" the firm (or any other organization) from those things that are "outside" of it. There is in a very real sense only a multitude of complex relationships (i.e., contracts) between the legal fiction (the firm) and the owners of labor, material and capital inputs and the consumers of output.[13]

Viewing the firm as the nexus of a set of contracting relationships among individuals also serves to make it clear that the personalization of the firm implied by asking questions such as "what should be the objective function of the firm," or "does the firm have a social responsibility" is seriously misleading. *The firm is not an individual.* It is a legal fiction which serves as a focus for a complex process in which the conflicting objectives of individuals (some of whom may "represent" other organizations) are brought into equilibrium within a framework of contractual relations. In this sense the "behavior" of the firm is like the behavior of a market; i.e., the outcome of a complex equilibrium process. We seldom fall into the trap of characterizing the wheat or stock market as an individual, but we often make this error by thinking about organizations as if they were persons with motivations and intentions. . . .

. . . [Compare] the behavior of a manager when he owns 100 percent of the residual claims on a firm to his behavior when he sells off a portion of those claims to outsiders. If a wholly owned firm is managed by the owner, he will make operating decisions which maximize his utility. These decisions will involve not only the benefits he derives from pecuniary returns but also the utility generated by various non-pecuniary aspects of his entrepreneurial activities

---

13. For example, we ordinarily think of a product as leaving the firm at the time it is sold, but implicitly or explicitly such sales generally carry with them continuing contracts between the firm and the buyer. If the product does not perform as expected the buyer often can and does have a right to satisfaction. Explicit evidence that such implicit contracts do exist is the practice we occasionally observe of specific provision that 'all sales are final.'

such as the physical appointments of the office, the attractiveness of the secretarial staff, the level of employee discipline, the kind and amount of charitable contributions, personal relations ("love", "respect", etc.) with employees, a larger than optimal computer to play with, purchase of production inputs from friends, etc. The optimum mix (in the absence of taxes) of the various pecuniary and non-pecuniary benefits is achieved when the marginal utility derived from an additional dollar of expenditure (measured net of any productive effects) is equal for each non-pecuniary item and equal to the marginal utility derived from an additional dollar of after tax purchasing power (wealth).

If the owner-manager sells equity claims on the corporation which are identical to his (i.e., share proportionately in the profits of the firm and have limited liability) agency costs will be generated by the divergence between his interest and those of the outside shareholders, since he will then bear only a fraction of the costs of any non-pecuniary benefits he takes out in maximizing his own utility. If the manager owns only 95 percent of the stock, he will expend resources to the point where the marginal utility derived from a dollar's expenditure of the firm's resources on such items equals the marginal utility of an additional 95 cents in general purchasing power (i.e., *his* share of the wealth reduction) and not one dollar. Such activities, on his part, can be limited (but probably not eliminated) by the expenditure of resources on monitoring activities by the outside stockholders. But . . . the owner will bear the entire wealth effects of these expected costs so long as the equity market anticipates these effects. Prospective minority shareholders will realize that the owner-manager's interests will diverge somewhat from theirs, hence the price which they will pay for shares will reflect the monitoring costs and the effect of the divergence between the manager's interest and theirs. Nevertheless, ignoring for the moment the possibility of borrowing against his wealth, the owner will find it desirable to bear these costs as long as the welfare increment he experiences from converting his claims on the firm into general purchasing power is large enough to offset them.

As the owner-manager's fraction of the equity falls, his fractional claim on the outcomes falls and this will tend to encourage him to appropriate larger amounts of the corporate resources in the form of perquisites. This also makes it desirable for the minority shareholders to expend more resources in monitoring his behavior. Thus, the wealth costs to the owner of obtaining additional cash in the equity markets rise as his fractional ownership falls.

We shall continue to characterize the agency conflict between the owner-manager and outside shareholders as deriving from the manager's tendency to appropriate perquisites out of the firm's resources for his own consumption. However, we do not mean to leave the impression that this is the only or even the most important source of conflict. Indeed, it is likely that the most important conflict arises from the fact that as the manager's ownership claim falls, his incentive to devote significant effort to creative activities such as searching out new profitable ventures falls. He may in fact avoid such ventures simply because it requires too much trouble or effort on his part to manage or to learn about new technologies. Avoidance of these personal costs and the anxieties that go with them also represent a source of on the job utility to him and it can result in the value of the firm being substantially lower than it otherwise could be. . . .

In the above analysis we have ignored the potential for controlling the behavior of the owner-manager through monitoring and other control activities. In practice, it is usually possible by expending resources to alter the opportunity the owner-manager has for capturing non-pecuniary benefits. These methods include auditing, formal control systems, budget restrictions, and the establishment of incentive compensation systems which serve to more closely identify the manager's interests with those of the outside equity holders, etc. . . .

We can also see from the analysis . . . that it makes no difference who actually makes the monitoring expenditures — the owner bears the full amount of these costs as a wealth reduction in all cases. Suppose that the owner-manager could expend resources to guarantee to the outside equity holders that he would limit his activities which cost the firm [some amount]. We call these expenditures "bonding costs", and they would take such forms as contractual guarantees to have the financial accounts audited by a public account[ant,] explicit bonding against malfeasance on the part of the manager, and contractual limitations on the manager's decision making power (which impose costs on the firm because they limit his ability to take full advantage of some profitable opportunities as well as limiting his ability to harm the stockholders while making himself better off). . . .

In general we expect to observe both bonding and external monitoring activities, and the incentives are such that the levels of these activities will satisfy the conditions of efficiency. They will not, however, result in the firm being run in a manner so as to maximize its value. . . .

The reduced value of the firm caused by the manager's consumption of perquisites . . . is "non-optimal" or inefficient in comparison to a world in which we could obtain compliance of the agent to the principal's wishes at zero cost or in comparison to a *hypothetical* world in which the agency costs were lower. But these costs (monitoring and bonding costs and 'residual loss') are an unavoidable result of the agency relationship. Furthermore, since they are borne entirely by the decision maker (in this case the original owner) responsible for creating the relationship he has the incentives to see that they are minimized (because he captures the benefits from their reduction). Furthermore, these agency costs will be incurred only if the benefits to the owner-manager from their creation are great enough to outweigh them. In our current example these benefits arise from the availability of profitable investments requiring capital investment in excess of the original owner's personal wealth.

In conclusion, finding that agency costs are non-zero (i.e., that there are costs associated with the separation of ownership and control in the corporation) and concluding therefrom that the agency relationship is non-optimal, wasteful or inefficient is equivalent in every sense to comparing a world in which iron ore is a scarce commodity (and therefore costly) to a world in which it is freely available at zero resource cost, and concluding that the first world is "nonoptimal"—a perfect example of . . . the "Nirvana" form of analysis.

The magnitude of the agency costs discussed above will vary from firm to firm. It will depend on the tastes of managers, the ease with which they can exercise their own preferences as opposed to value maximization in decision making, and the costs of monitoring and bonding activities. The agency costs will also depend upon the cost of measuring the manager's (agent's) performance and evaluating it, the cost of devising and applying an index for compensating the manager which correlates with the owner's (principal's) welfare, and the cost of devising and enforcing specific behavioral rules or policies. Where the manager has less than a controlling interest in the firm, it will also depend upon the market for managers. Competition from other potential managers limits the costs of obtaining managerial services (including the extent to which a given manager can diverge from the idealized solution which would obtain if all monitoring and bonding costs were zero). The size of the divergence (the agency costs) will be directly related to the cost of replacing the manager. If his responsibilities require very little knowledge specialized to the firm, if it is easy to evaluate his performance, and if replacement search costs are modest, the divergence from the ideal will be relatively small and vice versa.

The divergence will also be constrained by the market for the firm itself, i.e., by capital markets. Owners always have the option of selling their firm, either as a unit or piecemeal. Owners of manager-operated firms can and do sample the capital market from time to time. If they discover that the value of the future earnings stream to others is higher than the value of the firm to them given that it is to be manager-operated, they can exercise their right to sell. It is conceivable that other owners could be more efficient at monitoring or even that a single individual with appropriate managerial talents and with sufficiently large personal wealth would elect to buy the firm. In this latter case the purchase by such a single individual would completely eliminate the agency costs. If there were a number of such potential owner-manager purchasers (all with talents and tastes identical to the current manager) the owners would receive in the sale price of the firm the full value of the residual claimant rights including the capital value of the eliminated agency costs plus the value of the managerial rights.

Monopoly, competition and managerial behavior. It is frequently argued that the existence of competition in product (and factor) markets will constrain the behavior of managers to idealized value maximization, i.e., that monopoly in product (or monopsony in factor) markets will permit larger divergences from value maximization. Our analysis does not support this hypothesis. The owners of a firm with monopoly power have the same incentives to limit divergences of the manager from value maximization (i.e., the ability to increase their wealth) as do the owners of competitive firms. Furthermore, competition in the market for managers will generally make it unnecessary for the owners to share rents with the manager. The owners of a monopoly firm need only pay the supply price for a manager.

Since the owner of a monopoly has the same wealth incentives to minimize managerial costs as would the owner of a competitive firm, both will undertake that level of monitoring which equates the marginal cost of monitoring to the marginal wealth increment from reduced consumption of perquisites by the manager. Thus, the existence of monopoly will not increase agency costs.

Furthermore the existence of competition in product and factor markets will not eliminate the agency costs due to managerial control problems as has often been asserted . . . If my competitors all incur agency costs equal to or greater than mine I will not be eliminated from the market by their competition.

The existence and size of the agency costs depends on the nature of the monitoring costs, the tastes of managers for non-pecuniary benefits and the supply of potential managers who are capable of financing the entire venture out of their personal wealth. If monitoring costs are zero, agency costs will be zero or if there are enough 100 percent owner-managers available to own and run all the firms in an industry (competitive or not) then agency costs in that industry will also be zero.

The analysis to this point has left us with a basic puzzle: Why, given the existence of positive costs of the agency relationship, do we find the usual corporate form of organization with widely diffuse ownership so widely prevalent? If one takes seriously much of the literature regarding the "discretionary" power held by managers of large corporations, it is difficult to understand the historical fact of enormous growth in equity in such organizations, not only in the United States, but throughout the world. . . . How does it happen that millions of individuals are willing to turn over a significant fraction of their wealth to organizations run by managers who have so little interest in their welfare? What is even more remarkable, why are they willing to make these commitments purely as residual claimants, i.e., on the anticipation that managers will operate the firm so that there will be earnings which accrue to the stockholders?

There is certainly no lack of alternative ways that individuals might invest, including entirely different forms of organizations. Even if consideration is limited to corporate organizations, there are clearly alternative ways capital might be raised, i.e., through fixed claims of various sorts, bonds, notes, mortgages, etc. Moreover, the corporate income tax seems to favor the use of fixed claims since interest is treated as a tax deductible expense. Those who assert that managers do not behave in the interest of stockholders have generally not addressed a very important question: Why, if non-manager-owned shares have such a serious deficiency, have they not long since been driven out by fixed claims?

The role of limited liability. Manne and Alchian and Demsetz argue that one of the attractive features of the corporate form vis-a-vis individual proprietorships or partnerships is the limited liability feature of equity claims in corporations. Without this provision each and every investor purchasing one or more shares of a corporation would be potentially liable to the full extent of his personal wealth for the debts of the corporation. Few individuals would find this a desirable risk to accept and the major benefits to be obtained from risk reduction through diversification would be to a large extent unobtainable. This argument, however, is incomplete since limited liability does not eliminate the basic risk, it merely shifts it. The argument must rest ultimately on transactions costs. If all stockholders of GM were liable for GM's debts, the maximum liability for an individual shareholder would be greater than it would be if his shares had limited liability. However, given that many other stockholders also existed and that each was liable for the unpaid claims in proportion to his ownership it is highly unlikely that the maximum payment each would have to make would be large in the event of GM's bankruptcy since the total wealth of those stockholders would also be large. However, the existence of unlimited liability would impose incentives for each shareholder to keep track of both the liabilities of GM and the wealth of the other GM owners. It is easily conceivable that the costs of so doing would, in the aggregate, be much higher than simply paying a premium in the form of higher interest rates to the creditors of GM in return for their acceptance of a contract which grants limited liability to the shareholders. The creditors would then bear the risk of any non-payment of debts in the event of GM's bankruptcy.

It is also not generally recognized that limited liability is merely a necessary condition for explaining the magnitude of the reliance on equities, not a sufficient condition. Ordinary debt also carries limited liability.[33] If limited liability is all that is required, why don't we observe large corporations, individually owned, with a tiny fraction of the capital supplied by the entrepreneur, and the rest simply borrowed. . . .[34]

The "irrelevance" of capital structure. In their pathbreaking article on the cost of capital, Modigliani and Miller demonstrated that in the absence of bankruptcy costs and tax subsidies on the payment of interest the value of the firm is independent of the financial structure.* They later demonstrated that the existence of tax subsidies on interest payments would cause the value of the firm to rise with the

33. By limited liability we mean the same conditions that apply to common stock. Subordinated debt or preferred stock could be constructed which carried with it liability provisions; i.e., if the corporation's assets were insufficient at some point to pay off all prior claims (such as trade credit, accrued wages, senior debt, etc.) and if the personal resources of the 'equity' holders were also insufficient to cover these claims the holders of this 'debt' would be subject to assessments beyond the face value of their claim (assessments which might be limited or unlimited in amount).

34. Alchian-Demsetz [see their article in this volume] argue that one can explain the existence of both bonds and stock in the ownership structure of firms as the result of differing expectations regarding the outcomes to the firm. They argue that bonds are created and sold to 'pessimists' and stocks with a residual claim with no upper bound are sold to 'optimists'.

As long as capital markets are perfect with no taxes or transactions costs and individual investors can issue claims on distributions of outcomes on the same terms as firms, such actions on the part of firms cannot affect their values. The reason is simple. Suppose such 'pessimists' did exist and yet the firm issues only equity claims. The demand for those equity claims would reflect the fact that the individual purchaser could on his own account issue 'bonds' with a limited and prior claim on the distribution of outcomes on the equity which is exactly the same as that which the firm could issue. Similarly, investors could easily unlever any position by simply buying a proportional claim on both the bonds and stocks of a levered firm. Therefore, a levered firm could not sell at a different price than an unlevered firm solely because of the existence of such differential expectations. . . .

*[The Modigliani-Miller theorem is explained in their article in Chapter 8 of this volume—Eds.]

amount of debt financing by the amount of the capitalized value of the tax subsidy. But this line of argument implies that the firm should be financed almost entirely with debt. . . . Modigliani and Miller are essentially left without a theory of the determination of the optimal capital structure.

While the introduction of bankruptcy costs in the presence of tax subsidies leads to a theory which defines an optimal capital structure, we argue that this theory is seriously incomplete since it implies that no debt should ever be used in the absence of tax subsidies if bankruptcy costs are positive. Since we know debt was commonly used prior to the existence of the current tax subsidies on interest payments this theory does not capture what must be some important determinants of the corporate capital structure.

In addition, neither bankruptcy costs nor the existence of tax subsidies can explain the use of preferred stock or warrants which have no tax advantages, and there is no theory which tells us anything about what determines the fraction of equity claims held by insiders as opposed to outsiders which our analysis [above] indicates is so important. We return to these issues later after analyzing in detail the factors affecting the agency costs associated with debt.

In general if the agency costs engendered by the existence of outside owners are positive it will pay the absentee owner (i.e., shareholders) to sell out to an owner-manager who can avoid these costs. This could be accomplished in principle by having the manager become the sole equity holder by repurchasing all of the outside equity claims with funds obtained through the issuance of limited liability debt claims and the use of his own personal wealth. This single-owner corporation would not suffer the agency costs associated with outside equity. Therefore there must be some compelling reasons why we find the diffuse-owner corporate firm financed by equity claims so prevalent as an organizational form.

An ingenious entrepreneur eager to expand, has open to him the opportunity to design a whole hierarchy of fixed claims on assets and earnings, with premiums paid for different levels of risk. Why don't we observe large corporations individually owned with a tiny fraction of the capital supplied by the entrepreneur in return for 100 percent of the equity and the rest simply borrowed? We believe there are a number of reasons: (1) the incentive effects associated with highly leveraged firms, (2) the monitoring costs these incentive effects engender, and (3) bankruptcy costs. Furthermore, all of these costs are simply particular aspects of the agency costs associated with the existence of debt claims on the firm.

We don't find many large firms financed almost entirely with debt type claims (i.e., non-residual claims) because of the effect such a financial structure would have on the owner-manager's behavior. Potential creditors will not loan $100,000,000 to a firm in which the entrepreneur has an investment of $10,000. With that financial structure the owner-manager will have a strong incentive to engage in activities (investments) which promise very high payoffs if successful even if they have a very low probability of success. If they turn out well, he captures most of the gains, if they turn out badly, the creditors bear most of the costs. . . .

In principle it would be possible for the bondholders, by the inclusion of various covenants in the indenture provisions, to limit the managerial behavior which results in reductions in the value of the bonds. Provisions which impose constraints on management's decisions regarding such things as dividends, future debt issues and maintenance of working capital are not uncommon in bond issues. To completely protect the bondholders from the incentive effects, these provisions would have to be incredibly detailed and cover most operating aspects of the enterprise including limitations on the riskiness of the projects undertaken. The costs involved in writing such provisions, the costs of enforcing them and the reduced profitability of the firm (induced because the covenants occasionally limit management's ability to take optimal actions on certain issues) would likely be non-trivial. In fact, since management is a continuous decision making process it will be almost impossible to completely specify such conditions without having the bondholders actually perform the management function. All costs associated with such covenants are what we mean by monitoring costs.

The bondholders will have incentives to engage in the writing of such covenants and in monitoring the actions of the manager to the point where the "nominal" marginal cost to them of such activities is just equal to the marginal benefits they perceive from engaging in them. We use the word nominal here because debtholders will not in fact bear these costs. As long as they recognize their existence, they will take them into account in deciding the price they will pay for any given debt claim, and therefore the seller of the claim (the owner) will bear the costs just as in the equity case discussed [above].

In addition the manager has incentives to take into account the costs imposed on the firm by covenants in the debt agreement which directly affect the future cash flows of the firm since they reduce the market value of his claims. Because both the external and internal monitoring costs are imposed on the owner-manager it is in his interest to see that the monitoring is performed in the lowest cost way. Suppose, for example, that the bondholders (or outside equity holders) would find it worthwhile to produce detailed financial statements such as those contained in the usual published accounting reports as a means of monitoring the manager. If the manager himself can produce such information at lower costs than they (perhaps because he is already collecting much of the data they desire for his own internal decision making purposes), it would pay him to agree in advance to incur the cost of providing such reports and to have their accuracy testified to by an independent outside auditor. This is an example of what we refer to as bonding costs.

. . . [We] consider here the third major component of the agency costs of debt which helps to explain why debt doesn't completely dominate capital structures — the existence of bankruptcy and reorganization costs. . . .

If there were no costs associated with the event called bankruptcy the total market value of the firm would not be affected by increasing the probability of its incurrence. However, it is costly, if not impossible, to write contracts representing claims on a firm which clearly delineate the rights of holders for all possible contingencies. Thus even if there were no adverse incentive effects in expanding fixed claims relative to equity in a firm, the use of such fixed claims would be constrained by the costs inherent in defining and enforcing those claims. Firms incur obligations daily to suppliers, to employees, to different classes of investors, etc. So long as the firm is prospering, the adjudication of claims is seldom a problem. When the firm has difficulty meeting some of its obligations, however, the issue of the priority of those claims can pose serious problems. This is most obvious in the extreme case where the firm is forced into bankruptcy. If bankruptcy were costless, the reorganization would be accompanied by an adjustment of the claims of various parties and the business, could, if that proved to be in the interest of the claimants, simply go on (although perhaps under new management).

In practice, bankruptcy is not costless, but generally involves an adjudication process which itself consumes a fraction of the remaining value of the assets of the firm. Thus the cost of bankruptcy will be of concern to potential buyers of fixed claims in the firm since their existence will reduce the payoffs to them in the event of bankruptcy. These are examples of the agency costs of cooperative efforts among individuals (although in this case perhaps "non-cooperative" would be a better term). The price buyers will be willing to pay for fixed claims will thus be inversely related to the probability of the incurrence of these costs i.e., to the probability of bankruptcy. Using a variant of the argument employed above for monitoring costs, it can be shown that the total value of the firm will fall, and the owner-manager equity holder will bear the entire wealth effect of the bankruptcy costs as long as potential bondholders make unbiased estimates of their magnitude at the time they initially purchase bonds.

Empirical studies of the magnitude of bankruptcy costs are almost nonexistent. Warner in a study of 11 railroad bankruptcies between 1930 and 1955 estimates the average costs of bankruptcy as a fraction of the value of the firm three years prior to bankruptcy to be 2.5% (with a range of 0.4% to 5.9%). The average dollar costs were $1.88 million. Both of these measures seem remarkably small and are consistent with our belief that bankruptcy costs themselves are unlikely to be the major determinant of corporate capital structures. It is also interesting to note that the annual amount of defaulted funds has fallen significantly since 1940. . . . One possible explanation for this phenomenon is that firms are using mergers to avoid the costs of bankruptcy. This hypothesis seems even more reasonable, if, as is frequently the case, reorganization costs represent only a fraction of the costs associated with bankruptcy.

In general the revenues or the operating costs of the firm are not independent of the probability of bankruptcy and thus the capital structure of the firm. As the probability of bankruptcy increases, both the operating costs and the revenues of the firm are adversely affected, and some of these costs can be avoided by merger. For example, a firm with a high probability of bankruptcy will also find that it must pay higher salaries to induce executives to accept the higher risk of unemployment. Furthermore, in certain kinds of durable goods industries the demand function for the firm's product will not be independent of the probability of bankruptcy. The computer industry is a good example. There, the buyer's welfare is dependent to a significant extent on the ability to maintain the equipment, and on continuous hardware and software development. Furthermore, the owner of a large computer often receives benefits from the software developments of other users. Thus if the manufacturer leaves the business or loses his software support and development experts because of financial difficulties, the value of the equipment to his users will decline. The buyers of such services have a continuing interest in the manufacturer's viability not unlike that of a bondholder, except that their benefits come in the form of continuing services at lower cost rather than principle and interest payments. Service facilities and spare parts for automobiles and machinery are other examples.

In summary then the agency costs associated with debt consist of:

(1) the opportunity wealth loss caused by the impact of debt on the investment decisions of the firm,

(2) the monitoring and bonding expenditures by the bond-holders and the owner-manager (i.e., the firm),

(3) the bankruptcy and reorganization costs.

Why are the Agency Costs of Debt Incurred?

We have argued that the owner-manager bears the entire wealth effects of the agency costs of debt and he captures the gains from reducing them. Thus, the agency costs associated with debt discussed above will tend, in the absence of other mitigating factors, to discourage the use of corporate debt. What are the factors that encourage its use?

One factor is the tax subsidy on interest payments. . . . However, even in the absence of these tax benefits, debt would be utilized if the ability to exploit potentially profitable investment opportunities is limited by the resources of the owner. If the owner of a project cannot raise capital he will suffer an opportunity loss represented by the increment in value offered to him by the additional investment opportunities. Thus even though he will bear the agency costs from selling debt, he will find it desirable to incur them to obtain additional capital as long as the marginal wealth increments from the new investments projects are greater than the marginal agency costs of debt, and these agency costs are in turn less than those caused by the sale of additional equity discussed [above]. Furthermore, this solution is optimal from the social viewpoint. However, in the absence of tax subsidies on debt these projects must be unique to this firm or they would be taken by other competitive entrepreneurs (perhaps new ones) who possessed the requisite personal wealth to fully finance the projects and therefore [were] able to avoid the existence of debt or outside equity. . . .

The model we have used to explain the existence of minority shareholders and debt in the capital structure of corporations implies that the owner-manager, if he resorts to any outside funding, will have his entire wealth invested in the firm. The reason is that he can thereby avoid the agency costs which additional outside funding impose. This suggests he would not resort to outside funding until he had invested 100 percent of his personal wealth in the firm — an implication which is not consistent with what we generally observe. Most owner-managers hold personal wealth in a variety of forms, and some have only a relatively small fraction of their wealth invested in the corporation they manage. Diversification on the part of owner-managers can be explained by risk aversion and optimal portfolio selection.

If the returns from assets are not perfectly correlated an individual can reduce the riskiness of the returns on his portfolio by dividing his wealth among many different assets, i.e., by diversifying. Thus a manager who invests all of his wealth in a single firm (his own) will generally bear a welfare loss (if he is risk averse) because he is bearing more risk than necessary. He will, of course, be willing to pay something to avoid this risk, and the costs he must bear to accomplish this diversification will be the agency costs outlined above. He will suffer a wealth loss as he reduces his fractional ownership because prospective shareholders and bondholders will take into account the agency costs. Nevertheless, the manager's desire to avoid risk will contribute to his becoming a minority stockholder. . . .

We have assumed throughout our analysis that we are dealing only with a single investment-financing decision by the entrepreneur and have ignored the issues associated with the incentives affecting future financing-investment decisions which might arise after the initial set of contracts are consumated between the entrepreneur-manager, outside stockholders and bondholders. These are important issues which are left for future analysis. Their solution will undoubtedly introduce some changes in the conclusions of the single decision analysis. It seems clear for instance that the expectation of future sales of outside equity and debt will change the costs and benefits facing the manager in making decisions which benefit himself at the (short-run) expense of the current bondholders and stockholders. If he develops a reputation for such dealings he can expect this to unfavourably influence the terms at which he can obtain future capital from outside sources. This will tend to increase the benefits associated with "sainthood" and will tend to reduce the size of the agency costs. Given the finite life of any individual, however, such an effect cannot reduce these costs to zero, because at some point these future costs will begin to weigh more heavily on his successors and therefore the relative benefits to him of acting in his own best interests will rise. Furthermore, it will generally be impossible for him to fully guarantee the outside interests that his successor will continue to follow his policies.

The careful reader will notice that nowhere in the analysis thus far have we taken into account many of the details of the relationship between the part owner-manager and the outside stockholders and bondholders. In particular we have assumed that all outside equity is nonvoting. If such equity does have voting rights then the manager will be concerned about the effects on his long-run welfare of reducing his fractional ownership below the point where he loses effective control of the corporation — [t]hat is, below the point where it becomes possible for the outside equity holders to fire him.

A complete analysis of this issue will require a careful specification of the contractual rights involved on both sides, the role of the board of directors, and the coordination (agency) costs borne by the stockholders in implementing policy changes. This latter point involves consideration of the distribution of the outside ownership claims. Simply put, forces exist to determine an equilibrium distribution of outside ownership. If the costs of reducing the dispersion of ownership are lower than the benefits to be obtained from reducing the agency costs, it will pay some individual or group of individuals to buy shares in the market to reduce the dispersion of ownership. We occasionally witness these conflicts for control which involve outright market purchases, tender offers and proxy fights. . . . Warrants, convertible bonds and convertible preferred stock have some of the characteristics of non-voting shares although they can be converted into voting shares under some terms. Alchian-Demsetz provide an interesting analysis regarding the use of non-voting shares. They argue that some shareholders with strong beliefs in the talents and judgements of the manager will want to be protected against the possibility that some other shareholders will take over and limit the actions of the manager (or fire him). Given that the securities exchanges prohibit the use of non-voting shares by listed firms the use of option type securities might be a substitute for these claims.

In addition warrants represents a claim on the upper tail of the distribution of outcomes, and convertible securities can be thought of as securities with non-detachable warrants. It seems that the incentive effects of warrants would tend to offset to some extent the incentive effects of the existence of risky debt because the owner-manager would be sharing part of the proceeds associated with a shift in the distribution of returns with the warrant holders. Thus, we conjecture that potential bondholders will find it attractive to have warrants attached to the risky debt of firms in which it is relatively easy to shift the distribution of outcomes to expand the upper tail of the distribution to transfer wealth from bondholders. It would also then be attractive to the owner-manager because of the reduction in the agency costs which he would bear. This argument also implies that it would make little difference if the warrants were detachable (and therefore saleable separately from the bonds) since their mere existence would reduce the incentives of the manager (or stockholders) to increase the riskiness of the firm (and therefore increase the probability of bankruptcy). Furthermore, the addition of a conversion privilege to fixed claims such as debt or preferred stock would also tend to reduce the incentive effects of the existence of such fixed claims and therefore lower the agency costs associated with them. The theory predicts that these phenomena should be more frequently observed in cases where the incentive effects of such fixed claims are high than when they are low. . . .

A large body of evidence exists which indicates that security prices incorporate in an unbiased manner all publicly available information and much of what might be called "private information." There is also a large body of evidence which indicates that the security analysis activities of mutual funds and other institutional investors are not reflected in portfolio returns, i.e., they do not increase risk adjusted portfolio returns over a naive random selection buy and hold strategy. Therefore some have been tempted to conclude that the resources expended on such research activities to find under- or over-valued securities is a social loss. . . . [T]he analysis of this paper would seem to indicate that to the extent that security analysis activities reduce the agency costs associated with the separation of ownership and control they are indeed socially productive. Moreover, if this is true we expect the major benefits of the security analysis activity to be reflected in the higher capitalized value of the ownership claims to corporations and *not* in the period to period portfolio returns of the analyst. Equilibrium in the security analysis industry requires that the private returns to analysis (i.e., portfolio returns) must be just equal to the private costs of such activity, and this will not reflect the social product of this activity which will consist of larger output and higher *levels* of the capital value of ownership claims. Therefore, the argument implies that if there is a non-optimal amount of security analysis being performed it is too much not too little (since the shareholders would be willing to pay directly to have the "optimal" monitoring performed), and we don't seem to observe such payments.

Our previous analysis of agency costs suggests at least one other testable hypothesis: i.e., that in those industries where the incentive effects of outside equity or debt are widely different, we would expect to see specialization in the use of the low agency cost financing arrangement. In industries where it is relatively easy for managers to lower the mean value of the outcomes of the enterprise by outright theft, special treatment of favored customers, ease of consumption of leisure on the job, etc. (for example, the bar and restaurant industry) we would expect to see the ownership structure of firms characterized by relatively little outside equity (i.e., 100 percent ownership of the equity by the manager) with almost all outside capital obtained through the use of debt.

The theory predicts the opposite would be true where the incentive effects of debt are large relative to the incentive effects of equity. Firms like conglomerates, in which it would be easy to shift outcome distributions adversely for bondholders (by changing the acquisition or divestiture policy) should be characterized by relatively lower utilization of debt. Conversely in industries where the freedom of management to take riskier projects is severely constrained (for example, regulated industries such as public utilities) we should find more intensive use of debt financing.

The analysis suggests that in addition to the fairly well understood role of uncertainty in the determination of the quality of collateral there is at least one other element of great importance — the ability of the owner of the collateral to change the distribution of outcomes by shifting either the mean outcome or the variance of the outcomes. . . .

Agency Problems and the Theory of the Firm*

Eugene F. Fama

Economists have long been concerned with the incentive problems that arise when decision making in a firm is the province of managers who are not the firm's security holders. One outcome has been the development of "behavioral" and "managerial" theories of the firm which reject the classical model of an entrepreneur, or owner-manager, who single-mindedly operates the firm to maximize profits, in favor of theories that focus more on the motivations of a manager who controls but does not own and who has little resemblance to the classical "economic man." . . .

More recently the literature has moved toward theories that reject the classical model of the firm but assume classical forms of economic behavior on the part of agents within the firm. The firm is viewed as a set of contracts among factors of production, with each factor motivated by its self-interest. . . . In effect, the firm is viewed as a team whose members act from self-interest but realize that their destinies depend to some extent on the survival of the team in its competition with other teams. This insight, however, is not carried far enough. . . .

The main thesis of this paper is that separation of security ownership and control can be explained as an efficient form of economic organization within the "set of contracts" perspective. We first set aside the typical presumption that a corporation has owners in any meaningful sense. The attractive concept of the entrepreneur

*Source: 88 J. Pol. Econ. 288–306 (1980), reprinted with permission. Eugene F. Fama is Yntema Professor of Finance in the Graduate School of Business at the University of Chicago.

is also laid to rest, at least for the purposes of the large modern corporation. Instead, the two functions usually attributed to the entrepreneur, management and risk bearing, are treated as naturally separate factors within the set of contracts called a firm. The firm is disciplined by competition from other firms, which forces the evolution of devices for efficiently monitoring the performance of the entire team and of its individual members. In addition, individual participants in the firm, and in particular its managers, face both the discipline and opportunities provided by the markets for their services, both within and outside of the firm.

The Irrelevance of the Concept of Ownership of the Firm

To set a framework for the analysis, let us first describe roles for management and risk bearing in the set of contracts called a firm. Management is a type of labor but with a special role — coordinating the activities of inputs and carrying out the contracts agreed among inputs, all of which can be characterized as "decision making." To explain the role of the risk bearers, assume for the moment that the firm rents all other factors of production and that rental contracts are negotiated at the beginning of each production period with payoffs at the end of the period. The risk bearers then contract to accept the uncertain and possibly negative difference between total revenues and costs at the end of each production period.

When other factors of production are paid at the end of each period, it is not necessary for the risk bearers to invest anything in the firm at the beginning of the period. Most commonly, however, the risk bearers guarantee performance of their contracts by putting up wealth ex ante, with this front money used to purchase capital and perhaps also the technology that the firm uses in its production activites. In this way the risk bearing function is combined with ownership of capital and technology. . . .

However, ownership of capital should not be confused with ownership of the firm. Each factor in a firm is owned by somebody. The firm is just the set of contracts covering the way inputs are joined to create outputs and the way receipts from outputs are shared among inputs. In this "nexus of contracts" perspective, ownership of the firm is an irrelevant concept. Dispelling the tenacious notion that a firm is owned by its security holders is important because it is a first step toward understanding that control over a firm's decisions is not necessarily the province of security holders. The second step is setting aside the equally tenacious role in the firm usually attributed to the entrepreneur.

Management and Risk Bearing: A Closer Look

The entrepreneur (manager-risk bearer) is central in both the Jensen-Meckling and Alchian-Demsetz analyses of the firm. . . . [However, to] understand the modern corporation, it is better to separate the manager, . . . from the risk bearer . . . The rationale for separating these functions is not just that the end result is more descriptive of the corporation . . . The major loss in retaining the concept of the entrepreneur is that one is prevented from developing a perspective on management and risk bearing as separate factors of production, each faced with a market for its services that provides alternative opportunities and, in the case of management, motivation toward performance.

Thus, any given set of contracts, a particular firm, is in competition with other firms, which are likewise teams of cooperating factors of production. If there is a part of the team that has a special interest in its viability, it is not obviously the risk bearers. It is true that if the team does not prove viable factors like labor and management are protected by markets in which rights to their future services can be sold or rented to other teams. The risk bearers, as residual claimants, also seem to suffer the most direct consequences from the failings of the team. However, the risk bearers in the modern corporation also have markets for their services — capital markets — which allow them to shift among teams with relatively low transaction costs and to hedge against the failings of any given team by diversifying their holdings across teams.

Indeed, portfolio theory tells us that the optimal portfolio for any investor is likely to be diversified across the securities of many firms. Since he holds the securities of many firms precisely to avoid having his wealth depend too much on any one firm, an individual security holder generally has no special interest in personally overseeing the detailed activities of any firm. In short, efficient allocation of risk bearing seems to imply a large degree of separation of security ownership from control of a firm.

On the other hand, the managers of a firm rent a substantial lump of wealth — their human capital — to the firm, and the rental rates for their human capital signaled by the managerial labor market are likely to depend on the success or failure of the firm. The function of management is to oversee the contracts among factors and to ensure the viability of the firm. For the purposes of the managerial labor market, the previous associations of a manager with success and failure are information about his talents. The manager of a firm, like the coach of any team, may not suffer any immediate gain or loss in current wages from the current performance of his team, but the success or failure of the team impacts his future wages, and this gives the manager a stake in the success of the team. . . .

We come now to the central question. To what extent can the signals provided by the managerial labor market and the capital market, perhaps along with other market-induced mechanisms, discipline maangers? . . .

The Viability of Separation of Security Ownership and Control of the Firm: General Comments

The outside managerial labor market exerts many direct pressures on the firm to sort and compensate managers according to performance. One form of pressure comes from the fact that an ongoing firm is always in the market for new managers. Potential new managers are concerned with the mechanics by which their performance will be judged, and they seek information about the responsiveness of the system in rewarding performance. Moreover, given a competitive managerial labor market, when the firm's reward system is not responsive to performance the firm loses managers, and the best are the first to leave.

There is also much internal monitoring of managers by managers themselves. Part of the talent of a manager is his ability to elicit and measure the productivity of lower managers, so there is a natural process of monitoring from higher to lower levels of management. Less well appreciated, however, is the monitoring that takes place from bottom to top. Lower managers perceive that they can gain by stepping over shirking or less competent managers above them. Moreover, in the team or nexus of contracts view of the firm, each manager is concerned with the performance of managers above and below him since his marginal product is likely to be a positive function of theirs. Finally, although higher managers are affected more than lower managers, all managers realize that the managerial labor market uses the performance of the firm to determine each manager's outside opportunity wage. In short, each manager has a stake in the performance of the managers above and below him and, as a consequence, undertakes some amount of monitoring in both directions.

All managers below the very top level have an interest in seeing that the top managers choose policies for the firm which provide the most positive signals to the managerial labor market. But by what mechanism can top management be disciplined? Since the body designated for this function is the board of directors, we can ask how it might be constructed to do its job. A board dominated by security holders does not seem optimal or endowed with good survival properties. Diffuse ownership of securities is beneficial in terms of an optimal allocation of risk bearing, but its consequence is that the firm's security holders are generally too diversified across the securities of many firms to take much direct interest in a particular firm.

If there is competition among the top managers themselves (all want to be the boss of bosses), then perhaps they are the best ones to control the board of directors. They are most directly in the line of fire from lower managers when the markets for securities and managerial labor give poor signals about the performance of the firm. Because of their power over the firm's decisions, their market-determined opportunity wages are also likely to be most affected by market signals about the performance of the firm. If they are also in competition for the top places in the firm, they may be the most informed and responsive critics of the firm's performance.

Having gained control of the board, top management may decide that collusion and expropriation of security holder wealth are better than competition among themselves. The probability of such collusive arrangements might be lowered, and the viability of the board as a market-induced mechanism for low-cost internal transfer of control might be enhanced, by the inclusion of outside directors. The latter might best be regarded as professional referees whose task is to stimulate and oversee the competition among the firm's top managers. In a state of advanced evolution of the external markets that buttress the corporate firm, the outside directors are in their turn disciplined by the market for their services which prices them according to their performance as referees. . . .

This analysis does not imply that boards of directors are likely to be composed entirely of managers and outside directors. The board is viewed as a market-induced institution, the ultimate internal monitor of the set of contracts called a firm, whose most important role is to scrutinize the highest decision makers within the firm. In the team or nexus of contracts view of the firm, one cannot rule out the evolution of boards of directors that contain many different factors of production (or their hired representatives), whose common trait is that their marginal products are affected by those of the top decision makers. On the other hand, one also cannot conclude that all such factors will naturally show up on boards since there may be other market-induced institutions, for example, unions, that more efficiently monitor managers on behalf of specific factors. All one can say is that in a competitive environment lower-cost sets of monitoring mechanisms are likely to survive. . . .

To [better understand] the problem we are trying to solve, let us first examine the situation where the manager is also the firm's sole security holder, so that there is clearly no incentive problem. When he is sole security holder, a manager consumes on the job, through shirking, perquisites, or incompetence, to the point where these yield marginal expected utility equal to that provided by an additional dollar of wealth usable for consumption or investment outside of the firm. The manager is induced to make this specific decision because he pays directly for consumption on the job; that is, as manager he cannot avoid a full ex post settling up with himself as security holder.

In contrast, when the manager is no longer sole security holder, and in the absence of some form of full ex post settling up for deviations from contract, a manager has an incentive to consume more on the job than is agreed in his contract. The manager perceives that, on an ex post basis, he can beat the game by shirking or consuming more perquisites than previously agreed. This does not necessarily mean that the manager profits at the expense of other factors. Rational managerial labor markets understand any shortcomings of available mechanisms for enforcing ex post settling up. Assessments of ex post deviations from contract will be incorporated into contracts on an ex ante basis; for example, through an adjustment of the manager's wage.

Nevertheless, a game which is fair on an ex ante basis does not induce the same behavior as a game in which there is also ex post settling up. Herein lie the potential losses from separation of security ownership and control of a firm. There are situations where, with less than complete ex post settling up, the manager is induced to consume more on the job than he would like, given that on average he pays for his consumption ex ante. . . .

Suppose a manager's human capital, his stream of future wages, is a marketable asset. Suppose the manager perceives that, because of the consequent revaluations of future wages, the current value of his human capital changes by at least the amount of an unbiased assessment of the wealth changes experienced by other factors, primarily the security holders, because of his current deviations from contract. Then, as long as the manager is not a risk preferrer, these revaluations of his human capital are a form of full ex post settling up. The manager need not be charged ex ante for presumed ex post deviations from contract since the weight of the wage revision process is sufficient to neutralize his incentives to deviate.

It is important to consider why the manager might perceive that the value of his human capital changes by at least the amount of an unbiased assessment of the wealth changes experienced by other factors due to his deviations from contract. . . . Although his next wage may not adjust by the full amount of an unbiased assessment of the current cost of his deviations from contract, a manager with a multiperiod horizon may perceive that the implied current wealth change, the present value of likely changes in the stream of future wages, is at least as great as the cost of his deviations from contract. In this case, the contemporaneous change in his wealth implied by an eventual adjustment of future wages is a form of full ex post settling up which results in full enforcement of his contract. Moreover, the wage revision process resolves any potential problems about a manager's incentives even though the implied ex post settling up need not involve the firm currently employing the manager; that is, lower or higher future wages due to current deviations from contract may come from other firms. . . .

Conclusions

. . . No claim is made that the wage revision process always results in a full ex post settling up on the part of the manager. There are certainly situations where the weight of anticipated future wage changes is insufficient to counterbalance the gains to be had from ex post shirking, or perhaps outright theft, in excess of what was agreed ex ante in a manager's contract. . . .

The extent to which the wage revision process imposes ex post settling up in any particular situation is, of course, an empirical issue. But it is probably safe to say that the general phenomenon is at least one of the ingredients in the survival of the modern large corporation, characterized by diffuse security ownership and the separation of security ownership and control, as a viable form of economic organization.

NOTES AND QUESTIONS

1. Notice the importance that attitude toward risk, specifically risk aversion, plays in the economic analysis of the corporate firm in the selections in this chapter. For the sake of the reader who lacks any background in economics, it may be helpful if we spell out in somewhat greater detail than in the selections what economists mean by terms like "risk aversion" and "risk preference."

Where an outcome is uncertain, the economist speaks of it as an "expected" outcome. The "value" of an expected outcome is the dollar value (or cost) of the outcome if it occurs, "discounted" (i.e., multiplied) by the probability of its occurrence. Thus, the "value" of a lottery ticket which gives the holder a .0001 chance of winning $10,000 is $1.00. However, the "utility" of the expected outcome may differ from its "value." Utility may, for present purposes, be defined as the price that an individual would consider equivalent to the expected outcome. Stated differently, the utility of the expected outcome is the sum certain that is subjectively equivalent to the expected (uncertain) outcome. If the utility and value of an expected outcome are identical for some individual, that individual, at least as regards the transaction in question, is said to be "risk neutral." If the utility to him is less than the value, he is "risk averse"; if it is greater than the value, he is "risk preferring." Thus, in the above example, if the lottery ticket had a utility of less than $1.00 to the individual, he would be risk averse; if it had a utility of $1.00, he would be risk neutral; and if it had a utility of more than $1.00, he would be a risk preferrer. Gamblers are risk preferrers because the cost of the gamble always exceeds the value (in the special sense defined above) of the gamble. Can you see why?

Economists believe that most people in most settings are risk averse; studies of the securities markets by finance theorists have provided, as we shall see (in the Brealey reading in Chapter 6), quantitative evidence in support of this belief. Its theoretical basis is the principle of diminishing marginal utility of income—i.e., that one's second dollar confers less utility than one's first, one's third less than one's second. Can you see the connection between diminishing marginal utility of income and risk aversion?

Risk is normally measured in terms of the dispersion of expected outcomes. A lottery ticket with a .9999 chance of winning nothing and a .0001 chance of winning $10,000 would be said to be more risky than a lottery ticket with a .9 chance of winning nothing and a .1 chance of winning $10, even though the value of the two gambles is the same. (Can you relate this result to the principle of diminishing marginal utility of income?) Dispersion can be reduced by pooling independent risks—a principle illustrated by the fact that the average mortality of the American population ("life expectancy") varies much less than the mortality of the individual members of the population. The individual American may die at 20 or 40 or 90 but the average American dies at exactly 70.1. Can you relate this result to the propensity of risk-averse individuals to hold diversified portfolios? How would you define "diversification"? We shall return to these points, especially in Chapter 7.

2. Notice that Alchian and Demsetz criticize Coase as ascribing too much importance to the "fiat" elements in the method of organizing production through the firm. Yet they themselves emphasize

the importance of the firm's right to terminate the employment of members of the "team." Isn't the right to terminate employment an essential aspect of the "fiat" or hierarchical method of organizing production through the firm that distinguishes the firm from the contract as a method of organizing production? Of course, contracts, too, often provide for termination at will; and discharge of employees may be limited by collective-bargaining agreements or long-term employment contracts. Ordinarily, however, a refusal to do the work the employer wants is grounds for termination; and without such a right of termination the hierarchical organization of the firm would be impaired.

3. Do you think Jensen and Meckling are correct in suggesting that if there were no principle of limited liability of a corporation for its torts, the liability of the shareholder would be limited to his proportionate share of the tort liability of the corporation? Are they unaware of the principle of tort law (changed by statute in many jurisdictions, to be sure) that there is no right of contribution among joint tortfeasors? Or do they think the shareholders would enter into an agreement indemnifying any shareholder who paid more than his pro rata share?

4. The Williamson article utilizes an empirical technique which is very common in the social sciences and has been used extensively by economists and finance scholars in empirical studies of various dimensions of corporate behavior. This is not the place to attempt an explanation of regression analysis beyond the barest minimum necessary to make the Williamson article intelligible. For a good introduction to statistical inference with special reference to economics, see Thomas H. Wonnacott and Ronald T. Wonnacott, Introductory Statistics for Business and Economics (1972).

Briefly, regression analysis is a statistical technique for explaining (by regressing) one variable (the dependent variable) by (on) another or others (the independent variable or variables). In the regression analysis presented in Table 1 of Williamson's article, the dependent variable is the level of executive compensation and the independent variables are staff (administrative and selling expense), concentration, barriers to entry, and the composition of the board of directors (the proportion of management representatives on the board). The coefficient of each independent variable indicates the effect of that variable on the dependent variable. The sign of the coefficient (i.e., whether positive or negative) is very important. If the sign is positive, it means that an increase in the independent variable is associated with an increase in the dependent variable; if negative, it means that an increase in the independent variable is associated with a decrease in the dependent variable. Notice that all of the signs in Table 1 are positive, meaning that, as Williamson hypothesizes, executive compensation rises with increases in staff, concentration, barriers to entry, and the fraction of the board that consists of management.

In appraising the significance of the results, it is important to consider (among other factors that we won't try to explain) both the statistical significance of the coefficients and the size of the coefficient of determination (R^2). Statistical significance is a measure of the likelihood that a correlation (e.g., the positive correlation between concentration and executive compensation) is not just the result of chance. Conventionally, statistical correlations in social science research are considered significant if there is a five percent or less probability that the correlation is the product purely of chance — a condition satisfied if the coefficient is at least twice the size of its standard error. The ratio of the coefficient to its standard error is known as a t-statistic; a t-statistic of 2 or greater thus indicates that the coefficient is significantly different from zero at the five percent level. If, as with some of the correlations in Table 1, the significance level is greater than five percent (e.g., there is only a one percent chance that the correlation is the result of pure chance), so much the better.

The coefficient of determination indicates the percentage of variance in the dependent variable that is explained by the independent variables in the regression. For example, in Williamson's regression for 1953, 78.6 percent of the variance in executive compensation across the companies in the sample is explained by the independent variables in the regression. Generally, a low R^2 would suggest that the regression analysis had failed to identify the most important determinants of the dependent variable. However, a very high R^2 could result simply from a high correlation between the independent variables in the regression analysis and some omitted variable.

5. There have been recurrent proposals to place labor representatives on the boards of directors of corporations; such a proposal was recently implemented by Chrysler Corporation. And "codetermination" (as labor participation in management is sometimes called) has long been required of some companies under German corporation law. What are the effects of codetermination on the efficiency with which corporate assets are managed? They are summarized in Michael C. Jensen and William H. Meckling, Rights and Production Functions: An Application to Labor-Managed Firms and Codetermination, 52 J. Bus. 469, 503–504 (1979), as follows:

> Efforts to analyze the behavior of the codetermined firm face a serious problem just getting off the ground. We do not have a theory that will tell us how supervisory boards will behave, or at least none in which

we have any confidence. Even in the "parity" representation case the supervisory boards could end up behaving as if they represented only the stockholders. Given the German law, for example, where the chairman, who is elected by stockholders, has the deciding vote in case of ties and where one of the labor representatives is from the salaried ranks, it is possible that the stockholders will have complete control over the affairs of the firm. Certainly in the short run this is a reasonable prediction of how codetermination will work. In the long run, however, it is possible that codetermination will lead to the other end of the spectrum, that is, codetermination could end up effectively turning the firm over to labor.

If labor gets complete control of supervisory boards what will happen? Our prediction: It will likely turn into the Yugoslav-type system with state ownership of productive resources and all the problems of the pure-rental and Yugoslav firms. In brief, they will have (1) the horizon problem, induced by the truncated (nonperpetual) claims on firm cash flows; (2) the common-property problem, induced by the equal sharing of firm cash flows among employees; (3) the nontransferability problem, induced by the fact that workers' claims on firm cash flows are contingent on employment with the firm and are non-marketable; (4) the voting problem, induced by the rule requiring one vote per employee in the political process for decision making within the firm; (5) the savings-investment problem, induced by the illegality of personal investment in productive capital goods and the necessity for the state to set interest rates, choose projects, and supply all the producer capital.

Chapter 3

The Corporation's Social Responsibility

The selections in this chapter extend and illustrate the discussion in the last chapter of the separation of ownership and control in the large publicly-held corporation. That separation presumably frees corporate managers to pursue courses of action that sacrifice profits, not only to their own private enjoyment, but also to some broader conception of social welfare. This might take the form of gifts to charity, or avoiding imposition of harmful externalities (such as pollution) beyond the point of merely profit-maximizing compliance with law (or in the absence of any law on the subject), or paying workers more than their marginal product.

There are normative and positive issues here. The normative issue is whether it is a good thing for management to subordinate profit maximization to other goals. This issue is considered in the first selection in the chapter, which is excerpted from a recent article by David Engel. The positive question is whether there is sufficient separation of ownership and control to enable managers to pursue courses of action that sacrifice profits to other goals. This is the question investigated in Orace Johnson's paper in this chapter, using the example of corporate gifts to charity. The chapter closes with a selection by Robert Solow which wittily and concisely reviews the social responsibility issue as formulated by Professor Galbraith.

An Approach to Corporate Social Responsibility*

David L. Engel

. . . [I]s it sensible, or even possible, to ask about the social desirability of corporate altruism without also asking about the desirability of individual altruism?

I do think that the desirability of corporate voluntarism is to a significant degree a distinct topic. The fundamental reason for this — in very oversimplified form — may be thought of as the necessity that corporate altruism rest on a narrower social justification than is available to support individual altruism. Consider, for example, the case of cash gifts to organized charities. Any social justifications one might advance for the making of such gifts by for-profit corporations would almost surely apply as well to donations by individuals. But if all such common rationales for both corporate and individual donations were to prove unpersuasive, there would remain one vitally important justification applicable only to individual giving: the pleasure taken from it by the donors themselves — the aspect of charitable giving that resembles any consumption expenditure. The analogous rationale, with respect to corporate donations could not, as a practical matter, rest on any pleasure taken by the shareholders. Rather, it would have to involve the gratification felt by management. And as soon as the matter is put that way it becomes apparent, as a question of both law and policy, that this "consumption" justification just does not work with respect to corporate donations. . . .

It is (somewhat loose) first-year economics that "in competitive markets, a sustained commitment to any goal other than profitability will lead to bankruptcy unless collusion is permitted." But since most large public companies compete, at least in large part, in oligopolistic markets, this principle does not in any case throw much light on the debate about altruism by public corporations. Rather, the essential economic limit on the kinds of voluntarism we are discussing is the level of altruistic activity at which, were an outsider to try to wrest corporate *control* from the current managers and eliminate the altruistic practice, his expected gains from so doing would exceed his costs.

While this observation has been frequently made, two related ones have not. First, the degree of competitiveness in the product market is significant even where the outer limit on corporate altruism is the threat of takeover rather than of bankruptcy: The less

*Source: 32 Stan. L. Rev. 1-98 (1979), reprinted with permission. Copyright © 1979 by the Board of Trustees of the Leland Stanford Junior University. Formerly professor of law at Stanford University, David Engel now practices law in Boston.

competitive the product market, the more the costs of altruism will be borne by the firm's customers rather than its shareholders, and so the higher the level of altruism that can be practiced before it is worthwhile for an outsider to attempt to displace current management. Second, even monopolistic product markets would not seem to enable a firm to pass on to customers any of the costs of voluntarism if those costs are unrelated to volume of production. That is, a flat, one-time altruistic expense will not shift the firm's marginal cost curve upward, and so will not make it worthwhile for even a monopolistic firm to raise price and reduce volume; such a one-time expense will be borne entirely by the shareholders.

What is most striking out of all this is that, in the case of a large, publicly held corporation — the very kind of corporation at whom the corporate social responsibility proponents have in fact directed their proposals for structural reform — conditions allowing *substantial* management voluntarism in the course of operations are likely to be present even today. Many such corporations do compete in oligopolistic product markets; most forms of voluntarism in the course of operations may be expected to raise marginal (and not just fixed) costs to at least some degree; and, above all, it is generally very expensive to displace the management of a publicly held corporation. It is not surprising, then, that a broad range of people perceive the current managements of public corporations as having substantial "discretionary funds" at their disposal. And if public corporations were somehow restructured, so that an increased tendency toward altruism would be not just an isolated leaning by one management but rather a general and unavoidable phenomenon — a phenomenon not to be dispelled in any given corporation merely by taking control of, say, the insider directorships — then this perceived room for management discretion could only be increased. . . .

As I started the previous section by suggesting, public corporations should pursue only goals whose pursuit by corporations is supported by broad public consensus. The goals incorporated in the profit-maximization proxy are the ones most obviously likely to fulfill this requirement. . . . Insofar as the profit-maximization proxy fails at any time to direct corporate energies down routes supported by social consensus, the legislature has the power, at least in theory, to modify the profit consequences of any given corporate action, so as to nudge corporate behavior in the direction society prefers. The initial failure of the profit-maximization proxy would most likely be due to market imperfections, but conceivably also might result from society's wish to use corporate mechanisms to redistribute wealth, or perhaps even to accomplish goals that are in some sense "noneconomic." Whatever the source of the perceived shortcomings in the profit-maximization proxy, the legislature can enact liability rules, regulatory provisions backed by criminal sanctions, or other measures, to correct the shortcomings. At least as a first, rough presumption, the profit-maximization proxy at any given time may be taken to reflect—with more or less appropriate relative weights—the complex of social goals that society through its chosen representatives has decided that corporations should pursue. Moreover, the profit-maximization proxy communicates to corporate managements with relative clarity information about which available corporate actions are and are not likely to further society's chosen goals. . . .

A corporation that unremittingly pursued maximum profits would not, of course, be practicing social responsibility in our sense of the phrase. Therefore, given my starting proposition that public corporations should pursue only those social goals clearly signalled to them as supported by a social consensus, the central question of this essay—whether and when corporate voluntarism may be socially desirable—reduces to this: Are there other social goals, besides (or more accurately, instead of) those reflected in the profit-maximization proxy, whose pursuit by corporations is supported by broad social consensus, and whose dictates as applied to particular corporate decisions are signalled to management with reasonable clarity? . . .

[Rather than examine the conventional example of corporate social responsibility—gifts to charity—the author considers the question, should the corporation comply with laws beyond the point at which compliance is profit-maximizing? He begins with the example of a law that is enforced by] an arbitrary level of penalty meant to apply, at least in theory, to each instance of a given type of conduct without explicit dependence on the amount of damage actually caused in a given case. Whether such a flat-amount penalty is criminal or civil, it provides an ostensibly unambiguous dollar amount of liability for a given action. This makes it possible to argue that society, through its elected representatives, has reached a collective judgment that the damage from each such action shall be *deemed* to be $X. In the illustrative case of the pollution tax, for example, the legislature (through its delegates) would surely expend considerable effort trying to ensure that X would be set at a level, for each pollutant in each location, bearing some resemblance to actual damage. It could be argued that this legislative effort sanctions an altruistic decision by corporate management always to deem $X a cost of the relevant conduct—even if the conduct might well escape detection or prosecution.

Even in the case of flat-amount liabilities such as a pollution tax or criminal fines, the argument in this form is not persuasive. For the argument ignores, among other things, the likelihood that the nominal level of X will be set *above* the external social costs of the conduct at issue, *because* of the possibility of nondetection or nonprosecution. If one accepts the purely economic model of the criminal law — which surely contains significant insights for our purposes — then the legislature's estimate of external social costs is the product of $X and the probability of detection and conviction. Management's knowledge of the level of X, without also knowing the legislature's estimate of this probability, tells the corporation nothing. . . .

Fortunately for the proponents of corporate social responsibility, however, this economic model of the criminal law is itself far from totally persuasive. For one thing, it is disingenuous to accept the legislature's enactments as an accurate benchmark of appropriate behavior, while at the same time assuming deliberate corporate concealment of conduct whose public announcement might lead to more severe or different legislative reaction. Nondetection of a corporate violation of law may have two effects: First, the particular corporation whose conduct escapes detection cannot be prosecuted for it under current law; but second, concealment of the conduct may cause the legislature to underestimate the general level of the undesired activity in the society. Even if one were persuaded that the escape of some corporate conduct from prosecution never calls for corporate altruism because the legislature factors it into the penalty, the second effect is precisely one of legislative error, and may well be a basis for asking for some corporate voluntarism. However, at least as an initial matter, the form of voluntarism thus called for would seem to be altruistic *disclosure* rather than substantive abstention from disfavored conduct. As it happens, if a corporate management were persuaded to practice some voluntarism by this kind of case for altruistic disclosure, they would very likely end up practicing substantive voluntarism after all: Altruistic abstention from prohibited substantive conduct is likely to be cheaper than, for example, commiting a crime and then disclosing it. But this does not change the fact that the particular type of case of voluntarism we have just outlined is made out in the first instance as a case for altruistic disclosure. . . .

It is rather a different failing of the economic model of the criminal law that may be thought to support a case for *substantive* corporate voluntarism: Whatever the maximum level to which we are willing to raise the probability of detection and conviction of a given crime or, for example, instance of pollution, we may refrain, for a variety of reasons, from then setting the penalty for violation high enough so that its product with the detection/conviction probability accurately reflects external social costs. The general reluctance of many individual actors in the society to commit (particularly) crimes — a reluctance not fully explicable in terms of probability of detection/conviction and explicit penalties — somewhat compensates for this shortfall in punishment. It might well be argued that we need some equivalent compensation by corporate actors in their own spheres of operations; that is, that we want them — at least sometimes — to obey, for example, substantive criminal laws — or to spend money to keep lower-echelon employees within the laws — beyond the point dictated by profit-maximization.

But this just brings us back to the recurrent question: How is management to know *when* voluntary law-obedience is called for — or *how much* to spend beyond profit-maximizing investment on internal audit systems? . . .

[T]he proponents [of corporate voluntarism] might argue that we criminalize only those acts that we do not want performed in the society at all — regardless of cost. It is probably the perceived force of this argument, more than any other single factor, that explains why pleas are so much more common for voluntary corporate obedience of the criminal law than for any other particular form of corporate social responsibility. . . .

But . . . the argument that the socially optimal level of crime is zero seems particularly infirm in the corporate context. For there, except in the rare case where the board of directors systematically sanctions a criminal act or pattern of action by the corporation, every attempt by top management to reduce corporate crime involves the rather special costs of internal policy-promulgation, monitoring, and enforcement. It is not plausible to argue that *every* substantive crime represents a legislative judgment that *every* corporation should spend an *infinite* amount on an internal auditing system to ensure that *none* of its employees engages in the prohibited conduct. And yet as soon as the argument is diluted at all from this proposition, a moralistic approach to the meaning of substantive criminal law gives no guidance as to *how much* a corporation should spend to reduce lower-echelon crime. . . .

Where the level of liability explicitly depends on the amount of damage caused by each violation — as is the case with most ordinary civil liabilities — it seems even plainer that the only quantitative signal corporate management may be said to receive, as to the desirability of altruistic adherence to substantive legal norms, is its own estimate of the social costs [of violating the rule]. . . . [But] where the liability rule is unenforceable because of nondetection of violations, it seems probable that management will be ill-equipped to estimate external social costs at all — even though the legislature may have helped by narrowing the classes of bystanders whose costs should be included. Typically, it is difficult for a corporation to know how many people are likely to be damaged how much by, for example, its undetected pollution. Undetected conduct tends not to generate any experience about even the *nominal* amount of liability it should be deemed to entail under, for example, a civil damage rule. This lack of information does not eliminate all possibility of well-directed altruism by the undetected, polluting corporation. But, at least in the first instance, the only altruistic act that seems likely to be called for with reasonable clarity is to disclose the undetected pollution. . . .

Where, on the other hand, unenforceability is a result of expenses related to litigation, it seems a shade more likely to be accompanied by some management information about external social costs. Nevertheless, the information will not typically be good enough to constitute a clear signal of the socially desired substantive conduct. For one thing, it is unlikely even in this situation that data on external social costs will be at all precise; any such precision owes to something more than the presence of a liability rule. But even more generally, while a liability rule may well represent a legislative judgment that some kind of interpersonal utility comparisons by management are appropriate in a given substantive area, as soon as conviction (or for that matter detection) becomes less than certain it cannot just be assumed that a straight dollar-for-dollar cost-benefit comparison is what the legislature would have had in mind. That is, where nondetection or nonprosecution is possible, the legislature's failure to raise the ostensible penalty above, for example, actual damages may represent a judgment that the prospective corporate actor should weigh each dollar of its own potential benefit more heavily than each dollar of the bystander's cost. And so again, if a social consensus does call for straight dollar-for-dollar comparison in a given class of cases, it will take more than the presence of a liability rule to demonstrate this.

*Corporate Philanthropy: An Analysis of Corporate Contributions**

Orace Johnson

. . . Two alternative forces assumed most frequently to explain corporate giving are the traditional profit motive and, more recently, the evolving assertion of social responsibility or duty. Sometimes

*Source: 39 J. Bus. 489-504 (1966). Reprinted with permission of The University of Chicago Press. Orace Johnson is professor of accounting at the University of Illinois, and this article is drawn from the author's doctoral dissertation, Business Corporations and Philanthropy (University of Chicago, 1966).

these two different motives, profit and duty, lead to different predictions about the effect of firm size and industry structure on the extent of corporate contributions. We shall look for opportunities to make such predictions and then test them by reference to the data. . . .

At most points throughout this paper, the variable we seek to explain is the contribution ratio, which is the ratio of the dollar value of charitable contributions to the dollar amount of profits of various groupings of firms. Contributions will be defined as the dollar value of donations deducted in corporate income tax returns, as reported to the Internal Revenue Service (I.R.S.). Profits will be defined as "compiled net profit," also as reported to the I.R.S. . . .

A conventional view of the 5 per cent limit on deductibility of charitable contributions is that it is intended, as is the I.R.S. list of qualified tax-exempt organizations, to limit the firm's ability to avoid taxes and possibly to foster socially undesirable activities under the protection of the charitable deduction. Some writers, however, have argued that both the 5 per cent rule and the I.R.S. list should be interpreted as expressions of a social consensus that "responsible" firms *should* distribute 5 per cent of their pretax profits among the permitted donees.

Figure 1 shows, for the entire corporate economy from 1936 to 1961, the dollar amount of contributions from all active corporations. It also shows the contribution ratios for corporations having both net income and balance sheets; and also the aggregate ratios for all active corporations, including loss firms and those reporting no assets. Loss firms gave only 2 per cent to 3 per cent of the total contributions during 1940–61, and 5 per cent to 16 per cent in the late 1930's.

This record shows little evidence of any desire to exceed or even approach the 5 per cent limit. Whether firms have been unable to find sufficiently attractive opportunities for abuse of the contributions privilege or whether they have rejected the social directive to aid specified organizations, or possibly for still other reasons, it remains true that the aggregate contribution ratio exceeded 1 per cent in only three of the twenty-six years. These years, 1945, 1952, and 1953, were all years of high marginal tax rates on excess profits, and two of them (1945 and 1953) were followed by years in which the tax was removed and contributions fell sharply.

The effects of including loss corporations can be seen in the ratios for 1938, 1949, and 1958. In these recession years, the dollar volume of contributions dropped, but the ratio rose because profits fell even more.

The amount of contributions increased annually, except for five years: the three just mentioned plus 1946 and 1954. All five were

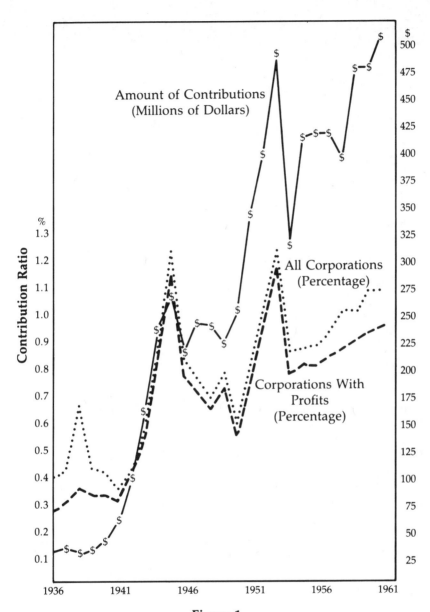

Figure 1
Corporate Contributions by All Industry, as Amount and as Percentage of Profits, for All Firms and Firms with Profits, 1936–1961

Source: Johnson, Figure 1, and Internal Revenue Service, Source Book of Statistics of Income, Corporation Income Tax Returns.

recession years. The sharpest drops occurred in 1946 and 1954 when excess-profits taxes were removed.

There are several possible explanations for the rising long-term trend in contributions, both as absolute amounts and as percentages of net profit. First, there might have been a gradual acceptance by both corporate management and stockholders of the previously mentioned concept of corporate responsibility, or at least of the importance of contributions as public relations.

Second, the increase might be more apparent than real. It might come from corporations gradually adapting to the newer category of tax deductions and deducting donations as contributions rather than as expenses. Thus, in 1951, the Tax Court would not allow an aircraft company to deduct as a business expense a donation to a local college for the establishment of a course in aeronautical engineering because the company had already reached the 5 per cent limit. If the 5 per cent limit cannot be exceeded by contributions masquerading as business expenses, then there might be the fear that a smaller percentage would be disallowed as an expense deduction while permitted as a contribution deduction. This explanation might seem to apply most clearly to the years soon after 1936 when the change occurred. Obviously, this "shifting" would tend to exhaust itself. Recent increases in donations are more likely to be real than apparent.

Finally, the increase in peacetime taxes, resulting in lower net costs to the corporation, might have increased corporate giving. This explanation is consistent with data summarized in Figure 1. Assuming that a majority of stockholders themselves would make equivalent contributions out of dividends, it is economical for the firm to contribute on their behalf. At high corporate tax rates, a stockholder might even be *willing* to accept a considerably different distribution of corporate contributions than he would make himself.

Some students have suggested that there is a positive relationship between an industry's concentration ratio and its contribution ratio. If concentration leads to or measures economic power, and if power somehow begets "responsibility" toward a wider range of groups, then firms in concentrated industries should have higher contribution ratios. Figure 2 shows the relationship between industrial concentration and the contribution ratio for selected industries in 1954 and 1958.

For 1954, Stigler identified fifteen industries in which the four largest firms shipped more than 60 per cent of the product in the national market. These percentages were paired with the aggregate contribution ratios for firms with more than $1 million assets. . . .

The negative relationship suggested by the scatter diagram is not consistent with the hypothesis that power leads to social respon-

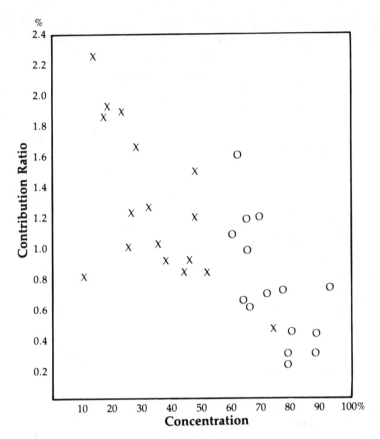

Figure 2
Industrial Concentration and Contribution to Philanthropy
Ratios for Selected Three-Digit [O] (1954) and Two-Digit
[X] (1958) Industries

Source: Johnson, Figure 2, and Internal Revenue Service, Source Book.

sibility. However, the concentration ratio is not necessarily related to other indexes of power, such as the absolute size of the largest firms, or monopoly. . . . A more precise analysis of industry structure and competitive behavior, one that goes beyond the simple concentration measures used in the second test, might lead to a different and better set of predictions of industry contribution ratios.

"If the corporation were in a perfectly competitive industry . . . no amount of charitable giving could be tolerated. Any increase in costs over those of competitors would result in the inability of the firm to survive." "Businessmen are free to practice the prerogatives of business statesmanship only to the extent that they are free from the compulsions of competition." By this reasoning, competitive industries will have comparatively low contribution ratios.

But the absence of competition is only a necessary but not a sufficient reason for contributions. The profit-maximizing monopolist is also free to make contributions at a very low level as well as a high one. Furthermore, gifts of product would more likely reduce sales for the monopolist than for the competitor. For these reasons, we should expect monopolistic industries to have low ratios if they are profit maximizers.

This leaves the industries that are at neither extreme. The term "rival" is used to designate firms that are oligopolistic, imperfectly or monopolistically competitive. Rival firms are more likely to seek a comparative advantage over each other by means that the atomistically competitive firms cannot, and the monopolistic firms need not, employ. Among these means, we can include contributions along with the conventional listing of advertising, product and marketing innovations, etc. . . .

Figure 3 contrasts the contribution ratios of the monopoly, competition, and rivalry categories for the entire period, 1936–61. The percentages shown are unweighted averages of the annual aggregate ratios for each industry sector. . . . The general picture is consistent with the hypotheses outlined at the beginning of this section. As predicted, monopoly and competition gave consistently at lower rates than rivalry sectors.

"The fundamental objection to bigness stems from the fact that big companies have monopolistic power. . . . " If this is so, then corporate giants will contribute at a comparatively low rate. Furthermore, the giants will exhibit a low rate if there are any economies of scale in buying good will with contributions. At the opposite extreme, if perfect competition is associated with the existence of firms of very small size, then the smallest firms will also contribute at a comparatively low rate. This again suggests that the in-between group of firms, middle sized and operating in industries where the middle-sized firms are relatively numerous, will have relatively higher contribution ratios. By this reasoning, the curve relating contribution rates to corporate size will be concave to the independent axis.

This prediction conflicts with the findings of two earlier studies. Andrews observed, "Indeed, in all asset classes the rate of giving as compared with profits showed a marked descent as the size of corporation increased." Watson said, "Although total dollar contributions of larger companies were bigger than those of smaller companies, the smaller companies were more generous in their contribu-

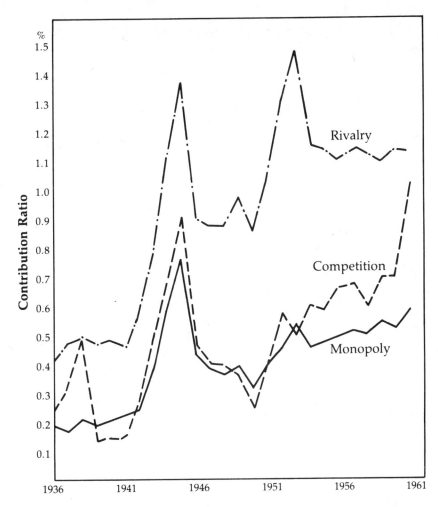

Figure 3
Industry Structure and Contribution Ratios, 1936–1961

Source: Johnson, Figure 3, and Internal Revenue Service, Source Book.

tions . . . as a percentage of income. . . ." Both studies were conducted in the absence of a theoretical framework for predictions. Consequently, the researchers misread their data, which actually show a curve that is not monotonically decreasing with increasing size. . . .

Figure 4 relates contribution ratios to asset size for all firms in three groupings of peacetime years and a pair of peak wartime years, 1945 and 1953. The horizontal scale, measuring asset size, is roughly geometric. The intervals progress usually by a factor of 2.

Class 1 has more than zero but less than $25,000 assets; class 2 has $25,000 but less than $50,000; class 3 has $50,000 but less than $100,000; and so on to class 14 which has $250 million and more. . . .

The significant association of rivalry with higher-than-average contribution ratios—and the lack of any general tendency for the largest-sized firms to give at the highest rates—confirms the predic-

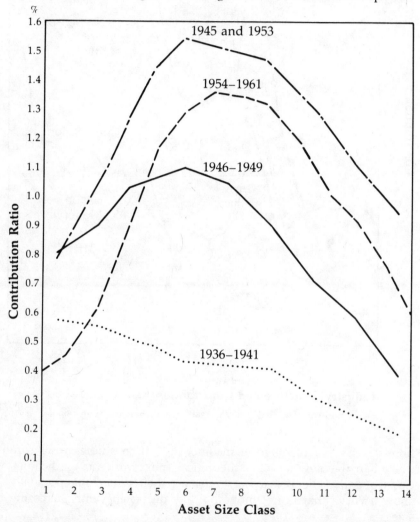

Figure 4
Corporate Size and Contribution Ratios Averages for Selected Time Periods

Source: Johnson, Figure 4, and Internal Revenue Service, Source Book.

tion that corporate contributions are motivated by a striving for competitive advantage. But this showing leaves much room for contributions to be affected by concepts of responsibility; even a perfect explanation of inter-industry *differences* in contribution ratios would not explain why all industries contribute something. . . .

The New Industrial State or *Son of Affluence**

Robert M. Solow

I shall try to summarize the main steps in Galbraith's argument [in The New Industrial State], and shall then return to discuss them, one by one.

(1) The characteristic form of organization in any modern industrial society is not the petty firm but the giant corporation, usually producing many different things, and dominating the market for most of them. Nor is this mere accident. The complicated nature of modern technology and the accompanying need for the commitment of huge sums of capital practically demand that industry be organized in large firms.

(2) With few exceptions, the giant corporation is in no sense run by its owners, the common stockholders. The important decisions are made—have to be made—by a bureaucracy, organized in a series of overlapping and interlocking committees. The board of directors is only the tip of an iceberg that extends down as far as technicians and department managers. The members of the bureaucracy are all experts in something, possibly in management itself. Galbraith calls them the "technostructure," but that awkward word is probably a loser.

(3) It is the nature of the highly-capitalized bureaucratically controlled corporation to avoid risk. The modern business firm is simply not willing to throw itself on the mercy of the market. Instead, it achieves certainty and continuity in the supply of materials by integrating backward to produce its own, in the supply of capital by financing itself out of retained earnings, in the supply of labor by bringing the unions into the act. It eliminates uncertainty on the selling side by managing the consumer, by inducing him, through advertising and more subtle methods of salesmanship, to buy what the corporation wants to sell at the price it wants to charge. The

*Source: Reprinted with permission of the author from 9 Public Interest 100-108 (Fall 1967). Copyright © 1967 by National Affairs, Inc. Robert M. Solow is professor at Massachusetts Institute of Technology.

major risk of general economic fluctuations is averted by encouraging the government in programs of economic stabilization.

(4) It would be asking much too much of human nature to expect that the bureaucracy should manage the firm simply in the interests of the stockholders. There is, therefore, no presumption that the modern firm seeks the largest possible profit. Nor does it. The firm's overriding goal is its own survival and autonomy; for security it requires a certain minimum of profit and this it will try to achieve. Security thus assured, the firm's next most urgent goal is the fastest possible growth of sales. (Since firms grow by reinvesting their earnings, this goal is not independent of profits; nevertheless, once the minimum target in profits is achieved, the modern firm will expand its sales even at the expense of its profits.) There are two lesser goals: a rising dividend rate, presumably to keep the animals from getting restless, and the exercise of technological virtuosity. . . .

There is a lot more in the book, much of it full of insight and merriment, but the main logic of the argument seems to be roughly as I have stated it. . . .

(1) Professor Galbraith is right that modern economics has not really come to terms with the large corporations. Specialists in industrial organization do measure and describe and ponder the operations of the very large firm. Occasionally some of these specialists propound theories of their financial or investment or pricing behavior. It cannot be said that any of these theories has yet been so successful as to command widespread assent. Perhaps for that reason, much economic analysis, when it is not directly concerned with the behavior of the individual firm, proceeds as if the old model of the centralized profit-maximizing firm were a good enough approximation to the truth to serve as a description of behavior in the large. But this is not always done naively or cynically. Professor Galbraith is not the first person to have discovered General Motors. Most close students of industrial investment or pricing do make room in their statistical behavior equations for behavior that is neither perfectly competitive nor simply monopolistic. . . .

There is, after all, a moderate amount of economic activity that is not carried on by General Motors, or by the 100 largest or 500 largest corporations. In fact, only about 55 percent of the Gross National Product originates in nonfinancial corporations at all. Not nearly all of that is generated by the giant corporations (of course, some financial corporations are among the giants). Nor is it entirely clear which way the wind is blowing. The giant corporation is preeminently a phenomenon of manufacturing industry and public utilities; it plays a much less important role in trade and services. If, as seems to be in the cards, the trade and service sectors grow relative to the total, the scope of the large corporation may be limited. Alternatively, big firms may come to play a larger role in industries that have so far been carried on at small scale.

Enough has been said to suggest that it is unlikely that the economic system can usefully be described either as General Motors writ larger or as the family farm writ everywhere. This offers at least a hint that it will behave like neither extreme. In any case, counting noses or assets and recounting anecdotes are not to the point. What is to the point is a "model" — a simplified description — of the economy that will yield valid predictions about behavior.

(2) The "separation of ownership from control" of the modern corporation is not a brand new idea. It is to be found in Veblen's writings and again, of course, in Berle and Means' The Modern Corporation and Private Property. Recent investigation shows that the process has continued; only a handful of the largest American corporations can be said to be managed by a coherent group with a major ownership interest. (The non-negligble rest of the economy is a different story.) I do not think the simple facts have ever been a matter for dispute. What is in dispute is their implications. It is possible to argue — and many economists probably would argue — that many management-controlled firms are constrained by market forces to behave in much the same way that an owner-controlled firm would behave, and many others acquire owners who like the policy followed by the management. I think it may be a fair complaint that this proposition has not received all the research attention it deserves. It is an error to suppose it has received none at all. Such evidence as there is does not give a very clear-cut answer, but it does not suggest that the orthodox presupposition is terribly wrong. Galbraith does not present any convincing evidence the other way, as I think he is aware. The game of shifting the burden of proof that he plays at the very end of this book is a child's game. Economics is supposed to be a search for verifiable truths, not a high-school debate.

(3) The modern corporation — and not only the modern corporation — is averse to risk. Many economic institutions and practices are understandable only as devices for shifting or spreading risk. But Galbraith's story that the industrial firm has "planned" itself into complete insulation from the vagaries of the market is an exaggeration, so much an exaggeration that it smacks of the put-on.

Galbraith makes the point that the planning of industrial firms need not always be perfect, that a new product or branch plant may occasionally go sour. By itself, therefore, the Edsel is not a sufficient argument against his position. His is a valid defense — but it is not one he can afford to make very often. No doubt the Mets "plan" to win every ballgame.

Consider the supply of capital. There is a lot of internal financing of corporations; it might perhaps be better if companies were forced more often into the capital markets. But external finance is hardly trivial. In 1966 the total flow of funds to nonfarm nonfinancial corporate business was about $96 billion. Internal sources accounted for $59 billion and external sources for the remaining $37 billion. Besides, depreciation allowances amounted to $38 billion of the internal funds generated by business, and much of this sum is not a source of net finance for growth. External sources provided about one half of net new funds. In 1966, bond issues and bank loans alone added up to about two-thirds of undistributed profits. Trade credit is another important source of external funds, but it is complicated because industrial corporations are both lenders and borrowers in this market. I don't know how the proportions of external and internal finance differ between larger and smaller corporations, but the usual complaint is that the large firm has easier access to the capital market. I do not want to make too much of this, because self-finance is, after all, an important aspect of modern industrial life. But there is, I trust, some point in getting the orders of magnitude right. There might also be some point in wondering if the favored tax treatment of capital gains has something to do with the propensity to retain earnings.

Consider the consumer. In the folklore, he (she?) is sovereign; the economic machinery holds its breath while the consumer decides, in view of market prices, how much bread to buy, and how many apples. In Galbraith's counterfable, no top-heavy modern corporation can afford to let success or failure depend on the uninstructed whim of a woman with incipient migraine. So the consumer is managed by Madison Avenue into buying what the system requires him to buy. Now I, too, don't like billboards or toothpaste advertising or lottery tickets of unknown — but probably negligible — actuarial value with my gasoline. (Though I put it to Professor Galbraith that, in his town and mine, the Narrangansett beer commercial may be the best thing going on TV.) But that is not the issue; the issue is whether the art of salesmanship has succeeeded in freeing the large corporation from the need to meet a market test, giving it "decisive influence over the revenue it receives."

That is not an easy question to answer, at least not if you insist on evidence. Professor Galbraith offers none; perhaps that is why he states his conclusion so confidently and so often. I have no great confidence in my own casual observations either. But I should think a case could be made that much advertising serves only to cancel other advertising, and is therefore merely wasteful.

If Hertz and Avis were each to reduce their advertising expenditures by half, I suppose they would continue to divide the total car rental business in roughly the same proportion that they do now. (Why do they not do so? Presumably because each would then have a motive to get the jump on the other with a surprise advertising campaign.) What would happen to the total car rental business? Galbraith presumably believes it would shrink. People would walk more, sweat more, and spend their money on the still-advertised deodorants. But suppose those advertising expenditures were reduced too, suppose that all advertising were reduced near the minimum necessary to inform consumers of the commodities available and their elementary objective properties? Galbraith believes that in absence of persuasion, consumers would be at a loss; total consumer spending would fall and savings would simply pile up by default.

Is there anything to this? I know it is not true of me, and I do not fancy myself any cleverer than the next man in this regard. No research that I know of has detected a wrinkle in aggregate consumer spending behavior that can be traced to the beginning of television. Perhaps no one has tried. Pending some evidence, I am not inclined to take this popular doctrine very seriously. (It is perhaps worth adding that a substantial proportion of all the sales that are made in the economy are made not to consumers but to industrial buyers. These are often experts and presumably not long to be diverted from considerations of price and quality by the provision of animated cartoons or even real girls.)

Consider the attitude of the large corporation to the economic stabilization activities of the Federal Government. It is surely true that big business has an important stake in the maintenance of general prosperity. How, then, to account for the hostility of big business to discretionary fiscal policy, a hostility only lately ended, if indeed traces do not still persist? Here I think Professor Galbraith is carried away by his own virtuosity; he proposes to convince the reader that the hostility has not come from the big business bureaucracy but from the old-style entrepreneurial remnants of small and medium-sized firms. Their fortunes are not so dependent on general prosperity, so they can afford the old-time religion. Professor Galbraith is probably wrong about that last point; large firms are better able than small ones to withstand a recession. He is right that the more Paleolithic among the opponents of stabilization policy have come from smaller and middle-sized business.

But up until very recently, the big corporation has also been in opposition. Even in 1961 there was considerable hostility to the investment tax credit, mainly because it involved the government too directly and obviously in the management of the flow of expenditures in the economy at large. It was only after further acquaintance with the proposal excited their cupidity that representatives of the large corporation came around. More recently still, they have generally opposed the temporary suspension of the credit as a counter-inflationary stabilization device, and welcomed its resumption. (This warm attachment to after-tax profits does not accord well with the Galbraith thesis.) There is a much simpler explanation for the earlier, now dwindling, hostility that would do no harm to the argument of the book: mere obtuseness.

(4) Does the modern industrial corporation maximize profits? Probably not rigorously and singlemindedly, and for much the same reason that Dr. Johnson did not become a philosopher—because cheerfulness keeps breaking in. Most large corporations are free enough from competitive pressure to afford a donation to the Community Chest or a fancy office building without a close calculation of its incremental contribution to profit. But that is not a fundamental objection to the received doctrine, which can survive if businesses merely *almost* maximize profits. The real question is whether there is some other goal that businesses pursue systematically at the expense of profits.

The notion of some minimum required yield on capital is an attractive one. It can be built into nearly any model of the behavior of the corporation. I suppose the most commonly held view among economists goes something like this (I am oversimplifying): for any given amount of invested capital, a corporation will seek the largest possible profits in some appropriately long-run sense, and with due allowance for cheerfulness. If the return on capital thus achieved exceeds the minimum required yield or target rate of return, the corporation will expand by adding to its capital, whether from internal or external sources. If the return on equity actually achieved (after corporation tax) is any guide, the target rate of return is not trivial. The main influence on profits in manufacturing is obviously the business cycle; for fairly good years one would have to name a figure like 12 percent, slightly higher in the durable-goods industries, slightly lower in nondurables. In recession years like 1954, 1958, 1961, the figure is more like 9 percent.

Alternatives to this view have been proposed. Professor Galbraith mentions William Baumol and Robin Marris as predecessors. Baumol has argued that the corporation seeks to maximize its sales revenue, provided that it earns at least a certain required rate of return on capital. This is rather different from Galbraith's proposal that corporations seek growth rather than size. These are intrinsically difficult theories to test against observation. Some attempts have been made to test the Baumol model; the results are not terribly decisive, but for what they are worth they tend to conclude against it. Marris's theory is very much like Galbraith's, only much more closely reasoned. He does propose that corporate management seeks growth, subject to a minimum requirement for profit. But Marris is more careful, and comes closer to the conventional view, because he is fully aware, as Galbraith apparently is not, of an important discipline in the capital market. The management that too freely sacrifices profit for growth will find that the stock market puts a relatively low valuation on its assets. This may offer an aggressive management elsewhere a tempting opportunity to acquire assets cheap, and the result may be a merger offer or a takeover bid, a definite threat to the autonomy of the management taken over. Naturally, the very largest corporations are not subject to this threat, but quite good-sized ones are.

Professor Galbraith offers the following argument against the conventional hypothesis. A profit-maximizing firm will have no incentive to pass along a wage increase in the form of higher prices, because it has already, so to speak, selected the profit-maximizing price. Since the modern industrial corporation transparently does pass on wage increases, it can not have been maximizing profits in the first place. But this argument is a sophomore error; the ideal textbook firm will indeed pass along a wage increase, to a calculable extent.

There is, on the other hand, a certain amount of positive evidence that supports the hypothesis of rough profit-maximization. It has been found, for instance, that industries which are difficult for outsiders to enter are more profitable than those which are easily entered and therefore, presumably, more competitive. It has been found, also, that there is a detectable tendency for capital to flow where profits are highest. Serious attempts to account for industrial investment and prices find that the profit-supply-demand mechanism provides a substantial part of the explanation, though there is room for less classical factors, and for quite a lot of "noise" besides. . . .

NOTES AND QUESTIONS

1. Is Engel correct in asserting that shareholders never derive a benefit from a corporation's gift to charity (or other altruistic deed)? Would this be true if the managers of the corporation were more efficient than the shareholders in gathering information regarding the relative worthiness of competing charities?

2. If corporate managers do not maximize corporate profits, does it follow that they embrace social goals? Isn't it necessary to show how their personal utility maximization entails social responsibility? Would it make a difference, so far as the likelihood of socially responsible behavior of corporations is concerned, whether the managers were maximizing their own utility (as suggested in the Williamson paper excerpted in Chapter 2) as its goal, or maximizing the sales, or growth in sales, of the firm (rather than its profits), as suggested by Professor Baumol? (See William J. Baumol, Business Behavior, Value and Growth [rev. ed. 1967]).

3. If contributions to charity are simply a form of advertising or public relations, as suggested in the Johnson piece, why should the contribution ratios of highly competitive firms be lower on average than those of imperfectly competitive firms? Does the definition of perfect competition somehow exclude expenditures on advertising and public relations? Why might it be thought to?

4. Why does Johnson say that "gifts of product would more likely reduce sales for the monopolist than for the competitor"?

5. Harold Demsetz, in Social Responsibility in the Enterprise Economy, 10 Sw. U.L. Rev. 1 (1978), suggests that the negative "externalities" (or harmful spillover effects) of monopolistic firms will be smaller than those of competitive firms; the former have a lower output (the charging of a monopoly price will reduce the demand for a firm's product), and so their undesired by-products such as pollution, which are presumably a function of their market output, will be fewer. Is there a fallacy in this argument? If the monopolized industry contracts, what will happen (in the long run) to the resources invested in that industry? Will the total physical output (including by-products such as pollution) of the economy necessarily be smaller when the economy has adjusted fully to the monopolization of a particular industry?

6. What is the optimal policy toward gifts to charity of a corporation that is in a lower federal income-tax bracket than its average shareholder, assuming that gifts to charity have no value to this corporation as advertising or public relations?

Part II

Limitations on Managerial Discretion: Protection of Shareholders

Chapter 4

Fiduciary Law and the "Competition in Laxity"

The preceding part has considered the corporation as a legal device for aggregating limited investments from many persons, most of whom have no intention of, capacity for, or interest in devoting their time to the conduct of the firm's business affairs. That means, as was noted, that those who do manage the firm have interests distinct from those of the stockholder-owners, but it does not mean that they are free to pursue those interests without constraint. In this part, we shall focus on the constraints, both legal and economic, on management disregard of shareholder welfare.

To the lawyer, the obvious and direct method of protecting shareholders from dishonest (though not from incompetent) managers is the imposition on the managers of legal obligations of fair dealing. The body of principles that lies at hand for such purposes is the law of fiduciaries, which governs for example the obligations of a trustee to the beneficiaries of the trust. State corporation codes make the corporate managers fiduciaries who are obligated to act in the best interest of the shareholders (in somewhat the same way that the trustee is a fiduciary of the trust beneficiaries), and impose personal liability for unfair self-dealing transactions, appropriations of corporate opportunities for personal gain, and other transgressions of the fiduciary principle.

The great problem that critics have seen in relying on the fiduciary provisions of the corporation codes is that corporate management can shop around among the states for a corporation code of their liking, perhaps because its fiduciary standards are not too strict, and then incorporate in that state. The states have a tax incentive to attract corporations to incorporate in them, and this "competition in laxity" or "race to the bottom" has been won by

Delaware.* That is the prevailing view, and it is challenged by Ralph Winter in the piece that opens this chapter. Winter argues that competition among the states for incorporations will lead to optimal, not inadequate, fiduciary principles protecting shareholders. The article by Peter Dodd and Richard Leftwich provides empirical evidence supporting Winter's conclusion.

The Winter reading discusses not only the competitive process among the states but also the contents of the fiduciary principles contained in corporation codes. An article by Alison Grey Anderson, excerpted in the Notes and Questions at the end of this chapter, provides a contrasting economic analysis of those principles.

The fiduciary principle relates not only to protection of shareholders from managers, but also to protection of minority shareholders from majority shareholders who might seek to "squeeze out" the minority under terms confiscatory of the value of the minority's shares. Indeed, one of the accusations against the Delaware code is that it provides insufficient protection to minority shareholders from unfair squeeze-outs. This issue is examined at the end of the chapter.

State Law, Shareholder Protection, and the Theory of the Corporation[†]

Ralph K. Winter, Jr.

The academic literature on the federal role in the shareholder-corporation relationship makes two claims. (1) Because state corporation codes do not require strict judicial scrutiny of many acts of corporate management, they leave shareholders in a vulnerable position. (2) The cause of this "tilt" in state corporation law lies in the operation of competitive legal systems. Because corporate chartering can generate substantial revenue for state treasuries, states compete for charters. Since the decision as to where to incorporate is a management decision and management's interests are adverse to those of shareholders, competitive legal systems tend to permissiveness so far as management conduct is concerned and to inadequate protec-

*See William L. Cary, Federalism and Corporate Law: Reflections Upon Delaware, 88 Yale L.J. 663 (1974). Similar charges have been leveled at the dual banking system. See Kenneth E. Scott, The Dual Banking System: A Model of Competition in Regulation, 30 Stan. L. Rev. 1 (1977).

†*Source:* Reprinted with permission from 6 J. Legal Stud. 251-292 (1977), copyright © 1977 by the University of Chicago Law School. Ralph K. Winter, Jr., is Townsend Professor of Law at Yale University.

tion for shareholders. The vast preponderance of academic opinion, and the conventional wisdom of those, such as Mr. Nader, who chronically favor further contraction of the private sector, is that the federal system works to benefit corporate management at a cost to shareholders and that federal regulation is necessary. . . .

No one denies that Delaware's open bidding for corporate charters has led to a steady lessening of the restrictiveness of state corporation law. Restrictions on the longevity of a corporation, the businesses in which it may engage, the issuance of stock, the classes of stock issued, dividend policy, discretion as to the holding of shareholder's meetings, charter amendments, means of electing directors, sales of assets, mortgaging, and the indemnification of officers, among others, have all been eliminated or diminished in a series of amendments to state corporation codes. It would further appear that the ability of a corporation to work fundamental changes, such as mergers or the elimination of minority shareholders, has been increased, as has management's power to work its will in a variety of matters, including some in which it may have a conflict of interest, e.g., management compensation.

The history of state corporation law is thus largely a history of drastic reduction of legal restrictions on management and of the legal rights of shareholders. This movement has not been at random but has rather occurred as corporations have sought charters in states with less restrictive codes. Other states have then adopted similar codes in response. As a result, the movement toward diminished restrictions has been national in scope and the Delaware Code is no longer significantly different from those of a number of other states.

An important mechanism generating change in American corporate law has thus been the competition among the states for charters. Both Delaware (40 per cent of the largest industrial corporations are chartered there) and its competitors candidly admit that the purpose of corporate code revisions has been the attraction of charters to their state in order to produce significant tax revenues. Delaware has benefitted in other ways. Not only is its corporation code an attraction to promoters and management but lawyers find it a hospitable jurisdiction in which to litigate issues of corporate law, with the result that the Wilmington Bar enjoys an unusually lucrative practice for a city of that size.

No one disputes these propositions. Rather, the controversy is over the effect on the governance of many of the nation's major economic units.

The most celebrated exposition of the conventional academic analysis, but avowedly not an original approach, is Federalism and Corporate Law: Reflections Upon Delaware, by Professor William

Cary of the Columbia University Law School,* a former Chairman of the Securities and Exchange Commission. Characterizing Delaware as leading a "movement toward the least common denominator" and a "race for the bottom," Professor Cary argues that Delaware's lessening of the restrictiveness of its corporation code has left shareholders an easy prey to self-dealing management. To this unhappy conclusion he adds an attack on the Delaware judiciary and argues that "Gresham's law applies" to its decisions, which "lean toward the status quo and adhere to minimal standards of director responsibility."

Having rejected full federal chartering as "politically unrealistic," Professor Cary calls for federal minimum standards legislation. This legislation, designed to "raise" the standards of management conduct, would, he claims, increase public confidence — and investment — in American corporations.

The claim, it is absolutely critical to note, is not that an overriding social goal is sacrificed by state law, but simply that Delaware is preventing *private* parties from optimizing their *private* arrangements. With all due respect both to Professor Cary and to the almost universal academic support for his position, it is implausible on its face. The plausible argument runs in the opposite direction: (1) If Delaware permits corporate management to profit at the expense of shareholders and other states do not, then earnings of Delaware corporations must be less than earnings of comparable corporations chartered in other states and shares in the Delaware corporations must trade at lower prices. (2) Corporations with lower earnings will be at a disadvantage in raising debt or equity capital. (3) Corporations at a disadvantage in the capital market will be at a disadvantage in the product market and their share price will decline, thereby creating a threat of a takeover which may replace management. To avoid this result, corporations must seek out legal systems more attractive to capital. (4) States seeking corporate charters will thus try to provide legal systems which optimize the shareholder-corporation relationship.

The conclusion that Delaware shares sell for less is implicit in Professor Cary's analysis, for if a "higher" legal standard for management conduct will increase investor confidence, investor confidence in Delaware stock must have been less than in stocks of other states for more than a generation. This lack of confidence would have long been reflected in the price of Delaware shares. Moreover, a reduction in the earnings of a corporation will affect its ability to raise debt capital, as well as equity, since the risk of a lender is

*[83 Yale L.J. 663 (1974) — Eds.]

thereby increased and a higher interest rate will be charged. Delaware corporations, therefore, not only face a lower share price but also must pay higher interest rates.

This analysis is not crucially dependent upon the consumer of securities or lenders understanding the intricacies of corporate law or knowing of the general permissiveness of the Delaware Code. That, indeed, must be what Professor Cary means when he argues that increased confidence will result from more protective legal systems. A simple comparison of earnings of various corporations, for example, will affect the price of Delaware stock. Moreover, institutional investors — not to mention investment counselors — cannot be unaware of such crucial facts and their role in the stock market is so critical that their knowledge alone will sharply affect share price. The claim that Delaware is leading a "race for the bottom" has been made so frequently and by so many that it can hardly be described as a carefully guarded secret. Recent work on the stock market strongly suggests that relatively obscure — even confidential — information is transmitted extremely swiftly and almost automatically affects share price. That the impact of a legal system on investors would be known only to law professors and Mr. Nader seems a rather tenuous proposition.

It is not in the interest of Delaware corporate management or the Delaware treasury for corporations chartered there to be at a disadvantage in raising debt or equity capital relative to corporations chartered in other states. Management must induce investors freely to choose their firm's stock instead of, among other things, stock in companies incorporated in other states or other countries, bonds, bank accounts, certificates of deposit, partnerships (general or limited), individual proprietorships, joint ventures, present consumption, etc. . . . [A] corporation's ability to compete effectively in product markets is related to its ability to raise capital, and management's tenure in office is related to the price of stock. If management is to secure initial capital and have continuous access to ready capital in the future, it must attract investors away from the almost infinite variety of competing opportunities. Moreover, to retain its position management has a powerful incentive to keep the price of stock high enough to prevent takeovers, a result obtained by making the corporation an attractive investment.

The Cary analysis thus seems implausible at an *a priori* level, because, when analyzed, it appears as little more than a claim that Delaware can facilitate the monopolization of the capital market, just as it can grant exclusive franchises for taxicabs in Wilmington. But the market for capital is international in scope and involves an undifferentiated product with no transportation costs. Delaware cannot create barriers which prevent it from flowing to the most attractive investments; any attempt at monopolization will only drive capital from that state.

The fact that other states have found it necessary to change their law in response to Delaware, therefore, strongly suggests that investors do not share Professor Cary's view and in fact believe that they do better under Delaware law than under the laws of the other states. . . .

Intervention in private transactions which impose no social cost can be justified only as a means of reducing the costs to the private parties. Thus, a prime function of state corporation codes is to supply standard terms which reduce the transaction costs, and thereby increase the benefits, of investing by eliminating costly bargaining which might otherwise accompany many routine corporate dealings. But substituting a mandatory legal rule for bargaining also may impose a cost in the form of the elimination of alternatives which the parties might prefer.

Much of the legal literature calling for further federal regulation either assumes that no costs will fall upon shareholders or merely undertakes a cursory "eyeballing" of the potential costs. To be sure, self-dealing and fraud exist in corporate affairs and their elimination is desirable. But at some point the exercise of control by general rules of law may impose costs on investors which damage them in both quantity and quality quite as much as self-dealing or fraud. A paradox thus results: maximizing the yield to investors generally may, indeed almost surely will, result in a number of cases of fraud or self-dealing; and eliminating all fraud or self-dealing may decrease the yield to shareholders generally.

For example, numerous proposals have been made to increase the power of shareholders over the corporate destiny by enabling them to initiate proposals to be submitted to shareholders, by requiring cumulative voting, by compelling management to make extensive information available to any requesting shareholder, by requiring shareholder votes on certain matters, and so on. There is, however, no established or even apparent connection between increasing shareholder power and increasing the yield to investors. To be sure, the lack of shareholder control may have led to some self-dealing, but the elimination of self-dealing by increasing that control involves a trade-off with corporate efficiency and may well reduce the return to shareholders generally. Whether the amount saved in eliminating isolated instances of self-dealing through increased shareholder control is greater than a general loss in corporate efficiency is the issue, and it is neither intuitively nor empirically self-evident that the Delaware Code is not a satisfactory resolution. . . .

Another example involves the standard of care required of directors. Here the Delaware decision attacked by Professor Cary held that directors might rely on summaries, reports and corporate records as evidence that no antitrust violations were being committed by the company, even though 19 years earlier the Federal Trade Commission had issued a cease and desist order against price fixing. Professor Cary's suggestion is that an internal control system to prevent repeated antitrust violations would have prevented the fines and treble damages paid by the company. The issue, however, is not whether damages might be avoided but whether, even employing a simple negligence calculus, the expected value of damages (probability times likely amount) is greater than the cost of avoiding them. Requiring perfect fail-safe systems in every corporation can be far more costly than any potential loss to shareholders, and Professor Cary presents an incomplete analysis in concluding that loss could have been avoided. He is on more solid ground in suggesting that the need for preventive measures was greater in the particular case in light of past conduct since that is relevant to the likelihood of loss. . . .

A state which rigs its corporation code so as to reduce the yield to shareholders will spawn corporations which are less attractive as investment opportunities than comparable corporations chartered in other states or countries, as well as bonds, savings accounts, land, etc. Investors must be attracted before they can be cheated, and except for those seeking a "one shot," "take the money and run," opportunity to raid a corporation, management has no reason to seek out such a code. Just as shareholder yield and management discretion rise together, so too they may descend in tandem. Low yields to shareholders mean low stock prices which mean low costs of takeover which, as explained above, reduce the parameters of management discretion. The chartering decision, therefore, so far as the capital market is concerned, will favor those states which offer the optimal yield to both shareholders and management.

It is in neither management's nor the shareholders' interest to see the ability of a corporation to raise capital impaired. As Professor Baumol has noted, even a relatively small need for capital from stock issues can impose discipline on a firm. Moreover, raising capital through equity or debt are closely related since investors and lenders both are making similar judgments about the long-run earning potential of the firm, and the management's power to drain off assets obviously affects either judgment. In short, the lower the stock price the higher the interest rate.

The availability of internal financing does not affect this since the true cost of using retained earnings as capital is the opportunity cost, the highest return available in alternative uses. If an investment of retained earnings in another venture would return 15 per cent, the true cost of using it within the firm is also 15 per cent. Thus, an efficient firm which can borrow at 12 per cent and invest its retained earnings will earn more than the inefficient firm which can borrow only at 18 per cent and must use its own retained earnings.

So far as the capital market is concerned, it is not in the interest of management to seek out a corporate legal system which fails to protect investors, and the competition between states for charters is generally a competition as to which legal system provides an optimal return to both interests. Only when that competition between legal systems exists can we perceive which legal rules are most appropriate for the capital market. Once a single legal system governs that market, we can no longer compare investor reaction. Ironically, in view of the conventional wisdom, the greater danger is not that states will compete for charters but that they will not. . . .

A single-minded focus on legal structure accompanied by an indifference to economic function has generated considerable unease among legal commentators over the present law governing transactions between directors and the corporations they serve. Because directors are said to be fiduciaries and, like trustees, owe a duty of loyalty to the shareholders, transactions with the corporation from which directors may profit are said to be tainted by a conflict of interest. Nineteenth-century law made all contracts in which a director was interested voidable at the instance of the corporation or shareholders no matter whether it was objectively fair. Today, the law is dramatically different. Generally, no such contract is voidable if, after disclosure, it is adopted by a majority of disinterested directors, ratified by the shareholders or unless a court finds it unfair to the corporation, a standard far below that imposed on fiduciaries such as trustees. This dramatic movement in corporate law is regarded by many critics as wholly unjustified and a source of considerable financial injury to shareholders.

For all the criticism, however, the shareholder losses are not visible to the naked eye. The movement from the legal rules which prevailed earlier (at a time labeled by these same critics as the Era of the Robber Barons) to those which prevail now has not been accompanied so far as one can tell by a corresponding decline in yield to shareholders or a movement by investors away from this alleged legalized robbery. These apparent nonevents are significant because few would doubt that similar changes in trust law would seriously injure trust beneficiaries and lead to a greatly reduced use, probably the disappearance, of that legal device. The failure of trust law to move in the same direction, moreover, may indicate that different economic forces are at work in the corporate area and the problem lies more in the analogy to trustees than in the competition for corporate charters.

Trustees by and large manage property within predetermined limits. Normally they operate under a trust instrument which both gives direction to their conduct and circumscribes their discretion as to risk, liquidity, etc. Their economic function is thus wholly dissimilar to that performed by corporate management. While trustees may face decisions as to portfolio mix, they are not charged with the entirely different task of hiring the most efficient mix of productive inputs or with monitoring the use of these inputs so as to avoid shirking. Trustees do not profit maximize in the context of the competitive market for products or services. They do not concern themselves with innovation in products or methods of production or distribution, the raising of capital or the choosing of personnel. Nor are they engaged in a team production effort which requires monitoring and the assignment of a residual share. Most important, trustees need not fear that beneficiaries may sell their interest to entrepreneurs who will install new trustees to manage the trust corpus. In short, trustees and corporate management have utterly different economic functions and operate under utterly different economic constraints. The movement of corporate law away from the strict trust analogy is the result, not of Delaware's perversity, but of the fact that the analogy is faulty.

. . . [M]anagement's participation in determining the share of the enterprise's earnings to go to it creates powerful incentives to profit maximize on the corporation's behalf and to keep the price of the company's stock high, just as the right to profits creates incentives for individual proprietors to manage their company well. Because corporate management's discretion in determining its own share of the corporate return is directly related to the market for management control and stock price, the incentives created benefit shareholders.

A single owner of an unincorporated business or general partners in a partnership also determine their "share" with an eye to what is necessary to hire capital, labor and raw materials and to maintain a healthy competitive stature. There is no calculation by which a fixed sum or percentage of the gross business is allocated to these "owners" as their "entitlement." Those who "own" management control in the corporate context operate under functionally similar circumstances which are obscured by an obsession with the shareholders' "ownership." The principal difference is simply that the fear of "looting" or "one-shot" raids is of no consequence in the case of the individual proprietorship (except perhaps as to creditors and thus the existence of a body of law about fraudulent conveyances) while it is a serious risk in the case of corporations.

Facts cited by corporate critics support the view that a residual share to management may benefit shareholders. Mr. Nader and his associates, for example, chose to demonstrate the "excessive" compensation received by corporate management through an appendix listing the corporate-related income of the executives of the fifty largest corporations. One supposes the critics chose these individuals because they are among the highest paid. Yet, if in fact management share and corporate or shareholder success go together, one should expect a rough correlation between size and executive compensation, at least to the extent there is a rough correlation between size and earnings. The point the critics are seeking to make would be better proven by demonstrating a correlation between *low* stock price, *low* earnings, and *high* executive compensation. Moreover, most of the individuals cited also held large blocs of stock in their corporations, a most peculiar investment if state corporation law allows them freedom to divert corporate income directly to themselves.

A "fairness" standard, of course, provides restraint only in egregious cases but closer judicial scrutiny may not be consistent with economic function. Fairness in this context is based on more than personal values since it involves objective comparisons with commercial arrangements of a known arm's-length nature and the economic health of the enterprise. This is consistent with the economic analysis above. The market constraints and incentives described operate only upon a management which views its future well-being in terms of a continuing relationship with the corporation (or in another corporation impressed by prior performance) and thus has an interest in maintaining stock price and avoiding a takeover. That management compensation will also be at a high level is the incentive to bring about this happy result. Shareholder vulnerability exists where a management undertakes a "one-shot" raid on the corporate assets and impairs the corporation.

The fairness rule seems an attempt to recognize both the incentives for management to increase stock price and the vulnerability of shareholders to "one-shot" raids. It permits distribution of a residual share to the team input monitor (management) but prohibits transactions which seem unlikely commercial arrangements when tested by arm's-length standards. It is thus a rule geared to economic function in the hope of optimizing efficiency rather than to legal analogy in the hope of creating a tidy legal structure for law professors.

The Market for Corporate Charters: "Unhealthy Competition" vs. Federal Regulation*

Peter Dodd and Richard Leftwich

Introduction

Competition among states for corporate charters is criticized in the legal literature where it is viewed as "unhealthy" because it supposedly results in a trend towards pro-management ("permissive") statutes. It is alleged that some states, in their quest to make their statutes more appealing to corporate management, provide management with so much freedom from stockholder control that shareholders receive inadequate protection. In support of their allegations, critics focus on the predominance of Delaware in the market for corporate charters and argue that the appeal of that state's corporation code to management is its disregard for the rights of stockholders. It is claimed that other states compete by offering similar codes, and Cary protests that Delaware is leading a "movement towards the least common denominator" and winning a "race for the bottom".

The proposed remedy for the deterioration of stockholder protection is federal intervention, with a body such as the Securities and Exchange Commission responsible for granting, and regulating the content of corporate charters. Only a central authority offers a solution to the "voting with the feet" problem, it is claimed, and congressional hearings have been held with a view to establishing federal chartering regulations.

Proponents of federal chartering present no empirical evidence to support their claims that stockholders of companies incorporated in Delaware (or in any of its counterparts) are at the mercy of management. The purpose of this paper is to investigate the case for federal chartering of corporations by examining evidence of the effect of the choice of a state of incorporation on the wealth of stockholders. . . .

The Market for Corporate Charters

Initial Incorporations

The numbers in Table 1 [omitted] support the contention that Delaware is a major supplier of corporate charters. In 1977, 436,170

*Source: Forthcoming in 53 J. Bus. (1980). Reprinted with permission of The University of Chicago Press. Peter Dodd and Richard Leftwich are assistant professors of accounting and finance at the Graduate School of Business, University of Chicago.

companies were newly incorporated in the United States, and 14,836 (3.40%) of these obtained their charters in Delaware. Only 6 states supplied more charters than Delaware, and each of these states is much larger than Delaware. When the states' chartering activity is scaled by population (as a measure of size, albeit crude), Delaware's chartering activity clearly dominates that of other states. Table 1 reveals that, in 1977, one company incorporated in Delaware for every 39 people in the state, compared with one company for every 220 people in Florida, the state with the next smallest ratio. Moreover, the dominance prevails across time. During the period 1945–1977, Delaware's share of new charters did not fall below 2.13% per year, and rose as high as 4.48% per year. When the state of incorporation of larger corporations is considered, the dominance of Delaware is striking, even in absolute numbers. For example, of all the firms listed on the New York Stock Exchange (NYSE) in 1977, approximately 40% were incorporated in Delaware.

Delaware's chartering activity is indeed impressive, especially for a state of its size. However, the sheer weight of numbers does not constitute evidence that stockholders of Delaware corporations suffer at the hands of management. The welfare of stockholders of Delaware corporations is not affected by the degree of protection afforded by the Delaware code, even if that code allows management to misappropriate stockholders' funds. Stockholders have an alternative means of protection — the price they are prepared to pay for the stock. The supposed lack of protection offered by the Delaware code is well-publicized. Provided stockholders' expectations are unbiased, the prices of shares of firms incorporated in any state reflect the costs that are expected to be imposed on stockholders by management. If, in the extreme, a particular state offered no protection at all (even to the extent of not enabling voluntary contracts to be enforced), shares of firms incorporated in that state would not sell for a positive price. This price protection argument represents an *a priori* challenge to the allegation that stockholders of firms incorporated in Delaware are disadvantaged.

Reincorporations

Even if a firm is incorporated in a state which offers shareholders extensive protection from management exploitation, shareholders cannot take that level of protection for granted. Firms can change their state of incorporation. Reincorporation in another state is usually achieved by establishing a subsidiary with the same name in the desired state. The parent is then merged into the subsidiary, and the subsidiary becomes the surviving corporation. According to the price protection argument, stockholders make unbiased estimates of the cost and probability of such switches when they make their initial purchase of the corporation's stock. When the switch to another state occurs (strictly, when it becomes known), most of the uncertainty associated with the event is resolved. If there is less protection for stockholders in the new state, the price of the stock falls to reflect the resolution of uncertainty and holders of the stock suffer a wealth loss. However, even in this scenario, stockholders are in no way fooled or exploited.

To assess the significance of Delaware in the market for reincorporations, we collected a sample of 140 New York Stock Exchange (NYSE) listed firms which changed their state of incorporation during the period 1927–1977. . . . The role played by Delaware is indeed overwhelming. Of the total of 140 switching firms, 126 (90.0%) changed to Delaware and only 6 (4.3%) left Delaware for other states. The states receiving the next largest number of changes were Connecticut, New Jersey, New York and Pennsylvania, each of which received only 2 (1.4%) switches. . . . The switching activity of the sample is heavily concentrated in the 1966–1977 period, but the dominance of Delaware pesists during the entire time period.

The dominance of Delaware in the market for reincorporations raises some interesting questions. Given that Delaware plays a large role in the market for new incorporations, but has some competitors, why does it have so little competition in the market for reincorporations? Why do switching firms incorporate elsewhere and then reincorporate in Delaware, and why does this behavior persist through time? We address these questions in the next section, and develop competing hypotheses concerning what motivates firms to incur the costs of changing their state of incorporation.

The Lure of Delaware: Competing Hypotheses

We discuss the following competing hypotheses concerning why firms change their state of incorporation to Delaware:
  (i) Stockholder Exploitation Hypothesis, and
  (ii) Cost Avoidance Hypothesis.

Stockholder Exploitation Hypothesis

Proponents of federal regulation of corporate charters argue that managers of firms change the state of incorporation to enrich themselves at the expense of stockholders. This hypothesis, which we call the stockholders exploitation hypothesis, has testable implications. Shareholders of firms which reincorporate in Delaware will, on average, suffer losses as the value of their shares falls to reflect an increase in the expected costs of exploitation by management. Note that, although we call this the exploitation hypothesis, it is entirely consistent with the price protection argument addressed above, and no one is fooled or exploited.

Those who propose arguments similar to the exploitation hypothesis allege that the predominance of Delaware in the market for charter switches is itself evidence in support of their arguments. Predominance, they contend, is consistent with the view that Delaware's appeal lies in the relative ease with which the state's code allows managers to exploit stockholders.

Cost Avoidance Hypothesis

We propose an alternative hypothesis to explain management's decision to change the state of incorporation. According to our cost avoidance hypothesis, management selects a state where the corporate code minimizes the expected costs of the firm's production-investment and financing activities. The attraction of a particular state may be not only the state code *per se,* but rather the interpretation of that code by the courts. For example, an often-quoted advantage of incorporation in Delaware is the long history of established precedents and predictable rulings of the Delaware judiciary. The predictability of court rulings lowers the legal costs of bringing and defending actions.

A decision to change the state of incorporation to avoid costs can be induced by two distinct types of events. First, the corporate code of the present "home" state or a potential "destination" state might have changed, resulting in lower costs for the firm in the destination state. Second, a particular firm can anticipate a change in its activities which results in a potential cost saving from switching states, given the states' corporate codes. For example, if a firm decides to undertake a policy of expanding by merger, it can switch to a state which reduces the cost of a merger by requiring a smaller percentage of stockholders to approve mergers. . . .

Whatever the event which is the source of the real cost savings, the cost avoidance hypothesis has empirical implications which are distinct from those of the shareholder exploitation hypothesis. If there are real cost savings associated with a switch, shareholders will not suffer losses when the switch is announced. To the contrary, the value of their shares could even increase. Whether shareholders of reincorporating firms suffer, on average, losses or reap gains is testable, and enables us to discriminate between the two hypotheses advanced above. In the next section of the paper, we describe the data we use to test the hypotheses.

Description of the Data

Moody's Industrial Manual (Moody's) provides a concise summary of the incorporation histories of industrial firms listed on the NYSE, American Stock Exchange, and regional exchanges. Utilities, transportation firms, banks, and finance corporations are not included in the manual.

We searched the 1977 edition of Moody's and discovered 199 NYSE firms which had changed their state of incorporation since 1927. That sample is neither complete nor unbiased, since it is comprised of surviving firms only, i.e., it does not include firms which have been delisted as a result of mergers or bankruptcy. To complete the sample, we collected a sample of switches for non-surviving NYSE firms during the period 1927–1977. Using the CRSP file of monthly security prices, we obtained the names of all firms delisted from the NYSE since 1927. There were 1,147 such corporations and we searched the history of incorporation for each of those corporations in the edition of Moody's immediately prior to its delisting. This process yields a sample of 81 switches for non-surviving NYSE firms, resulting in a total sample of 280 switches.

Our methodology requires information concerning the stock prices of the sample firms for months prior to and after the announcement of the change in state of incorporation.* When we imposed these minimum data requirements on the firms, our eligible sample size fell to 140, of which 26 were non-survivors. . . .

Initially, we obtained the month of the switch from Moody's also. Subsequently, we searched the Wall Street Journal Index for the period 1958–1977 for each firm in our sample to obtain the earliest date of the announcement to change states. For each of our 140 sample firms, we used the earliest date of announcement we were able to discover. The dates included in our study refer to: the date of mailing proxy material to stockholders, the date of stockholder approval of the merger with the dummy corporation, or the date of formal registration of the new charter. . . .

Results

The major results of this study are summarized in Table 5 [omitted] and Figure [5] where the monthly average prediction errors and

*[For an explanation of the research methodology used in this study, see the selection by G. William Schwert in Chapter 6 — Eds.

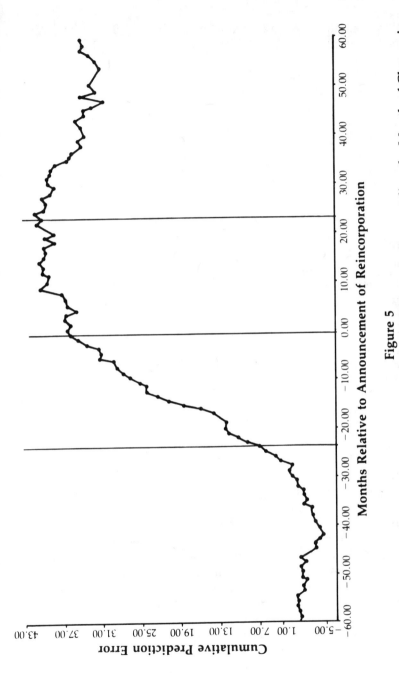

Figure 5

Plot of Cumulative Average Prediction Errors for the 120 Months Surrounding the Month of Change in State of Incorporation for 140 NYSE Firms

Source: Dodd and Leftwich, Figure 1.

105

cumulative monthly average prediction errors for 60 months before and after the month of change in state of incorporation are presented. The cumulative average prediction error can be interpreted as an index of the total abnormal price changes from 60 months prior to the switch. These cumulative average prediction errors are the sum of the monthly average prediction errors from month −60, i.e., from 60 months before the switch.

The most striking aspect of the data in Table 5 and Figure [5] is that shareholders of switching firms earn persistent positive abnormal returns over the 25 month period prior to and including the month of the switch. The cumulative average prediction error for this period is 30.25%. These positive abnormal returns follow a period of slight positive performance from months −60 to −25 where the cumulative average prediction error rises from zero to 5.90%.

After the switch, the average prediction errors fluctuate randomly around zero, and there is no obvious pattern in the cumulative average prediction error. This post-switch behavior is as expected in an efficient capital market where the stock price reflects all publicly available information. . . .

Interpretation and Extension of the Results

Pre-Switch Performance

The two hypotheses tested in this study have distinctly different predictions concerning the effect of a change in state of incorporation on stockholder returns. The stockholder exploitation hypothesis predicts negative returns to stockholders and the cost avoidance hypothesis predicts positive returns. The results above are consistent with the cost avoidance hypothesis. There is no evidence of any negative market reaction after reincorporation. Stockholders of switching firms earn positive abnormal returns of 30.25% over the 25 month period preceding and including the month of the change.

The absolute magnitude and pattern of pre-switch positive performance raise some interesting questions. If the announcement of a change in the state of incorporation is viewed as good news for stockholders, we expect to see a discrete positive reaction in the month that the information becomes known. From Table 5, it can be seen that the average prediction error in the month of the change (our month zero) is 1.58%. There are 9 larger monthly average prediction errors during the 24 months prior to the event. One interpretation of this persistent abnormal performance is that these firms switched after experiencing a period of abnormally good performance. However, before accepting that interpretation we investigate an alternative explanation.

It is possible that our results are induced by the procedure we use to select our month zero. As noted [above], our sample of incorporation changes is taken from Moody's, with some cross-checking to the Wall Street Journal. The date we use sometimes refers to the date of first public announcement of the proposed reincorporation, but, in many instances, it is the date of the merger of the former corporation with a dummy corporation established in the new state to effect the change. Thus, our month zero does not always represent the initial public announcement of the switch.

Because the month we designate as our event month is subsequent to the month of the first public announcement of the event, the persistent positive abnormal returns prior to our month zero could be induced by the lag in the data. The gradual increase in the cumulative average prediction error would then imply that, across our sample, the initial knowledge of the change is uniformly distributed over the 24 months prior to our month zero.

To obtain more insight into the persistent pre-switch abnormal positive performance, we revise our calculations of the CPE for months −25 to 0. For each firm, we eliminate the largest prediction error for months −25 to 0 inclusive, and then recalculate the monthly average prediction errors and cumulative average prediction errors over this 25 month period. . . . If the maximum prediction error is removed, the CPE rises to only 5.78% at month 0, far short of its level of 30.25% at month 0 when all observations are included. Over 80% of the abnormal performance of the sample over the period from −25 to 0 is accounted for by one observation for each firm. It appears that in the 25 months up to and including the switch, each firm in our sample was the subject of one piece of particularly good "news." Moreover, the timing of that news announcement was spread uniformly over the 25 month period. . . .

Performance on Announcement Days

The piece of particularly good news that affected the firms in our sample over the 25 month period prior to month zero could be news of the switch itself or news of some other event affecting the firms. Undoubtedly information about the proposed reincorporation was released sometime prior to our month zero. However, it is unlikely that this earlier announcement would precede our month zero by more than 6 months. With precise announcement dates it is possible to determine the impact of the switch *per se*. We do not have such precise dates for our sample of 140 firms, but we do have more accurate announcement dates for a subset of 50 firms in our sample.

. . . Over the 80 day period around the announcement, there is evidence of slight positive abnormal performance and the cumulative average prediction error is 2.89% at day +40. There is no evidence of any market reaction to the announcement itself and the average prediction error at day 0 is −0.01%. For this same subsample of 50 firms the cumulative average prediction error over the 24 months prior to the announcement is 11.65%. It appears that firms switch state of incorporation after experiencing a period of positive abnormal returns. Again there is no evidence of any negative market reaction to the switch, and the results of this subsample are consistent with the cost avoidance hypothesis. . . .

Conclusions

Proponents of federal chartering of corporations contend that the existing competition among states for corporate charters results in an inadequate standard of protection for stockholders. They argue that federal intervention is required to prevent managements from electing to incorporate in states offering less restrictive corporate charters. In support of these claims, they cite the predominance of Delaware in the market for corporate charters. That predominance, they conjecture, is a direct result of Delaware's corporate code which allows management to expropriate stockholder wealth.

We examine Delaware's share of the market for corporate charters, and conclude that it has a disproportionate share of new incorporations and clearly dominates the market for reincorporations. We offer evidence that, contrary to the allegations of the supporters of federal regulation, stockholders are not made worse off when firms switch state of incorporation, even when they switch to that much-maligned state of Delaware. Surprisingly, over the two years preceding the month of the switch, stockholders earn positive abnormal returns. Although we do reject the stockholder exploitation hypothesis, we are not able to identify the economic events causing this positive pre-switch performance of our sample firms. When daily abnormal returns are estimated for a subsample of firms, there is evidence of only slight positive performance around the day of announcement of the change in state of incorporation. It appears that firms reincorporate following a period of positive abnormal performance. At the date of the switch, and subsequently, there is no evidence of any negative impact on stockholder wealth.

Our study reveals that the case for federal chartering is not supported by the evidence. The evidence is consistent with our hypothesis that managers of a firm take advantage of the competition among states to locate in a state which offers an efficient set of restrictions on the firm, given the firm's anticipated production-investment and financing decisions.

NOTES AND QUESTIONS

1. Is it a fair inference that Winter considers fiduciary principles rather unimportant in the corporate context, because he believes that there is rarely a real conflict of interest between managers and shareholders, at least in a long-term perspective? A contrasting view is presented in Alison Grey Anderson, Conflicts of Interest: Efficiency, Fairness and Corporate Structure.*

Just as contract and warranty law and consumer protection legislation can promote both efficiency and fairness by providing standardized rules for transactions with high contracting and monitoring costs, corporation codes can perform a similar function by providing standardized rules to govern shareholder-management relations. The transaction costs are reduced and the free-rider problem is eliminated if managerial discretion is restricted not by individual contract, but by corporation codes which prohibit or require specified behavior by management. Such standardized restrictions on managerial discretion are undesirable, however, if they are likely to limit managerial flexibility to act in the interests of the shareholders. As a result, most corporation statutes do not contain detailed codes of behavior for managers, but instead provide managers with the greatest possible flexibility in using their control for any corporate purpose they choose.

Such "enabling" statutes have been recently subjected to substantial criticism. The criticism is aimed not at the efficiency of such laws, which is well-recognized, but at their fairness. The "contract" between managers and shareholders resulting from such statutes is in effect a contract of adhesion; corporate managers or those associated with them have had the greatest influence in formulating state corporation laws. Critics of existing state corporation laws do not suggest that they be reformed by providing for true arms' length bargaining between managers and shareholders. Instead, it is suggested that uniform federal standards be imposed by law, providing greater restrictions on managerial misbehavior. Such provisions would preserve the efficiencies associated with standardized contract terms, while correcting the imbalance of bargaining power resulting from the high information and transaction costs which prevent shareholders from protecting their own interests by contract or state sta-

*25 U.C.L.A. L. Rev. 738, 781–783 (1978). Reprinted with permission. Alison Grey Anderson is Professor of Law at the University of California, Los Angeles.

tute. Like standardized provisions for insurance policies, they would protect the reasonable expectations of the more numerous, less expert parties to the contract without imposing on society the costs associated with true arms' length bargaining by such persons.

Commentators have not described the proposed federal restrictions in great detail, and the problem remains one of designing restrictions which limit managerial abuse of discretion without limiting managerial discretion to act quickly and efficiently in the shareholders' interests. It is hard to envision legal restrictions which can effectively control managerial failure to maximize corporate wealth. Similarly, it is hard to imagine specific restrictions on the discretion of management to make acquisitions, set financial policy, choose between growth in sales and enhanced net profits, and make other basic decisions which directly or indirectly affect their compensation, position, or status. Conflicts of interest of this type, which are inherent in management's position in the corporation, cannot be significantly restricted without restricting management's ability to manage the corporation as efficiently as possible and thus benefit the shareholders.

Where conflicts of interest are not inherent in management's function of making decisions on behalf of the corporation, there are fewer costs associated with strict regulation of managerial discretion. Transactions between managers and the corporation involving the purchase or sale of property are not an inherent part of the managerial job. An absolute prohibition on such self-dealing would not, in most cases, significantly affect a manager's ability to manage the corporation efficiently. The argument that an absolute prohibition would prevent the corporation from benefiting from advantageous propositions can be answered by a rule allowing such transactions only when the manager can show that this property is uniquely valuable to the corporation. Tighter restrictions on self-dealing of this sort would provide fair treatment for shareholders without imposing very great costs in efficiency.

Is there really a conflict between "fairness" and "efficiency" considerations? Isn't conflict of interest just another name for the agency costs discussed by Jensen and Meckling in the selection reprinted in Chapter 2? How is Professor Anderson's analysis affected by Winter's analysis of competition among the states?

2. Anderson also stresses that information and transaction costs, especially in the setting of the publicly-held corporation, are so substantial as greatly to impair effective monitoring of managers by shareholders through either contractual provisions or active oversight. Would those factors equally impair effective monitoring of managers for fiduciary violations under legal liability rules?

The fragmented nature of holdings in the public corporation, coupled with the "free rider" problem, makes monitoring or enforcement action by individual stockholders generally unprofitable. The deterrent effect of fiduciary liability rules depends largely on the award of attorney fees to plaintiff's counsel in a derivative suit or class action. Judicial determination of the amount of such fees defines the incentive for members of the plaintiff's bar to invest in monitoring management — in investigating, acquiring information, pressing suit. Since the fee will be only a fraction, sometimes a small one, of the amount of any damage recovery, one can expect under-investment in enforcement of fiduciary rules. On the economics of private enforcement, with special reference to class actions, see, e.g., Gary S. Becker and George J. Stigler, Law Enforcement Malfeasance, and Compensation of Enforcers, 3 J. Legal Stud. 1 (1974); Kenneth W. Dam, Class Actions: Efficiency, Compensation, Deterrence, and Conflict of Interest, 4 J. Legal Stud. 47 (1975); Kenneth E. Scott, Two Models of the Civil Process, 27 Stan. L. Rev. 937 (1975).

3. The idea of corporation law as a kind of standard or form contract which economizes on negotiation costs between managers and shareholders and between the corporation and its creditors is a recurrent one in the economic analysis of the corporation. See, e.g., the Posner selection in Chapter 8.

4. Why does Delaware have such a commanding position in reincorporations but only a modestly disproportionate share of original incorporations? A possible answer is that Delaware has tailored its law to the needs of the large public corporation; if states are competing for charter business, wouldn't one expect some product specialization? In fact, in recent years, quite a few states have adopted special statutes or provisions to deal with the special needs of small, closely-held corporations. Another part of the answer is that incorporation in a foreign state, solely for charter purposes, subjects a local business to an extra layer of taxation. In short, the advantages of a Delaware charter may outweigh the additional Delaware taxes only for businesses attaining a certain scale of operations. So the cost avoidance hypothesis may have a size implication, and not simply a new-activity implication as Dodd and Leftwich suggest.

5. Are Dodd and Leftwich correct in suggesting, under the cost avoidance hypothesis, positive abnormal returns for the shareholders of companies switching to Delaware? Assuming that Delaware does offer a minimum-cost law for corporations of a certain size, the legal and printing and mailing and other costs of effecting a transfer can nonetheless be substantial — hundreds of thousands or even millions of dollars for a large corporation. Wouldn't rational management make the move as soon as the savings on legal and administrative costs afforded by the Delaware law represent a normal return on the transfer expenditure?

6. *"Squeeze-out" mergers.* At least until some recent decisions,*

*See Singer v. Magnavox Co., 380 A.2d 969 (Del. 1977), and Tanzer v. International General Industries, 379 A.2d 1121 (Del. 1977).

the Delaware corporation law was viewed as permitting majority stockholders to eliminate minority interests whenever they wished. For example, a parent corporation could get rid of public stockholders in a subsidiary by the device of merging the subsidiary into the parent or another wholly-owned subsidiary; the minority stockholders would receive cash or parent stock, as provided in the merger agreement. While the minority stockholders might challenge the price being paid through invoking a dissenters' appraisal statute remedy, they were in any event being forced to sell their stock. The economic rationale for such a rule is discussed in Boyd Kimball Dyer, An Essay on Federalism in Private Actions Under Rule 10b-5:*

"In effect, under Delaware law, the majority may treat the minority as though they were parties to a contract which the majority is free to breach on penalty of merely paying damages equal to the value of the minority shares. This theory has been called the 'value approach.'

"The opposite theory is that a shareholder's interest in his stock is more like ownership of real property and cannot be taken without his consent. This theory is called the "vested-shareholder-interest" approach. . . .

"Of course, the laws of contracts and real property do not divide sharply with respect to the two approaches. Some contracts will be specifically enforced while some interests in real property are protected only through damage remedies. It is not the area of law, but the theory of protection that is important. Predictably, other state corporate laws with respect to squeeze outs do not unanimously support either approach. Some states follow the Delaware approach, others lean strongly to the vested-shareholder-interest approach. . . .

"The chief argument for the value approach is economic efficiency. Suppose a corporation is worth one hundred dollars, of which sixty dollars or sixty percent is owned by a single majority shareholder and forty dollars or forty percent is owned by two thousand minority shareholders. Assume that if the corporation can go private, the total value of the corporation would increase from one hundred dollars to one hundred and ten dollars. It is unimportant how or where the ten dollars would be realized. The point is simply that economic efficiency would be served if the corporation were privately owned.

"Economic efficiency is a cold term. It could be stated more appealingly as the principle that shareholders should obtain the best possible return and that no single shareholder should be able to thwart this by demanding more money per share than any other shareholder — majority or minority.

*1976 Utah L. Rev. 7. Reprinted with permission.

"If a state follows the value approach, the majority will squeeze out the minority and the economic benefit will be realized. In contrast to the value approach, the vested-shareholder-interest approach makes going private extremely difficult. If the majority could negotiate directly with the minority as a class — all bound by the decision of a majority of the minority — the two sides could work out a total price for the minority of between forty dollars (below which the minority would be better off not selling), and fifty dollars (above which the majority would be better off not buying), but the majority must negotiate simultaneously with each of the minority shareholders since each has an individual vested interest. Not only will each minority shareholder have his own idea of the total benefit from going private, but each may disagree on how that benefit should be divided between minority and majority and how the portion allocated to the minority should be divided between its members. In effect, each minority shareholder is simultaneously bargaining with the majority and with each other minority shareholder and no one bargain can be settled until all are settled.

"In conclusion, Delaware's choice of the value approach to squeeze outs is defensible on the grounds of economics and equity, defining equity as treating shareholders alike with respect to their holdings. Of course, equity in this sense will not be achieved unless a fair price is set for the minority interest, but this is a separate question and will be discussed below. . . .

"Up to this point, the assumption has been made that the price the minority would receive for their stock is fair — that the benefit of the squeeze out is shared by both the majority and minority shareholder proportionately, share for share.

"Appraisal under the Delaware statute does not assure this result. First, the valuation of the corporation is 'exclusive of any element of the value arising from the expectation or accomplishment of the merger.' Second, the method of determining the value of a corporation for appraisal purposes focuses on a 'true' or 'intrinsic' value rather than the value obtained by the majority.

"In the context of an acquisitive merger it is reasonable that the stockholder who will not join in the merger should not be permitted to benefit from it. But in a squeeze out the minority would participate if it were possible. Presumably the benefit would accrue to all shareholders if the corporation were liquidated and its assets sold for the best price obtainable. This would be paid by a purchaser who would hold the assets as a close corporation so as to realize the benefit of private ownership that motivates the squeeze out.

"The second problem is that under Delaware law the value of the corporation is determined by a weighted average of its asset value (value in liquidation), its capitalized earnings, the market value of its stock and, occasionally, its dividend value. The general aim is to value the corporation as a going concern. The difficulty with this approach is it treats value as an average, and does not isolate the determinations of value from the influence of the majority shareholder. In a squeeze out the majority is, in a sense, exercising a power of eminent domain over the minority. It seems wise to look for the highest value of the corporation available to the majority in setting the minimum value for appraisal purposes, adding to that value an increment for the value of going private."

A more critical view of the Delaware squeeze-out provisions appears in an unpublished paper, Tender Offers and Two-Step Acquisitions (1978), by Stephen C. Peck and Jerald H. Udinsky, from which the following excerpt is taken with permission:

". . . [I]t appears that in the majority of consolidations, the dissenting shareholders of the subsidiary will possess the right to receive the 'fair market value' of their shares in cash and that the legal literature treats th[is] appraisal remedy as an important defense for the minority shareholders . . . .

". . . [Authoritative commentators have noted that frequently] 'fair market value' has been computed as a weighted average of net asset value, market value and investment value. For example, the Delaware courts require the appraiser to state the weights which he has assigned to each factor . . . . The Delaware cases have assigned assets a weight ranging from 20% to 50% with a figure of 30% being an average value. The remaining 70% should be allocated between market value and earnings value. If dividends are given independent weight, they could be regarded as a subcategory of earnings hence reducing the weight given to earnings. Thus a recommended starting allocation might be a 30% weight to assets, and a 35% weight to each of market value and earnings value. Starting from an initial allocation, the weights could be modified . . . . Finally, an important point for our study is that where there has been a two-step acquisition the 'fair market value' is not determined solely by the tender offer price. This is shown clearly in the Olivetti-Underwood case.

"From 1960 onward, Olivetti Underwood, a wholly owned subsidiary of Olivetti Italy, owned 69% of Underwood shares. On May 21, 1963, Olivetti Italy made a tender offer at $14.50 for approximately 836,000 outstanding shares of Underwood. In the accompanying circular, Olivetti stated that it intended to acquire the business and assets of Underwood whatever the outcome of the tender offer either by voting its shares in a sale of Underwood's assets or by a short form merger if its shareholdings rose to 90% as a result of the tender. As a result of the offer, Olivetti Italy captured more than 600,000 of the publicly held shares and in a position of a 90% parent could compel liquidation under the short form merger statutes. In evaluating the market value component of the 'fair market value,' the appraiser fixed and the court agreed to a market value of $14.25 where the difference between that price and the tender offer price was the 'premium that Olivetti Italy was willing to pay for control.' And even though market value was assigned a high weight (50%), the 'fair market value' was only $9.78 because net asset value and investment value were low.

"We now provide an argument that 'fair market value' should be uncorrelated with the stock market during the period between the tender offer completion and the merger. We do this by showing that the majority of the components of the 'fair market value' would not be expected to move with the stock market. First, consider earnings value; as mentioned above, the Delaware courts, which are influential and deal with the majority of 'fair market value' cases, predict future earnings by taking an average of the past five years earnings. Also the discount rate which is used to capitalize the earnings is frequently computed according to rather conservative rules which are most probably unrelated to current movements of the stock market. Second, consider the stock's market value; according to the . . . cases introduced above it is the price prior to the tender offer in the first case and prior to the transfer of control in the second which should provide a basis for evaluating the stock's market value. . . . Finally, consider the net asset value component; this may in fact move with the stock market. When business is booming, the stock market may well be high and the present cost of reproducing phsyical assets may be relatively high; similarly the rental stream of property may be relatively high. However it seems obvious that the correlation between net asset value and the level of the stock market will be far from perfect and also as was reported above, net asset value receives a weight of only 30% in a typical case and it therefore follows that the 'fair market value' of a share should be only slightly correlated with the stock market.

"Who bears the costs of the appraisal varies from jurisdiction to jurisdiction. In Virginia the corporation bears the cost of appraisal in every case, in Pennsylvania the corporation bears the cost whenever the proceedings were brought in good faith, in Delaware the court may in its discretion apportion the costs among the parties and in California the burden may depend on whether the award exceeds the amount which the corporation offered to pay. In addition, a New York provision permits the court discretion to assess the corporation for reasonable compensation of the shareholder's experts if the final judgement materially exceeds the corporation's offer or if the corporation made no offer.

"Notwithstanding the fact that in many jurisdictions the corporation bears the cost of appraisal, it has generally been recognized by legal scholars that the appraisal remedy is very costly for the shareholder. Thus, Eisenberg has called appraisal a 'remedy of desperation.' Dean Manning has pointed out that frequently the amount of the award will be quite uncertain and that when the award is made, it may be taxable where the transaction dissented from may have produced tax-free benefits to the shareholder. In addition the process of litigation is lengthy and technical.

"From these considerations it would appear that appraisal would provide protection only in cases of extreme rapacity of the parent corporation. But this is a superficial interpretation because the corporation as well as the shareholder bears costs if an appraisal suit is brought. If the corporation perceives its own costs as being sufficiently high, then it may offer a generous price in the merger negotiations in order to prevent an appraisal hearing. Dean Manning has argued that the costs of appraisal to the parent corporation are high and that 'these statutes can be a frightful nuisance, drain and burden.' This is so for the following reasons. First, the corporation cannot know in advance how many dissenters there will be, hence there may be a 'sudden and largely unpredictable drain . . . imposed upon the corporation's cash position. This demand for a cash payout to shareholders often comes at a time when the enterprise is in need of every liquid dollar it can put its hands on.' Second, the time surrounding a merger may be a time when 'uneasy trade creditors, suppliers or banks may decide that they would be happier to have cash in their pockets rather than a claim against the still untried combined enterprise.' Hence, if a large cash settlement is suddenly made in favor of the minority, a run of creditors may be started. Manning points out that it is possible to write into a merger agreement conditions such that the merger can be annulled if there are sufficiently many dissenters but he argues further that such conditions 'introduce an extraneous element of contingency into the transaction' and that 'the availability of the kickout tends to poison the whole atmosphere of the negotiation and to expose other terms of the transaction to continuous redickering.' Eisenberg does not find any of these arguments of Manning to be persuasive and presumably believes therefore that the cost of an appraisal hearing to the parent corporation is low. . . .

" . . . Our empirical results [in a previous paper indicated] that a target's share price behavior subsequent to a tender offer is inconsistent with shareholders believing that they are protected solely by the appraisal statutes. Our results are based on a small sample of tender offers carried out prior to 1968. If those results hold up for a larger sample of more recent tender offers, then the intricate detail spent on valuing the shares of minority shareholders after a merger offer for a previously widely held company may be misplaced. This is so because the major advantages of these procedures for minority shareholders may be to provide another means for aggravating the parent so that he will settle for a 'fair' price. Much of this effort could be avoided by a change in the law which would guarantee to minority shareholders the tender offer price modified by some index of overall stock market performance between the time of the tender offer and the merger. This is in the spirit of the proposal by Brudney and Chirelstein that minority shareholders should possess the right to have their shares purchased in the second step of a two-step acquisition at a price equal to the tender offer price. . . . "

Can Peck and Udinsky's analysis be reconciled with the empirical findings of Dodd and Leftwich? Consider the following argument: if the appraisal remedy is known to be incomplete, then ex ante the price of shares to minority shareholders, or to shareholders likely to become minority shareholders, will be decreased as a way of compensating them for the expected losses from being squeezed out. Under what circumstances might this be a more efficient form of compensation than having a more comprehensive appraisal remedy?

Chapter 5

Insider Trading

The subject of insider trading is taken up next because it can be viewed as yet another form of "discretionary" behavior by management—an example of the use of corporate office for self-enrichment, but one subject to attack under federal rather than state law. This area was put in the domain of federal law by two provisions of the Securities Exchange Act of 1934: Section 16(b) and, as it turned out, Section 10(b). Section 16(b) is relatively clear and specific; it applies only to officers, directors and major stockholders of companies with securities registered under the Act, and imposes liability for any profit that can be generated by matching a purchase and a sale that occurred within six months of each other. The reasons for the matched transactions, and whether they depended in any way on the knowledge of non-public information, are irrelevant. The liability is automatic, sometimes bizarre, and probably of little overall significance.

Section 10(b) is another matter. It authorizes the SEC to prescribe rules "necessary or appropriate in the public interest" to prohibit any "manipulative or deceptive device or contrivance" in securities transactions. Rule 10b-5* was promulgated in 1942, to deal with the situation of a company president who was telling his stockholders that the business was doing very badly (when the opposite was true) and then buying their stock.[†] The rule prohibited material misrepresentations or half-truths in connection with the purchase as well as sale of securities, but its reach has been extended far beyond the situation of simple fraud in direct dealings with which it began. In particular, the Court of Appeals for the Second Circuit, in the famous *Texas Gulf Sulphur* decision,[‡] used the rule to impose liability on persons who had purchased a company's stock over the exchange without disclosing "inside information" material to its value.

*17 C.F.R. §240.10b-5 (1979)
[†]See M. Freeman, 22 Bus. Law 922 (1967).
[‡]401 F.2d 833 (2d Cir. 1968).

Much, if not most, of the judicial discussion of insider trading has been in terms of fairness and equal treatment of all investors — for example, the court's opinion in *TGS* declares that "the Rule is based in policy on the justifiable expectation of the securities marketplace that all investors trading on impersonal exchanges have relatively equal access to material information . . . " The implications of the concept of fairness that is embodied in the insider trading decisions are analyzed, and compared to those of other rationales for the rule that have been advanced, in the first article in this chapter, by Kenneth E. Scott. He finds justification for the rule to be considerably more limited than its present, and potential, scope. A more sweeping attack on the rule, and defense of insider trading, has been made by Professor Henry Manne, both in the article that is excerpted in this chapter and in his book, Insider Trading and the Stock Market (1966).

A factual examination of insider trading is also worth considering. Do insiders have valuable information, and trade on the basis of it, often enough for the phenomenon to be detectable? From a "fairness" standpoint, or any other, of what magnitude is the practice and problem?

One of the first careful investigations of the question was by James Lorie and Victor Niederhoffer of the University of Chicago, in Predictive and Statistical Properties of Insider Trading, 11 J. Law & Econ. 35 (1968). Using for the first time data based on the stock price on the day of the insiders' transactions, Lorie and Niederhoffer concluded, unlike most prior studies, that insider trading tended to be profitable and to forecast successfully stock price movements: "When insiders accumulate a stock intensively, the stock can be expected to outperform the market during the next six months. Insiders tend to buy more often than usual before large price increases and to sell more than usual before price decreases." Similar conclusions, using a more sophisticated methodology, were reached in Jeffrey Jaffe, Special Information and Insider Trading, 47 J. Bus. 410 (1974). The most comprehensive and recent study, by Joseph Finnerty, confirmed their findings and is briefly excerpted.

The recent studies cover periods long after the enactment of Section 16(b) or promulgation of rule 10b-5, so it is evident that those legal rules have not ended the practice — a point made earlier by Manne. But no one expects perfect compliance with, or enforcement of, any legal rule. Just how sensitive has insider trading been to the increasing attention and stringency displayed by the SEC and the courts? Jeffrey Jaffe undertook some measurements in his study that concludes this chapter.

Insider Trading: Rule 10b-5, Disclosure and Corporate Privacy*

Kenneth E. Scott

. . . It is . . . possible, from the abundant if not very rewarding materials available, to extract three differing conceptions of the rule [10b-5] and its objectives. The first and most common view is that the rule is principally intended to serve the ends of fairness and equity — to prevent, in the words of the Commission, "the inherent unfairness involved where a party takes advantage of [inside] information knowing it is unavailable to those with whom he is dealing." This we will denominate the Fair Play concept of the rule. Its implication is that the damaged party is the one with whom the insider traded and took unfair advantage, who should be made whole by a remedy of rescission.

A second view of the rule is that it facilitates the flow of information to the market, so that it may better perform its functions of security evaluation and capital allocation. To quote the Second Circuit in a later case: "As we have stated time and again, the purpose behind Section 10(b) and rule 10b-5 is to protect the investing public . . . by promoting full disclosure of inside information so that an informed judgment can be made by all investors who trade in such markets." Though not unrelated to the first concept, the focus here is on the entire market rather than the particular trading partner, and the implication is that damages were incurred by all investors who traded in the market in the opposite direction from the insiders during the period of nondisclosure. This rationale for the rule we will refer to as the Informed Market.

The third view of the functions of the rule is that it affords protection to the property rights of the firm in inside information, which was described by the Commission in its pathbreaking *Cady, Roberts* decision as "information intended to be available only for a corporate purpose and not for the personal benefit of anyone." This function is quite clear in a case like *Texas Gulf Sulphur*, where unusual trading by the drill site geologist and others with knowledge of the drill core assay analysis would be likely to contribute to rumors of a strike and raise the costs of acquisition of the surrounding land by the company. The implications of this Business Property view, however, would be that the injured party was the company, and that damages would be better measured by the increase in land acquisition costs than by stock market price movements.

Source: Forthcoming in 9 J. Legal Stud. (1980), with permission. Kenneth E. Scott is professor of law at Stanford Law School.

These different conceptions of the rule are not necessarily mutually exclusive, but they lead to different conclusions about who should be the plaintiff in the damage action and what should be the measure of damages. And in fact, the cases have exhibited considerable confusion and uncertainly about precisely those issues. We will proceed to explore the premises and implications of each of these views at greater length.

Fair Play

The fair game approach to rule 10b-5, which seems to have some kinship with the layman's attitude that the stock market is just another form of gambling, focuses on the individual parties to a particular trade and asks whether one has an "unfair advantage" over the other in some respect. If pushed far enough, of course, it will always be found that the parties are not on a parity in all regards; there will be disparities in knowledge or intelligence or experience or capital or whatever. Among all these advantages and disadvantages, which are "unfair" and why? Judging by the opinions and commentaries, unfairness is one of those qualities which exist in the eye of the beholder and elicit little effort at explanation. There are, however, a number of brief formulations of that aspect of equity with which the rule is supposed to be concerned. An early case in this line of development saw the rule as "an attempt to provide some degree of equalization of bargaining position." Along the same line, the First Circuit in 1966 stated that "the law has deliberately tried to equalize bargaining power" between seller and buyer. If equality in bargaining position or bargaining power is the objective, and one thinks of the trade as a direct transaction (as it was in the cases just mentioned) and not an exchange over organized and competitive markets, then logically the rule should not be confined to informational disparities; there are others of equal or greater importance, and the rule's potential for yet more expansion is clear.

In *Texas Gulf Sulphur* the court was dealing with stock exchange transactions and formulated the rationale in a less open-ended fashion: "the Rule is based in policy on the justifiable expectation of the securities marketplace that all investors trading on impersonal exchanges have relatively equal access to material information . . . " The "equal access to information" view of fairness became the dominant approach, although some other conceptions were still alluded to from time to time in the cases. The opinions usually concluded by noting that fair play in this sense is necessary to protect the integrity of the securities markets and maintain public confidence in them.

If equal access to information is the purpose of the rule, then it would seem proper to extend it to any material nonpublic information, whether obtained from an "inside" source or any other source. There is . . . no reference in the language of the rule to insiders or inside information; that is a limiting gloss that has been added, and may be removed, by the courts. At least a partial removal was attempted by the Second Circuit in the recent case of United States v. Chiarella,[13] a criminal prosecution for a willful violation of rule 10b-5 by an employee of a financial printing house, Pandick Press. On five occasions he received coded proof copy of the documents that have to be filed with the SEC and furnished to stockholders in connection with takeover bids, and proceeded to purchase shares in the target company prior to the public announcement. Obviously his information did not come from within the company whose shares he bought, but the court still made some effort to fit him into an insider category: "A financial printer such as Chiarella is as inside the market itself as one could be." More dispositive of the affirmance of his conviction, however, was the court's emphatic feeling that "betting on a 'sure thing' is anathema to the ideal of 'fair and honest markets' established as the foundation" of our securities laws.

However, the Supreme Court, in its opinion in *Chiarella* reversing the Second Circuit, saw the aspirations of the rule in much more limited terms. The Court held that "not every instance of financial unfairness constitutes fraudulent activity under Section 10(b)" and that, in particular, silence in connection with the purchase or sale of securities may operate as a fraud actionable under Section 10(b) only where it breaches "a duty to disclose arising from a relationship of trust and confidence between parties to a transaction." Such a duty may exist between corporate insiders and the company's stockholders, but not between complete strangers dealing through impersonal markets.

The Court's "breach of trust" definition of the rule obviously represents a less ambitious concept of fair play than the ones that had been pursued by various lower courts, and correspondingly it raises fewer problems of coverage and implementation. Nonetheless, questions have been raised as to the justification for even this more modest version of the rule. Some commentators, prominent among them Henry Manne, have objected that the only effect the insiders' trades can have is to move the market in the correct direction, so that the other party to the transaction, if affected at all, receives a better price than if the insider had dutifully stayed out of the market.[16] In that event, how can the other party claim injury or

13. 588 F. 2d 1358 (2d Cir. 1978), reversed 100 S. Ct. 1108 (1980)
16. See Manne, Insider Trading and the Stock Market 77-110 (1966).

show damages? The rather supple answer of the Second Circuit is that, under the TGS "disclose or abstain" rule, the insider having chosen to trade thereby incurred (and breached) the duty to disclose first, so the other party is injured by the nondisclosure and entitled to damages measured by the effect of disclosure on the market price.[17]

What that answer does not deal with is the question of why, if the trade itself is not harmful but beneficial to the trading partner, the law should be interpreted to create a duty which stifles such trades. Most of the commentators who reject Manne's conclusions, as practically all of them do, fall back at this point on simply asserting that insider trading is not right . . . .

In terms of our earlier gambling analogy, secondary trading is apparently seen as a zero-sum game in which insiders are playing with . . . "percentage dice" and therefore winning abnormally often. It is indeed true that the recent studies of insider trading in general, using the reports filed with the SEC or exchanges by officers, directors, and substantial (10%) stockholders of listed and registered companies, have shown insiders obtaining excess returns. The level of excess return found has been on average from 2% to 8%, and trading in the companies and periods involved constitutes a small fraction of all secondary trading. Nonetheless, although the magnitude may be small, a detectable percentage edge for insiders seems reasonably well established.

But is the conclusion from the gambling analogy a valid one? In modern finance theory, shareholders are seen as investors seeking a return proportionate with that degree of systematic or market-related risk which they have chosen to incur. Unsystematic risk, related to factors specific to a given company or industry, may be diversified away in a portfolio, so investors are not compensated for it. The rate of return for any given level of risk is established by an efficient market where security prices reflect all publicly-available information. In such a perspective, the limited knowledge or ability of the individual investor is largely irrelevant. He is "protected" by the price established by the market mechanism, not by his personal bargaining power or position; this assumes that, as in the recent cases, we are dealing with transactions over organized exchanges and not with directly negotiated purchases in inactive markets, as in the cases where the rule began.

That is not to deny that those with superior (nonpublic) information can reap higher returns; in a sense, they are "selling" their information, and correcting the market price in the process. But does that mean other investors are not receiving the expected rates

17. Shapiro v. Merrill Lynch, 495 F.2d 228, 238–240 (2d Cir. 1974).

of return? Insider trading is hardly an unknown or unanticipated phenomenon; the returns expected by investors would not include any gains unique to insiders. To return to the gambling analogy, if I know you are using percentage dice, I won't play without an appropriate adjustment of the odds; the game is, after all, voluntary.

Nor do the excess returns received by insiders necessarily represent some sort of "unfair" or windfall gain for them. If a certain corporate position carries with it the prospect of being able to obtain on occasion some insider trading profits, the value of that prospect constitutes part of the total compensation attaching to that position and, like any other fringe benefit, affects the level of direct salary payments. The opportunities for significant insider trading profits are no doubt rather infrequent and unpredictable, however, so that management is in effect receiving long-shot lottery tickets as part of its compensation, and that may well be an inefficient form of compensation. The value of such lottery tickets to their recipients may be substantially less than their expected cost to the owners of the firm, but that is a different issue.

From a private standpoint, then, the fairness concern proves to have surprisingly little substance, when viewed in terms of the game as a whole rather than in terms of a single, isolated play. What is presented to a court, of course, is precisely that—a single, isolated event, and the court's perspective tends to be defined accordingly. Neither the courts nor the SEC take an ex ante view of a diversified portfolio; instead they take an ex post view of a particular transaction. Since the individual transaction involves a wealth gain by an insider, and to that extent leaves others worse off in the immediate period, they make an implied jump to the conclusion that under such circumstances the game itself is unfair.

On the other hand, from a social standpoint, do not insider trading and the associated nondisclosure (or delays in disclosure) constitute a part, though no doubt a very small part, of the total level of systematic risk in the economy? Investors have to be compensated for bearing that risk, so the issue is not one of fairness, but a lower level of risk and uncertainty would benefit the society as a whole. In essence, the argument is that there is a social cost in the nondisclosure of already available information, and that leads us to the next rationale for the rule.

The Informed Market

This conception of the rule sees it as intended to enhance the flow of information to the market, in order to contribute to the accurate pricing of securities and the efficient allocation of capital resources. But why is any species of mandatory disclosure rule needed to serve those ends? If information about the company is valuable to investors or reduces the risk and uncertainty associated with the company's securities, investors have incentives to pay for information and companies have incentives to furnish it in order to lower their cost of capital. Given those incentives, is there any reason to believe inadequate information is supplied? The usual answer is that such information has the characteristics of an underproduced public good. There are "free riders"; the producers of such information cannot capture its full value because of customer resales or transfers, or externalities. Thus there is a need for a government agency to mandate production and disclosure of the information the public wants — always assuming that can be said to describe what the SEC actually does.

Furthermore, the firm may be in a position of natural monopoly in producing many kinds of information about its own operations, having large cost advantages as compared to an outsider. But when it comes to disclosure, there are more benefits and incentives for the firm to voluntarily reveal positive information about itself than negative information. Therefore the disclosure rules properly emphasize the production and disclosure of negative information about the firm.

The foregoing arguments are not beyond challenge, but for our purposes we will accept them as constituting the premises of the SEC disclosure system. Even in that context, it is appropriate to inquire whether the rule makes any significant contribution to the disclosure objective. As interpreted by the courts in *Texas Gulf Sulphur* and subsequent cases, the rule affords an option: disclose the inside information or abstain from trading. Upon disclosure, obviously, that opportunity for trading profit disappears, so the insider has no reason to disclose in order to trade. How then does the rule promote fuller disclosure? Mainly, it is said, by removing an incentive to *delay* the release of corporate information so that insiders may first take a trading profit. Delay for that purpose alone should not normally involve more than a few weeks at most, so the contribution to fuller and faster disclosure seems minor at best. . . .

But let us examine further the proposition that the *TGS* rule does serve to reduce to at least a small degree delays in disclosure of available corporate information. When the information is positive (giving rise to an increase in stock price), the proposition is plausible; if insiders cannot profit from a trading delay, they otherwise have ample incentives promptly to release the information (after any requisite corporate action, such as the land acquisition in *TGS*, is

completed). Good news benefits stockholders, which usually includes the insiders, and correlates with increases in management
compensation. But if the news is bad, the immediate incentives for
insiders now point in the other direction, and therefore it is to be
expected that one should be quite sure of the facts before making a
release, which should be framed to avoid over-reactions by ill-in-
formed investors, and so on.[24] In this situation, the TGS rule does
not help, since insiders can delay or avoid the negative disclosure
simply by not trading. Indeed, the rule makes the situation worse,
for by cutting off insider selling it also cuts off an activity that is
itself a source of information to the marketplace and removes an
incentive for full disclosure promptly upon completion of trading.

In terms of promoting disclosure to inform the market, therefore, it is easy to argue that the *TGS* interpretation of rule 10b-5 is
ill-conceived and overly restrictive. Why limit it to insiders and inside information? Isn't the functioning of an informed market improved by the revelation of *all* material nonpublic information,
whether possessed by an insider or an outsider? Putting the issue
another way, Hirshleifer has pointed out that the use of resources to
obtain foreknowledge of impending developments, purely for trading purposes, may be very profitable in private terms but is of no
social value.[26] Perhaps trading disclosure rules should be broadened,
then, to prevent that social waste.

Nor does the rule have to stop there. Why should the company
or its insiders be able to avoid disclosure by not trading? An express
expansion of the rule to require, regardless of trading, insider disclosure of any material nonpublic information has not yet been accomplished, but it may be on the way.[27] For example, in another part of
the *TGS* case the company and an officer were held liable, for issuing on April 12 an initial press release that was deemed too discouraging and thus misleading, to persons who had thereafter sold their
stock, even though the company and officer were themselves engaging in no stock transactions during this period.[28] While that case
involved a representation and not pure non-disclosure, a company
is always issuing statements and reports; the failure to release cer-

24. The main countervailing consideration would seem to be a long-run interest
in enhancing the reputation for accuracy and reliability of the company's financial
statements and other disclosures, and of the managers themselves.
26. Hirshleifer, The Private and Social Value of Information and the Reward to
Inventive Activity, 61 Am. Econ. Rev. 561 (1971).
27. See the discussion of grounds for liability in Financial Industrial Fund v.
McDonnell Douglas Corp., 474 F.2d 514 (10th Cir. 1973).
28. Reynolds v. Texas Gulf Sulphur Co., 309 F. Supp. 548 (D. Utah 1970), aff'd
sub nom. Mitchell v. Texas Gulf Sulphur Co., 446 F.2d 90 (10th Cir. 1971), cert.
denied, 404 U.S. 1004 (1971).

tain information can readily be seen as converting other statements into half-truths, and the category of pure nondisclosure is swallowed up and disappears.

In short, to face the question squarely, should rule 10b-5 be read (as its amorphous language would certainly permit) as a blanket disclosure rule, not tied to any company relationship or trading by the defendant? All persons with material nonpublic information about a firm, who knowingly[29] failed to disclose it, would be liable to all persons who were disadvantaged by trading at a price which did not impound that information. That seemed until recently to be the position toward which the courts, hesitantly and uncertainly, were drifting.

Put that baldly, it is evident that the administrative and enforcement difficulties could be horrendous. Some people might be covered by the rule without any awareness of their status. Others would have no reliable way of telling whether their information qualified as material or nonpublic. No mechanism exists, or can readily be imagined, for effecting meaningful disclosure of purported information from such a mix of sources and of degrees of value. Even in the relatively clear cases, detection and enforcement would be either very expensive or very haphazard, or quite possibly both. The measure of damages, since we are outside of the category of trading defendants and rescission remedies, would seem to be determined by the volume of market trading over what might be an extended period, and hence might be ferocious. A rule whose objective was a reduction of investment risks and costs would have ended up increasing them.

But those are not the only drawbacks to such a blanket rule. Another kind of objection is that a requirement of free disclosure destroys incentives to *produce* information, and not all information is of the socially worthless, valuable only for private trading purposes, type referred to earlier. A discussion of two more recent and celebrated cases may help clarify the issues. In the *Douglas Aircraft* case, [30] the company headquarters was advised by its aircraft division on June 14, 1966, that it was encountering production delays and had a several million dollar loss for May. Auditors were sent in, a substantial inventory writedown was decided upon, and on June 24 the

29. In Ernst & Ernst v. Hochfelder, 425 U.S. 185 (1976), the Supreme Court imposed a "scienter" or intent requirement on rule 10b-5 damage actions. But the logic of a blanket disclosure rule would tend to erode the rigor of any requirement of a genuinely fraudulent intent.

30. Financial Industrial Fund v. McDonnell Douglas Corp., 474 F.2d 514 (10th Cir. 1973); Shapiro v. Merrill Lynch, Pierce, Fenner & Smith, 495 F.2d 228 (2d Cir. 1974); Investors Management Co., Rel. No. 34-9267, CCH Fed. Sec. L. Rep. §78,163 (July 29, 1971).

company issued a press announcement that earnings for the last six months were 12 cents a share, as compared to an earlier announcement of 85 cents a share for the first five months. At the time, Douglas was in registration for a new issue of debentures and kept its lead underwriter, Merrill Lynch, informed of these developments. Beginning June 21, Merrill Lynch disclosed the information to certain institutional clients, who sold out their existing Douglas positions and also sold the stock short; the stock price went from $90 on June 21 to $69 on June 27. Merrill Lynch and the investors it tipped off were found liable, to a class consisting of all purchasers of Douglas stock the same week, for violation of rule 10b-5; the case was returned to the district court for a determination of appropriate damages, and subsequently settled. Douglas was also sued by a purchaser, but was found to have exercised due care and its good business judgment in investigating and issuing the release; the court of appeals therefore reversed a judgment against the company.

The *Equity Funding Corporation of America* case was one of the most massive frauds in recent history, involving the fabrication of millions of dollars of fake insurance policies to support fictitious growth in sales and earnings. With the aid of a disgruntled former Equity Funding employee (Secrist), a securities analyst (Dirks) investigated the company's affairs and became sufficiently convinced of the fraud by March 12, 1973 to advise clients of the story and urge them to sell; rumors of trouble became widespread, and trading was suspended on March 27; the company promptly went into bankruptcy. An SEC administrative proceeding has found that Dirks and his selling clients violated the insider trading rules.[31]

Both cases can be seen as "tippees" selling on the basis of negative inside information, but there are differences. *Douglas* seems to represent a relatively pure 'foreknowledge trading' situation, accomplishing nothing but some wealth transfers. *Equity Funding*, however, represents an outsider expending efforts to discover fraud, and fraud detection is a socially valuable activity; resources are consumed both in producing and in guarding against fraud. The SEC position is that Dirks' clients could not sell without informing the SEC and the buyers of the foundations for their belief in the scandal at Equity Funding. If that removes most of the incentive for securities analysts to discover such frauds, it is all justified by the preservation of the fairness and integrity of the stock-trading system.

Neither a blanket or total disclosure rule, nor the present *TGS* rule as it has been applied make any distinction between positive

31. In the Matter of Boston Company Institutional Investors, CCH Fed. Sec. L. Rep. §81,705 (September 1, 1978).

and negative information or between mere trading on fore-knowledge and socially valuable discovery. To gain, arguably, a bit of market efficiency through more rapid disclosure of favorable inside information, such rules would sacrifice a considerable amount of socially productive discovery. It is encouraging to note, therefore, that in its recent *Chiarella* decision the Supreme Court refused to recognize "a general duty between all participants in market transactions to forego actions based on material, nonpublic information." While the Court's position was grounded on its reading of congressional intent, it finds considerable support in policy considerations as well. These observations bring us to the third conception of rule 10b-5.

Business Property

Many of the rule 10b-5 decisions stress the importance of the fact that the defendant acquired the information in some fiduciary capacity, knowing that it was intended for a corporate purpose and not for personal benefit. In this view, the wrong committed is essentially that of theft or conversion; the information belongs to the firm, but an employee appropriates it for his own use and gain. It becomes quite important, then, where and how the trader acquired his knowledge, an aspect less central to the Fair Play or Informed Market approaches, but it is quite unimportant whether the information is inside or outside. And in the tipping situation, the tippee becomes comparable to one receiving stolen property.

The application of this concept to a case like *TGS* is quite straightforward; by buying on their knowledge of the strike, the trading insiders fed the rumor mill, to the likely detriment of their employer. What Manne saw as entrepreneurial compensation comes out in this instance as an agent acting in his own interest and contrary to the interest of his principal, what Jensen and Meckling refer to as an agency cost.[33] The application is also clear in a case like *Chiarella* where the Second Circuit found it awkward to explain why the acquiring company could make market purchases with advance knowledge of the tender offer while the layout man could not; the trading printer is tending to drive up the price of the target company, to his own ultimate gain but to the detriment of the acquirer, from whom he is appropriating the information of the impending bid. In neither case, however, did the court draw the conclusion that

33. See Jensen and Meckling, Theory of the Firm: Managerial Behavior, Agency Costs and Ownership Structure, 3 J. Fin. Econ. 305 (1976). [Included in Chapter 2 of this volume — Eds.]

the injured party was the owner of the stolen information, as opposed to sellers in the stock market.[34]

In both the foregoing cases the firm had invested resources to make socially useful discoveries — new mineral deposits, companies that could be made more productive and profitable. Applying rule 10b-5 in such situations to debar insider trading merely serves to protect the firm's property rights in the discovery it has made.[35] Presumably express provisions in employment and other contracts could accomplish much the same objective, but the incorporation of a legal rule may well be the more efficient method.

But does the interest in the protection of information as valuable property fit all of the cases at which we have looked? To return to the *Douglas* case, was the company injured by the trading with foreknowledge of the imminent downward earnings adjustments? Not in any obvious way, although one can develop a line of argument about maintaining a reputation for management integrity. Nonetheless, agency law requires agents to account to their principals for any profits gained through the use of confidential information, even if the principal was not harmed.[36] Was there a social loss incurred? Perhaps yes, to the extent resources were used in obtaining foreknowledge and effecting trades, but that does not seem to affect the value to the company of the information it produced. The property protection rationale, then, by no means finds application to all the situations in which rule 10b-5 has been invoked, but it provides clear guidance both for the function and the beneficiary of the rule in some cases.

In Defense of Insider Trading*

Henry G. Manne

. . . In the entire literature on insider trading there does not exist one careful analysis of the subject. Lawyers have been having a

34. That conclusion has been reached in a few cases under state corporate fiduciary law, outside rule 10b-5: Brophy v. Cities Service Co., 31 Del. Ch. 241, 70 A.2d 5 (1949); Diamond v. Oreamuno, 24 N.Y.2d 494, 248 N.E.2d 910 (1969).

35. In *Chiarella* the opinion for the Supreme Court majority did not reach the merits of the misappropriation or conversion theory of rule 10b-5, on the ground that it was not included in the instructions to the jury which convicted him; four of the concurring or dissenting justices, however, seemed to endorse such an interpretation of the rule.

36. Restatement (Second) of Agency §388 comment c.

Source: 44 Harv. Bus. Rev. 113–122 (November–December 1966). Reprinted with permission; copyright © 1966 by the President and Fellows of Harvard College; all rights reserved. Henry G. Manne is Director of the Law and Economics Center at the University of Miami Law School.

field day arguing about the meaning of words or the reach of the last case or any of a thousand technical and legal issues. Unfortunately, however, most lawyers do not have the skills to develop a careful economic analysis of the subject, and economists have offered no assistance. The tone of debate has remained essentially moralistic and question-begging. Logic has been totally lost to emotion. . . .

Careful analysis of insider trading requires consideration of at least three major questions:

(1) Who gains and who loses from insider trading? (We cannot assume that the shareowners who should be protected are necessarily the same people who are in danger of being hurt.)

(2) What are the long-run consequences of disallowing insider trading? (Even if some individuals may be hurt by it, the economy may be hurt more if we remove the incentive effect of such trading.)

(3) Can insider trading be prevented, and at what financial and social cost? (There are many indirect devices for trading in information, and they can be very subtle and hard to trace.) . . .

What, if any, advantages would flow to participants in the stock market if insider trading were effectively stopped? Here we come to one of the most astounding facts in this whole astounding business: the only stock market participants who are likely to benefit from a rule preventing insider trading are the short-term speculators and traders, not the long-term investors who are regularly stated to be the objects of the SEC's solicitude.

The initial error of most commentators is the assumption that the persons who sold to insiders before disclosure of important news would not have sold at all if the insiders were not in the market. Obviously this is absurd; the average seller has no way in the world of knowing the identity of his buyer. One of the great virtues of an organized securities market is its automaticity, which results in anonymity of traders. Publicly traded companies are quite different in this respect from small, closely held corporations, and the rules governing them should also be different. . . .

To discover the identity of sellers who would not trade but for the insider's activities, we must first distinguish two types of shareholders — investors and traders. This distinction has certainly been overworked for many purposes, but it is of considerable value in the present analysis:

Investors, the long-term shareholders, tend to select stocks based on so-called "fundamental" factors, such as earning potential, dividend history, growth prospects, or the reputation of management, to mention just a few. And they select stocks suitable for their own particular investment needs. They tend to sell either because their estimate of the fundamental factors proved wrong or because of some change in their personal circumstances or needs. They almost never buy or sell because of short-swing fluctuations in the price of a security.

Short-swing traders, whether we call them "speculators" or not, may also trade on so-called "fundamental" factors. But many of them, unlike any of the true investors, also buy or sell simply because of recent changes in the price of a security. That is, they assume their ability to predict future price changes from previous changes in price and volume — so-called "technical" factors. And very many of these traders simply are gambling.

. . . The importance of this trading for our purposes is that any price change is taken as a signal by the "technicians" in the market, or by the gamblers, to buy or sell. Consequently, as insiders cause a price rise by adding their buying power to the market, the selling necessary to complete the additional transactions will ordinarily be supplied by short-term traders.

Though statistically this is probably not significant, the long-term investor may turn out to be the individual who in fact sells to the insider. But since he is normally selling for reasons unrelated to the insider's trading, and would be selling in any event, he should be indifferent to the identity of his buyer. Actually, he may benefit from the insider's buying on good news, as the average price received may be higher with than without insider trading. For example:

Let us assume that a stock is selling at $50, with undisclosed good news which will *ultimately* cause the stock to sell for $60, and that no factors other than the good news will affect the price.

Suppose, further, that with insider trading the price of the shares rises *gradually* to $60. The average price at which shares sell during this period is somewhere in the neighborhood of $55 (more or less depending on the shape of the time-price curve). At $60, anyone who has held his shares will have received the full benefit of the new information whether it is disclosed to him or not. This advantage to the ultimate holder remains even if we effectively prevent insider trading.

Without insider trading, however, the position of those who sell during the time required for the price to rise from $50 to $60 is radically altered. No longer do they receive an average price of $55. Assuming that the ultimate disclosure is made at the same time under either rule, they receive only $50 for their shares without insider trading. In short, they get less than they would with insider trading.

It may be argued that this overstates the direct advantages from insider trading. For, in fact, during the same relevant time period investors will be buying as well as selling, and — to take the same example — with insider trading they might buy at an average price of $55, while without it they would buy at an average price of $50. If the number of buyers among investors is the same as the number of sellers, then we are simply back where we started; the gains and losses cancel out (though not necessarily for the same individuals). It may be true, however, that a gradual price increase will cause fewer investment decisions to buy relative to decisions to sell than would be the case with an abrupt price change. (The difference, of course, is accounted for by other traders.) On balance, therefore, insider trading may still benefit investors. . . .

. . . Only rarely will all the necessary conditions for effective, regular insider trading be met. Great developments, measured in stock price impact, do not happen very often in any company. And news of these occurrences is not always the exclusive property of a few insiders. Therefore really significant trading by insiders is probably not a very common occurrence.

If this is all that could be said for or against insider trading, the matter would not be a very interesting one. But there is another and far more crucial facet to the issue, one which has not been noted in the existing literature. Basically, the argument is that profits from insider trading constitute the only effective compensation scheme for entrepreneurial services in large corporations.

I should begin this discussion with some explanation of what is meant by the "entrepreneurial function." The term is used here in a technical, economic sense, and the function differs in critical respects from that performed by managers:

Entrepreneur — An Innovator. Fundamentally the entrepreneur is a man who finds a new product or a new way to make or sell an old one. He may reorganize corporate administration, or he may be responsible for the merger of two companies. He may be a corporate promoter, or he may perform the job of selecting and guiding the managers. In short, he is the individual responsible for having or taking a new idea and causing it to be put into effect. A critical part of this definition is the "new idea," but there is no payoff unless the idea is put into effect successfully.

Since the value of an entrepreneur's contribution cannot be known until it has been made, there is rarely any way of appraising his services in advance. This is undoubtedly why early economists, including Adam Smith, did not see the entrepreneurial function as being distinct from the capitalist's function, for in the eighteenth century one was generally required to risk his own money to prove the value of his innovation. The return for successful innovation looks, superficially at least, like the return to the owner of capital.

Today, however, a sizable portion of economic literature, introduced principally by the late Joseph A. Schumpeter of Harvard University, has been built on the distinction between the entrepreneur and the capitalist, though it has not yet had a great impact on popular thinking.

Manager — A Technician. The management function is, in the pure sense, simply to administer a business along lines already determined. Though it may be extraordinarily complex and highly paid, the manager's job is basically that of a technician. As soon as he begins to reorganize the existing arrangement, then and only then is the executive performing an innovational or entrepreneurial activity, rather than a management function. Again the distinction between functions remains even though the same individual performs both. As Schumpeter commented, it is "just as rare for anyone always to remain an entrepreneur through the decades of his active life as it is for a businessman never to have a moment in which he is an entrepreneur, to however modest a degree."

In return for performing its function, management receives its compensation, generally termed by economists the "wage." This wage is simply the market price for managerial skills. No one knowingly pays more or takes less. Similarly, the capitalist receives "interest," which, whatever the legal form might be called, is the economic return to him. It may be relatively certain, as in the case of bonds, or it may be very indefinite, as with speculative securities; but its economic nature remains the same. Although the degrees of risk may vary greatly, interest is the price that has to be paid for the use of money over time.

But in the sense that wages and interest are the market return for capital and management, there is no such thing as a market price for entrepreneurial skills. In fact, almost by definition, it is impossible to value entrepreneurial activities *before they have paid off in some other form.* Economic theorists do, however, have a word for the entrepreneurial return; it is termed "profit," although that particular usage of the word has not received popular acceptance. But, aside from having a word for it, we have little knowledge about the particular form that this "profit" may take, or even whether it can redound to the benefit of entrepreneurs in large corporations.

Here it is important to turn once more to Schumpeter. Perhaps his greatest contribution in modern economic theory was the concept of dynamic competition. Schumpeter pointed out that where enterprise is allowed a free rein, no one can afford to stand still. His famous "perennial gale of creative destruction" is the process by which the most significant competition occurs. This is the competition created by the true entrepreneur, and it is a fierce thing.

Schumpeter thought that price competition, so loved by anti-trusters, was effete indeed compared to the competitive effects of new products, new markets, and new ways of doing things. On this point he may well have been right. Price competition could probably be administered by pure managers, corporate bureaucrats, or today even by carefully programmed computers. But that kind of activity could never withstand the onslaught of the real entrepreneur.

For all his brilliance in developing the theory of entrepreneurship and dynamic competition, Schumpeter made a serious and well-known error concerning the American corporate system. This error occurred in his famous Capitalism, Socialism and Democracy, published in 1942. Briefly, it was that the system of corporate capitalism simply could not survive. He believed that large corporations would become completely bureaucratized and management-oriented. He felt that innovation had been routinized, and the "romance of earlier commercial adventure" no longer characterized business leaders' activities. This routinization of innovation would first destroy the capitalist entrepreneurs as a class, and eventually capitalism would disappear for lack of an effective champion. "The true pacemakers of socialism," he said, "were not the intellectuals or agitators who preached it but the Vanderbilts, Carnegies, and Rockefellers."

It requires no argument to realize how wrong Schumpeter was in this prediction. For all their organization and bureaucratization, American corporations seem as dynamic, innovative, and entrepreneurial today as they have ever been. What, then, could explain such a gross misconception by one of the leading economic scholars of the century? The answer to this question seems to have eluded theoreticians up to now.

Closer examination of Schumpeter's arguments may explain his error. Schumpeter stated that any form of compensation for corporate executives other than salaries and bonuses was either "illegal or semi-illegal." Yet he realized that salary and bonuses were appropriate forms of compensation only for the pure management function. Entrepreneurs would require something much grander, though less certain. And since Schumpeter felt that this could not be made available to them in the large corporation, he assumed that they would disappear from the large corporate scene.

But he did not see the possibility of using insider information as an appropriate form of compensation for entrepreneurs in large corporations.

One cannot argue with Schumpeter's theory of what would happen to large corporations *if in fact* no entrepreneurs within them could receive an appropriate return. Government agencies and heavily regulated or protected industries are probably sufficient proof of the validity of this idea. On this basis the prediction for which Schumpeter has been frequently criticized could be closer to the mark than his critics have realized — that is, if misguided proposals to abolish our most effective system for rewarding entrepreneurs in large corporations (insider trading in one form or another) are adopted.

To provide an effective incentive, entrepreneurial compensation has to be available when the benefits are realized by the corporation, and it must vary with the value of the contribution. Since neither of these eventualities can ordinarily be predicted in advance, most existing compensation plans are inadequate for the task. Obviously, salary is inappropriate. The amount of salary has to be decided on in advance, it does not allow for distinguishing the manager who only manages from one who also innovates, and it is not flexible enough to reward particular contributions.

At first glance the bonus does seem to answer most of these objections. However, most bonuses today are formulated in advance and depend on total profits rather than individual contributions. Bonus plans are incentive devices, but they probably tend to generate managerial improvements, such as small cost-cutting, rather than radical innovations. The bonus plan, as opposed to the special bonus, will not serve the entrepreneur's purpose.

The special bonus can, of course, be used to reward great innovations, though there are legal restrictions if authorization is not established in advance. But the main drawback is that the true value of a particular contribution, in the form of higher profits, may not be known for many years. So there frequently are gross disparities in judgment between the bonus committee and the executive as to the latter's true worth. This misjudgment may become even more serious if the innovation has caused the price of the stock to rise but has not yet affected profits, though the stock price rise is precisely what the entrepreneur should be rewarded for.

In addition, the entrepreneurial type who is motivated by the possibility of "getting rich quick" probably does not like the idea of negotiating his reward after his contribution has been made. This distinction is like that between a patent system and a system of bonuses or government awards for inventions. Few will be found to argue that the latter system encourages as much invention as the former.

Stock options also add some incentive to efficiency for managers, but it is doubtful that they can serve the needs of the entrepreneur for massive reward for great innovations. The difficulty should be obvious. The number of shares to be optioned to various executives normally has to be determined in advance of any entrepreneurial innovation. If the options are granted after the innovation, they are the same as the special bonus, except that payment is made in the form of a free call on corporate stock rather than in the form of cash. Stock options undoubtedly add greatly to incentive, but they may still promise too little to entrepreneurial types with ambition, enthusiasm, and a large measure of self-confidence.

On the other hand, free trading by insiders in a company's securities meets the objections mentioned for other compensation schemes and has special advantages of its own. Perhaps this can best be seen by comparing systems of compensation for patentable and nonpatentable innovations.

Basically the patent system is designed to allow inventors to receive an appropriate reward for successful innovations by preventing others from copying and participating in profits which we might say were not earned by them. The granting of a temporary monopoly to the patentee assures two goals: (1) it excludes the would-be interloper; (2) it provides the patentee with a substantial reward for his idea, although that reward will vary with the economic importance of the invention.

The patent system seems to work reasonably well, but only for patentable ideas. How can we guarantee a similar reward to inventors of nonpatentable ideas? In this area our legal system has been rather weak and ineffective; it has developed few really successful techniques for the protection of such ideas. Most businessmen recognize that secrecy and speed of marketing are the two principal devices for realizing substantial profits for their companies from nonpatentable innovations — secrecy to keep competitors away and speed because they cannot be kept away for long. But nothing in this scheme provides any protection or reward for the individual who has an important, nonpatentable idea which he personally is in no position to exploit.

For the man who has not founded his own business to exploit his idea — historically the traditional course for an entrepreneur — trading in the stock market on inside information provides a reward system, and is the only effective device available for the entrepreneur who is employed by a large corporation.

Insider trading allows any individual who works for a publicly traded corporation to play the entrepreneurial role, a very important advantage. Individuals can, in effect, sell their own ideas without the necessity of having large amounts of capital available. The increase in stock price, though not perfect, will provide as accurate a gauge of the value of the innovation as can be found, and it will leave little room for argument about an individual's worth.

Large corporations will be able to compete more effectively for entrepreneurial talent with closely owned companies, since they can now hold out the promise of very great rewards for the successful innovator. The image of corporate executives as gray bureaucrats can and should be erased. Large corporations can furnish as much romance, excitement, and opportunity for rapid economic and social advancement as any other avenues pursued today. But if corporations get hung up on foolish moralizing, such as characterizes most discussions of insider trading, they cannot hope to compete successfully or to survive the subtle attacks of government agencies.

If there really is an economic service or function that can be termed entrepreneurship, then we must have some way of compensating it. The cases are legion of new corporate managers bringing in fresh, imaginative, but often untested ideas. If these individuals were to be limited to the same compensation as their dull unimaginative, and overly conservative predecessors, what incentive would they have to innovate? Their salaries, bonuses, and pensions are usually secure, and few large companies face imminent bankruptcy. Their stock options and bonus plans will give some motivation to improve things, but not to take very great personal risks. For the true entrepreneur, the possibility of great riches will elicit more risk-taking activities and enterprise than will the possibility of smaller though more certain gain. . . .

There are some objections that can be raised to insider trading as a compensation device, although on balance they are not very significant.

Windfall Benefits. Here the argument goes that individuals would benefit fortuitously from good news which they have not produced. This does not seem too serious an objection, since innovators rarely receive the full value of their contribution anyway. With any nonpatentable invention, competitors flock in fast to copy and to claim entrepreneurial profits for themselves. Similarly, both stockholders and other executives will ordinarily share in the corporate entrepreneur's gains. When we view insider trading as an appropriate *form* of compensation rather than a device for accurately valuing innovations and paying a precise number of dollars, the windfall argument does not seem strong at all.

Unearned Returns. It may often appear that individuals who have not contributed anything to the corporation in years, if ever, will be regularly privy to inside information. But appearances may be deceiving. Frequently these individuals may be participating in an information exchange (to be discussed shortly), or perhaps an obligation is being met with valuable information rather than money.

One individual seldom has sole possession of information and so is unable to control its dissemination both within and outside his company, although insiders will have strong incentive to police the dissemination of information efficiently. But this does not mean that it will be economical to secure perfect policing, and therefore some leakage is bound to occur.

Trading on Bad News. Nor should the fact that profits can be made in the market by selling short on bad news deter us from adopting this theory of compensation. If the appropriate incentives and constraints are built into the modern corporation system, they will generate a desire to create good news, not bad. And if this is so, the fact that one may incidentally profit from bad news should be of no more significance for this discussion than the fact that one may profit from good news which he did not personally produce.

Stock "Manipulation." Here the argument is that if insiders are allowed to trade freely, they will manipulate the affairs of the corporation so as to maximize their own trading profits rather than the company's earnings. There are many different forms to this argument, though critics of insider trading never clearly distinguish the different kinds of manipulation that are possible. Space does not allow detailed consideration of this matter, but some observations may be made:

There are few incentives for manipulation of stock prices that conflict with the long-run interests of the corporation and its shareholders.

Manipulation which takes the form only of changing the time at which disclosure is made is of no consequence to all outsider investors considered as a group.

The grosser forms of manipulation can be dealt with quite effectively through less drastic techniques than preventing insider trading. . . .

Under Section 16(b) of the Securities Exchange Act of 1934, profits resulting from any combination of a purchase and a sale of equity securities by an insider within a six-month period inure to the benefit of the corporation and may be claimed by any shareholder on behalf of the corporation in a simplified legal action. Monthly reporting of any changes in the holdings of officers, directors, and 10% shareholders is also required. The section applies to any corporation with $1 million in assets and . . . 500 shareholders. . . .

Note that only the simplest form of insider trading is specifically restricted by Section 16(b) of the Securities Exchange Act of 1934 and by shareholders' suits based on that law. It would be an unimaginative business community which would allow perhaps billions of dollars in stock market profits to sift through its hands like sand because direct trading is outlawed. The stakes are too large, and the alternative techniques are too easy.

Since direct exploitation of valuable information is ruled out, the next step is to find an indirect method of exchanging this valuable but unusable information for valuable and usable information. This may be done by a simple exchange of information. Undoubtedly many social relationships, such as club memberships, golf four-somes, and luncheon groups, provide opportunities for these mutually beneficial exchanges. There will always be some uncertainty in advice gained this way; but when the source is reliable, it is as different from the run-of-the-mine tip or the average broker's advice as gold is from clay.

But simple barter is never a very efficient exchange mechanism compared to using a medium of exchange like money. The parties may disagree on the value of their respective contributions; one may develop considerable information of value, while nothing important happens in the other's company; and neither can effectively control the further dissemination of information once it has been given out. The last point is especially important, since businessmen with property of great value should not be assumed to toss it away carelessly as they might a cigar wrapper.

To make this barter system function effectively, some sort of bank or clearinghouse operation is required. Here valuable information can be "deposited," and the ensuing credit drawn on in the form of information about other companies when the depositor is in a legal and financial position to use it.

Clearly, the operator of the clearinghouse will have to be completely trustworthy, privy to fantastic amounts of very valuable information about many corporations and familiar with the roles played by the executives of these companies. The order may seem like a large one, but it is probably being filled regularly by familiar figures on the financial scene — the investment bankers. Some of the techniques used by investment banking houses in the operation of this information "bank" have long been evident but simply unidentified as such:

Boards of directors — The first and most obvious of these techniques is the control of one or more seats on various boards of directors. This may be used either as a method of allowing an individual to "draw" on his credits or to secure information for the common fund, as was alleged in Blau v. Lehman. But, as the SEC's Special Study of Securities Markets suggested, bankers and brokers making markets in shares can get all the information they need without "deputing" anyone to sit on the board.

Priority lists — Another familiar device for operating an information bank is the preference or priority list. These lists simply designate certain individuals who are to be made privy to a specific bit of valuable information. This may be done either by disclosure of the information itself or simply by a recommendation to buy the stock. This method has the advantage of not requiring that the "information banker" also be the recipient's broker, but it has the disadvantage of causing a loss of control over further disclosures. It may also be too slow to be useful in some circumstances, though there are a number of variations on this technique which can improve its efficiency.

Discretionary accounts—Perhaps the most efficient device, at least since the outlawing of stock pools, is the so-called discretionary account. Here the information banker simply agrees to manage an investment fund of a stated amount. He may thus carefully control the value drawn from the common information fund, and there is no problem of policing the information since no disclosure is made. This device has considerable flexibility and can be used with a high degree of speed and precision. Furthermore, in its more complicated forms, it can thwart all but the most extreme methods of government policing. . . .

In spite of the Supreme Court's admonition not to expand the coverage of 16(b), the SEC has continued to try to develop a stronger weapon against insider trading through administrative acts. In 1942 it adopted what is now known as the "SEC fraud rule," rule 10b-5, which, among other things, makes it illegal to issue an untrue or misleading statement, or omit a material fact in a statement, or commit any act of fraud or deceit in connection with the purchase or sale of a security. It purports to follow from Section 10(b) of the Securities and Exchange Act of 1934, though its operative terms are far broader than those of the act. In fact, the important language is taken from Section 17 of the Securities Act of 1933, which applied only to sales of securities and was therefore useless in dealing with most insider trading.

Strangely enough, during the early development of 10b-5 as an insider trading provision, neither the SEC nor the most influential commentators saw it as very important. The general view was that the provision merely codified common law in the states, applied their doctrine in federal cases, and covered transactions in stocks listed on exchanges.

Whether this somewhat restrained view of 10b-5 was intended by the SEC or not, the courts began to use language strongly suggesting that the provision outlawed all forms of stock market trading with undisclosed information. . . .

Concluding Note

The insider trading scheme for compensating entrepreneurs is not a neat, one-for-one exchange arrangement. It may sometimes appear highly arbitrary. But it is probably the best scheme we can devise for compensating the entrepreneurial function in large corporations. There is undoubtedly much that we need to learn about how this scheme actually works in practice, but we know enough now to have serious reservations about the prevailing attitude on the subject.

The SEC has reflected, as well as helped to develop, this attitude toward insider trading. There is strong reason to believe that this has been a real disservice to the American shareholder. The public's indignation with the defendants at the outset of the *Texas Gulf Sulphur* case may well have been directed toward the wrong party in the action.

Insiders and Market Efficiency*

Joseph E. Finnerty

The strong-form of the efficient market hypothesis assumes all available public and private information is fully reflected in a security's market price. The strong-form, in terms of market participants, also assumes that no individual can have higher expected trading profits than others because of monopolistic access to information. One possible test of the strong-form is to determine whether insiders earn better than average profits from their market transactions. To ascertain if the market is truly efficient will involve determining how well insiders do relative to the market in general. To date, some work has already been done in evaluating rates of return earned by insiders trading for their own accounts. Jaffe, Pratt and DeVere, Rogoff, and Glass have calculated rates of return earned by insiders trading for their own accounts and their work lends some support to the hypothesis that insiders do, in fact, earn above average profits. A major shortcoming of these studies centers on data availability, as no precise price per share or date of insider trades were reported to the S.E.C. prior to 1965. Further, except for Jaffe, the studies do not incorporate an explicit adjustment for risk. . . .

The time period for this study runs from January, 1969 to December, 1972. The data are from the S.E.C.'s Official Summary of Stock Transactions for NYSE firms. The data file contains identification of the company and the individual insider, date of the transaction, number of shares traded, end of the month holding of the

*Source: 31 J. Fin. 1141–1148 (1976), reprinted with permission. Joseph E. Finnerty is professor of finance at the University of Massachusetts.

insider, buy or sell code, and closing price on the day of the trade. Data are adjusted for stock splits or dividends. For the total period, there are recorded over 30,000 individual transactions: 9,602 buy transactions and 21,487 sell transactions.

Common stock acquired by the exercise of options or through compensation plans was excluded from the insider sample, because of the difficulty in getting price information associated with the exercise of options and in determining the worth of the shares received as compensation. Any bias introduced by this omission would tend to understate the returns earned by the insiders, because of the bargain prices generally associated with these transactions. Gifts and private sales were also excluded because of the lack of a market determined price. Late reports were included in their proper transaction month. Since the major concern of this study is with the stong-form of market efficiency, no bias is introduced by including late reports in their proper month.

An insider buy portfolio and an insider sell portfolio are formed for each month of the time period. The buy (sell) portfolio for the *i*th month is comprised of the securities of those companies for which any insider engaged in a buy (sell) transaction during that *i*th month. Each security is weighted in the portfolio for the *i*th month by the number of times insiders bought that particular security in the *i*th month. Thirty-six such buy (sell) portfolios are formed, starting with January 1969 and ending with December 1971. Portfolio returns for each of the thirty-six buy (sell) portfolios are computed for the portfolio formation month and for each of the eleven subsequent months. . . .

The results of the regressions are presented in Table [3]. For each portfolio for each holding period the following data are presented: the excess return, *t*-statistic, and level of significance.

The intercept term of the buy portfolios is always positive and significantly different than zero, at the 10% significance level. This implies that insiders earn above average returns when they buy securities of their respective corporations. . . .

Since the market fell substantially during 1969 and the first half of 1970, and then recovered during the latter half of 1970 and the first half of 1971, to be followed by another drop during the last half of 1971, the returns of the individual insiders may not have been positive. The point is that their investments were doing better than the market.

All of the sell portfolios have negative differential returns which are significantly different than zero at the 10% level, except the returns for the fifth and seventh months. The results indicate that the securities the insiders were selling fell more than the general

Table 3
Monthly Differential Returns

	Buy Portfolio				Sell Portfolio			
Month From Trade	Monthly Excess Return	Standard Error	t-Statistic	Signi-ficance	Monthly Excess Return	Standard Error	t-Statistic	Signi-ficance
0	.0368	.0128	2.875	.0420	−.0090	.0042	−2.143	.0403
1	.0101	.0053	1.905	.0731	−.0045	.0012	−3.750	.0007
2	.0085	.0026	3.230	.0042	−.0043	.0012	−3.583	.0009
3	.0037	.0012	2.972	.0054	−.0042	.0012	−3.500	.0009
4	.0053	.0013	4.252	.0002	−.0047	.0011	−4.272	.0003
5	.0026	.0011	2.440	.0200	−.0033	.0018	−1.277	.1581
6	.0049	.0013	3.832	.0005	−.0031	.0014	−2.214	.0438
7	.0016	.0012	1.433	.1010	−.0026	.0019	−1.368	.1173
8	.0018	.0011	1.606	.0951	−.0037	.0011	−3.363	.0019
9	.0021	.0012	1.808	.0675	−.0034	.0015	−2.266	.0468
10	.0040	.0012	3.369	.0019	−.0028	.0010	−2.833	.0421
11	.0020	.0012	1.750	.0891	−.0026	.0012	−2.166	.0398

Source: Finnerty, Table 1.

market decline of the period. These results for both the buy and sell portfolios bear out the fact that insiders, because probably of their access to privileged information, can outperform the market in their stock selections.

From the monthly differential returns for the buy portfolio, most of the above average returns, are realized in the first six months. The first month has the greatest amount of above average return [and] this may indicate either that the information on which the insiders act soon becomes public knowledge and is discounted by the market quite quickly or that the knowledge that insiders have been accumulating certain stocks prompts the public to acquire the same stocks and thereby bid up the prices. Whichever the case, it is clear that after the insider acts, the short-term effect is to have the market follow.

The monthly differentials for the sell portfolios present a different picture, with most of the below average performance taking place uniformly throughout the subsequent months. Of particular interest is the relatively small differentials compared to the buy portfolio in the first three months. It would appear that initially as the insiders are selling, either the information they are selling on is not immediately released, or the fact that insiders are selling is not immediately discounted by the market.

From the results it is apparent that in the short-run insiders are able to identify profitable as well as unprofitable situations in their own companies.

To sum up the findings of this study, it corroborates those of Pratt and DeVere and Jaffe: Insiders are able to outperform the market. Insiders can and do identify profitable as well as unprofitable situations within their corporations. This finding tends to refute the strong-form of the efficient market hypothesis.

The Effect of Regulation Changes on Insider Trading*

Jeffrey F. Jaffe

The effect of government regulation on the trading of insiders is a matter of great concern in legal circles, as the proliferation of law journal articles and court cases on the subject will testify. The legal literature has been concerned primarily with the presumed injustice of knowledgeable insiders' benefiting at the expense of other investors.

Economists, by contrast, typically have been more involved with the effect of insiders on capital market efficiency—and there is much disagreement. On the one hand, Friend states that one purpose of security regulation is "to prevent insiders' profiting thereby at the expense of shareholders." He concludes that "I have never thought there was any equity or economic justification for revoking that part [of the Securities and Exchange Act] which deals with disclosure of insider trading." On the other hand, Demsetz argues that secrecy is not necessarily an evil, for it prevents "the rapid communalization of rewards" from information. Demsetz also views the costs of policing insider trading as substantial. Manne adds that regulation may actually increase secrecy by lengthening the time between the production of information and its release to the market.

Though lawyers and economists have speculated about the consequences of effective insider regulation, empirical research has yet to establish whether the regulation of insiders is even effective. The techniques of this study permit judgments to be made on the effectiveness of regulation.

The results of previous studies suggest that insiders possess special information. The present study compares the extent of their use of that special information in various time periods with the

*Source: 5 Bell J. Econ. & Man. Sci. 93-121 (1974). Reprinted with permission; copyright © 1974 by the American Telephone and Telegraph Company. Jeffrey F. Jaffe is professor of finance at the Wharton School, University of Pennsylvania.

degree of regulation in effect during these periods. After the Securities and Exchange Act of 1933–1934, all important changes in insider trading regulation resulted from case law. Three of the most significant regulatory events concerning insider trading are:

(1) the *Cady, Roberts* decision (November 8, 1961),

(2) the Texas Gulf Sulphur indictment (April 19, 1965), and

(3) the *Texas Gulf Sulphur* decision (August 19, 1966).

These three important cases signaled changes in the attitude of the courts and law enforcement agencies towards insider trading. Therefore, we shall compare the behavior of insider trading immediately before and after each of these three regulatory changes. This technique should reduce the effect of other economic influences, such as changing market conditions, which have plagued studies comparing periods separated by many years. The combined effect of the three decisions is also measured. . . .

In order to estimate the profitability of insider trades, this study examines the performance of a security subsequent to specific types of insider trades in that security, which we call insider trading events. We define the performance of a security to be that part of its return not explained by price movement in the stock market as a whole. The performance of a security, when measured in this way, is commonly referred to as the security's residual. . . .

It is meaningful to consider the effect of regulation on the speculation of insiders only if it can first be shown that insiders earn profits above those accruing to investors with no special information. This section presents results suggesting that insiders do earn abnormal profits. First, an initial sample, containing randomly chosen insider trades, is selected as a benchmark. Next, samples consisting of large trades and trades from months of intensive insider activity are studied.

The initial sample is composed of insider trades from the 200 largest securities listed on the Stock Price Tape of the Center for Research in Security Prices (CRSP) of the University of Chicago. For each of these securities, insider trades are observed in five separate months during the interval from 1962 to 1968. The individual months of observation for a particular security are separated in time by 12 to 18 months. The exact number of months between two observations is determined by the selection of a random number from 12 to 18.

In any calendar month an individual trader is classified as a purchaser if the number of days during the month in which he buys stock is greater than the number of days in which he sells stock. Conversely, he is classified as a seller if the number of days in which he buys stock is less than the number of days in which he sells stock. If he purchases stock on just as many days as he sells it, he is not included in the sample. (Exercises of options are excluded from this and all other samples in this study because it is felt that options are exercised due to institutional factors rather than as a result of special information.)

For each company in the initial sample, a month is classified as a month of net purchasers or a month of net sellers depending on whether the number of purchasers is greater or less than the number of sellers. Months during which the number of purchasers equals the number of sellers are excluded. Months of net purchasers and months of net sellers are defined as insider trading *events*. In this and all other samples in the study, events are excluded if companies are not listed on the CRSP tape for fifty months before the event and ten months after the event. This restriction assures sufficient data to form portfolios and to calculate residual variances. There are 952 trades in the initial sample. Many companies have more than one trade in a month, so that the number of months of net purchasers plus the number of months of net sellers is only 362.

Cumulative average residuals are calculated via the method explained [above]. . . . The magnitude of the residuals from this sample, as well as the statistical significance of the residuals is examined. The average residual of month 1, the cumulative average residual from month 1 to month 2, and the cumulative average residual from month 1 to month 8 are presented in Table 2 [omitted]. These three time intervals are chosen in order to study both the short-term and long-term predictive power of insiders. The cumulative average residual rises to 0.0136 within eight months. This value is of small magnitude, as it would not cover normal transactions costs of two or three percent on a round-trip transaction. Almost one half of that rise, 0.0060, occurs in the first month. This suggests that insiders are better able to predict short-term than longer-term movement in stock price. . . .

Though the evidence of the initial sample suggests that insiders possessed and used special information, certain subsamples might yield more convincing results. In particular it was felt that insiders with information might trade large blocks of stock. All transactions from the initial sample whose values are greater than $20,000 are assembled into a subsample. This subsample contains 370 trades, representing 39 percent of the original sample of 952. The previous classification scheme is employed to separate months of net purchasers from months of net sellers. As shown in Table 2, the cumulative average residuals and the *t*-values are of similar magnitude to the residuals and *t*-values from the initial sample. These results suggest successful forecasting by insiders, though they do not indicate that large transactions contain more information than other transactions contain.

The work of Glass, Lorie-Neiderhoffer, and Rogoff suggest that months of intensive insider trading preceded significant stock price movement. As these studies employed small samples and ignored the relative risk of different securities and general market conditions, this paper also examines intensive trading months. Any company with at least Y more purchasers than sellers in a month is classified as an intensive buying company for that month. Conversely, any company with at least Y more sellers than purchasers in a month is classified as an intensive selling company for the month. In the following sample, Y will assume the value of three.

The present sample includes all intensive trading companies listed on the CRSP tape during the months from April to October 1961; from December 1961 to November 1962; from January 1964 to March 1965; from May to December 1965; and from September 1966 to March 1967. Using the methods explained [above], the cumulative average residuals and t-values are calculated. . . . The residuals rise approximately 5 percent in eight months, with 3 percent of the rise occurring in the last six months. These figures are quite large, as they are much greater than transaction costs. The t-values are clearly significant as they range from 3.65 to 5.23. The results from this sample support the previous research cited above.

The above results were checked by selecting a sample of intensive trading companies from a different time period. For this sample Y assumes the values of four, five, and six, All intensive trading months occurring during the period from January 1953 to December 1955 and January 1958 to December 1959 for the companies listed on the CRSP tape are included in the sample. The results from these samples are also presented in Table 2.

For the sample when Y equals four, the cumulative average residuals rise over 5 percent in eight months, suggesting that insiders possess special information. The t-values are large, as each of the three is greater than 3.0. The residuals when Y equals four are lower than the t-values in the former sample due to a smaller sample size. When Y equals six, the residuals are smaller and the t-values are not significant. As this sample contains only eighty observations, the results are not so decisive as those of the total sample.

The findings from these intensive trading samples also suggest that insiders are earning abnormal profits. However, as the cumulative average residuals do not increase as Y increases, the results do not suggest that the profit of insiders is an increasing function of the intensity of the trading.

The study has examined three different samples: the initial

sample and two independent samples of intensive trading companies. Each of these samples exhibits evidence of special information among insiders. The sample of intensive trading companies yields particularly strong evidence of special information as residuals from some of the subsamples rose above 5 percent in eight months, while some *t*-values were above five. Because evidence has been provided that insiders can earn significant profits, there is now reason to examine the effect of security regulation on the profits of insiders.

The effect of regulation on the securities market is a subject of much current interest. For the most part, it has simply been assumed that regulation accomplishes its objectives. Only rarely is it possible to directly measure the effects of a particular type of governmental control. The regulation of insiders is one of these exceptions. Since we have seen in the previous section that insiders do possess special information, we can now compare the extent of their use of that information in various periods of time with the degree of regulation in effect in these periods.

As previously mentioned, three of the most significant changes in security regulation have resulted from the *Cady, Roberts* decision, the Texas Gulf Sulphur indictment, and the *Texas Gulf Sulphur* decision. Though the Securities and Exchange Act of 1934 empowered the SEC with authority over insiders, this authority was not enforced until the *Cady, Roberts* decision in November, 1961. The decision penalized a brokerage firm for trading with secret information on behalf of its clients and thus established the precedent that corporate officials trading on inside information were liable for civil prosecution. In April 1965 the SEC indicted* officials of Texas Gulf Sulphur for trading on, as well as suppressing, information related to the company's vast mineral strike. Since the *Cady, Roberts* decision was merely an administrative ruling, the Texas Gulf Sulphur civil indictment can be viewed as an extension of regulatory law. To the surprise of many lawyers and corporate officials, the decision in August 1966 upheld most of the counts of the April 1965 indictment. This ruling showed insiders that the courts, as well as the SEC, would punish speculation on special information. In recent years, the courts have handled other cases involving misuse of inside information, and have heard appeals on the *Texas Gulf Sulphur* case. However, since the *Cady, Roberts* decision and the Texas Gulf Sulphur indictment and decision appear to be the most important, the effects of only these three actions are examined. In this section, we compare the properties of insider trading immediately before and

*[The SEC suit was a civil action for injunctive and other equitable relief, not a criminal prosecution — Eds.]

after each of these regulatory changes. Since a regulatory decision could conceivably affect both the profitability and the volume of insider trades, the existence of these possible effects is investigated below.

Effect on profitability. Prior research and the results [above] suggest that an examination of intensive trading companies yields the most convincing evidence of successful forecasting by insiders. Below we compare the performance of intensive trading companies prior to each decision with the performance of intensive trading companies subsequent to it. For this section of the study, any company with at least three more purchasers than sellers in a month is classified as an intensive buying company for that month, i.e., we set $Y = 3$. Conversely, any company with at least three more sellers than purchasers in a month is classified as an intensive selling company.

As the *Cady, Roberts* decision occurred in November 1961, we select a sample including every company listed on the CRSP tape with an intensive trading month during the period from April 1961 to October 1961, and another sample including every company listed on the CRSP tape with an intensive trading month during the period from December 1961 to November 1962. We use the methods explained [above] and calculate the cumulative average residuals and *t*-values for the two samples. . . . In the first sample, the cumulative average residuals are large, as they rise approximately 0.08 in eight months following trading events. Insiders appear to be forecasting returns many months ahead, as the value of the cumulative average residuals increases when we move from one to eight months. However, as the cumulative average residuals *per month* decline, one suspects that insiders are better able to predict stock price movement in the immediate future than in the more distant future. All of the *t*-values for the pre-*Cady, Roberts* sample are larger than 2.00, indicating with high probability that insiders earned excess returns during this period. The cumulative average residuals are large in the second sample and the same general pattern of increasing cumulative average residuals but decreasing cumulative average residuals per month is observed here. We also find high *t*-values in this sample. However, the cumulative average residuals are lower than in the pre-*Cady, Roberts* sample, possibly indicating an effect due to the decision.

To examine the hypothesis that the *Cady, Roberts* decision had no effect on the profitability of insider trading, a difference of the means test is constructed. . . . As values this low imply that the differences might well be due to chance, the hypothesis that the Cady, Roberts decision did not affect the profitability of insider trading cannot be rejected.

In order to measure the effects of the Texas Gulf Sulphur indictment on the profitability of insider trading, two samples are used. The first sample includes all intensive trading months during the period from January 1964 to March 1965 for any company listed on the CRSP tape, while the second sample includes all intensive trading months during the period from May to December, 1965. For each of the two samples, the results from residual analysis and the portfolio method are presented in Table 2. The cumulative average residuals are large in these samples, though smaller than those from the *Cady, Roberts* samples. All six *t*-values are large and positive, suggesting that insiders were earning profits both before and after the Texas Gulf Sulphur indictment. It is interesting that insiders actually perform slightly better *after* the indictment, as all three cumulative average residuals are higher in the post-*TGS* sample.

To examine the null hypothesis that insiders were not influenced by the Texas Gulf Sulphur indictment, the average standardized residuals from the pre-*TGS* sample are tested against the average standardized residuals from the post-*TGS* sample. . . . More important, as none of the *t*-values is statistically large, there is not sufficient evidence to reject the hypothesis that the Texas Gulf Sulphur indictment did not affect the profitability of insider trades.

Though the Texas Gulf Sulphur indictment did not appear to have a deterrent effect on the profitability of insider trading, the decision on August 19, 1966, may have had such an effect. To test this, a sample containing all the intensive trading events of companies listed on the CRSP tape from September 1966 to March 1967 is collected. Statistics from residual analysis are presented in Table 2 [omitted]. The cumulative average residuals from this sample are as large, if not larger, than those from prior samples. The eight-month value of 0.0840 is particularly high, suggesting that the three regulatory decisions may have had only a slight, if any, effect on the performance of insiders. This sample is compared to the one running from May to December, 1965. (Statistics on this latter sample are also presented in Table 2.) The one- and two-month cumulative average residuals are larger in the 1965 sample than in the 1966 to 1967 sample, while the eight-month cumulative average residual is smaller. . . .

The cumulative effect of the three cases is measured by comparing the pre-*Cady, Roberts* decision data with the post-*Texas Gulf Sulphur* decision data. From Table 2, we find that the one- and two-month cumulative average residuals are higher in the pre-*Cady, Roberts* data, while the eight-month cumulative average residuals are almost identical in the two samples. The results of difference of the means tests between the average standardized residuals of the pre-*Cady, Roberts* sample and the average standardized residuals of the post-*Texas Gulf Sulphur* sample are presented in Table 3 [omitted]. The *t*-values are negative, indicating better performance in the pre-*Cady, Roberts* sample. However, since the *t*-values are small (all are above −1.0), the evidence is not sufficient to reject the hypothesis that there was no cumulative effect of the three events.

In this section, we have examined the individual effects of three regulatory events on the profitability of insider trades. On the one hand, there was a drop in the average profitability of insider trades following both the *Cady, Roberts* decision and the *Texas Gulf Sulphur* decision. On the other hand, there appeared to be an increase in profitability following the Texas Gulf Sulphur indictment. However, for each of the three regulatory events, the average profitability of insider trades before an event was not significantly different from the average profitability of insider trades after that event. In addition, the performance of insiders in a period prior to the three events was not significantly different from the performance of insiders in a period subsequent to all three events. Hence, the results of this section do not suggest that regulation changes had an effect on the profitability of insider trading.

Effect on insider trading volume. As the total profit to insiders per period might be related to the frequency of trades, the trading activity in the months surrounding our three case law changes is examined. A sample is selected containing the total number of insider traders in months before and after each regulation change. Options are excluded in the formation of the sample. . . .

In this section, the effect of the three decisions on the volume of trading was investigated. Initially, monthly data were used. Time series of the number of insider traders per month were formed and the data were standardized by total monthly market volume on the NYSE. First months, as well as lagged effects of each decision, were examined. Both the standardized and unstandardized time series did not indicate an effect on volume from any of the three decisions. Daily data were also employed for the last two regulatory events. The results did not indicate any effect due to either event, as the insider trading volume actually increased in the days following the indictment and the decision. Thus, the data do not suggest that the regulation changes in the 1960s influenced the volume of insider trading.

In order to assess the effectiveness of changes in the regulation of insiders, this study examined certain properties of insider trading immediately before and after three important events in case law. There appeared to be few changes in the characteristics of trading attributable to the three cases. Only the *Texas Gulf Sulphur* decision seems to have had even a slight effect on the profitability of insider trading, and there is no evidence of any cumulative effect of the three events on profitability. Furthermore, the data do not suggest that the regulatory changes affected the volume of insider trading. The volume actually increased slightly after each of the three events, though none of these changes in volume could be called statistically large.

The nature of the regulations and their enforcement may explain why their effect is so small. Though new developments have increased the restrictiveness of the old laws, these laws still prohibit only the most flagrant examples of speculation on inside information. In order to prosecute an insider, the SEC must prove not only that the individual made abnormal profits, but that he was also trading on "material" information not known to the general public. We previously showed in our intensive trading samples that, on average, insiders reaped excess returns of approximately 4 percent per trade. Though insiders earning these small returns may actually be receiving material information, movements in stock prices of this order are likely to be due to events undetectable by a regulatory agency. . . .

The results of this paper do not suggest that the recent regulation of insiders is effective, casting doubt on the value of this regulation to society. However, before policy decisions can be made, much new research is needed in this area. This paper has attempted only to measure the power of current insider regulation. Future work might investigate the factors impeding effective regulation and suggest new techniques to increase the influence of our laws. In particular, methods to restrict the trading of tippees would be valuable. Furthermore, an examination of the costs to taxpayers of security regulation would be both important and interesting.

More generally, insider trading regulation should be related to discussions of social welfare. Though the important works of Demsetz, Fama-Laffer, Friend, Hirshleifer, Manne, and Marshall have gone far in this regard, certain questions are not yet satisfactorily answered. For example, are we interested in the fairest solution or the most efficient one? How much money is it worth to society to prevent the redistribution of a dollar from naive investors to insiders? When these and other questions have been answered, empirical work can be better put into perspective.

NOTES AND QUESTIONS

1. Manne relies on two main propositions in his justification of insider trading. The first is that insider trading represents a superior incentive compensation device for entrepreneurs. To what extent are the beneficiaries of insider trading actually "entrepreneurs"? In

Texas Gulf, the largest trader was the geologist at the drill site, together with the friends to whom he passed on the good news. In the *Douglas Aircraft* case,* the traders were institutional clients of a brokerage house who sold on advance word of a sharp drop in earnings. And does Manne skip too quickly over the possibility that insider trading would reduce managerial incentives to perform well, by enabling them to profit from an unexpected decline in the value of the company? If the managers knew that the company was, perhaps because of their mismanagement, about to suffer a substantial loss not discounted in the market price of its stock because not yet known to the market, couldn't they (in the absence of any legal barriers) make handsome profits by selling the stock short? In short, wouldn't insider trading give managers an incentive to produce unexpected fluctuations in the market value of their companies' stock, rather than to maximize the present value of their companies? Does the Fama selection in Chapter 2 provide an answer for this concern?

How could one distinguish empirically between the Manne thesis on insider trading and the view that it is harmful to good management? Could one ask whether insider trading was ever forbidden in employment contracts before being forbidden by law, or is ever forbidden by contract today in countries that still have no laws against the practice?

2. Manne's second point is that insider trading is a force that works to move market prices in the correct direction, toward levels that reflect the value of the undisclosed information.† More rapid disclosure of that information would, of course, serve the same end even more effectively. Which is likely to produce more prompt and accurate market pricing—signals from insider trading or legal disclosure requirements? The answer seems necessarily empirical, not theoretical.

3. Finnerty, like Jaffe, found that insider trading generated excess returns that were not only significant but also persisted over periods of eight or twelve months after the trade. If insiders can forecast price movements that far ahead, the efficient market seems to be overlooking a good bet, since insider trades are reported to the SEC and available to the public within a month or so. Much quicker adjustment was found in a study of large secondary distributions by Myron Scholes, professor of finance at the Graduate School of Business, University of Chicago: The Market for Securities: Substitution versus Price Pressure and the Effects of Information on Share Prices, 45 J. Bus. 179–211 (1972).

*Shapiro v. Merrill Lynch, Pierce, Fenner & Smith, 495 F.2d 228 (2d Cir. 1974).
†See also Hsiu-Kwang Wu, An Economist Looks at Section 16 of the Securities Exchange Act of 1934, 68 Colum. L. Rev. 260 (1968)

Chapter 6

Modern Finance Theory and the Efficient Market Hypothesis

We have deferred to this, the second part of the book, a systematic consideration of what many would think the fundamental economic concepts relevant to corporation law: the concepts, relating to shareholder and investor behavior, that have been developed by the theorists of the subfield of economics known as "finance." Finance is the study of capital markets, e.g., the New York Stock Exchange. The corporation is fundamentally a device for raising capital, and the large, publicly held companies often raise their capital on one of the public securities markets.

The theory of finance is by no means limited to the formal capital markets such as the NYSE, but its best demonstrated findings pertain to those markets because it is there that the data are available for testing the hypotheses of finance theory. The most celebrated findings of these theories is that the organized securities markets are "efficient," in the sense that all information publicly obtainable about a security is impounded in its market price, so that there are no gains to be had from trying to outguess the market. This is also known as the "random walk" theory of the stock market, and is explained in the article by Eugene Fama. The theory of efficient markets has important implications for corporation law, but that theory is itself only one relevant aspect of modern finance theory; some other central concepts are introduced in the selection that follows from a book by Richard A. Brealey. A slightly more technical introduction to the field is given in the article by Franco Modigliani and Gerald A. Pogue, from which we have borrowed just a few pages. The reader may also consult the excellent second part of the article which appears in the Financial Analysts Journal for May–June 1974 at page 69.

The "market model" of finance theory has also proved to be a powerful research tool for measuring the impact of unanticipated events or regulations on the value of the firm. The technique is explained in the paper by G. William Schwert and finds application in many of the articles in this book. Although the explanation is necessarily technical, its mastery will afford access to an important and rapidly growing body of empirical studies.

Random Walks in Stock Market Prices*

Eugene F. Fama

In order to put the theory of random walks into perspective we first discuss, in brief and general terms, the two approaches to predicting stock prices that are commonly espoused by market professionals. These are (1) "chartist" or "technical" theories and (2) the theory of fundamental or intrinsic value analysis.

The basic assumption of all the chartist or technical theories is that history tends to repeat itself, i.e., past patterns of price behavior in individual securities will tend to recur in the future. Thus the way to predict stock prices (and, of course, increase one's potential gains) is to develop a familiarity with past patterns of price behavior in order to recognize situations of likely recurrence.

Essentially, then, chartist techniques attempt to use knowledge of the past behavior of a price series to predict the probable future behavior of the series. A statistician would characterize such techniques as assuming that successive price changes in individual securities are dependent. That is, the various chartist theories assume that the *sequence* of price changes prior to any given day is important in predicting the price change for that day.

The techniques of the chartist have always been surrounded by a certain degree of mysticism, however, and as a result most marked professionals have found them suspect. Thus it is probably safe to say that the pure chartist is relatively rare among stock market analysts. Rather the typical analyst adheres to a technique known as fundamental analysis or the intrinsic value method. The assumption of the fundamental analysis approach is that at any point in time an individual security has an intrinsic value (or in the terms of the

*Source: 21 Fin. Analysts J. 55–99 (September–October 1965), reprinted with permission.

economist, an equilibrium price) which depends on the earning potential of the security. The earning potential of the security depends in turn on such fundamental factors as quality of management, outlook for the industry and the economy, etc.

Through a careful study of these fundamental factors the analyst should, in principle, be able to determine whether the actual price of a security is above or below its intrinsic value. If actual prices tend to move toward intrinsic values, then attempting to determine the intrinsic value of a security is equivalent to making a prediction of its future price; and this is the essence of the predictive procedure implicit in fundamental analysis.

Chartist theories and the theory of fundamental analysis are really the province of the market professional and to a large extent teachers of finance. Historically, however, there has been a large body of academic people, primarily economists and statisticians, who adhere to a radically different approach to market analysis — the theory of random walks in stock market prices. The remainder of this article will be devoted to a discussion of this theory and its major implications.

Random walk theorists usually start from the premise that the major security exchanges are good examples of "efficient" markets. An "efficient" market is defined as a market where there are large numbers of rational, profit-maximizers actively competing, with each trying to predict future market values of individual securities, and where important current information is almost freely available to all participants.

In an efficient market, competition among the many intelligent participants leads to a situation where, at any point in time, actual prices of individual securities already reflect the effects of information based both on events that have already occurred and on events which, as of now, the market expects to take place in the future. In other words, in an efficient market at any point in time the actual price of a security will be a good estimate of its intrinsic value.

Now in an uncertain world the intrinsic value of a security can never be determined exactly. Thus there is always room for disagreement among market participants concerning just what the intrinsic value of an individual security is, and such disagreement will give rise to discrepancies between actual prices and intrinsic values. In an efficient market, however, the actions of the many competing participants should cause the actual price of a security to wander randomly about its intrinsic value. If the discrepancies between actual prices and intrinsic values are systematic rather than random in nature, then knowledge of this should help intelligent market participants to better predict the path by which actual prices will move towards intrinsic values. When the many intelligent traders attempt to take advantage of this knowledge, however, they will tend to neutralize such systematic behavior in price series. Although uncertainty concerning intrinsic values will remain, actual prices of securities will wander randomly about their intrinsic values.

Of course intrinsic values can themselves change across time as a result of new information. The new information may involve such things as the success of a current research and development project, a change in management, a tariff imposed on the industry's product by a foreign country, an increase in industrial production or any other *actual or anticipated* change in a factor which is likely to affect the company's prospects.

In an efficient market, *on the average,* competition will cause the full effects of new information on intrinsic values to be reflected "instantaneously" in actual prices. In fact, however, because there is vagueness or uncertainty surrounding new information, "instantaneous adjustment" really has two implications. First, actual prices will initially overadjust to changes in intrinsic values as often as they will underadjust. Second, the lag in the complete adjustment of actual prices of successive new intrinsic values will itself be an independent, random variable with the adjustment of actual prices sometimes preceding the occurrence of the event which is the basis of the change in intrinsic values (i.e., when the event is anticipated by the market before it actually occurs) and sometimes following.

This means that the "instantaneous adjustment" property of an efficient market implies that successive price changes in individual securities will be independent. A market where successive price changes in individual securities are independent is, by definition, a random walk market. Most simply the theory of random walks implies that a series of stock price changes has no memory — the past history of the series cannot be used to predict the future in any meaningful way. The future path of the price level of a security is no more predictable than the path of a series of cumulated random numbers.

It is unlikely that the random walk hypothesis provides an exact description of the behavior of stock market prices. For practical purposes, however, the model may be acceptable even though it does not fit the facts exactly. Thus although successive price changes may not be strictly independent, the actual amount of dependence may be so small as to be unimportant.

What should be classified as unimportant depends, of course, on the question at hand. For the stock market trader or investor the criterion is obvious: The independence assumption of the random walk model is valid as long as knowledge of the past behavior of the series of price changes cannot be used to increase expected gains. More specifically, if successive price changes for a given security are independent, there is no problem in timing purchases and sales of that security. A simple policy of buying and holding the security will be as good as any more complicated mechanical procedure for timing purchases and sales. This implies that, for investment purposes, the independence assumption of the random walk model is an adequate description of reality as long as the actual degree of dependence in series of price changes is not sufficient to make the expected profits of any more "sophisticated" mechanical trading rule or chartist technique greater than the expected profits under a naive buy-and-hold policy.

Over the years a number of empirical tests of the random walk theory have been performed; indeed, so many that it is not possible to discuss them adequately here. Therefore in describing the empirical evidence we limit ourselves to a brief discussion of the different approaches employed and the general conclusions that have evolved.

The main concern of empirical research on the random walk model has been to test the hypothesis that successive price changes are independent. Two different approaches have been followed. First there is the approach that relies primarily on common statistical tools such as serial correlation coefficients and analyses of runs of consecutive price changes of the same sign. If the statistical tests tend to support the assumption of independence, one then *infers* that there are probably no mechanical trading rules or chartist techniques, based solely on patterns in the past history of price changes, which would make the expected profits of the investor greater than they would be with a simple buy-and-hold policy. The second approach to testing independence proceeds by testing directly different mechanical trading rules to see whether or not they provide profits greater than buy-and-hold.

Research to date has tended to concentrate on the first or statistical approach to testing independence; the results have been consistent and impressive. I know of no study in which standard statistical tools have produced evidence of *important* dependence in series of successive price changes. In general, these studies (and there are many of them) have tended to uphold the theory of random walks. . . . In all of these studies, the sample serial correlation coefficients computed for successive price changes were extremely close to zero, which is evidence against important dependence in the changes. Similarly, Fama's analysis of runs of successive price changes of the same sign, and the spectral analysis techniques of Granger and Morgenstern, and Godfrey, Granger, and Morgenstern also support the independence assumption of the random walk model.

We should emphasize, however, that although the statistical techniques mentioned above have been the common tools used in testing independence, the chartist or technical theorist probably would not consider them adequate. For example, he would not consider either serial correlations or runs analyses as adequate tests of whether the past history of series of price changes can be used to increase the investor's expected profits. The simple linear relationships that underlie the serial correlation model are much too unsophisticated to pick up the complicated "patterns" that the chartist sees in stock prices. Similarly, the runs tests are much too rigid in their manner of determining the duration of upward and downward movements in prices. In particular: in runs-testing, a run is considered as terminated whenever there is a change in sign in the sequence of successive price changes, regardless of the size of the price change that causes the change in sign. The chartist would like to have a more sophisticated method for identifying movements — a method which does not always predict the termination of the movement simply because the price levels has temporarily changed direction.

These criticisms of common statistical tools have not gone unheeded, however. For example, Alexander's filter technique is an attempt to apply more sophisticated criteria to the identification of moves. Although the filter technique does not correspond exactly to any well-known chartist theory, it is closely related to such things as the Dow Theory. Thus, the profitability of the filter technique can be used to make inferences concerning the potential profitability of other mechanical trading rules.

A filter of, say, 5 percent is defined as follows: if the daily closing price of a particular security moves up at least 5 percent, buy and hold the security until its price moves down at least 5 percent from a subsequent high, at which time simultaneously sell and go short. The short position is maintained until the daily closing price rises at least 5 percent above a subsequent low, at which time one should simultaneously cover and buy. Moves less than 5 percent in either direction are ignored.

It is, of course, unnecessary to limit the size of the filter to 5 percent. In fact, Professor Alexander has reported tests of the filter technique for filters ranging in size from 1 percent to 50 percent. The tests cover different time periods from 1897 to 1959 and involve daily closing prices for two indices, the Dow-Jones Industrials from 1897 to 1929 and Standard and Poor's Industrials from 1929 to 1959. In Alexander's latest work, it turns out that even when the higher broker's commissions incurred under the filter rule are ignored, the filter technique can not consistently beat the simple policy of buying and holding the indices for the different periods tested. Elsewhere I have tested the filter technique on individual securities. Again the simple buy-and-hold method consistently beats the profits produced by different size filters. It seems, then, that at least for the purposes of the individual trader or investor, tests of the filter technique also tend to support the random walk model.

As stated earlier, chartist theories implicitly assume that there is dependence in series of successive price changes. That is, the history of the series can be used to make meaningful predictions concerning the future. On the other hand, the theory of random walks says that successive price changes are independent, i.e., the past cannot be used to predict the future. Thus the two theories are diametrically opposed, and if, as the empirical evidence seems to suggest, the random walk theory is valid, then chartist theories are akin to astrology and of no real value to the investor.

In an uncertain world, however, no amount of empirical testing is sufficient to establish the validity of a hypothesis beyond any shadow of doubt. The chartist or technical theorist always has the option of declaring that the evidence in support of the random walk theory is not sufficient to validate the theory. On the other hand, the chartist must admit that the evidence in favor of the random walk model is both consistent and voluminous, whereas there is precious little published discussion of rigorous empirical tests of the various technical theories. If the chartist rejects the evidence in favor of the random walk model, his position is weak if his own theories have not been subjected to equally rigorous tests. This, I believe, is the challenge that the random walk theory makes to the technician.

There is nothing in the above discussion, however, which suggests that superior fundamental or intrinsic value analysis is useless in a random walk-efficient market. In fact the analyst will do better than the investor who follows a simple buy-and-hold policy as long as he can more quickly identify situations where there are non-negligible discrepancies between actual prices and intrinsic values than other analysts and investors, and if he is better able to predict the occurrence of important events and evaluate their effects on intrinsic values.

If there are many analysts who are pretty good at this sort of thing, however, and if they have considerable resources at their disposal, they help narrow discrepancies between actual prices and intrinsic values and cause actual prices, on the average, to adjust "instantaneously" to changes in intrinsic values. That is, the existence of many sophisticated analysts helps make the market more efficient which in turn implies a market which conforms more closely to the random walk model. Although the returns to these sophisticated analysts may be quite high, they establish a market in which fundamental analysis is a fairly useless procedure both for the average analyst and the average investor. That is, in a random walk-efficient market, on the average, a security chosen by a mediocre analyst will produce a return no better than that obtained from a randomly selected security of the same general riskiness.

There probably aren't many analysts (in fact, I know of none) who would willingly concede that they are no better than the "average" analyst. If all analysts think they are better than average, however, this only means that their estimate of the average is biased downward. Fortunately, it is not necessary to judge an analyst solely by his claims. The discussion above provides a natural benchmark with which we can evaluate his performance.

In a random walk-efficient market at any point in time the market price of a security will already reflect the judgments of many analysts concerning the relevance of currently available information to the prospects of that security. Now an individual analyst may feel that he has better insights than those that are already implicit in the market price. For example, he may feel that a discrepancy between market price and intrinsic value exists for some security, or he may think the intrinsic value of the security is itself about to change because of some impending piece of new information which is not yet generally available.

These "insights" of the analysts are of no real value, however, unless they are eventually borne out in the market, that is, unless the actual market price eventually moves in the predicted direction. In other words, if the analyst can make meaningful judgments concerning the purchase and sale of individual securities, his choices should consistently outperform randomly selected securities of the same general riskiness. It must be stressed, however, that the analyst must *consistently* produce results better than random selection, since, by the nature of uncertainty, for any given time period he has about a 50 percent chance of doing better than random selection even if his powers of analysis are completely nonexistent. Moreover, not only must the analyst do consistently better than random selection, but he must beat random selection by an amount which is at least sufficient to cover the cost of the resources (including his own time) which are expended in the process of carrying out his more complicated selection procedures.

What we propose, then, is that the analyst subject his performance to a rigorous comparison with a random selection procedure. One simple practical way of comparing the results produced by an analyst with a random selection procedure is the following: Every time the analyst recommends a security for purchase (or sale), another security of the same general riskiness is chosen randomly. A future date is then chosen at which time the results produced by the two securities will be compared. Even if the analyst is no better than the random selection procedure, in any given comparison there is still a 50 percent chance that the security he has chosen will outperform the randomly selected security. After the game has been played for a while, however, and the results of many different comparisons are accumulated, then it will become clear whether the analyst is worth his salt or not.

In many circumstances, however, the primary concern is with the performance of a portfolio rather than with the performance of individual securities in the portfolio. In this situation one would want to compare the performance of the portfolio in question with that of a portfolio of randomly selected securities. A useful benchmark for randomly selected portfolios has been provided by Fisher and Lorie. They computed rates of return for investments in common stocks on the New York Stock Exchange for various time periods from 1926 to 1960. The basic assumption in all of their computations is that at the beginning of each period studied the investor puts an equal amount of money in each common stock listed at that time on the Exchange. This amounts to random sampling where the sampling is, of course, exhaustive. Different rates of return are then computed for different possible tax brackets of the investor, first under the assumption that all dividends are reinvested in the month paid, and then under the assumption that dividends are not reinvested.

A possible procedure for the analyst is to compare returns for given time periods earned by portfolios he has managed with the returns earned for the same time periods by the Fisher-Lorie "randomly selected" portfolios. It is important to note, however, that this will be a valid test procedure only if the portfolios managed by the analyst had about the same degree of riskiness as the Fisher-Lorie "market" portfolios. If this is not the case, the Fisher-Lorie results will not provide a proper benchmark. In order to make a proper comparison between the results produced by the analyst and a random selection policy, it will be necessary to define and study the behavior of portfolios of randomly selected securities, where these portfolios are selected in such a way that they have about the same degree of riskiness as those managed by the analyst.

If the claims of analysts concerning the advantages of fundamental analysis have any basis in fact, the tests suggested above would seem to be easy to pass. In fact, however, the only "analysts" that have so far undergone these tests are open end mutual funds.

In their appeals to the public, mutual funds usually make two basic claims: (1) because it pools the resources of many individuals, a fund can diversify much more effectively than the average, small investor; and (2) because of its management's closeness to the market, the fund is better able to detect "good buys" in individual securities. In most cases the first claim is probably true. The second, however, implies that mutual funds provide a higher return than would be earned by a portfolio of randomly selected securities. In a separate paper I reported the results of a study which suggest that if the initial loading charges of mutual funds are ignored, on the average the funds do about as well as a randomly selected portfolio. If one takes into account the higher initial loading charges of the funds, however, on the average the random investment policy outperforms the funds. In addition, these results would seem to be consistent with those of the now famous Wharton study of mutual funds.

An Introduction to Risk and Return from Common Stocks*

Richard A. Brealey

The price of a stock only changes when investors change their expectations for its price in the future. Fluctuations in price, therefore, are caused by fluctuating opinions as to the stock's prospects, so that, for investors in general, uncertainty and price volatility are directly related. This need not necessarily be the case for any single investor, for he may have private information that is not reflected in the price of the stock; but for most investors, for most of the time, private information is unlikely to be of sufficient quality to shift a stock into an altogether different risk category.

The margin for error in forecasting company prospects is liable to be greater if either the range of possible outcomes is wide or there is little information on which to base a forecast. The former condition will arise when the concern is, in the broadest sense, highly leveraged, the latter condition when either the business is very individualistic in character or management is very secretive about opera-

*Source: Richard A. Brealey, An Introduction to Risk and Return from Common Stocks, 42–46, 48–54, 115–131 (1969), reprinted with permission. Richard A. Brealey is Professor of Portfolio Investment at the London School of Business.

The author wishes to acknowledge his indebtedness to the following writers, whose research is relied on in the text: Shannon Pratt, George Douglas, Fred Arditti, William Sharpe, Edward Thorp, S. Kassouf, William Peters, John Lintner, James Tobin, Harry Markowitz, Jack Gaumnitz, Arthur D. Little, Inc., and Paul Samuelson.

tions. It seems improbable that these characteristics are typically transitory. For example, most metal-refining companies are likely to continue to possess high operating leverage, advanced-technology businesses should continue to be very individualistic, and companies working on classified contracts should continue to be secretive. If this reasoning is correct and the causes of uncertainty do persist over time, it is probable that stocks that are most volatile in one period will tend to be the most volatile in the next.

Suppose the existence of five investors with differing attitudes to risk. Each is presented in December 1957 with the task of selecting a portfolio. Each assumes that the past volatility of a stock provides a useful indication of its future behavior. Investor A, the most cautious member of the group, therefore includes in his portfolio the 20% of the NYSE stocks that have shown the least variation in their returns over the previous three years. Investor E, in contrast, as befits his position as the speculator of the group, includes in his portfolio the 20% of the NYSE stocks that have shown the most variability over the previous three years. Each of Investors B, C, and D selects in turn, according to his attitude to risk, another 20% of the NYSE stocks on the basis of earlier volatility. If these investors are correct in their belief that past variation in returns is an indicator of the future variation, A's portfolio should exhibit greater stability than B's over the ensuing years. Similarly, B's portfolio should exhibit less volatility than C's, and so on.

Imagine now that an identical situation has occurred in each month from January 1929 through the end of 1957. Therefore, instead of testing the subsequent behavior of just one set of five portfolios, it may be tested on 348 such sets.

Table [4] summarizes in index form the average subsequent experience of the 348 sets of portfolios.

This average experience provides some justification for the ac-

Table 4
Subsequent Volatility of Portfolios of Stocks Selected on the Basis of Prior Volatility

	Year After Formation	Three Years After Formation
A's Portfolio	100	100
B's Portfolio	137	126
C's Portfolio	164	147
D's Portfolio	194	184
E's Portfolio	244	224

Source: Brealey, Table 7; after Pratt, Shannon P., Relationship Between Risk and Rate of Return for Common Stocks, unpublished DBA dissertation, Indiana University, 1966, used with permission.

tions of the five mythical investors. However, averages are liable to conceal a diversity of experience. It does not necessarily follow that the five portfolios formed in any one month would have behaved in such an accommodating fashion. But at least the odds are in favor of their having done so.

If, on the average, A's portfolio tended to show less violent changes in value than E's, it is probable that over any one period he would have been less likely to suffer an actual loss. Table [5] lists the proportion of the 348 occasions on which each investor would have been involved in loss. As expected, those portfolios that were composed of stocks that had been less variable in former years resulted less frequently in loss.

These results have all been in terms of differences in the behavior over time of the return on the five portfolios. It would also be interesting to examine the movement of the individual stocks that composed these portfolios in order to determine whether, over any single time period, the stocks forming the lower grade portfolios tended to display a wider diversity of experience than those included in the high-grade portfolios. If it can be demonstrated both that the more volatile stocks as a group have shown greater subsequent fluctuations over time and that the owner could have had less reliance that in a given period the behavior of any one stock in that group would be similar to that of the others, then it can truly be said that these stocks, individually or en masse, were more risky investments. Confirmation for this view is provided by Table [6], which shows in index form the disparity among the price changes of the individual stocks. Clearly, Investor A could have had far more confi-

Table 5
Probability of Subsequent Loss on Portfolios of Stocks Selected on the Basis of Prior Volatility

Size of Loss	Probability of Loss After One Year (%)				
	Investor A	Investor B	Investor C	Investor D	Investor E
Greater than 50%	0.9	1.4	2.3	3.2	3.2
Greater than 34%	2.3	3.7	4.6	5.7	6.9
Greater than 18%	5.6	6.9	8.0	10.9	14.4
Greater than 2%	16.7	21.0	26.1	28.2	34.5

Size of Loss	Probability of Loss After Three Years (%)				
	Investor A	Investor B	Investor C	Investor D	Investor E
Greater than 45%	0	0	0.3	0.9	3.4
Greater than 25%	0	0.9	4.0	5.2	9.3
Greater than 5%	4.6	8.6	11.1	10.8	14.2

Source: Brealey, Table 8, after Pratt.

Table 6
Divergent Subsequent Behavior of Holdings Within Portfolios of Stocks on the Basis of Prior Volatility

	Divergence One Year After Portfolio Formation	Divergence Three Years After Portfolio Formation
A's Portfolio	100	100
B's Portfolio	126	127
C's Portfolio	148	158
D's Portfolio	178	195
E's Portfolio	228	240

Source: Brealey, Table 9, after Pratt.

dence than Investor E that any one of his holdings would behave like the rest of the group.

This study was concerned with the behavior of about 1,000 stocks over 29 years. When only the portfolios formed after 1931 were considered, the results were similar. Neither did changing the lengths of the periods over which the volatility was measured affect the conclusions. Altogether, therefore, there is considerable evidence that the relative volatility exhibited by any stock has tended to persist over time. It is reasonable to suppose that this will continue to be true in the future. If so, this characteristic offers the investor a valuable means of estimating the degree of fluctuation that his holdings are likely to exhibit and, accordingly, the risk that their value at any time may be below his expectations. . . .

If it is true that investors dislike incurring risk, they will do so only if they are compensated for it. The fact that common stocks have tended over a long period to give a higher rate of return than bonds supports this belief. It seems reasonable to suppose, therefore, that the returns on individual common stocks will also vary according to their inherent risks. . . .

In order to determine whether the owners of the portfolios were compensated according to the risk they assumed, the return on each portfolio was computed over periods of one and three years after its formation. Table [7] shows the average returns realized by each investor. With the exception of Investor E, whose experience was slightly inferior to that of C and D, the investors with the lower grade portfolios would have been rewarded with higher average returns.

Support for this conclusion was furnished by two other studies. One examined the annual returns of a sample of 616 stocks between 1946 and 1963. The other considered the annual returns over the same period of the 500 stocks composing the Standard and Poor's Composite Index. In both cases the magnitude of a stock's return

Table 7
Subsequent Returns Received from Portfolios of
Stocks Selected on the Basis of Prior Volatility

	One-Year Return	Three-Year Return, Annual Rate
Investor A	9.8%	10.8%
Investor B	11.0	12.8
Investor C	11.2	13.5
Investor D	11.2	13.6
Investor E	10.9	13.2

Source: Brealey, Table 10, after Pratt.

was positively correlated with the amount of variation it displayed. On the average, those who have taken increased risks in their investment do seem to have been compensated by some increase in return. However, it is not yet determined whether the compensation was, in retrospect, adequate.

The return on a short government bond represents the reward that the investor requires for not having access to his money for a period. The return on a common stock may be regarded as composed of this time value of money, together with a premium for accepting risk. It is possible, therefore, to segregate the risk premium for each of the five sets of portfolios by deducting from their returns an estimated 3% for the time value of money between 1929 and 1960. This has been done in Table [8].

It is now possible to assess whether each of the five investors received a reward commensurate with the risk he incurred. Table [9] shows in index form the rewards per unit of risk.

Each increase in risk appears to have been accompanied by a less than proportionate gain in reward. This shortfall seems to have

Table 8
Subsequent Risk Premiums Received from
Portfolios of Stocks Selected on the Basis
of Prior Volatility

	Risk Premium	
	One-Year Return	Three-Year Return, Annual Rate
Investor A	6.8%	7.8%
Investor B	8.0	9.8
Investor C	8.2	10.5
Investor D	8.2	10.6
Investor E	7.9	10.2

Source: Brealey, Table 11, after Pratt.

Table 9
Subsequent Rewards per Unit of Risk Received
from Portfolios of Stocks Selected on the
Basis of Prior Volatility

	Risk Premium per Unit of Risk	
	One-Year Return	Three-Year Return
Investor A	100	100
Investor B	86	100
Investor C	74	92
Investor D	62	74
Investor E	48	58

Source: Brealey, Table 12.

been particularly marked for the more volatile stocks. Indeed, as was observed above, for Investor E the increase in risk was marked by an actual fall in return.

A study of 34 mutual funds between 1954 and 1963 provides some further evidence on the subject. The average annual return and the variability of return for each fund are illustrated in Figure [6].

The first thing to notice is that, in general, the funds with the greatest volatility tended to give the highest returns. Indeed, 70% of the difference in return between funds could be explained solely in terms of the differences in riskiness. Since the closeness of stock prices to a random walk has already suggested the difficulty of obtaining superior information for a given group of stocks, this finding is not surprising.

Again using 3% as an estimate of the rate of return on a riskless bond, it is a simple matter to compute the reward for risk per unit of risk for each fund during this period. In order to measure whether the lower risk funds tended to provide a higher reward per unit of risk than their more volatile rivals, the funds were ranked according to both their volatility and the reward per unit of risk. The correspondence between these two sets of rankings was measured by the rank correlation coefficient. A coefficient of zero would indicate no correspondence between the two lists, a coefficient of plus one, perfect correspondence. The actual result was a rank correlation coefficient of + 0.44. This provides some corroboration for the earlier suggestion that higher risk stocks have not, on the average, provided their owners with commensurately higher rewards.

What this meant to the fund holder can be illustrated by an example. If an investor had held half his assets in the form of one of the seven most volatile of the 34 funds and had invested the re-

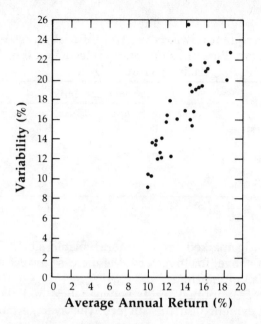

Figure 6
Scatter Diagram of Average Annual
Return and Variability of Return for
34 Mutual Funds, 1954–1963

Source: Brealey, Figure 14, after William F.
Sharpe, Mutual Fund Performance, 39 J. Bus.
119 (1966), with permission.

mainder in short-term government bonds, the total risk that he
would have incurred on his assets would have been almost identical
to the risk that would have resulted from investing all his assets in
one of the seven least volatile funds. Yet his annual return over the
period would have averaged 1.6 percentage points less than he
could have obtained with the latter strategy.

Several qualifications to these findings may be made. . . . The
inferior ratio of reward to risk provided by the more volatile funds
may reflect a relative deficiency in management rather than a characteristic of the type of stock that they hold. For example, it may be that
the return has been reduced by the high rate of portfolio turnover that
appears to distinguish these funds.

Return was defined above as the sum of dividend income and
capital appreciation. No allowance was made for the effects of taxation. Since dividends and capital gains may be taxed at different
rates, the net return may constitute a different proportion of the

gross return for each of the five sets of portfolios. Therefore, if after-tax returns could be substituted in the study, different conclusions might be indicated.

The risk premium, it will be remembered, consists of the total return less the reward that would be provided by a riskless security. The selection of a value for the latter was necessarily arbitrary to some degree. The general conclusion, however, would not be affected by most changes in the assumed rate of interest.

There undoubtedly have been errors such as these in measurement, but they are unlikely to have been important enough to constitute a complete explanation of the results. Two other causes have probably worked to lower the premium received for accepting very high risks in the equity market.

Many investors, seeking high rates of return, have the option of buying high-risk securities or of borrowing funds for the purchase of somewhat lower risk stocks. For others, however, the latter opportunity is not available. Their access to funds is so restricted that, if they require high returns, they have no option but to invest all their assets in the highest risk stocks available. As long as no alternative means of achieving their aims is possible and as long as such stocks do not actually offer lower expectations of gain, these investors will be willing to pay up for such stocks. This competition for the ownership of assets that provide a substitute for leverage is even more evident in the overpricing that occurs in the market for short-term warrants.

A second explanation for the apparent overpricing of high-risk stocks is simply that investors have persistently exaggerated the chances of gain from them. This may represent a phenomenon peculiar to the 1929 to 1960 period or some part of it. However, there appears to be, in many spheres, a tendency to overestimate the probability of success in long-odds situations. For example, there is evidence that the odds quoted on outsiders in horse racing typically overstate the probability of a victory. Similar excessive optimism may have caused some overpricing of high-risk stocks.

The broad conclusion of this chapter, that increased risk tends to be compensated by increased rewards, was both expected and well supported. The subsidiary conclusion, that the premiums received on high-risk stocks have tended, in retrospect, to be inadequate, must in contrast be considered one of the least reliable in this book. The suggestion strikes directly at the popular cult of the more volatile stocks. Many of the latter's disciples would be shocked at the suggestion that by simultaneously reducing their liquidity and shifting their stock portfolio toward the less volatile securities they could both increase their expectation of gain and reduce their exposure to risk. The results of the chapter, however, must at least sow the seeds of doubt. . . .

It is a commonly held view that the mix of common stocks maintained by an investor should depend on his willingness to bear risk. According to this view, a broker or investment counselor is a kind of financial interior decorator, skillfully designing portfolios to reflect his client's personality.

This chapter argues that the "interior decorator" concept of portfolio management is based on a fundamental misconception of investment risk. An investor's attitude to risk should be reflected not in the character of his common stock portfolio but in its size. The widow should put at risk a smaller proportion of her savings than the speculator, but the sum that each is willing to venture should be invested in the same stocks and in the same proportions.

An investor faced with the task of selecting a common stock portfolio usually has a large number of candidates to choose from. These are likely to offer both differing expectations of return and differing degrees of risk. Since there is a tendency for higher risk stocks to offer prospects of greater reward, the available choices, when plotted as a scatter diagram, should look something like Figure [7].

By holding these stocks in varying proportions, an unlimited number of different combinations of risk and return can be secured. The expected gain on any of these portfolios would be equal to the average of the gains expected from each of the holdings. However,

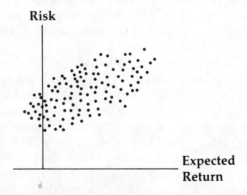

Figure 7
Attainable Combinations of Risk and Return with Full Investment in a Single Common Stock

Source: Brealey, Figure 24.

the equivalent does not hold true of the risk. As long as the outlook for each of the stocks is not completely conditional on the occurrence of the same set of events, risks may be reduced by diversification.

The range of combinations of risk and return that might be secured from these portfolios is illustrated in Figure [8] by the continuous dark line. The [dots] continue to represent the single stock portfolios. Any other point on or within the continuous line can be achieved by holding two or more of these stocks.

It is now possible to give a partial answer to the question, "Which portfolio should the investor choose?" For any given level of risk, an investor will prefer the portfolio that offers the highest expected return. He should therefore not accept any portfolio on the graph if there is another portfolio to the right of it, for the latter would improve his return without increasing the risk. The only combinations that offer no such opportunities for improvement are represented by the portion of the boundary lying between A and B in Figure [8].

This has narrowed the choice, but the curve AB could represent a large number of different combinations of stocks. So far, however, only full investment in common stocks has been considered, although the investor has the alternative of retaining all or part of his portfolio in the form of cash. This cash may be invested in insured savings accounts to earn a fixed and certain return, which is completely unrelated to movements of common stocks. The expected return on a portfolio consisting partly of cash and partly of a mix of common stocks would be a weighted average of the returns on each.

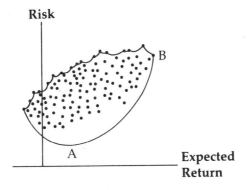

Figure 8
Attainable Combinations of Risk and
Return with Full Investment in a Port-
folio of One or More Common Stocks

Source: Brealey, Figure 25.

Because the return on cash is certain, the risk of such a portfolio varies in direct proportion to the amount invested in common stocks. Thus, not surprisingly, a portfolio only 50% invested in common stocks would have only half the risk of a portfolio fully invested in common stocks. The combinations of return and risk obtainable by varying the proportions invested in cash and any group of common stocks may be represented graphically by a straight line. Thus, once the possibility of lending cash is introduced, the boundary of available opportunities is extended to the area enclosed by the solid line in Figure [9]. The question, "Which portfolio should the investor choose?" can be repeated. Applying the former criterion, he should choose any one of the portfolios lying along the boundary XB. But the portfolios between X and Y merely represent different proportions of the assets allotted to cash and to common stock portfolio Y, so the mix of common stocks would not be affected by choosing different points along that segment of the boundary. Only if the investor opted for one of the portfolios between Y and B, which are fully invested in common stocks, would he change the mix of stocks.

Thus, the introduction of the option of lending cash has resulted in a considerable narrowing of the variety of stock portfolios that the investor should choose from. As a third and final stage in the argument, the possibility of borrowing cash will be introduced. This may be thought of as negative bank lending. The point X in Figure [10] represents 100% lending to the bank, M represents lending 50% of the portfolio to the bank, Y represents lending none of the portfolio.

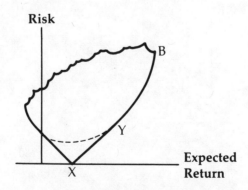

Figure 9
Attainable Combinations of Risk and Return with Any Combination of Cash and Common Stocks

Source: Brealey, Figure 26.

The effect of a negative loan may be seen by extending the line beyond Y, as illustrated. Here, Z represents a portfolio that would be achieved by borrowing from the bank and investing this cash, together with all the investor's original cash, in portfolio Y. Such a policy would involve both increased expectations of return and increased risks. The available opportunities given the possibility of borrowing lie within the two solid lines in Figure [10]. As long as there is no limit to the borrowing, there is no limit to the distance that these lines may extend upwards.

The best of these available opportunities again lie along the extreme right boundary, for only then is there room for increasing the return with no increase in risk. But the right boundary is now a straight line, and that straight line represents different sums of cash being borrowed from or lent to the bank and the balance always invested in the same mix of common stocks, designated Y on the graph. Which of these combinations should the investor choose? That is a matter between him and his courage. However, regardless of his willingness to accept risk, his mix of stocks remains unchanged, and only the proportion of assets committed to common stocks is allowed to vary.

. . . [T]he return on common stocks can be regarded as the sum of two components. The first consists of the reward required by the investor for parting with the use of his money. This is the rate of interest. The portion of the return that is in excess of the rate of interest represents a reward paid to the investor for accepting risk.

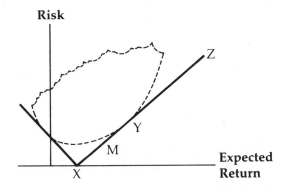

Figure 10
Attainable Combinations of Risk and Return with Any Combination of Cash and Common Stocks, Including the Option to Borrow

Source: Brealey, Figure 27.

The distinguishing characteristic of portfolio Y is that it offers the highest attainable reward for risk per unit of risk. . . .

The argument presented in this chapter does not imply that all investors should have the same mix of stocks, but only that they should have the same mix *if* they are faced with the same set of opportunities and are agreed on the odds of realizing various levels of return. In practice, of course, such agreement is rare. Even if they do share identical views of each stock's prospects, differences in the costs to which they are liable could result in differences in their expectations of return. For example, high-yielding stocks offer very low returns to investors with a high tax rate. Similarly, a diversified portfolio is an expensive luxury to an investor with very limited funds. The important message of this chapter, however, is that for any investor, the problem of how much to invest in stock should be wholly separate from the problem of which stocks to own. His willingness to bear risks should influence only the former decision. . . .

A portfolio composed of stocks in sound, well-established companies is clearly likely to provide less risk than one composed of the stocks of fly-by-night enterprises. Yet the risk of a portfolio will usually be less than the risk of its separate parts and will depend on the manner in which these risks are spread. Other things being equal, the larger the number of holdings, the less the portfolio is likely to lose as the result of one company's misfortune. It is also important, though, to insure that the prospects for each of the companies are not contingent on the occurrence of the same set of events. Otherwise, the circumstances that would cause failure to one company would bring failure to them all. In summary, therefore, portfolio risk is a function of:

1) The riskiness of each individual holding;
2) The number of holdings;
3) The degree to which the risks are independent of each other.

This chapter will argue that while the first and third determinants are important, increasing the number of holdings beyond a relatively small figure typically has little impact on risk.

As a first step, a hypothetical portfolio will be examined in which the number of holdings is varied while all else is held constant. For this purpose, three simplifying assumptions will be made. First, all holdings in the portfolio are assumed to be of equal size. Second, all holdings are assumed to be equally risky. Third, the risks of each pair of holdings in the portfolio are equally independent.

It is desirable at this stage to quantify the extent to which the outlook for any two stocks is likely to be dependent on the occurrence of the same set of events. . . . Chapter 5 [omitted] concluded from an examination of past price changes that, on the average, in recent years about 30% of a stock's price movement has been contingent on what was happening to the market as a whole. Of course, any two stocks taken from the same industry group would have had considerably more in common than just this 30%. However, since the object is to measure the maximum effect that diversification can reasonably be expected to have, it will be assumed that such duplication is never necessary in a portfolio and that the stocks share only the market influence in common.

The last paragraph discussed the relationships between actual price movements over a succession of past periods. Yet the portfolio manager is, in practice, concerned only with the degree of dependence between possible price changes over a single future period. This is not the same thing. However, just as the amount of past price volatility may be used as a reasonable measure of the risk being faced by investors in general, so the amount of dependence between past price changes may be used as a measure of the relationship between the changes that investors in general believe to be possible.

Given the three earlier assumptions, the maximum theoretical benefits from diversification would be secured with a portfolio composed of an infinitely large number of holdings. If the only relationship between any two holdings in a portfolio lies in the fact that 30% of each stock's prospects is contingent on the behavior of the market, then it can be demonstrated that no amount of diversification can reduce the risk, or standard deviation of possible returns, beyond 74% of that of a one-stock portfolio.

Not only is the potential benefit from diversification fairly limited, but a large part of this potential can be realized with a portfolio of relatively few stocks. This is demonstrated in the first column of Table [10]. A portfolio of ten stocks provides 88.5% of the possible advantages of diversification; one of twenty stocks provides 94.2% of these advantages.

Columns 2 and 3 express these results in a different form. The former shows the risk of a diversified portfolio as a percentage of the risk of a single stock. For example, a ten-share portfolio is shown to involve 77.0% of the risk of a one-share portfolio. The third column shows the reduction in risk contributed by the addition of that one last holding. Thus, the effect of going from a nine- to a ten-stock portfolio is a fall in risk of only 0.4%. It is interesting to consider the diversification policies of some European funds in the light of the figures shown toward the bottom of this column.

Yet if, beyond a certain point, the number of holdings has a negligible effect on portfolio risk, the other two determinants — the riskiness of each holding and the extent of the dependence between

Table 10
A Theoretical Illustration of the Effect of Diversification on Risk

No. of Holdings	Reduction in Risk as % of Potential	Risk as % of One-Stock Portfolio	Effect on Risk of Last Holding
2	46.3%	88.0%	−12.03%
3	63.2	83.6	− 5.00
4	72.0	81.3	− 2.74
5	77.4	79.9	− 1.73
6	81.0	78.9	− 1.19
7	83.7	78.3	− 0.87
8	85.7	77.7	− 0.66
9	87.2	77.3	− 0.52
10	88.5	77.0	− 0.42
11	89.5	76.7	− 0.35
12	90.4	76.5	− 0.29
13	91.1	76.3	− 0.25
14	91.7	76.2	− 0.21
15	92.3	76.0	− 0.19
16	92.7	75.9	− 0.16
17	93.2	75.8	− 0.14
18	93.5	75.7	− 0.13
19	93.9	75.6	− 0.12
20	94.2	75.5	− 0.10
30	96.1	75.0	− 0.05
50	97.7	74.6	− 0.02
100	98.83	74.31	− 0.0041
500	99.76	74.07	− 0.0002
1,000	99.88	74.04	− 0.00004
2,000	99.94	74.02	− 0.00001

Source: Brealey, Table 34.

these risks—are both important. Reduce the risk of the individual holdings by so much, and the portfolio risk is reduced in the same proportion. The effect of holding securities whose fortunes are less dependent on the same circumstances is more complex and can best be illustrated by an example. The first column of Table [11] is extracted from Table [10]. It shows the reduction in risk that would be achieved with varying degrees of diversification, given that 30% of the outlook for a group of stocks is dependent on the occurrence of the same set of events. In the second column of Table [11], this assumption has been changed so that only 25% of the outlook is conditional on the same events. A portfolio of ten securities formed from this second group of stocks would have 3.7% less risk than a ten-security portfolio formed from the original group. Perhaps a more striking demonstration that the quality of the diversification is

Table 11
A Theoretical Illustration of the Effect on Risk of Holding Stocks with Less Interrelated Prospects

Number of Holdings	Risk as % of One-Stock Portfolio Group 1	Risk as % of One-Stock Portfolio, Group 2
2	88.0%	86.6%
3	83.6	81.6
4	81.3	79.1
5	79.9	77.5
6	78.9	76.4
7	78.3	75.6
8	77.7	75.0
9	77.3	74.5
10	77.0	74.2
11	76.7	73.9
12	76.5	73.6
13	76.3	73.4
14	76.2	73.2
15	76.0	73.0
16	75.9	72.9
17	75.8	72.8
18	75.7	72.6
19	75.6	72.5
20	75.5	72.5
30	75.0	71.9
50	74.6	71.4
100	74.31	71.06
500	74.07	70.78
1,000	74.04	70.75
2,000	74.02	70.73

Source: Brealey, Table 35.

more important than the quantity is the fact that an eleven-security portfolio drawn from the second group would be less risky than a 2,000-stock portfolio formed from the first.

A somewhat less artificial, if less precise, demonstration of the progressively diminishing effects of diversification is provided by a study of the stocks of 140 large corporations. From this sample, five portfolios, each consisting of just three stocks, were selected at random. This exercise was repeated six times; on each successive occasion, the portfolios comprised a larger number of holdings. The volatility of the monthly returns of each portfolio was computed for the period 1960 to 1963. Table [12] provides a summary of the results. On the average, the volatility of the five least diversified port-

Table 12
An Empirical Illustration of the Effect of Diversification on Risk

Number of Holdings	3	6	11	18	26	36	44
Average Risk of Five Portfolios*	126	112	107	105	101	105	107

*Expressed as % of risk of 140-stock portfolio.
Source: Brealey, Table 36.

folios was 26% greater than that of a portfolio composed of all 140 stocks. However, as the number of holdings was increased, the avoidable risk diminished rapidly. Indeed, beyond about 18 holdings, the degree of diversification seems to be a far less important consideration than which stocks came out of the hat.

These examples demonstrate generally that increasing diversification beyond a certain point is unlikely to be an effective way of reducing exposure to risk. They suffer, however, from the artificiality embodied in their assumptions. One such limitation stems from the supposition that holdings are always equal in size. Usually this neither is, nor ought to be, the case. Yet if the risks are not spread evenly, a larger number of holdings is required to achieve the same reduction.

The other assumptions constitute a more serious drawback. Thus, all stocks are not equally risky, as the simple model suggested. If an increase in the number of holdings involved the addition of higher risk securities, the net effect could be an increase rather than a fall in risk. In a similar way, all stocks are not equally independent. For example, stocks within the same industry group have more in common than stocks from different industries. In consequence, increasing the number of holdings is likely to prove far less effective when it reaches the stage of duplicating representation in an industry. The force of these remarks is that whereas the above examples could demonstrate that diversification beyond about 20 securities cannot reduce risk by a meaningful amount, they were unable to provide nformation as to whether such diversification, in practice, offers any reduction in risk at all. What is needed is some indication of the stage at which the benefits of increasing diversification typically begin to be outweighed by the concomitant disadvantages. In other words, it would be useful to know how many securities are likely to be held in a portfolio that is constructed to minimize risk.

Given a measure of the risk of the eligible stocks and of the relationship between each pair of stocks, there are straightforward mathematical techniques for determining the composition of this minimum-risk portfolio. The problem is to determine these quantities. One method is to ask the investor to describe, either directly or indirectly, his degree of conviction about each stock's prospects and the relationships between these prospects. Whenever this has been tried, the computed minimum-risk portfolio has typically consisted of no more than five holdings. The objection to this approach is that there is no assurance that the investor is describing his beliefs accurately. Therefore, it is probably more appropriate to base the computations on historical data and to assume that risk is directly proportional to the degree of volatility and that the dependence between possible price changes over a single period is equal to the dependence between actual price changes over a number of periods.

To this end, a representative sample of 100 NYSE stocks was selected. Measures of individual risk and dependence were calculated from the monthly price changes between 1963 and 1967. Of all the possible portfolios that could have been selected from these 100 stocks, the portfolio with the least risk consisted of just 15 holdings.

This result is the more striking when considered in conjunction with the conclusion of the last chapter. It was argued there that an investor should only be interested in selecting from a short list of possible candidates, which are represented as lying along the line AB in Figure [8]. The characteristic shared by each of these candidates is that no other portfolio can be constructed with the least possible risk is represented by point A, and of all the candidates for the investor's consideration, this portfolio contains the largest number of holdings. The stock portfolio in the example above is therefore the most diversified of the short list candidates. Whether the investor should choose this portfolio or one with an even smaller number of holdings would depend upon which offered the highest reward for risk per unit of risk.

Only if the investor considers that the risks of stocks are far less interrelated than their past history indicates should he be willing to accept a much larger number of holdings than the example suggests. . . .

For both the individual and the corporate investor this chapter should provide some lessons. It has been estimated that the average number of stocks directly owned by the individual investor is between three and four. It can be shown that, given some degree of uncertainty on the part of the investor and a choice of securities whose returns are imperfectly correlated, it will always pay to own more than one security. This chapter has argued that the benefits of diversification will usually continue to accrue at least beyond three or four holdings. A large number of portfolios of individual investors are therefore inadequately diversified.

One of the advantages claimed by investment institutions is that they provide the only opportunity for individuals to gain the full benefit of diversification. While such an argument has much to recommend it, the number of holdings necessary to achieve an optimum amount of diversification may not be out of the reach of many individual investors.

If most individual investors own too few holdings, the reverse usually holds true of institutions. The benefits that they gain from their large number of holdings are at best minimal and are probably more than outweighed by an inclusion of securities that offer lower expectations of reward per unit of risk.

An Introduction to Risk and Return: Concepts and Evidence*

Franco Modigliani and Gerald A. Pogue

. . . [W]hile some risks can be eliminated via diversification, others cannot. Thus we are led to distinguish between a security's "unsystematic" risk, which can be washed away by mixing the security with other securities in a diversified portfolio, and its "systematic" risk, which cannot be eliminated by diversification. This proposition is illustrated in [Figure 11]. It shows total portfolio risk declining as the number of holdings increases. Increasing diversification gradually tends to eliminate the unsystematic risk, leaving only systematic, i.e., market-related risk. The remaining variability results from the fact that the return on nearly every security depends to some degree on the overall performance of the market. Consequently, the return on a well diversified portfolio is highly correlated with the market, and its variability or uncertainty is basically the uncertainty of the market as a whole. Investors are exposed to market uncertainty no matter how many stocks they hold. . . .

. . . [W]e now need a way of quantifying the systematic risk of a security and relating the systematic risk of a portfolio to that of its component securities. This can be accomplished by dividing security return into two parts: one dependent (i.e., perfectly correlated), and a second independent (i.e., uncorrelated) of market return. The first component of return is usually referred to as "systematic," the second as "unsystematic" return. Thus we have

*Source: 30 Fin. Analysts J. 68, 76–77 (March–April 1964), reprinted with permission. Franco Modigliani is Institute Professor at the Sloan School of Management, Massachusetts Institute of Technology, and Gerald A. Pogue is chairman of the Economics and Finance Department at Baruch College, City University of New York.

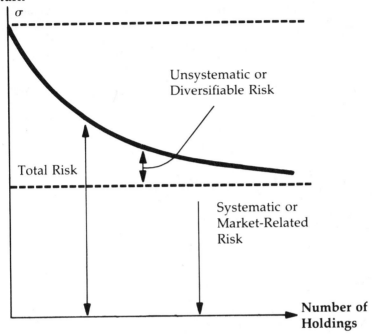

Standard
Deviation of
Portfolio
Return

σ

Unsystematic or
Diversifiable Risk

Total Risk

Systematic or
Market-Related
Risk

Number of
Holdings

Figure 11
Systematic and Unsystematic Risk

Source: Modigliani and Pogue, Exhibit 6.

Security Return = Systematic Return + Unsystematic Return. (4)

Since the systematic return is perfectly correlated with the market return, it can be expressed as a factor, designated beta (β), times the market return, R_m. The beta factor is a market sensitivity index, indicating how sensitive the security return is to changes in the market level. The unsystematic return, which is independent of market returns, is usually represented by a factor epsilon (ϵ'). Thus the security return, R, may be expressed

$$R = \beta R_m + \epsilon'. \tag{5}$$

For example, if a security had a β factor of 2.0 (e.g., an airline stock), then a 10 per cent market return would generate a systematic return for the stock of 20 per cent. The security return for the period would be the 20 per cent plus the unsystematic component. The unsystematic component depends on factors unique to the company, such as labor difficulties, higher than expected sales, etc.

The security returns model given by Equation (5) is usually written in a way such that the average value of the residual term, ϵ', is zero. This is accomplished by adding a factor, alpha (α), to the model to represent the average value of the unsystematic returns over time. That is, we set $\epsilon' = \alpha + \epsilon$ so that

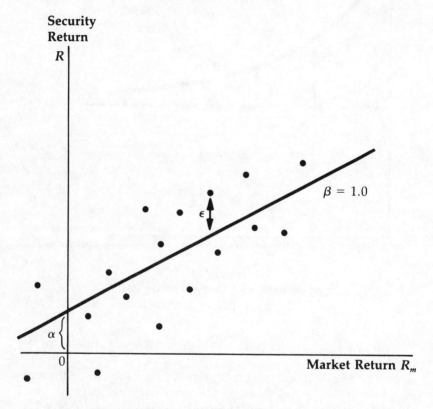

Beta (β), the market sensitivity index, is the slope of the line.

Alpha (α), the average of the residual returns, is the intercept of the line on the security axis.

Epsilon (ϵ), the residual returns are the perpendicular distances of the points from the line.

Figure 12
The Market Model for Security Returns

Source: Modigliani and Pogue, Exhibit 7.

$$R = \alpha + \beta R_m + \epsilon, \tag{6}$$

where the average ϵ over time is equal to zero.

The model for security returns given by Equation (6) is usually referred to as the "market model". Graphically, the model can be depicted as a line fitted to a plot of security returns against rates of return on the market index. This is shown in [Figure 12] for a hypothetical security.

The beta factor can be thought of as the slope of the line. It gives the expected increase in security return for a one per cent increase in market return. In [Figure 12], the security has a beta of 1.0. Thus, a ten per cent market return will result, on the average, in a ten per cent security return. The market-weighted average beta for all stocks is 1.0 by definition.

The alpha factor is represented by the intercept of the line on the vertical security return axis. It is equal to the average value over time of the unsystematic returns (ϵ') on the stock. For most stocks, the alpha factor tends to be small and unstable.

Using Financial Data to Measure Effects of Regulation*

G. William Schwert

The positive analysis of government regulation, measuring the actual rather than the intended effects of regulation, is an increasingly popular topic of research. Often, this analysis concentrates on the "wealth effects" of regulation. At one extreme, the "public interest" or consumer protection hypothesis predicts that regulation confers net benefits on consumers at the expense of regulated firms. At another extreme, the "capture" or producer protection hypothesis predicts that regulated firms net benefits at the expense of consumers. Yet another possibility is that regulators themselves receive net benefits at the expense of both consumers and regulated firms. All of these hypotheses make predictions about the effects of regulation on the value of the regulated firm. . . .

The efficient markets/rational expectations hypothesis posits that security prices reflect all available information. Hence, unanticipated changes in regulation result in an immediate change in security prices, and the price change is an unbiased estimate of the value

*Source: Excerpted with permission from Working Paper no. GPB78-7, Center for Research in Government Policy and Business, Graduate School of Management, University of Rochester, where Schwert is professor of finance.

of the change in the future cash flows to the firm. This fact underlies a variety of methods for estimating the effects of unanticipated regulatory change on shareholder wealth.

The efficient markets/rational expectations hypothesis also implies that it is impossible to test the effects of existing or anticipated regulation by using security returns. If regulation has implications for the value of securities, the effects of regulation are impounded into prices at the time when they are first anticipated. Subsequent security returns will only reflect the equilibrium expected returns to assets of comparable risk, unless the actual effects of regulation deviate from the originally anticipated effects. . . .

Tests of Changes in the Regulation of Individual Firms or Industries

The main difficulty with measuring the effects of regulatory change on security prices is identifying when the market first anticipates the effects of the change on future profitability. In an efficient market, any regulatory change, including new regulation or different enforcement of existing regulations, that affects future cash flows will cause a change in asset prices as soon as the regulatory change is anticipated by the market.

The magnitude of the effect on asset prices depends on the time pattern of regulatory effects on future cash flows and on the discount rate. . . .

In general, it is difficult to separate the effects of regulatory change on the expected value and the risk of future cash flows, especially if the discount rate is not the same for all future periods. Nevertheless, an efficient capital market sets the prices of assets equal to the present value of the anticipated future cash flows, thus reflecting the total impact of regulatory change on shareholder wealth.

Review of Capital Market Theory and Evidence

1. *The Efficient Markets/Rational Expectations Hypothesis.* . . . Fama formalizes the efficient markets model by stipulating that deviations of returns to asset $i, \tilde{R}_{it}$, from their equilibrium expected values, $E(\tilde{R}_{it}|\phi_{t-1})$, conditional on the information set available at time $t-1$, ϕ_{t-1}, are not systematically different from zero. In other words, the "fair game" variable,

$$\tilde{\epsilon}_{it} \equiv \tilde{R}_{it} - E(\tilde{R}_{it}|\phi_{t-1})$$

has a mean of zero. Given some economic model of equilibrium expected returns to assets, which might incorporate risk premia, term premia, or other differences among assets, market efficiency can be tested by examining the statistical properties of the fair game variable, $\tilde{\epsilon}_{it}$.

The "random walk" hypothesis is a special case of the efficient markets model in which expected returns are assumed to be constant over time for each asset, although expected returns can differ among assets. Voluminous empirical evidence supports the random walk hypothesis for the prices of New York Stock Exchange (NYSE) common stocks. Rates of return to NYSE stocks seem to be serially uncorrelated from day to day, or month to month. In addition, Fama argues that monthly returns to NYSE stocks are approximately normally distributed, which provides a statistical basis for deciding when observed returns are abnormally high or low in association with unanticipated regulatory changes.

The "market model" posits that there is a common factor in the returns to all assets which can be represented by the regression model,

$$\tilde{R}_{it} = \alpha_i + \beta_i \tilde{R}_{mt} + \tilde{\epsilon}_{it} \qquad (1)$$

where $\tilde{R}_{mt}$ is the return on a value-weighted portfolio of all marketable assets. Conditional on the information set, ϕ_{t-1}, and the contemporaneous return on the market portfolio, R_{mt}, the equilibrium expected return to asset i is,

$$E(\tilde{R}_{it}|\phi_{t-1}, R_{mt}) = \alpha_i + \beta_i R_{mt}$$

so that the disturbance $\tilde{\epsilon}_{it}$ in (1) is a fair game variable. This model has been used to analyze the effects of firm-specific events, such as stock splits, secondary distributions of securities, or announcements of accounting data, on the prices of the firm's securities. Using the market model (1) to control the market-wide variation in returns to all assets yields more precise estimates of the firm-specific effects on asset returns. There is a substantial amount of evidence that the market model is a well-specified time series regression model when monthly returns to NYSE stocks are analyzed . . . Thus, the market model provides another basis for defining abnormal returns to securities which will generally improve the precision of the estimates of regulatory effect relative to the random walk model.

2. *The Capital Asset Pricing Model.* Sharpe, Lintner, and others derive a model of capital market equilibrium that quantifies the trade-off between risk and expected return. Jensen surveys further

developments of the theory and some tests of the capital asset pricing model (CAPM). The CAPM predicts that the expected return to asset i is linearly related to the risk of the asset in the portfolio of all marketable assets,

$$E(\tilde{R}_{it}) = R_{ft} + \beta_i[E(\tilde{R}_{mt}) - R_{ft}] \qquad (2)$$

where R_{ft} is the return on the risk-free asset, such as a treasury bill, $E(\tilde{R}_{mt})$ is the expected return on the value-weighted market portfolio, and $\beta_i = \text{cov}(\tilde{R}_{it}, \tilde{R}_{mt})/\sigma^2(R_{mt})$, and is interpreted as the risk of asset i relative to the market portfolio. The covariance of $\tilde{R}_{it}$ with $\tilde{R}_{mt}$, $\text{cov}(\tilde{R}_{it}, \tilde{R}_{mt})$, measures the contribution of asset i to the variance of the return to the market portfolio, $\sigma^2(\tilde{R}_{mt})$. Thus, if portfolio risk is measured by the variance of the rate of return, β_i is a standardized measure of marginal risk. According to the CAPM, the only differences among the equilibrium expected returns to assets are attributable to differences in "systematic risk," β_i. . . .

Although there have been numerous refinements of the CAPM, the important result for the purpose of measuring the effects of regulation is that the CAPM provides an estimable relationship between risk and expected return. The CAPM can be viewed as a specific model of equilibrium expected returns which, along with market efficiency, can be used to measure abnormal changes in asset values in association with unanticipated regulatory changes.

The CAPM can also be used to determine how regulation affects the risk of firms. If regulation changes the risk of the firm, it is possible to estimate the risk change by estimating the market model using samples from both before and after the regulatory change. In this way, it is possible to separate out the effects of regulation on the expected value and the risk of future cash flows. . . .

Changes in Regulation Which Affect Firms Simultaneously

1. *Methodological Issues.* Many legislative regulations affect a large number of firms at the same point in time. Also, major legal precedents that change the enforcement of existing legislation can affect a large number of firms simultaneously. In such cases, the common effect of regulation on a set of firms can be measured by analyzing the returns to a portfolio of affected assets. . . .

In order to measure the full effect of an unanticipated regulatory change on the value of the regulated firm, it is necessary to measure the rates of return to all of the firm's securities. Because market price data are not readily available for most corporate debt securities, most studies to date have concentrated on common stock returns. Nevertheless, unless the regulatory change substantially alters the probability that the regulated firm will default on its debt commitments, it seems unlikely that the concentration on common stock returns causes serious biases.

There are important statistical reasons for using portfolio returns instead of analyzing the returns to each individual asset in association with a regulatory change. There is substantial evidence that returns to NYSE common stocks are contemporaneously correlated, and this is probably true for other assets as well. Thus, probability statements based on the analysis of several individual asset returns for the same time period are not independent, and there is no direct way to combine the single asset tests into a joint probability statement about the entire set of assets. On the other hand, the portfolio return, $\tilde{R}_{pt}$, directly incorporates the cross-sectional dependence of its components, facilitating joint tests of significance. . . .

In general, to measure abnormal returns it may be desirable to use a model of equilibrium expected returns that is more sophisticated than the random walk model. For example, either the market model (1) or the capital asset pricing model (2) can be used to control for market-wide changes in asset values that occur at the same time, but that are unrelated to the regulatory change. By controlling for variation in $\tilde{\epsilon}_{it}$ that is unrelated to the regulatory change, it is possible to get a more precise estimate of the impact of regulation on shareholder wealth.

There is an important problem which has been glossed over in this stylized illustration: it is often difficult to determine when a regulatory change is first anticipated by the market. Many regulatory changes result from a series of public hearings, or a study, or some other prolonged process. The market will use this information to determine the probability that regulatory change will occur, and every time these probabilities are revised the market will adjust security prices accordingly. Hence, in many instances it is necessary to look at abnormal security returns many periods before the actual implementation of the regulatory change in order to measure the full effect of regulation. . . . Of course, when the effects of regulation are spread over longer time intervals it becomes more difficult to measure them, because the random variability in security returns increases with the length of the measurement interval. Therefore, it is important to specify the timing of changes in expectations about regulation as accurately as possible.

Finally, it is important to note that the efficient markets/rational expectations hypothesis does not imply that investors have perfect foresight about the future effects of regulation (or anything else).

Security prices change to reflect the most accurate unbiased prediction of what will happen in the future, but it is certainly possible that the actual effects of regulation will turn out to be very different from what was expected at the time of the regulatory change. In principle, it should be possible to determine whether the actual effects of regulation deviate substantially from the expected effects by measuring the returns to affected securities after the regulatory change. For example, if there is a sequence of identifiable events which provide successively more information about the effects of a particular regulation, it would be necessary to sum the abnormal returns associated with all of these events in order to measure the actual impact of regulation. . . .

Regulatory Changes Which Affect Firms at Different Times

1. *Methodological Issues.* Some changes in public regulation occur through case law, or administrative law, or because of decisions by government regulatory agencies. In many instances a specific type of regulatory change will affect different firms at different times. . . .

Fama, Fisher, Jensen, and Roll [1969] pioneered the analysis of abnormal security returns in "event time." For example, the effect of filing an antitrust suit can be measured by averaging the abnormal returns to all defendant firms' securities in the period of the event,

$$\bar{\epsilon}_t = \frac{1}{N} \sum_{i=1}^{N} \epsilon_{it} \tag{3}$$

where the event time, t, will generally be a different calendar date for each firm in the sample. The pattern of effects can be analyzed by computing an average abnormal return for several periods before and after the event occurs. This is especially important if there is some doubt about the time when the regulatory change is first anticipated by the securities market, since some of the effects may occur before or after the designated event period.

If all of the firms in a particular sample have regulatory events on different calendar dates, the individual firm abnormal returns should not be intercorrelated and the variance of the average abnormal return,

$$\text{Var}(\bar{\epsilon}_t) = \frac{1}{N^2} \cdot \sum_{i=1}^{N} \text{Var}(\epsilon_{it})$$

is proportional to the sum of the variance of the individual abnormal returns. However, if some firms have regulatory events on the same date, it is more difficult to get a direct measure of the variability of the average abnormal return, because the returns which occur on the same date are likely to be correlated.

Another technique which has been used to analyze the impact of regulation which occurs at different times for different firms is to form a portfolio which is composed of all affected firms at each calendar date. This can be thought of as a trading strategy where the investment rule is to buy securities which are likely to be positively affected by regulation and to short sell securities which are likely to be negatively affected. The return to this strategy, properly adjusted for risk, provides a measure of the impact of the regulatory change. The average of the time series of abnormal trading strategy portfolio returns is conceptually similar to the cross-sectional average abnormal return in (3). In fact, if the trading strategy portfolio never contains more than one security at any calendar date, the two measures will be identical. The trading strategy portfolio method can be used to analyze anticipation or lag effects by including all firms which have regulatory events in a span of several months either side of the event date.

NOTES AND QUESTIONS

1. The implication of modern capital-markets theory that the current market price of a security is the best estimate of its value has led to the creation of a number of "index funds." These are mutual funds or other investment pools which practice a passive "buy and hold" strategy, while minimizing diversifiable risk by holding a much larger portfolio than any actively managed fund. For discussion of index funds see John H. Langbein and Richard A. Posner, Market Funds and Trust-Investment Law, parts I and II.* The authors discuss some implications of the index fund for issues of corporate governance (1977 at 13–16):

> It may be argued that the passive strategy would aggravate the various problems that are alleged, in an extensive literature, to result from the divorce between ownership and control in the large corporation. The corporation is owned by its shareholders, but the practical day-to-day control of the company is in the hands of hired managers who, to the extent that they are free from effective shareholder control, can run the corporation for their own benefit, with resulting harm to the shareholders and perhaps to the efficiency of the firm.

*1976 American Bar Foundation Res. J. 1 and 1977 id. 1. Reprinted with permission.

Arguably, this problem would be aggravated by widespread adoptions of the passive strategy since even fewer corporate owners than at present would be exercising oversight of managerial performance.

The premise of the argument is debatable. While corporate shareholders are not in effective control of the day-to-day management of major corporations, it does not follow that hired managers are free to conduct corporate affairs in any manner they like or that they do not as a rule act in the interest of the shareholders. This is not the place to rehearse in detail the arguments that have been made pro and con on this issue, but one should note the considerable harmony of interests between managers and shareholders (especially where managerial compensation is based on corporate performance), the effect of competition in the corporation's product markets in constraining managerial discretion, the pressures exerted by creditors (especially large lenders), and the existence of various mechanisms for displacing unsatisfactory management, notably the tender offer (take-over bid).

Current discussion of the market for corporate control focuses on the tender offer, in part because the effectiveness of the tender offer as a method of corporate take-over does not depend on the degree to which stockholders are involved in the actual management of the corporation's business. . . .

But what if a majority of a company's stock were held by institutions committed to the passive strategy — institutions that engaged in no trading whatsoever (except as necessary for redemptions or to maintain the desired level of diversification)? If another company believed it could manage that company's assets more profitably than the present management, how would it go about obtaining majority control? If it approached each of the (passive) institutional investors with an attractive tender offer, presumably they would refuse to sell, on the ground that their policy was never to sell any stock except when necessary for purposes of redemption or diversification. Existing management, however dishonest or inept, would be immune from the threat of take-over because a majority of the shareholders would refuse to consider any offer to sell their stock.

Although this is a potential problem worthy of concern, it can be solved by a slight modification in (or clarification of) the decision rules governing passive investors, including trustees, so as to permit (indeed, presumptively to require) the investor to accept the (highest) cash tender offer if it is significantly above the market price of the stock. This approach seems congenial to the assumptions of the passive approach, which posits that the current market price of a stock is the best estimate of its true value. If the market price of a share of stock is $20 and a tender offer of $30 is made, the inference from modern capital market theory is that $20 is the best estimate of the value of the corporation's stock *under present management* and therefore a price of $30 is presumptively an attractive one at which to dispose of the stock. Typically in take-over situations the defending management will argue that the stock of the corporation is undervalued — not only at its current price but at the (often much) higher price offered by the firm seeking to take over the corporation. This argument has a hollow ring from the standpoint of efficient-market theory.

While it is thus a reasonable extension of the passive strategy for the passive investor to respond affirmatively to tender offers, he should not be required to accept the first tender offer made. He should sell at the highest possible price. Often there will be a succession of competing tender offers bidding up the price of the stock. He will have to determine when the bidding process has been completed.

There is an argument for declining tender offers. It runs as follows: if the offeror offers $30, he must—unless he is a "raider"—think the value of the stock will exceed $30 if he obtains control; therefore the shareholder should decline to tender, since the stock is really worth more than the tender-offer price. Moreover, if he does sell his stock, he may have to buy it right back in order to maintain his desired level of diversification. However, by declining the tender offer, the shareholder (depending on the size of his holdings) may defeat the take-over bid—and then he is $10 a share poorer. It would seem therefore that any shareholder (including a trustee) who has such a large share of the company's stock that his refusal to tender might defeat the take-over attempt would be well advised to accept the best tender offer, though he need not tender more shares than sought by, or necessary to, the offeror. But the wisdom of attempting these nice strategic calculations depends on their cost, and most trustees will be better advised, we suspect, to adopt an automatic policy of responding affirmatively to tender offers.

A related question is that of the trustee's optimal expenditure of time and money on deciding how to vote on merger, squeeze-out, and related management proposals that might reduce (or enhance) the value of the trustee's holdings. The well-diversified trustee may conclude that the net gains from researching these questions is negative—so long as a majority of the stock of a corporation in which he has invested is *not* controlled by passive investors. Should a time come when there are corporations so controlled, the prudent trustee may decide that the active exercise of his rights as a shareholder is appropriate to protect his investment from management overreaching. The problem, however, is at present remote and conjectural.

This problem aside, once the decision rule that we have advocated were adopted, the concern that the market-fund concept might result in aggravating the alleged separation of corporate ownership from control would disappear. Indeed, the passive investor's automatic rejection of management claims that the current price of the corporation's stock is less than the "true" value of the stock would promote the operation of the market in corporate control. The passive investor who utilizes the decision rule urged here would be quicker to respond to take-over bids than the conventional investor who listens carefully to the management argument that the tender-offer price undervalues the corporation's stock.

2. What is the relationship between the "random walk" component of modern capital-market theory and the emphasis the theory places on *beta*, a measure of systematic risk (as explained in the Modigliani-Pogue reading), as determining the expected return of a security?

3. What is the theoretical reason why the *alpha* factor discussed

in the Modigliani-Pogue reading is, in their words, "small and unstable"? How is that conclusion related to Brealey's discussion of the return to highly volatile stocks? Does his discussion imply that stocks of low volatility might have a consistently positive *alpha*?

4. Why, if bankruptcy costs were zero, would shareholders have nothing to gain from the acquisition of firm *A* by firm *B* even if the risks of the two firms were negatively correlated? Would the conclusion that (in the absence of positive bankruptcy costs) shareholders have nothing to gain from such a merger hold if there are substantial costs to the individual of holding a diversified portfolio of common stocks? How does Brealey's discussion of diversification bear on this issue?

Chapter 7

Acquisitions and the Market For Corporate Control

This chapter considers corporate acquisitions in relation to the fundamental theme of the separation of ownership and control introduced in Part I. The study of merger activity bears on that issue in two ways. First, a study of the effect of mergers on the wealth of the shareholders of the *acquiring* firm may help one distinguish empirically between profit maximization and rival hypotheses of management behavior. (These hypotheses can be viewed as derived ultimately from the Berle-Means thesis, since if the shareholders are in control they will insist that management maximize profits, i.e., shareholder wealth.) If mergers, while increasing the size, reduce the profits of the acquiring firm, that is evidence against the hypothesis of profit maximization. However, the selection from an article by Gershon Mandelker which begins this chapter rejects that conclusion, as have most although not all empirical studies of the question. See, e.g., D. Kummer and J.R. Hoffmeister, Valuation Consequences of Cash Tender Offers, 33 J. Fin. 505 (1978), and the summary of studies in the Notes and Questions at the end of this chapter.

The effect of acquisitions on the wealth of shareholders of the *acquired* firm also bears on the question whether management controls the modern corporation to the detriment of the shareholders. If the shareholders of the acquired firm profit from the acquisition, as found by Mandelker (and, again, by most studies — see, e.g., P. Dodd and R. Ruback, Tender Offers and Stockholder Returns: An Empirical Analysis, 5 J. Fin. Econ. 351 (1977)), that is evidence that mergers may be a method for protecting shareholders from dishonest or incompetent management by transferring the control of the corporation to a new management that will manage the corporation in the shareholders' interest and thus increase the value of their shares. It is not conclusive evidence against the Berle-Means thesis, however — first, because it implies there was some interval during which the shareholders *were* exploited, and, second, because it does not show how much better off the shareholders are made (perhaps the chief effect of the merger is to transfer wealth from one group of managers to another), and, third, because the fact that some inefficiently or dishonestly managed firms are acquired doesn't mean that there aren't many other corporations in which shareholders are also exploited but which are not acquired.

The study by Peter Holl, the second selection in this chapter, bears on the latter question, though it hardly settles it conclusively. He asks to what extent the threat of takeover operates to discipline corporate managers by inducing them to take steps that will raise a below-average valuation ratio (his measure of the degree to which the corporation is being managed in the shareholders' interests).

Thus, the "market for corporate control" (a term, and idea, introduced into the literature by Henry G. Manne in his article Mergers and the Market for Corporate Control, 73 J. Pol. Econ. 110 (1965)) emerges as a potentially important constraint on management misconduct or inefficiency. However, the effectiveness of the constraint depends on several factors. First, the costs of using the market for control are apparently high. One recent study found that the transaction costs involved in making a tender offer were on average 13 percent of the post-offer market price of the shares tendered for. See Robert Smiley, Tender Offers, Transaction Costs and the Theory of the Firm, 58 Rev. Econ. & Stat. 22 (1976). The paper by Daniel Fischel discusses how the costs of takeovers have been increased by the Williams Act, a federal statute regulating tender offers. Second, Sanford Grossman and Oliver Hart point out the problems for effective offers created by free-riding shareholders who do *not* tender — a group whose interests the SEC is currently much concerned with protecting.

These articles suggest that conglomerates — firms which specialize in acquisitions of companies in unrelated lines of business — can serve an important efficiency function. With antitrust law creating formidable obstacles to horizontal and vertical mergers, the conglomerate acquisition becomes the main avenue for such a displacement of inefficient management. Is that the sole explanation for the existence of conglomerates and conglomerate mergers? Professor James H. Scott, Jr., considers some of the purely financial benefits that may also account for conglomerate acquisitions, in another paper in this chapter.

The last paper in this chapter, by Michael Bradley, suggests an alternative theory of takeovers to the management-discipline theory that has dominated the literature: a "synergy" theory. Certain mergers increase the value of both firms and Bradley views the takeover process as the process by which the merger combination which will maximize the joint value of the firms is found.

Risk and Return: The Case of Merging Firms*

Gershon Mandelker

Mergers are a controversial issue in economic literature. At one extreme is the view that in the acquisitions market "big business" uses its power to exploit imperfections in the capital market to gain monopolistic power in the product market. It is frequently argued that stockholders of acquiring firms earn abnormal returns from mergers. In discussing mergers, many textbooks present famous mergers of successful firms, and conclude that mergers are profitable. Consequently frequent waves of mergers have been regarded as a threat to the free enterprise system for which the heavy hand of the regulator is needed.

At the other extreme is the position that assumes the separation of control from ownership in the modern multi-owner corporation. In this view management pursues size maximization, often at the expense of maximization of owners' wealth. That implies that firms engage in acquisitions even when the marginal cost of acquisition is higher than the marginal increase in the value of the firm. Stockholders are thus expected to earn lower than normal returns. This approach seems to have considerable empirical support. Indeed most of the empirical studies on the profitability of the acquiring firms yield the surprising result that, on the average, mergers are unsuccessful. In a recent survey article which reviews the last fifty years' empirical research on the profitability of mergers, Hogarty concludes that mergers have a *negative* effect on the profitability of the acquiring firms, and a neutral effect on the *sum* of acquired plus acquiring firms. He believes that acquiring firms engage in this unprofitable activity because "mergers are an attractive form of investment for those firms whose managers are risk takers . . . (since) some mergers produce extraordinary profits . . ." while most produce losses to the acquiring firms. However, previous studies suffer

Source: 1 J. Fin. Econ. 303-335 (1974), reprinted with permission. Gershon Mandelker is associate professor of business administration at the Graduate School of Business, University of Pittsburgh.

from various shortcomings. Most employ small sample sizes and use rather primitive models, i.e., they neither adjust for risk nor do they take into consideration changes in risk. In this study we attempt to incorporate these factors.

In contrast to the above two views, the basic presumption of this study is that the expected return from an acquisition is the same as from any other investment-production activity with similar risk. That is, we expect the market for acquisitions to operate competitively. Consequently two basic questions will be examined:

(a) Are mergers in fact associated with abnormal positive or negative returns? If so, how are the abnormal returns shared between the shareholders of acquired and acquiring companies?

(b) Is the capital market efficient with respect to mergers? That is, is information on mergers reflected immediately in the stock prices of the merging firms? Statements that contradict the Efficient Capital Markets Hypothesis by assuming a long period for learning are found quite often in the literature on mergers. We hope to bring some evidence to bear on this. . . .

In a perfectly competitive market, competition will equate the expected rates of return on assets of similar risk. If the acquisitions market offers higher expected returns than equivalent activities of similar risk, more resources will be directed to this activity until expected rates of return are reduced to a competitive level. The reverse holds if the acquisitions market has lower expected returns than equivalent activities of similar risk. The PCAM hypothesis implies that for an acquiring firm there are no monopolistic sources of gains due solely to merging as a way of obtaining productive capacity.

We could, however, envisage an acquisitions market in which perfect competition prevails on only one side. For example, the acquiring firms might be in a perfectly competitive acquisitions market [PCAM], but the firms to be acquired might have some "unique" resources. In this situation only the acquiring firms' stockholders will earn normal levels of expected returns from an acquisition. If a firm to be acquired has some resources which are not used effectively and which could provide economic gains to other firms by merger, then competition among these firms will cause any abnormal returns from the merger to go to the stockholders of the acquired firm. We can envisage situations in which such unique resources can be released only by the agreement to merge (e.g., the acquired firm has had large losses which it cannot hope to use against future profits to lower taxes).

Some economists argue that firms merge to achieve synergy. However, in a steady-state economy this argument is inconsistent with a perfect market in business organizations. In a perfect market firms are able to achieve synergy equally by internal or external growth. They are not expected to be able to acquire a firm at prices which are lower than the cost of reproducing that firm's assets internally.

The efficient capital markets hypothesis says that stock prices adjust instantaneously to new information. Thus stock prices provide unbiased signals for efficient resource allocation. If the capital market is efficient with respect to mergers, then any information about a merger should be incorporated instantaneously into the corresponding stock prices. The efficient markets hypothesis does not rule out monopolistic elements in the acquisitions market. Mergers could imply gains for either the acquiring or for the acquired firms. The hypothesis states only that the stock market reacts efficiently to information about a forthcoming merger.

In fact, many of the reasons for mergers proposed in the literature are based on the assumption that the capital market is inefficient. Some of these arguments are presented below. . . .

The "abnormal gains" hypothesis. This hypothesis states that information concerning a forthcoming acquisition is generally considered "good" news for the stockholders of the acquiring firm. Various reasons for economic gains from mergers are usually given. These include economies of scale, attainment of monopoly or economic power that stems from "bigness," financial advantages, tax considerations, undervalued securities, diversification, improvement of the "marketability" of stocks, and others.

One of the most comprehensive articles written in support of this hypothesis is Lintner's most recent attempt to develop a theory of mergers. He presents many diverse reasons why mergers are bound to provide abnormal returns to the acquiring firm's stockholders and summarizes thoroughly most of the traditional arguments. Among those he mentions: "gains from favorable tax treatment, gains from greater leverage and/or lower borrowing costs due to size, and possible gains from merging imperfectly correlated income streams to preserve expected returns with reduced risk." . . .

The "chain letter" hypothesis. The second view found in the mergers literature is the "chain letter" hypothesis. It states that investors rely on very few sources of information, the main ones being financial and accounting numbers. Lintner mentions that mergers enhance opportunities for accountants to manipulate accounting income numbers in reports to stockholders by means of "dirty pooling," suppression of asset costs at the time of the merger in order to mislead shareholders. Also, instantaneous increases in earnings per share from *P/E* ratio differences among the merging firms tend to raise stockholders' assessments of future earnings. Thus he argues, "the current aggregate value of the merging companies in equilibrium will be raised, ceteris paribus, even in a pure conglomerate case in strictly perfect securities markets . . ."

The "chain letter" hypothesis implies that shareholders are misled by manipulation of accounting numbers so that the announcement of a forthcoming merger is followed by a rise in stock prices of the acquiring firm. But in this context, the information conveyed by the E.P.S. and other accounting numbers would be misleading. If we assume that equilibrium in the stock prices is eventually reached, then stock prices have to adjust downward finally, to reflect their equilibrium values. In any case, the "chain letter" hypothesis is based on the assumption that capital markets operate inefficiently.

The third view that has received much support lately in the literature in light of recent empirical results is the "growth maximization" hypothesis. This hypothesis is presented by Mueller as follows:

> . . . managers maximize, or at least pursue as one of their goals, the growth in physical size of their corporation rather than its profits or stockholder welfare . . . both the pecuniary and nonpecuniary rewards which managers receive are closely tied to the growth rate of their firm. Managerial salaries, bonuses, stock options, and promotions all tend to be more closely related to the size or changes in size of the firm than to its profits. Similarly, the prestige and power which managers derive from their occupations are directly related to the size and growth of the company and not to its profitability.

Thus, due to the separation of control from ownership in the modern giant corporation, the managers can pursue their own personal goals. The firm's goal, therefore, is not to maximize profits. However, if companies merge not for the sake of increasing profits, but merely for the sake of increasing size, their profits or rates of return on common stock should be abnormally low when this policy becomes known to the market. Reid in his comprehensive empirical work supports this conclusion. Indeed other empirical studies, some of which were mentioned earlier also suggest that mergers result in low returns to stockholders of the acquiring firms. . . .

[In order to understand the results of Mandelker's empirical study, which appear next in the reprinted article, an additional word about the "capital-asset pricing model" on which that study is based may be helpful. The model, which was presented in Chapter 6, postulates that the return to the owner of a security is a function of a number of factors, including the risk of the security relative to the risk of the securities market as a whole; this risk is called the security's *beta* (β). The higher the *beta* (or "relative risk"), the higher the expected return to the security. This results from the facts that shareholders are averse to risk and that *beta* is a form of undiversifiable risk. (These are matters that were taken up in greater detail in Chapter 6.) To the extent that regressing a security's return on the various factors identified in the model as influencing its return leaves some of that return unexplained, the unexplained portion is called the "residual." It can be either positive or negative, implying returns either greater or less than could have been anticipated from the objective factors incorporated in the capital-asset pricing model. In Mandelker's study, the residual is computed for each firm in the study on a monthly basis and in addition is cumulated over several months, yielding a "cumulative average residual" or C.A.R., to which he refers frequently.]

Table 1 [omitted] presents the C.A.R. of acquiring firms for the period (− 40 to + 40), i.e., from 40 months before the merger to 40 months after the merger. . . . The C.A.R. rises during the 40 months prior to the merger by 5.1 percent and decreases during the next 40 months by 1.7 percent. The average β decreases by approximately eight percent, five percent of which occurs after the merger. The results of Table 1 appear to be consistent with the theories that postulate positive results (either temporary or permanent) of mergers on stock prices of acquiring firms:

(a) The "abnormal gains" hypothesis states that mergers cause either economies of scale, monopoly power, or advantages that Lintner's new arguments suggest. Accordingly, news about a forthcoming merger should result in higher returns for stockholders of the acquiring firm.

(b) The "chain letter" hypothesis states that mergers cause an increase in stock prices because of their positive effect on the price-earning ratio or on earnings-per-share, even though the merger may not cause any real economies at all.

These results suggest that the informational impact of a forthcoming merger is spread over approximately thirty months before the event. The subsequent decrease in C.A.R. after the merger might be viewed as consistent with the hypotheses which assume that people are fooled by acquisitions. Accordingly, it has been argued that people believe that a merger implies higher performance of the acquiring firm and therefore revise their expectations upward. However, on the average, they are "overshooting" and after the merger they revise their expectations downward.

Since leaks of information into the market about a forthcoming merger would include the identity of both the acquiring and the acquired firms, we turn now to analyze the performance of the acquired firms. This may help us both to identify the period in which such information becomes available to the market and to evaluate the performance of the stocks involved.

Table 2 [omitted] shows the C.A.R. of acquired firms for the period (− 40 to − 1). Since most of the acquired firms cease to be listed on the New York Stock Exchange in the month of the merger, we are able to present results up to one month before the merger.

In contrast to Table 1, the C.A.R. in Table 2 shows a dramatic rise of about 14 percent (an average of 2 percent per month) during the last seven months before the merger. However, the C.A.R. is slightly negative during period (− 35 to − 7), and its lowest level is in month (− 9). During the 12-month period (− 20 to − 9) eight of the monthly average residuals are negative. The percentage of negative residuals . . . is consistently low during the last seven months before the merger and especially so in the last 4 months. This may indicate that for some mergers, positive information regarding acquisitions, or any other "good" news correlated with acquisitions, starts leaking out to the market about 7 months before the merger.

It should be noted that the increase in the cumulative average residuals during the period (− 7 to − 1) does not necessarily imply normal returns for those investors who purchase stocks of firms to be acquired after the acquisition has been announced. The residuals of individual stocks typically do not follow the behavior of the average residuals across stocks. Plots of successive residuals of individual stocks indicate that they are independent. Each stock has some high residuals in some months and these differ from stock to stock. The average residuals are high for all seven months because the timing of abnormal residuals differs from stock to stock. In the next section we employ some probability tests in order to examine whether the C.A.R. of Tables 1 and 2 are significantly different from zero. . . .

Table 3 [omitted] presents results for . . . *acquired* firms. The *t*-values* are very high, i.e., 5.8 to 13.8, and imply that during the last 5 months before the merger the average residual terms are significantly greater than zero, and amount to about 2 to 3 percent per month. This is consistent with the results in Table 2 and indicates that there is a very low probability of their occurrence by pure chance.

In Table 4 [omitted] we present some probability tests for the average residuals of the acquiring firms. . . . The acquiring stocks do not have such "significant" results. The *t*-values are very low, and thus the low level of the average residuals could have been obtained by pure chance. It is difficult to say whether the stockholders of the acquiring firms gain from mergers. For example, the average residuals of portfolios formed for the period (− 7 to − 4) is 0.24% per

*[This is a test of statistical significance. See the Notes and Questions at the end of Chapter 2—Eds.]

month, and the t-statistic is 0.74, which is far from being significant. However, the true average residual might amount to 0.7% or 1.0% per month and this would mean that the stockholders gain from acquisitions. On the other hand, the true average residual might be zero and this would be consistent with no abnormal gains to stockholders. Anyway our results seem to be inconsistent with abnormal losses to stockholders from acquisitions. . . .

Our results for the acquired firms are consistent with the hypothesis that mergers are a mechanism by which the market system replaces incompetent management. If managers of a firm do not operate efficiently, the stock prices of the firm will fall and the firm might become a good buy. Replacement of the incumbent management may then be a source of gains for the acquired entity. This explanation is also consistent with some other empirical studies.

In Table 2 the cumulative average residuals of the acquired firms are indeed negative and continue to decrease up to month ($-$ 9). In addition, the percentage of negative residuals is high. . . . The C.A.R. is negative up to month ($-$ 7). During the 7-month period ($-$ 15 to $-$ 9) only one average residual is positive. (The C.A.R. accumulates by $-$ 2.0 percent.)

If the firm to be acquired has relatively inefficient management, then this information should have been impounded in its stock prices at some point in time in the past. Afterwards its stockholders should earn "normal" returns. Since for each firm this information is revealed in a different month, we would not expect to detect its effect on the stock prices, in any specific month, for the sample as a whole. The level of the stock prices will reflect both the relative inefficiency of the firm's operations and the probability that this management will be replaced. However, incumbent management can resist an acquisition. As long as the management continues to successfully resist a take-over, the stock prices will probably continue at low levels. Indeed, it is very difficult to acquire a firm if its management resists forcefully.

In a competitive acquisitions market where there are other firms who expect, similarly, to improve the operations of the firm to be acquired, competition among potential acquiring firms will raise the price of the former. Consequently, the acquiring firm should earn a normal rate of return. However, if only one firm can make such an improvement, then the two constituent firms will share equally any abnormal profits. The stockholders of the acquired firms may gain in both cases.

This hypothesis is also consistent with the view that there exists a market for corporate control. As noted by Manne, "under almost all state statutes the board of directors of a corporation must ap-

prove a merger before it is submitted to shareholders for a vote . . ."
When a firm is confronted with a tender offer a conflict of interest
between management and shareholders may result. Although the
stockholders of the acquired firm are likely to profit from the merger
more than any other party involved, incumbent management may
stand to lose the most, for they may forfeit their controlling position
with all the accompanying benefits. If the incumbent management
objects to a take-over, the bidding firm has the option of making
either a proxy fight or a tender offer. However, these latter types of
acquisitions are relatively rare. They are usually considered to be too
expensive, because incumbent management has, to a certain degree,
all the economic resources of the firm at their disposal to resist an
undesired merger.

Some other possible reasons for higher returns to the stockholders of the acquired firms are suggested below:

(1) One hypothesis is that firms are acquired due to new positive information about their business. That is, the acquisition occurs
after some new positive information has been impounded into its
stock prices. So, there is a rise in the stock prices of the firm to be
acquired without any relation to the subsequent acquisition. We
have not tested this hypothesis. But it remains at least as one reason
why our results could also be consistent with a perfectly competitive
market for acquisitions on both sides, i.e., for the acquiring as well
as for the acquired firms.

(2) Tax considerations: In many cases the stockholders of the
acquired firms have to pay capital-gains taxes. Therefore the price
paid for the acquired common stocks should be sufficiently higher to
compensate for the costs involved in paying taxes that the owner
may otherwise have to pay only at an actual sale of his stocks. This
assumes that capital gains do, in fact, exist.

(3) Relative size of acquisition: In mergers where there are expectations for synergism if the two constituent firms share equally
any synergy gains, then the stockholders of the smaller firm may
gain proportionately more. While we have seen that stockholders of
acquired firms enjoy abnormal gains, we see in Table 5 [omitted]
that the acquiring firms' stocks do not show any abnormal gains,
during the period (-7 to -1). Another way to check this hypothesis is to look at the percentage of positive (or negative) residuals
before the merger. A comparison of these measures in Tables 6
[omitted] or 2, with those of tables 5 or 1 at period (-7 to -1)
reveals that the percentage of positive residuals of stocks of acquiring firms is about the same as in any other period. On the other
hand, stocks of the acquired firms show exceptionally high percentages of positive residuals during that period. Nevertheless, this hy-

pothesis, too, could account for part of the abnormal gains observed, at least for some individual acquiring firms.

Control Type and the Market for Corporate Control in Large U.S. Corporations*

Peter Holl

In recent years various attempts have been made to investigate the effect which the separation of ownership from control has on corporate behaviour. . . . This problem is investigated further in the present paper by bringing into the analysis the market for corporate control. This market is concerned with the buying and selling of voting stock and their effects on company control. If the market for corporate control operates efficiently all companies will be constrained to maximize profits and there will be an identity of interests among managers and owners; if not, the separation of ownership from control will have behavioural implications for those management-controlled firms that are able to evade, or are unaffected by, market discipline. It then becomes possible for the management of each of these firms to divert funds away from the owners in the sense that profits are lower than they would be if the firm were constrained to maximize profits. The burden of the present paper is to see whether the market for corporate control is effective and to consider its effect on the relationship between control type and company performance. . . .

The market for corporate control is concerned with the relationship between the market value of a company's common stock and the value of the assets to which it relates. If the former is divided by the latter we obtain the valuation ratio which provides an index showing how rewarding it would be for an outside interest to purchase control of a company — other things being equal, the lower the ratio the more profitable the purchase. A management which is not maximizing returns to the owners of the company will find this fact reflected in a lower common share price. As the market value of equity falls in relation to the value of physical assets (i.e., as the valuation ratio falls) it may become advantageous for an outside party to purchase those shares and, with them, control of the company. If this market is fully efficient management cannot do anything but maximize returns to owners as the only alternative is to

*Source: 25 J. Ind. Econ. 259-273 (1977), reprinted with permission. Peter Holl is Lecturer in Econometrics, The City University, London.

forfeit corporate control. The market for corporate control then be-comes a constraint which prevents management from directing re-turns away from the owners and ensures that the interests of man-agement and owners are synonymous.

The discipline exercised by this market is of two kinds which for convenience can be referred to as being punitive and corrective. Punitive discipline involves corporate takeover and can be thought of as discipline in the short run. It represents discipline in its most extreme form. A takeover bid will occur when the valuation ratio of a company falls low enough to encourage an outsider to attempt to buy control of the company, a low valuation ratio in this context being one that is less than the average for the industry from which it comes. Since a takeover is usually followed by the removal of the incumbent management, and the loss of income and perquisites associated with top managerial positions, it is a move that managers fear. . . . An alert management will usually know if it is ripe for a takeover bid and is likely to have contingency plans ready for such an event. While the existence of these plans will not guarantee that a bid will be successfully rejected it does suggest that defending man-agement has a definite advantage over an acquisition minded firm and that the punitive discipline exercised by the market for corpo-rate control is likely to be only partially effective.

It is partly because of this advantage of defending management over the raider firm that we see the market exercising what was previously referred to as corrective discipline. If a takeover is thwarted by raising the dividend or by purchasing its own shares in the open market the price of the company's stock will increase. This in turn will increase the valuation ratio and the cost of the takeover to the raider firm. Another situation in which such corrective discip-line may be exercised occurs when purchasing control results in expenditure so large that it has to be distributed over a long period of time. When an attempt is made to purchase control in this way a defending management will soon become aware of it as shareholder lists are continually updated, and there will be sufficient opportu-nity to introduce policy adjustments which result in an increase in the valuation ratio. The continued purchasing of control will then be far less attractive. In general if the market operates efficiently a firm cannot remain an attractive takeover possibility in the long run; the corrective discipline of an efficient market for corporate control con-strains a firm to pursue policies which result in its valuation ratio moving towards the long run industry average.

It has been seen that the punitive discipline of the market may be only partially operative and this may be true of the corrective discipline also. This will particularly be so in the case of large firms where buying control is likely to be a risky venture. A premium for this risk will have to be reflected in the valuation ratio and it could be that the valuation ratio of a company is low but not low enough to include an adequate risk premium for a potential buyer. The risk element involved may also result in there being few buyers in the market so that demand and supply may be out of phase in much the same way that those seeking employment in the labour market may not match the vacancies that exist. Moreover, as Stigler has pointed out, knowledge is not a free good and including the cost of information necessary for the decision-making process might make an otherwise profitable venture into an unprofitable one. For any one of these reasons, then, it is possible that corporate management can escape both the punitive and corrective discipline of the market for corporate control and it is this fact that has implications for the relationship between corporate performance and the separation of ownership from control. If the market operates imperfectly it may be possible for the management of some firms to pursue goals which are not in line with those of the owners, that is to say, management will be able to divert returns away from the owners. Thus, instead of comparing the behaviour of owner-controlled firms with that of management-controlled firms, as done in previous studies, it is necessary to compare the behaviour of owner-controlled firms with the behaviour of management-controlled firms that are able to overcome or evade the discipline of the market for corporate control. In order to test this line of reasoning it is first necessary to investigate empirically whether such a market exists. This is considered in the next section. . . .

The evidence presented below relates to the corrective action of the market for corporate control investigating whether there is a tendency for the distribution of the valuation ratios among firms to move towards a long run average value over time. . . .

[In an omitted section the author finds that] while the corrective discipline of the market for corporate control quite clearly operates it does so rather imperfectly.

In the previous section it was suggested that this imperfection may be in part a direct function of corporate size, and it is possible to consider this further with the information collected since the largest company in the sample (General Motors) is almost 100 times larger than the smallest (Detroit Steel) and this amount of size variation may well be sufficient to allow the market to have a differential impact within the sample. In order to investiate this possibility the entire group of companies was divided into four subgroups . . . Thus, group one contains companies ranked 1–125, group two contains companies ranked 126–250, etc. For companies ranked 1–125 there is a movement towards the long run average valuation ratio but while the slope coefficient* of 0.85 is less than unity at a 95% level of confidence it is not so using 99% limits. This weaker result is confirmed further by the results for companies ranked 126–250. For these companies b is estimated to be 1.01. With a standard error of 0.06 this value is consistent with a population coefficient of 1 suggesting that for these companies market discipline is non-existent. For . . . companies ranked 251–375 and 376–500 respectively, the situation is quite different. In each equation the estimated slope coefficient is clearly significantly less than 1 and has a value lower than any of the previous values. This change of emphasis resulting from change in corporate size is seen more clearly in equations (2.6) and (2.7). The former relates to companies ranked 1–250 (groups 1 and 2 combined) and the estimated value of 0.943 is not less than unity at even 95% limits. This situation is reversed in (2.7) for companies ranked 251–500 (groups 3 and 4 combined) where $b = 0.77$ is significantly less than 1 at a 99% significance level.

These results, however, are marred by the fact that they are disproportionately dependent on the presence of just one company. This company, Avon Products ranked 192, had valuation ratios of 12.59 and 16.84 for successive five-year periods and this one observation which is highly atypical biases the slope coefficient . . . in an upward direction. . . . Clearly, adjusting the samples in this way is not good practice but, conversely, confidence in the results must be weakened when they are heavily dependent on the presence of just one company in a fairly large sample. . . .

In general, the evidence presented and discussed suggests two main conclusions. First, a market for corporate control exists though its discipline is somewhat imperfect; second, the amount of imperfection probably increases with company size. The implication of both conclusions taken together is that there is room for some management-controlled firms to behave differently from owner-controlled firms, particularly amongst the biggest firms in the country.

If the market for corporate control affects the relationship between control type and corporate performance the problem that immediately arises is how to analyse this empirically. One possibility that suggests itself follows from the argument developed in the previous section. If a firm has a low valuation ratio for the period 1960–64 one of three things can happen in the period 1965–69. First, it can be taken over; this possibility, however, is ruled out here since the

*[In the omitted section, the author explained that a slope coefficient, or b, equal to or greater than 1, indicated an absence of corrective discipline of the market — Eds.]

360 firms of interest continued in existence throughout the period. Second, it can be subject to the corrective discipline of the market. . . . Third, it may be unaffected by the market. . . . If one party owns at least 30% of the common stock the firm is classed as strong owner control [OC]; more than 10% but less than 30% is akin to weak owner control, while the rest (<10%) are management controlled (MC). Only one measure of corporate performance is directly important in the results presented below, namely profits. In previous studies profits have usually been defined as net return on stockholders' equity: that is, net income over net worth. But a model based on the maximization of owners' utility requires a profit measure that includes dividend return and stock price appreciation. Results were generated using both measures though only those relating to the latter measure — total return — are presented [in Table 13]. . . .

Before carrying out any significance tests using these figures various adjustments have to be made. An observed difference between any two figures taken from the table may result from the effect of extraneous variables rather than from the two-way classification used. In particular, it is known that profitability is affected by corporate size and by product market structure. The effect of these variables on the profitability figures given in the table [below] has been brought under control by taking matched samples, that is to say, in the comparison of any two cells each company included in one cell is matched in the other cell by a company of the same size that operates in a comparable market structure. . . .

There are two comparisons that are of interest, the first being the comparison of profitability of all owner-controlled firms with all management-controlled firms. Using information given in Table [14] this involves comparing the values of 12.09 with 10.03. Using the

Table 13
Average Profitability Across Firms Using Two-Way Classification

	Strong OC	Weak OC	MC	All OC	All OC and MC
Companies with $VR_i < \hat{VR_i}$ in 1965–69*	12.44	8.88	7.72	10.22	8.59
	(17)	(28)	(84)	(45)	(129)
Other companies	13.11	13.32	11.41	13.24	12.03
	(28)	(45)	(141)	(73)	(214)
Total	12.86	11.62	10.03	12.09	10.74
	(45)	(73)	(225)	(118)	(343)

Figures in parentheses are numbers in relevant cells.
*[VR means valuation ratio, and this expression refers to companies with persistent below-average valuation ratios — Eds.]
Source: Holl, Table III.

Table 14
Average Profitability Across Firms Using Matched Samples

	Sample	OC	MC	MC*	t
All companies	1	12.09	10.03		2.45[a]
		(118)	(225)		
Matched by size	2	11.93	10.06		1.93[a]
		(113)	(113)		
Matched by size and	3	10.98	9.89		0.95
structure		(81)	(31)		
All companies	4	12.09		7.72	4.86[b]
		(118)		(84)	
Matched by size	5	11.38		7.78	2.95[b]
		(64)		(64)	
Matched by size and	6	11.26		6.73	3.10[b]
structure		(40)		(40)	

Figures in parentheses are numbers in samples for relevant cells.
[a]Significant difference in average values, 95% limit, one tail test.
[b]Significant difference in average values, 99% limit, one tail test.
Source: Holl, Table IV.

standard t test for testing for differences in means we obtain a t value of 2.45; the null hypothesis of no difference between mean values is rejected using 95% confidence limits for a one tail test. When companies are matched by size the respective profit figures are 11.93 and 10.06 with 113 observations for each group. The t statistic when firms are matched by size is 1.93 which again leads to rejection of the null hypothesis of no difference between mean values. When companies are matched by size and market structure the profit figures become 10.98 (OC) and 9.89 (MC) with 81 firms in each group. Here we find that the profit figures matched by size are biased upwards in each case (though more so for OC than for MC firms) and that the new t statistic of 0.95 reverses the previous conclusions, that is, when the bias resulting from differing size structures and market structures is removed the resulting difference in profitability is not significantly different from zero. This is consistent with the results of a number of previous studies.

The central comparison of interest involves OC firms and those MC firms able to evade the discipline of the market for corporate control, the latter group being designated MC*. For each pair of mean values for OC and MC* firms the observed difference is highly significant. Removing the effect of bias resulting from corporate size, that is moving from sample 4 to sample 5, lowers profits of the OC companies while marginally increased those of MC*. Moving from sample 5 to 6 and removing the effect of differing market structures lowers further the profits of both MC* firms and OC firms. The resulting differential is 4.53 percentage points and the associated t ratio of 3.10 suggests that the probability of this difference not being significant is extremely small. Clearly imperfections in the market for corporate control allow some MC firms to report profit figures markedly below those reported by OC firms in general.

Efficient Capital Market Theory, the Market for Corporate Control, and the Regulation of Cash Tender Offers*

Daniel R. Fischel

The market for corporate control and the threat of cash tender offers in particular are of great importance in creating incentives for management to maximize the welfare of shareholders. Theoretically, shareholders may oust poor management on their own initiative, but the costs to individual shareholders of monitoring management performance and campaigning for its defeat in shareholder elections when performance is poor are prohibitive. On the other hand, inefficient performance by management is reflected in share price thus making the corporation a likely candidate for a takeover bid. Since a successful takeover bid often results in the displacement of current management, managers have a strong incentive to operate efficiently and keep share prices high.

Section 13(d) of the Williams Act provides that any person who obtains more than a five percent beneficial interest in a company must file with the SEC. Under rule 14D-1, any person seeking to make a tender offer that will result in his becoming the owner of more than five percent of a class of equity securities must file a schedule 14D-1 statement with the SEC. Rule 14D-1 also requires that an offeror make extensive disclosures to the target company's shareholders. The information to be disclosed includes the name and background of the offeror (including any criminal convictions within the past five years), the highs and lows at which the target company's security has been traded in each quarter during the past two years, the offeror's source of funds, the offeror's financial condition, and any contracts or negotiations within the past three years between the target and the offeror concerning a merger or takeover. The offeror must also disclose the purpose of the tender offer includ-

*Source: 57 Tex. L. Rev. 1-46 (1978), reprinted with permission. Daniel R. Fischel is assistant professor of law at Northwestern University.

ing any plan for a future merger, reorganization, liquidation, transfer of any material amount of the target's assets, or any intended
change in the existing board of directors or management. Moreover,
section 14(e), the general antifraud provision of the Act, has been
interpreted to require disclosure of material information known to
the offeror while the offer remains outstanding, even if such information was not otherwise required. Some commentators have
argued that such diverse items as financial statements of the offeror
and the basis for setting the tender offer price are material and
should be disclosed to investors. . . . One of the leading supporters
of the Williams Act has argued in a famous article that disclosures
by the offeror are necessary "if public investors are to stand on an
equal footing with the acquiring person in assessing the future of
the company and the value of its shares." The legislative history of
the Act also reflects this concern.

The argument has a surface plausibility. Shareholders faced
with a tender offer must decide whether to tender their shares. If
they decide to sell, they will no longer have any interest in the
company, and therefore information concerning the background and
future plans of the offeror is irrelevant to them. While shareholders
who follow this course receive a premium above market, they relin-
quish the right to participate in growth of the company under new
management if the tender offer is successful. Some shareholders,
perhaps those who believe that the offeror would not pay a premium for control unless it thought it could turn the target around,
may prefer not to tender their shares in order to retain an equity
participation after the takeover. Of course, this strategy requires that
not too many shareholders follow it because the success of the
tender offer depends on a sufficient number of shares being
tendered. The risk that the tender offer will fail if not enough shares
are tendered imposes a cost on the shareholder who refuses to
tender in hopes of participating in the company under new management. If the tender offer is defeated, shareholders who refused to
sell lose the premium they could have received had they tendered.
Thus, shareholders must balance the cost of not tendering—the lost
premium of the tender offer price above market—against expected
gains under new management. While shareholders can readily ascertain the cost of not tendering by simply multiplying the premium
by the number of shares they own, the expected gains under new
management are speculative. The rational shareholder in making a
decision whether to tender may well desire such information as the
basis for setting the offer price and any future plans of the offeror.
Nevertheless, it is doubtful that the offeror should be required to
provide this information. . . .

For the market for corporate control to function effectively, outsiders must have adequate incentives to produce information. Outsiders are not generally privy to inside information about a potential target. A decision to tender only occurs after an offeror determines that the target will be more profitable in its control and that a tender offer is likely to succeed. These decisions involve research costs. The incentive to produce this information is the expected gain from the appreciation of the offeror's equity investment after obtaining control. Any legal constraint that limits the ability of owners of privately produced information to realize its exchange value will discourage devoting resources to produce new information. In other words, a failure to recognize a property right in privately produced information will decrease the incentives to produce this information.

Recognition of a property right in information — a right or entitlement to invoke the coercive machinery of the state to exclude others from its use — is not unusual in the American legal system. The granting of a patent is a familiar example of a legally enforceable property right. Another way in which the legal system can grant a property right in information is by allowing a party who possesses valuable information to enter into and enforce contracts without having to disclose the information to the other party. Imposing a duty of disclosure is tantamount to requiring that the benefit of the information be publicly shared. This requirement of disclosure is antithetical to the basic notion of a property right, which by definition entails the legal protection of private appropriation for private benefit.

The disclosure requirements of the Williams Act — justified by a goal of ensuring parity of information between the offeror and shareholders — dilute the value of the property right in privately produced information. Provisions like the filing requirements and requirements of disclosure of identity and source of funds increase the cost of a tender offer and thereby diminish takeover incentives. Other provisions such as the requirement of disclosure of intentions have a more serious impact. This requirement is perhaps the most objectionable feature of the Williams Act. The securities laws generally impose no corresponding requirement on incumbent management. If management and another party agree to a merger, for example, there is no duty to disclose until the agreement is closed. It is highly unlikely that an outsider will know with any certainty what his future plans are. The premature and tentative nature of any outsider's plans create a great uncertainty over when such disclosure is required. This uncertainty has resulted in considerable litigation. Indeed, a favored defensive tactic of management to frustrate a tender offer is to charge that an offeror has violated the Williams Act by not disclosing its intentions. The cost of uncertainty is a deterrent to tender offers. More fundamentally, disclosure of intentions forces an offeror to share information that he has used resources to produce, without receiving any compensation in return. In other securities transactions, inequalities of bargaining power attributable to superior intelligence, research, or diligence are not only permitted but are considered to be integral to a free market economy. The law does not require a purchaser of stock in an exchange or over-the-counter market to inform a seller why he believes the value of stock is or will be greater than the purchase price despite the fact this information would be extremely useful to the seller. Yet a tender offeror who believes that a company would be more profitable if managed in a different way, merged, or even liquidated must, under the Williams Act, disclose his intentions. There is no sound reason why investors should stand on an "equal footing" in the latter situation but not the former. A proponent may defend the duty of disclosure for insiders on the grounds that insiders are likely to acquire information, not by superior efforts, but by virtue of their superior access. Thus, a rule requiring insiders to disclose does not significantly deter the production of new information. But this justification is inapplicable to the typical tender offeror, and the Williams Act, by imposing on outsiders a quasi-fiduciary duty of disclosure instead of recognizing a property right in privately produced information, greatly reduces the incentive to undertake a takeover attempt. . . .

Takeover Bids, the Free Rider Problem, and the Theory of the Corporation*

Sanford J. Grossman and Oliver D. Hart

In all but the smallest groups social choice takes place via the delegation of power from many to few. A fundamental problem with this delegation is that no individual has a large enough incentive to devote resources to ensure that the representatives are acting in the interest of the represented. Since the representatives serve the public good, the social benefit to monitoring their activities is far larger than the private benefit to any individual. That is, the Public Good is a public good and each person attempts to be a free rider in its production.

*Source: 11 Bell J. Econ. 42–64 (1980), reprinted with permission. Sanford J. Grossman is professor of economics and finance, Wharton School, University of Pennsylvania, and Oliver H. Hart is lecturer in economics and fellow of Churchill College, Cambridge University.

It is often suggested that in a corporation the free rider problem can be avoided by use of the takeover bid mechanism. Suppose that the current directors of the corporation are not acting in the shareholders' interest, but that each shareholder is too small for it to be his interest to devote resources to overthrowing management. It is thought that this situation will not persist because an entrepreneur can make a takeover bid; i.e., he can buy the company at a low price, manage it well, and then sell it back at a high price. We show that this argument is false. Any profit a raider can make from the price appreciation of shares he purchases represents a profit shareholders could have made if they had not tendered their shares to the raider. In particular, suppose each shareholder is so small that his tender decision will not affect the outcome of the raid. Then, if a shareholder thinks that the raid will succeed and that the raider will improve the firm, he will not tender his shares, but will instead hold on to them, anticipating a profit out of their price appreciation. As a result a takeover bid may not be profitable even though current management is not acting in the interest of shareholders. Hence, even in a corporation, the public good (of the shareholders) is a public good.

There is a real resource cost in operating the takeover mechanism. A raid should take place if the social benefit is larger than the social cost. The raider bears the full social cost, but because shareholders attempt to free ride by not tendering their shares, he may be able to get only a small part of the social benefit. As a result there may be many raids which should take place, but which do not because it is not profitable for a raider to carry them out.

There is a way for shareholders to overcome this free rider problem. Specifically, they can write a constitution for the firm which permits the raider to exclude minority shareholders (i.e., shareholders who do not tender their shares to the raider and who hold shares in the post-raid company) from sharing in all the improvements in the firm brought about by the raider. One method for doing this is for the shareholders to permit a successful raider to sell off the firm's assets or output to another company owned by the raider at terms which are disadvantageous to minority shareholders. This enables the raider to get compensation from the raid which is above and beyond his share of the company's profits. This compensation is at the expense of other shareholders and represents a voluntary dilution of their property rights. . . .

On the Theory of Conglomerate Mergers*

James H. Scott, Jr.

Mergers can be exciting, however their effects on stockholders remain unclear. Mandelker found that the average firm that acquired another firm in the 1940's and 1950's did not benefit its stockholders. Given bleak findings such as this, it is not surprising to find theoretical controversy over what constitutes a good merger.

From a theoretical standpoint, a number of benefits are obvious, though they may be difficult to estimate in practice. For example, the profitability of a merger is enhanced by positive synergistic effects, i.e., real gains due to the effective integration of productive facilities, distribution networks, etc. Tax loss carry-forwards can also be a source of merger benefits. Another benefit is possible if, in an inefficient market, one large firm has better access to external sources of funds than do two smaller firms.

However, if these and other real factors are swept aside, and if the securities markets are efficient, are there any purely financial benefits to merging? The answers to this question constitute the theory of conglomerate mergers and are the subject of this paper.

The first major result of this theory concerns diversification per se. Is it worthwhile to merge two firms with dissimilar earnings streams to get a smoother path of earnings over time? If both firms are traded in a single, efficient capital market and if bankruptcy is not possible, Alberts, Myers, Levy and Sarnat, Adler and Dumas, and others have argued persuasively that investors can obtain the same diversification themselves by purchasing appropriate amounts of unmerged firms. Thus a conglomerate merger will not alter the total value of the combining firms. If no premium is paid to the shareholders of the acquired firm then the stock prices of both firms will remain unchanged. If there is a premium, the stockholders of the acquired firm gain what those of the acquiring firm lose.

Assuming that corporate bankruptcy is possible, Levy and Sarnat, and Lewellen have argued that if a merger reduces the probability that one of the firms would default on its debt, then the value of the debt will increase and the merger will be beneficial. However, Higgins conjectured that if bankruptcy is costless then any increase in the value of the firms' debt will be exactly offset by a decrease in the value of the equity. Higgins' conjecture has been proven rigorously by Rubinstein, Higgins and Schall, and Galai and Masulis.

On the other hand assuming bankruptcy is costly, Rubinstein

*Source: 32 J. Fin. 1235-1250 (1977), reprinted with permission. James H. Scott, Jr., is an associate professor at the Graduate School of Business, Columbia University.

suggested that conglomerate mergers which reduce the probability of bankruptcy may be capable of benefiting both stockholders and bondholders. Higgins and Schall considered the issue explicitly and argued that the effects of bankruptcy costs are ambiguous.

This paper deals with five unexplored or unresolved issues. First, what objective function should one consider when analyzing conglomerate mergers? For example, should an optimizing firm seek to maximize the value of its equity, or the total value of all of its outstanding securities? . . .

Second, the paper examines the effect on mergers of a class of corporate liabilities neglected by other studies. These are noncontractual obligations and include such things as damages awarded in law suits and sales taxes. Third, more can be said about the impact of bankrupty costs on the profitability of mergers, especially when the cash flow of the merging firms are similar.

Fourth, under the assumption that bankruptcy is possible, Higgins and Schall have argued that the corporate income tax will have no effect on the profitability of conglomerate merger. The analysis presented below argues to the contrary that the corporate income tax provides a slight encouragement to merger. Finally, Lewellen has argued that conglomerate mergers are profitable because the debt capacity of the merged firm exceeds the sum of the debt capacities of the unmerged firms. Although Lewellen's assertion may be true in many cases, this paper uses the state preference approach to optimal capital structure suggested by Kraus and Litzenberger to show that it is not true in general. . . .

[A] conglomerate merger of all equity firms can never be profitable. Intuitively, this type of merger is unprofitable because the limited liability protection of a merged firm is weaker than that of two unmerged firms. In general the merged firm goes bankrupt less frequently than do the unmerged firms. In future states where the merged firm remains solvent while one of the unmerged firms would have gone bankrupt, cash flows from the solvent firm are used to pay the noncontractual creditors of the otherwise bankrupt firm. Had there been no merger the firm would have gone bankrupt, and the firm's noncontractual creditors would not have been paid, or at least would not have been paid in full. A merger simply transfers wealth from stockholders to noncontractual creditors. Under these circumstances, a firm seeking to maximize stockholder wealth will engage in conglomerate divestitures. . . .

. . . When the firm has both debt and equity outstanding, the problem is more complex. Within the neoclassical framework two possible, and possibly conflicting, objectives are usually discussed: the maximization of the market value of currently outstanding equity and the maximization of the market value of all of the firm's currently outstanding securities.

These objectives can conflict with each other because some policies which maximize equity value do not maximize total value and vice versa. It is well known that these conflicts can arise with respect to decisions involving investment and capital structure policy as well as merger policy. With respect to mergers, a conglomerate merger that leaves total market value unchanged can decrease the market value of equity. Thus stockholders might oppose a merger which all the firm's security holders, taken as a group, would find a matter of indifference.

In order to simplify the discussion, assume that firms only issue debt and equity and that a firm's . . . decisions change only the market values of that firm's securities. [The second] assumption rules out conflicts that occur when an investor owns equity in each of two firms, and a decision by one firm affects the value of the other.

Many theorists assume that firms maximize total market value, because all of the firm's security holders, taken as a group, are better off if that criterion is followed. . . . Unfortunately, the problem is complicated because stockholders may decide to maximize the market value of equity. Since they have the legal power to make the firm's decisions, there is the possibility that stockholders may find it in their own best interest to follow a policy which is suboptimal from the point of view of all of the firm's security holders.

Fama and Miller propose one possible solution to this dilemma. A stockholder controlled firm will maximize total value (1) if stockholders and bondholders are free to make side payments to each other, and (2) if both parties negotiate with each other on a rational basis. In this case, bondholders will find it both possible and profitable to bribe stockholders to insure the maximization of total value.

A second possible solution to the dilemma follows from the fact that a stockholder controlled firm will maximize total value if the firm's stockholders happen to hold a sufficient amount of its debt. . . . Unfortunately a firm's stockholders are also its bondholders only in unusual circumstances, and while Fama-Miller type renegotiation clauses commonly exist in debt contracts, side payments are relatively rare because negotiations between stockholders and bondholders can be expensive. Thus one should expect to find additional mechanisms which mediate the potential conflict between stockholders and bondholders, i.e. additional mechanisms that induce stockholder controlled firms to maximize total value.

As Haley and Schall point out, the maximization of shareholder wealth will always maximize total value as long as the market value of the firm's outstanding debt cannot be altered by management decisions. Thus equity maximization and total value maximization can be made consistent if some way can be found to insulate the market value of debt from changes in firm policies. The inclusion of two covenants in the debt contract is sufficient to obtain this result.

First, the debt must be "perfectly protected" in the sense that the protective covenants attached to it must effectively prohibit management from making any operating, financial, or investment decisions which would decrease the market value of the debt *unless* bondholders are exactly compensated for their losses. Given such a covenant, stockholders would not benefit from a merger which increased equity value solely because it made debt riskier, because they would have to compensate bondholders by exactly the amount of the increase in equity.[6]

Second, as has been suggested by Higgins and Schall, the debt contract must allow the firm to repurchase or call all of its outstanding debt by paying a price equal to the market price of the debt an instant before the call is announced. This type of perfect callability insures that stockholders will not avoid projects which increase total firm value but would, in the absence of perfect callability, decrease equity value.[7]

These two covenants effectively insulate bond values from changes in management policies (but not from changes in exogenous factors such as general interest rates), and thus change the incentive structure faced by stockholders. If these covenants are included in all of the firm's debt then rational stockholders will seek

6. In practice it is difficult to write protective covenants which are comprehensive, and the perfect protection described above is seldom obtainable. However the various restrictions on working capital, dividend policy, security agreements, debt policy, seniority arrangements, and permissible investments can be viewed as an attempt to approximate this degree of protection. Although the above discussion implicitly assumes that the costs of creating and enforcing protective covenants are negligible, the more costly covenants are, the more likely the debt is to be imperfectly protected. In practice many of these costs are reduced by the inclusion of protective covenants in the legal system. Recent examples of laws which give creditors legal rights simply because they are creditors include the Uniform Commercial Code and the Uniform Fraudulent Conveyance Act.

7. One might suppose that even without perfect callability a firm can simply repurchase debt as its premerger or predecision market value. In general this will not be the case. For example if a firm has to raise external capital to repurchase its debt, it may have to announce what it plans to do with the capital to be raised. The announcement of an impending repurchase (or even an unannounced attempt to repurchase) may be taken by the market as a signal that the debt is worth more than its current price. Thus its price would rise before a repurchase could be completed. Other examples involving heterogeneous expectations or capital gains taxes can also be constructed. Note that the aspect of callability discussed here is in addition to its more frequently discussed function as a hedge against shifts in the rate of interest. Kraus has persuasively argued that in an efficient market this more familiar aspect of callability is a zero sum game.

policies that maximize total firm value. Furthermore, investors in a perfect capital market will value such a firm more highly than an identical firm which follows an objective inconsistent with total firm maximization. As a result since the total value of the firm is higher with covenants and since it is stockholders who ultimately receive any proceeds raised from a sale of debt, it is in stockholders' best interest to include these covenants in the debt they issue.

This rationale for the existence of protective covenants differs from that of Fama and Miller and of Haley and Schall, who argue that bondholders demand covenants to protect themselves. On the contrary, given an efficient market, bondholders simply determine the price they are willing to pay for the bonds. The inclusion or omission of covenants in a particular firm's debt contract may change the price of the debt, but that price will fairly reflect the market's expectations and preferences for risk and rate of return. Covenants do not exist because investors demand them, but because it is in stockholders' interest to design debt contracts that create [an] optimal incentive structure vis a vis the firm's security holders.

Finally, note that the value of claims to noncontractual creditors is not included in the total value of the firm's outstanding securities, and thus does not appear in the firm's objective function. The present value of these claims (e.g. sales taxes) is omitted because (1) as long as the firm does not default, these creditors have no ownership rights, and (2) unlike debt, these claims are not or cannot be protected from stockholder actions which decrease their value.

In summary, it is in stockholder's interest to issue debt which can be renegotiated, or if renegotiation is costly to issue perfectly callable, perfectly protected debt. Given that, the maximization of the total value of a firm's outstanding securities is a necessary condition for shareholder wealth maximization. Thus the following sections will investigate the effects of conglomerate mergers on the total value of the firm's outstanding securities.

According to the argument in the previous section, a merger will be profitable if the total value of the merged firm exceeds the total value of the two unmerged firms. [A] conglomerate merger does not change cash flows in future states where both A and B would have remained solvent. Thus if bankruptcy is impossible, a conglomerate merger will not change total firm values. This familiar result indicates that in a complete market conglomerate mergers are profitable or unprofitable because of their effects on the present value of cash flows upon bankruptcy.

There are three separate ways that the possibility of bankruptcy affects merger profitability. The first effect flows from the provisions of the corporate income tax and is distinct from the well known encouragement given mergers by tax loss carry forwards. Carry forwards are not modeled in this paper, however the tax deductibility of debt payments is, and this deductability also encourages mergers. . . .

Intuitively, a merger reduces future tax payments if there are future states where one of the merging firms would have gone bankrupt while the other would have remained solvent. In these states a merger makes the losses of the bankrupt firm available to lower the taxes that would have been paid by the solvent one.

In contrast to this result, Higgins and Schall have contended that the tax structure has no effect on the profitability of mergers. To reach their conclusion Higgins and Schall assume that (1) interest payments are tax deductible, (2) though a firm may default on a principal payment, its earnings never fall so low that it defaults on an interest payment, (3) taxes are strictly proportional and upon bankruptcy either the government is willing to pay a tax rebate to the bankrupt estate, or the bankrupt firm is able to sell its tax loss to someone else, and (4) there are no noncontractual creditors . . .

This set of assumptions is sufficient to guarantee that the amount of taxes paid by the merged firm in any future state will equal the taxes that would have been paid by the unmerged firms. By contrast this paper recognizes that it is possible for a firm to default on tax deductible debt payments.

The second effect of bankruptcy results from the noncontractual obligations and can either decrease or increase the profitability of a conglomerate merger. . . . Other things equal, a merger tends to be unprofitable to the extent that there are future states in which the merged firm remains solvent while one of the unmerged firms would have gone bankrupt. In states such as these, security holders receive less because part of the cash flow of the otherwise solvent (unmerged) firm is used to pay the noncontractual creditors of the otherwise bankrupt (unmerged) firm. Conversely security holders are better off to the extent that there are future states where the merged firm goes bankrupt while of the unmerged firms would have remained solvent. In such states, payments which would have been made by the solvent (unmerged) firm to noncontractual creditors are diverted to pay the bondholders of the otherwise bankrupt (unmerged) firm.

The costs of bankruptcy constitute the third and perhaps most important factor affecting the profitability of conglomerate mergers. [A] merger tends to be profitable to the extent that there are future states where, by means of a merger, one firm is able to save another from bankruptcy and its costs. On the other hand . . . a merger is unprofitable to the extent that there are future states in which because of the merger one firm pulls an otherwise solvent firm into bankruptcy and its costs. Roughly speaking this implies that a merger between a larger stable firm and a small, profitable, but unstable firm may tend to reduce the present value of future bankruptcy costs and thus increase value. Conversely, a merger between a small stable firm and a large volatile one may reduce value by increasing present value of future bankruptcy costs.

Corporate strategists often argue that there are positive benefits to diversification, so that, other things equal, firms should avoid merging when the earnings streams of the two companies are highly correlated. However, most mergers involve firms in the same industry, where high correlations can be expected. Although most of these mergers are based on expectations of positive synergy, it is interesting to note that these mergers can provide financial benefits as well.

For example, assume a merger of two firms whose cash flows are positively related in the sense that if they were unmerged, they would have gone bankrupt in the same future states and remained solvent in the same future states. . . .

This type of merger is profitable because of the economies of scale in bankruptcy costs. Quite simply, it is cheaper for one big firm to go bankrupt than for two little ones to do so.

Interfirm Tender Offers and the Market for Corporate Control*

Michael Bradley

It is commonly believed that the interfirm cash tender offer is an attempt by the bidding firm to purchase the target shares and profit from their subsequent market appreciation. This belief is inconsistent with the available evidence. While acquiring firms earn a positive return from the tender offer, they do not realize a capital gain from the target shares that they purchase.

In the 161 successful offers in this study, bidding firms paid target shareholders an average premium of 49% for the shares they purchased. This premium is calculated relative to the closing price of a target share two months prior to the announcement of the offer. The average appreciation of the target shares through one month subsequent to the execution of the offer was 36%, relative to this

*Source: Forthcoming in J. Bus. (1980), with permission. Michael Bradley is assistant professor at the University of Rochester's Graduate School of Management.

same benchmark. In sum, target stockholders realized a 49% capital gain on the shares purchased by acquiring firms and a 36% capital gain on the shares they retained. Thus, bidding firms suffered a 13% loss on the target shares they purchased. However these same acquiring firms realized an average 9% increase in the market value of their own shares as a result of the offer.

The paradoxical result that acquiring firms profit from the successful completion of an interfirm tender offer, yet suffer a capital loss on the target shares that they purchase, can be reconciled by considering an alternative model of tender offers. This theory views the acquisition of the target shares as a means of securing control of the target firm. The target shares are demanded by the bidding firm only insofar as they confer control. The (post-execution) premium paid tendering stockholders is viewed as payment for the right to control the assets of the target firm.

The model developed and tested in this paper assumes that the tender offer is an attempt by the bidding firm to secure control of the target shares and implement an operating strategy that will increase the value of both firms. These gains are assumed to stem from a synergy created by consolidating the two firms. The increase in the equity values of the acquiring and target firms — in the wake of a successful offer — is compelling evidence for a synergy theory of tender offers. In the successful offers of this study, the equity value of the average acquiring firm increased by $7.7 million, in spite of the average offer premium of $7.7 million paid to tendering stockholders. This capital gain is calculated over the period two months before the offer through two months thereafter. The value of the outstanding shares of successful target firms increased an average of $31 million over the same period. Thus these data indicate that consolidating the control of the two firms via an interfirm tender offer is a wealth-increasing investment for the stockholders of both firms.

The theory of tender offers that is advanced in this paper recognizes the existence of rivalrous firms that compete for the right to control the target resources. It is assumed that the information produced as a result of an interfirm tender offer enables other firms — including the managers of the target firm — to make a value-increasing change in the operations of the target firm. In other words, it is assumed that at least a portion of the return to preparing and effecting a tender offer becomes appropriable with the formal offer announcement. Thus, the announcement of a tender offer is presumed to alert other firms to the general intent of the bidding firm and initiate a competitive (auction-type) process for the target shares.

Target stockholders are assumed to be a diffuse group of homogeneous, wealth-maximizing price takers. It follows that the target shares will flow to that firm (management team) that makes the best offer in terms of the price offered for the sought-after or controlling shares, and the expected post-execution value of the target shares that are not demanded.

Viewing the tender offer in terms of the model sketched above yields several implications that are at once consistent with the available data and contrary to some popular notions concerning the nature of interfirm tender offers. The first is that successful bidding firms will be forced to pay a premium — relative to the pre-announcement as well as the post-execution market price — for the target shares that they purchase. Under the assumptions of the analysis, acquiring firms cannot consistently earn abnormal returns through the market appreciation of the target shares. The data of this study indicate that they do not; on average they suffer a 13% capital loss on the target shares that they purchase. This is not to say that acquiring firms will not profit from the tender offer. On the contrary, the underlying synergy is presumed to have a value-increasing effect on the shares of both firms.

A second implication of the theory advanced in this paper is that acquiring firms cannot profit from purchasing a simple majority of the target shares and "raiding" the assets of the target firm. Such offers will be anticipated by the target shareholders and competing bidding firms. Competitive alternatives will preclude such bids from being successfully executed. The fact that the post-execution market price of the target shares is 36% higher than the pre-announcement level indicates that corporate "raiding" is not an important explanation for interfirm tender offers. A corporate raiding strategy would result in a post-execution fall in the market price of the target shares. The data reveal no such price decrease.

Finally, the theory of this paper provides an explanation for the empirical fact that not all tender offers are accepted by the target stockholders. Of the 258 offers in this study, 97 were rejected by the stockholders of the target firm. According to the theory of this paper, an unsuccessful tender offer can be explained as a rational response to the alternatives that arise in a competitive market for corporate control. Clearly, bidding firms will not make an offer if they do not expect to be successful. However, once the offer is announced and new information regarding the value of the target resources is revealed (produced), the ultimate allocation of these resources is uncertain. Competing bidding firms or the target managers themselves may be able to exploit this new information and effect the optimal (highest-valued) allocation of the target resources.

Target stockholders will reject those offers that become dominated by a higher bid or a higher-valued production/investment plan proposed by the target managers. If this explanation for the occurrence of unsuccessful tender offers is correct, then on average, the value of a target share after the expiration of the offer will be greater than the rejected offer price. The data show that this is in fact the case.

In a sample of 97 unsuccessful tender offers, target stockholders realized an average capital gain of 45%. This average post-offer return exceeds the average premium of these rejected offers which is 29%. The data support the contention that refusing a given tender offer may be a value-maximizing investment for the target stockholders — even though the rejected offer price is significantly greater than the pre-offer market price of a target share.

This finding lends support to an implication of the theory that target managers may be acting in their stockholders' interests by opposing an outstanding offer. Target managers may have information that would induce a higher bid or a higher valuation of the target resources if disclosed. Lodging a formal opposition to an outstanding offer would be an effective means of communicating this type of information.

The distinction between target managers opposing an outstanding offer and preventing a bidding firm from even making an offer should be appreciated. While the theory admits that the former can increase the welfare of target stockholders, the theory assumes that the latter cannot. Opposing an outstanding offer is viewed as a means of communicating information to the target stockholders and other market participants. However, precluding an offer by, say, using the powers of the state, can only be viewed as a way of limiting the alterntives facing target stockholders. According to the theory, this cannot increase their welfare. . . .

NOTES AND QUESTIONS

1. The findings of Mandelker's study are confirmed, and clarified, by an analysis by Peter Dodd of Rochester of all proposals made to acquire NYSE-listed firms during the seven-year period 1971–77. The 151 merger proposals during this time period resulted in 71 acquisitions and 80 offers that terminated unsuccessfully; both groups were studied. In Merger Proposals, Management Discretion and Stockholder Wealth (forthcoming in 8 J. Fin. Econ. (1980), printed here with permission), Dodd summarizes his conclusions as follows:

State corporate codes require that the incumbent board of directors approve any merger proposal before putting it to a stockholder vote. Since these codes give the management of a target firm veto power over all merger proposals, management's response to specific proposals provides an opportunity to assess whether the accept/reject decision is made in the best interests of stockholders.

In this study the daily abnormal returns to stockholders of bidder and target firms in both completed and cancelled merger proposals for NYSE firms are reported. The main results are summarized in Table [15].

Stockholders of target firms earn large positive abnormal returns from the announcement of merger proposals, irrespective of the outcome of the proposal. In both completed and cancelled merger proposals, target stockholders on average, earn approximately 13% abnormal return at the time the offer is initially announced. There is significant market reaction to the revisions of uncertainty of the outcome of the proposals after the first announcement. For those merger proposals that are completed, target stockholders earn positive abnormal returns after the inital announcement of negotiations. Over the duration of the merger proposal (defined as 10 days before the first announcement, through 10 days after approval by target stockholders) these stockholders earn abnormal returns of 33.96% on average.

For merger proposals that are subsequently cancelled, stockholders of target firms earn, on average, significant negative normal returns on the date of the announcement of the termination of negotiations. Over the duration of the proposal (defined as 10 days before the first announcement through 10 days after the termination) these stockholders earn abnormal returns of 3.68%. However, when the sample of cancelled merger proposals is classified on the basis of whether or not the target firm's management terminate the negotiations, the market reaction is different. Where the merger proposal is vetoed by incumbent management, target stockholders earn, on average, 10.95% over the duration of the proposal and this represents a permanent revaluation of the target shares. In the remaining cancelled proposals it is not clear from the termination announcement that the incumbent managements have used their veto power—either bidder firm managements retract their offers or no reason for the terminations are given. Stockholders of target firms in these cases earn only 0.18% over the duration of the proposal, i.e., after an initial gain of 13.43% at the time of first announcement of the merger proposal, the stock price returns to its pre-proposal level.

For stockholders of bidder firms, in both completed and cancelled merger proposals, there is evidence of negative abnormal returns of − 7.22% and − 5.50% respectively, over the duration of the proposals.

2. What is the meaning to an economist of the term "value of physical assets"? Does the term mean book value? If not, does this suggest a problem with Holl's empirical technique?

Table 15

Summary of Percentage Abnormal Returns to Stockholders of Target and Bidder Firms in Completed and Cancelled Merger Proposals

	Completed Merger Proposals				Cancelled Merger Proposals			
	Sample Size	Average Abnormal Returns Around First Public Announcement of Merger Proposals[a]	Average Abnormal Returns Around Date of Stockholder Approval of Merger Proposals[a]	Average Cumulative Abnormal Returns From First Public Announcement through Date of Stockholders Approval of Merger Proposals[b]	Sample Size	Average Abnormal Returns Around First Public Announcement of Merger Proposals[a]	Average Abnormal Returns Around Date of Announcement of Termination of Merger Proposals[a]	Average Cumulative Abnormal Returns from First Public Announcement through Termination of Merger Proposals[b]
Target Firms								
(A) All targets	71	13.41%	0.76%	33.96%	80	12.73%	−8.68%	3.68%
(B) Target terminations					26	11.18%	−5.57%	10.95%
(C) Other than target terminations					54	13.43%	−9.75%	0.18%
Bidder Firms								
(A) All bidders	60	−1.09%	−0.29%	−7.22%	66	−1.23%	1.24%	−5.50
(B) Target Terminations					19	−0.04%	0.86%	−3.12%
(C) Other than target terminations					47	−1.70%	1.38%	−6.47%

[a] Sum of average prediction errors at day − 1 and 0.
[b] Cumulated from 10 days before first public announcement through 10 days after approval or termination.
Source: Dodd, Table 8.

3. Empirical evidence to support Fischel's analysis of the costs of the Williams Act is found in a recent study by Robert Smiley:

The most striking finding in this study is that the Williams Amendment has had a substantial impact on costs in tender offers, increasing them by between 13 percent and 27 percent. Whether or not this was the desired effect of this piece of legislation is unclear (it probably was for some interest groups involved in lobbying in favor of the amendment). But this impact should be considered the next time a legislative body begins consideration of a market mechanism which could (if left alone or encouraged) be instrumental in providing market imposed discipline on managers of U.S. firms.

Smiley, The Effect of the Williams Amendment and Other Factors on Transaction Costs in Tender Offers, 3 Industrial Organization Rev. 138, 145 (1975). On the adverse effect of the Williams Act on the small investor in the acquired firm see Comment: Economic Realities of Cash Tender Offers, 20 Maine L. Rev. 237 (1968).

4. Reanalyze the "squeeze-out" question discussed at Note 6 in the Notes and Questions for Chapter 4, in light of Grossman and Hart's analysis. How seriously do they undermine the concept of the market for·corporate control?

5. Paul Asquith of the Harvard Business School, in an unpublished paper, has summarized the economic studies of the market for corporate control as follows:

"The empirical literature on mergers covers the period from 1962 to 1979 and uses several different methodologies. The samples analyzed sometimes overlap, as do the questions studied, but not systematically or completely. The results confirm each other on several points.

"The dominant result is that the acquired firm's stockholders receive large premiums at the time of the merger. Hayes and Taussig[24] found a 16 percent premium for tender offers; Dodd and Ruback[25] found a similar 19 percent or 20 percent premium depending on whether the offer was unsuccessful or successful; and Bradley[26] mentions an average 40 percent premium for tender offers. The results from Lorie and Halpern[27] indicate that acquired firms' stockholders gain from a merger, as do Gort and Hogarty[28] and

24. Hayes and Taussig, Tactics of Cash Takeover Bids, 45 Harv. Bus. Rev. 135 (1967).
25. Dodd and Ruback, Tender Offers and Stockholder Returns: An Empirical Analysis, 5 J. Fin. Econ. 351 (1977).
26. M. Bradley, A Theory of Tender Offers (University of Chicago mimeograph).
27. Lorie and Halpern, Conglomerate Mergers: The Rhetoric and the Evidence, 13 J.L. & Econ. 149 (1970).
28. Gort and Hogarty, New Evidence on Mergers, 13 J.L. & Econ. 167 (1970).

Haugen and Undell.[29] More recently Mandelker,[30] Langetieg,[31] and Asquith[32] all found gains that accrue to acquired firms' shareholders ranging from 14 percent to 20 percent at the time of merger.

"Whether the acquiring firm's stockholders gain at the time of merger is somewhat less clear. Halpern[33] indicates that the gains from merger were evenly split between large and small firms, but this is the only study to indicate such results. Mandelker[34] and Langetieg[35] found no significant gain or loss accruing to the acquiring firm at the time of merger. Dodd and Ruback[36] and Bradley[37] found a small gain of approximately 2.5 percent at the time of merger to successful bidding firms in a tender offer. Asquith[38] found that the acquiring firm had a gain of 1.36 percent in the month the merger was announced but no gain or loss at the time of merger. The results seem to indicate, in sum, that the acquiring firm's stockholders receive a small gain (if any) from the merger, particularly when compared with the very large premium accruing to the acquired firm's stockholders.

"The period prior to the merger has been studied several times. Hale and Hale[39] found that 34.8 percent of the acquiring firms in the sample felt they could manage the acquired firm better than it was being managed. Hayes and Taussig[40] found that ⅔ of the target firms in tender offers had a high average surplus liquidity. Hindley[41] concluded that acquired firms were not efficiently managed. Finally, Asquith[42] found that acquired-firm stockholders suffer larger abnormal losses prior to the merger announcement. Three studies question whether acquiring firms were doing well before the merger. All three — Dodd and Ruback,[43] Asquith,[44] and Langetieg[45] — find that

29. Haugen and Udell, Rates of Return to Stockholders of Acquired Companies, J. Fin. & Quantitative Analysis (Jan. 1972).

30. Mandelker, Risk and Return: The Case of Merging Firms, J. Fin. Econ. 303 (1974).

31. T. Langetieg, An Application of 3-Factor Performance Index to Measure Stockholder Gains from Merger (University of Southern California mimeograph).

32. P. Asquith, Mergers and the Market for Acquisitions (University of Chicago mimeograph).

33. P. Halpern, Empirical Estimates of the Expected Economic Gains from Mergers (1971, Ph.D. dissertation).

34. See note 30 supra.

35. See note 31 supra.

36. See note 25 supra.

37. See note 26 supra.

38. See note 32 supra.

39. Hale and Hale, More on Mergers, 5 J.L. & Econ. 119 (1962).

40. See note 24 supra.

41. Hindley, Separation of Ownership and Control in the Modern Corporation, 13 J.L. & Econ. 185 (1970).

42. See note 32 supra.

43. See note 25 supra.

44. See note 32 supra.

45. See note 31 supra.

the acquiring firm's stockholders do well prior to tender offers, merger announcements, and mergers, respectively.

"The greatest dispersion of study results occurs for the consolidated firm after the merger. Whether the merger creates a firm which is able to reap abnormal gains is an important question. The major conflict in the results, however, is not whether there are gains but whether the consolidated firm suffers losses or not. Weston and Mansinghka[46] found that acquiring conglomerates were relatively more profitable in 1968 than in 1958. Lev and Mandelker[47] showed that acquiring firms were more profitable for the five-year period before merger, but the results were not a clear test of the impact of the merger. Reid[48] found that firms that made many mergers did much worse on profitability indexes than firms which did not engage in mergers. Hogarty[49] concludes, from mixed results, that acquiring firms perform poorly on average. Mandelker[50] found that after merger the consolidated firm earns a return consistent with its risk. Langetieg,[51] using several measures, found conflicting results — sometimes the merged firm performed poorly, sometimes competitively. The study concludes that the results are ambiguous. Dodd and Ruback,[52] on tender offers, and Asquith,[53] on mergers, both found no statistically significant gains or losses for the period of up to a year after merger. In sum, the evidence here is not clear-cut, but if any gains or losses occur after merger they are certainly not large and the returns are probably competitive. One other significant finding should be noted: Goldberg[54] found that conglomerate mergers had no impact on the concentration ratios in merger industries.

"These results present a fairly consistent pattern. Acquired firms perform poorly before acquisition and gain significantly upon acquisition. Acquiring firms appear to do well before merger and probably gain a small amount at the time of merger. The performance of the consolidated firm after merger is somewhat in dispute in the studies but overall appears to perform competitively.

"These results . . . show that acquired firms typically benefit from being acquired because their performance prior to merger was

46. Weston and Mansinghka, Tests of the Efficiency Performance of Conglomerate Firms, 26 J. Fin. 919 (1971).

47. Lev and Mandelker, The Microeconomic Consequences of Corporate Mergers, 45 J. Bus. 85 (1972).

48. S. Reid, Mergers and the Economy (1968).

49. Hogarty, The Profitability of Corporate Mergers, 43 J. Bus. (1970).

50. See note 30 supra.

51. See note 31 supra.

52. See note 25 supra.

53. See note 32 supra.

54. Goldberg, Effects of Conglomerate Mergers on Competition, 16 J.L. & Econ. 137 (1973).

below average and was improved by the acquisition. This confirms that the corporate merger is indeed a device for transferring assets out of the hands of less competent managers and into the hands of more competent ones. . . ."

6. Is the existence of positive costs of bankruptcy a plausible explanation for conglomerate mergers? Even if those costs are substantial, they would have to be discounted, would they not, by the probability of bankruptcy, in order to form an estimate of the expected cost savings of the merger? Other explanations for conglomerate mergers, or more broadly for the existence of diversified firms, have been offered. Professor Oliver E. Williamson emphasizes the advantages of decentralized, versus the traditional hierarchical, mode of firm organization which diversification enables. See Oliver E. Williamson, Corporate Control and Business Behavior (1970); Markets and Hierarchies: Analysis and Antitrust Implications, Chs. 8–9 (1975).

7. What does Bradley's study suggest is the optimal strategy of corporate management wishing to maximize the shareholders' wealth if a tender offer is made for the corporation's shares?

Part III

The Position of Creditors

Chapter 8

Capital Structure

At this point our attention shifts from the position of stock-holders, and the relation of their interests to those of the management of the firm, to a consideration of the role of creditors and debt claims in the financing of the corporation. Why are funds raised in these different forms? What determines the proportion of debt and equity capital that a firm chooses to employ — is there an "optimal" mix?

A characteristic of the corporate form is that it permits the issuance of a remarkably wide and varied range of security types to obtain funds for investment in the assets of the business. There are debt claims, such as secured bonds and unsecured debentures and subordinated notes; there are equity claims, such as preferred stock series and common stock; there are hybrids, such as convertible issues of either debt or preferred stock; there are as many variants and special provisions as the needs of issuers and investors and the imagination of the draftsman can generate.

All of these securities are claims on the income stream to be produced by the assets of the business. The uncertainty of the yields of those assets defines the riskiness of the business, and both the income and the risk are allocated among the various classes of securities in accordance with their priorities and provisions. Since, for any given business, debt claims have priority over and are therefore less risky than equity claims, we would expect them to have lower rates of return.

Does that mean that, quite apart from any effect of the tax laws, debt financing is cheaper for the firm than equity financing, to such an extent that the use of leverage lowers the total cost of capital and enhances the value of the stock by enhancing the amount of residual earnings left to it? That became the prevailing view:

Theoretically it might be argued that the increased hazard from using bonds and preferred stocks would counterbalance this additional income and so prevent the common stock from being more attractive than when it had a lower return but fewer prior obligations. In practice, the extra earnings from 'trading on the equity' are often regarded by investors as more than sufficient to serve as a 'premium for risk' when the proportions of the several securities are judiciously mixed. (Guthmann and Dougall, Corporate Financial Policy 245 (3d ed. 1955).)

Thus the substitution of some debt in an all-equity firm would, in this view, increase stock value, while an excessive proportion of debt would be so risky and costly as to depress stock value. Somewhere in between there should be a particular mix or range which would minimize the total cost of capital to the firm and maximize the value of its stock, and this would constitute the optimal capital structure for the firm.

It is this view that was attacked by Franco Modigliani and Merton Miller ("M & M") in a famous paper, the first selection in this chapter, which argued that a firm's average cost of capital was completely independent of its capital structure. Their proposition was based on a number of assumptions, in particular those of no corporate income taxes and of perfect capital markets. Interest payments to debt holders are deductible by the corporation as a business expense, while the earnings paid to stockholders as dividends or retained as part of the stockholders' equity in the business are post-tax earnings. When the investor's transaction costs in effecting his own leverage and the firm's tax savings from interest deductions are taken into account, what picture emerges? William Baumol and Burton Malkiel, in The Firm's Optimal Debt-Equity Combination and the Cost of Capital, 81 Q.J. Econ. 547, 571 (1967), concluded as follows:

It has been shown that in practice there *is* an optimal capital structure for the firm, and that its existence really follows from the logic of the M and M analysis supplemented only by a few simple institutional observations. In general, the tax advantages of bond financing and the near zero transactions costs incurred in *un*doing leverage make it desirable for the firm to employ as much debt as is consistent with considerations of financial prudence.

What are the "considerations of financial prudence" that would keep a firm from being almost 100% debt-financed, given the differential treatment afforded debt and equity payments by our tax laws? These issues are addressed by Nevins D. Baxter in the next article in this chapter, on the role of bankruptcy costs.

Is the result of the M & M hypothesis, in the final analysis, to bring us back in the real world to concepts of an optimal capital structure for the firm after all? The reasoning may be different from that employed twenty years ago, but the outcome may be hard to distinguish in practice. And in fact, this subject has not been rich so far in empirical research. On the theoretical level, however, Merton Miller has returned to the fray, to assert the irrelevance of leverage to the value of the firm even in a world of corporate income taxes. The paper excerpted here was his presidential address at the 1976 annual meeting of the American Finance Association.

Apart from the issue of the location of optimum leverage, the M & M hypothesis also sheds light on the clash of interests of debt holders and equity holders. For any given firm, an increase in leverage tends to increase the riskiness of the debt and hence of the expected return required by investors in that debt. If debt is issued at one price, reflecting the required yield for an existing degree of business risk and leverage, and subsequently that leverage is increased, the value of the debt will fall and the value of the equity will rise. (Similarly, the sale of additional equity may improve the position of outstanding risky debt without an offsetting reduction in its yield — unless it is callable.) Thus, even if the total market value of the firm were unchanged, changes in leverage can benefit one ownership class at the expense of the other. To try to protect themselves against such maneuvers, debt holders can extend credit of very short maturity (e.g., trade creditors), obtain asset liens that put them in a risk position largely unaffected by subsequent debt issuance (e.g., secured creditors), or obtain contractual controls over the issuance of additional debt or reduction of equity (e.g., protective covenants in debenture indentures and loan agreements). Some of these measures are analyzed by Clifford Smith and Jerold Warner in a lengthy paper from which the opening and concluding portions are excerpted.

Are the various techniques whereby creditors undertake to protect their interests nonetheless in some way inadequate? An affirmative answer to that question is implicit in the decisions that depart from the rule of limited liability for stockholders in order to "pierce the corporate veil." The basis for those decisions is analyzed, and criticized, in the article by Richard A. Posner which concludes this chapter.

The Cost of Capital, Corporation Finance and the Theory of Investment*

Franco Modigliani and Merton H. Miller

I. The Valuation of Securities, Leverage, and the Cost of Capital

A. The Capitalization Rate for Uncertain Streams

As a starting point, consider an economy in which all physical assets are owned by corporations. For the moment, assume that these corporations can finance their assets by issuing common stock only; the introduction of bond issues, or their equivalent, as a source of corporate funds is postponed until the next part of this section.

The physical assets held by each firm will yield to the owners of the firm — its stockholders — a stream of "profits" over time; but the elements of this series need not be constant and in any event are uncertain. This stream of income, and hence the stream accruing to any share of common stock, will be regarded as extending indefinitely into the future. We assume, however, that the mean value of the stream over time, or average profit per unit of time, is finite and represents a random variable subject to a (subjective) probability distribution. We shall refer to the average value over time of the stream accruing to a given share as the return of that share; and to the mathematical expectation of this average as the expected return of the share. Although individual investors may have different views as to the shape of the probability distribution of the return of any share, we shall assume for simplicity that they are at least in agreement as to the expected return. . . .

The next assumption plays a strategic role in the rest of the analysis. We shall assume that firms can be divided into "equivalent return" classes such that the return on the shares issued by any firm in any given class is proportional to (and hence perfectly correlated with) the return on the shares issued by any other firm in the same class. This assumption implies that the various shares within the same class differ, at most, by a "scale factor." Accordingly, if we adjust for the difference in scale, by taking the *ratio* of the return to the expected return, the probability distribution of that ratio is identical for all shares in the class. It follows that all relevant properties of a share are uniquely characterized by specifying (1) the class to which it belongs and (2) its expected return.

*Source: 48 Am. Econ. Rev. 261–297 (1958), reprinted with permission. Franco Modigliani and Merton H. Miller were then professors of economics at Carnegie Institute of Technology.

The significance of this assumption is that it permits us to classify firms into groups within which the shares of different firms are "homogeneous," that is, perfect substitutes for one another. We have, thus, an analogue to the familiar concept of the industry in which it is the commmodity produced by the firms that is taken as homogeneous. To complete this analogy with Marshallian price theory, we shall assume in the analysis to follow that the shares concerned are traded in perfect markets under conditions of atomistic competition.

From our definition of homogeneous classes of stock it follows that in equilibrium in a perfect capital market the price per dollar's worth of expected return must be the same for all shares of any given class. Or, equivalently, in any given class the price of every share must be proportional to its expected return. . . .

B. Debt Financing and Its Effects on Security Prices

Having developed an appartus for dealing with uncertain streams we can now approach the heart of the cost-of-capital problem by dropping the assumption that firms cannot issue bonds. The introduction of debt-financing changes the market for shares in a very fundamental way. Because firms may have different proportions of debt in their capital structure, shares of different companies, even in the same class, can give rise to different probability distributions of returns. In the language of finance, the shares will be subject to different degrees of financial risk or "leverage" and hence they will no longer be perfect substitutes for one another.

To exhibit the mechanism determining the relative prices of shares under these conditions, we make the following two assumptions about the nature of bonds and the bond market, though they are actually stronger than is necessary and will be relaxed later: (1) All bonds (including any debts issued by households for the purpose of carrying shares) are assumed to yield a constant income per unit of time, and this income is regarded as certain by all traders regardless of the issuer. (2) Bonds, like stocks, are traded in a perfect market, where the term perfect is to be taken in its usual sense as implying that any two commodities which are perfect substitutes for each other must sell, in equilibrium, at the same price. It follows from assumption (1) that all bonds are in fact perfect substitutes up to a scale factor. It follows from assumption (2) that they must all sell at the same price per dollar's worth of return, or what amounts to the same thing must yield the same rate of return. This rate of return will be denoted by r and referred to as the rate of interest or, equivalently, as the capitalization rate for sure streams. We now can derive the following two basic propositions with respect to the valuation of securities in companies with different capital structures:

Proposition I. . . . Proposition I asserts that . . . the *market value of any firm is independent of its capital structure and is given by capitalizing its expected return at the rate ρ_k appropriate to its class.*

This proposition can be stated in an equivalent way in terms of the firm's "average cost of capital." . . . That is, *the average cost of capital to any firm is completely independent of its capital structure and is equal to the capitalization rate of a pure equity stream of its class.*

To establish Proposition I we will show that as long as the [above] relations . . . do not hold between any pair of firms in a class, arbitrage will take place and restore the stated equalities. We use the term arbitrage advisedly. For if Proposition I did not hold, an investor could buy and sell stocks and bonds in such a way as to exchange one income stream for another stream, identical in all relevant respects but selling at a lower price. The exchange would therefore be advantageous to the investor quite independently of his attitudes toward risk. As investors exploit these arbitrage opportunities, the value of the overpriced shares will fall and that of the underpriced shares will rise, thereby tending to eliminate the discrepancy between the market values of the firms. . . .

Proposition II. From Proposition I we can derive the following proposition concerning the rate of return on common stock in companies whose capital structure includes some debt: . . . *the expected yield of a share of stock is equal to the appropriate capitalization rate ρ_k for a pure equity stream in the class, plus a premium related to financial risk equal to the debt-to-equity ratio times the spread between ρ_k and r . . .*

Effects of the Present Method of Taxing Corporations. The deduction of interest in computing taxable corporate profits will prevent the arbitrage process from making the value of all firms in a given class proportional to the expected returns generated by their physical assets. Instead, it can be shown [that "arbitrage" will make values within any class a function not only of expected after-tax returns, but of the tax rate and the degree of leverage.]* . . .

Effects of a Plurality of Bonds and Interest Rates. In existing capital markets we find not one, but a whole family of interest rates varying with maturity, with the technical provisions of the loan and, what is most relevant for present purposes, with the financial condition of the borrower. Economic theory and market experience both suggest that the yields demanded by lenders tend to increase with the debt-equity ratio of the borrowing firm (or individual). . . .

*Excerpted from Modigliani and Miller, Corporate Income Taxes and the Cost of Capital: A Correction, 53 Am. Econ. Rev. 433, 434 (1963).

Proposition I is actually unaffected in form and interpretation by the fact that the rate of interest may rise with leverage; while the average cost of *borrowed* funds will tend to increase as debt rises, the average cost of funds from *all* sources will still be independent of leverage (apart from the tax effect). This conclusion follows directly from the ability of those who engage in arbitrage to undo the leverage in any financial structure by acquiring an appropriately mixed portfolio of bonds and stocks. Because of this ability, the ratio of earnings (*before* interest charges) to market value — i.e., the average cost of capital from all sources — must be the same for all firms in a given class. . . .

D. The Relation of Propositions I and II to Current Doctrines

The propositions we have developed with respect to the valuation of firms and shares appear to be substantially at variance with current doctrines in the field of finance. . . . [T]he conventional view among finance specialists appears to start from the proposition that, other things equal, the earnings-price ratio (or its reciprocal, the times-earnings multiplier) of a firm's common stock will normally be only slightly affected by "moderate" amounts of debt in the firm's capital structure. . . . [This implies that] for any given level of expected total returns after taxes . . . the value of the firm must tend to *rise* with debt, whereas our Proposition I asserts that the value of the firm is completely independent of the capital structure. Another way of constrasting our position with the traditional one is in terms of the cost of capital. . . . According to [the traditional view], the average cost of capital is not independent of capital structure as we have argued, but should tend to *fall* with increasing leverage, at least within the relevant range of moderate debt ratios. . . . Or to put it in more familiar terms, debt-financing should be "cheaper" than equity-financing if not carried too far. . . .

Although the falling, or at least U-shaped, cost-of-capital function is in one form or another the dominant view in the literature, the ultimate rationale of that view is by no means clear. The crucial element in the position — that the expected earnings-price ratio of the stock is largely unaffected by leverage up to some conventional limit — is rarely even regarded as something which requires explanation. It is usually simply taken for granted or it is merely asserted that this is the way the market behaves. To the extent that the constant earnings-price ratio has a rationale at all we suspect that it reflects in most cases the feeling that moderate amounts of debt in "sound" corporations do not really add very much to the "riskiness" of the stock. Since the extra risk is slight, it seems natural to suppose that firms will not have to pay noticeably higher yields in order to induce investors to hold the stock.

A more sophisticated line of argument has been advanced by David Durand. He suggests that because insurance companies and certain other important institutional investors are restricted to debt securities, nonfinancial corporations are able to borrow from them at interest rates which are lower than would be required to compensate creditors in a free market. Thus, while he would presumably agree with our conclusions that stockholders could not gain from leverage in an unconstrained market, he concludes that they can gain under present institutional arrangements. This gain would arise by virtue of the "safety superpremium" which lenders are willing to pay corporations for the privilege of lending.

The defective link in both the traditional and the Durand version of the argument lies in the confusion between investors' subjective risk preferences and their objective market opportunities. Our Propositions I and II, as noted earlier, do not depend for their validity on any assumption about individual risk preferences. Nor do they involve any assertion as to what is an adequate compensation to investors for assuming a given degree of risk. They rely merely on the fact that a given commodity cannot consistently sell at more than one price in the market; or more precisely that the price of a commodity representing a "bundle" of two other commodities cannot be consistently different from the weighted average of the prices of the two components (the weights being equal to the proportion of the two commodities in the bundle).

An analogy may be helpful at this point. . . . Our Proposition I states that a firm cannot reduce the cost of capital — i.e., increase the market value of the stream it generates — by securing part of its capital through the sale of bonds, even though debt money appears to be cheaper. This assertion is equivalent to the proposition that, under perfect markets, a dairy farmer cannot in general earn more for the milk he produces by skimming some of the butter fat and selling it separately, even though butter fat per unit weight, sells for more than whole milk. The advantage from skimming the milk rather than selling whole milk would be purely illusory; for what would be gained from selling the high-priced butter fat would be lost in selling the low-priced residue of thinned milk. Similarly our Proposition II — that the price per dollar of a levered stream falls as leverage increases — is an exact analogue of the statement that the price per gallon of thinned milk falls continuously as more butter fat is skimmed off.

It is clear that this last assertion is true as long as butter fat is worth more per unit weight than whole milk, and it holds even if, for many consumers, taking a little cream out of the milk (adding a little leverage to the stock) does not detract noticeably from the taste (does not add noticeably to the risk). Furthermore the argument remains valid even in the face of institutional limitations of the type envisaged by Durand. For suppose that a large fraction of the population habitually dines in restaurants which are required by law to serve only cream in lieu of milk (entrust their savings to institutional investors who can only buy bonds). To be sure the price of butter fat will then tend to be higher in relation to that of skimmed milk than in the absence such restrictions (the rate of interest will tend to be lower), and this will benefit people who eat at home and who like skim milk (who manage their own portfolio and are able and willing to take risk). But it will still be the case that a farmer cannot gain by skimming some of the butter fat and selling it separately (firm cannot reduce the cost of capital by recourse to borrowed funds). . . .

II. Implications of the Analysis for the Theory of Investment

A. Capital Structure and Investment Policy

On the basis of our propositions with respect to cost of capital and financial structure (and for the moment neglecting taxes), we can derive the following simple rule for optimal investment policy by the firm:

Proposition III. If a firm in class k is acting in the best interest of the stockholders at the time of the decision, it will exploit an investment opportunity if and only if the rate of return on the investment, say ρ^*, is as large as or larger than ρ_k. That is, *the cut-off point for investment in the firm will in all cases be ρ_k and will be completely unaffected by the type of security used to finance the investment.* Equivalently, we may say that regardless of the financing used, the marginal cost of capital to a firm is equal to the average cost of capital, which is in turn equal to the capitalization rate for an unlevered stream in the class to which the firm belongs. . . .

To illustrate, suppose the capitalization rate for uncertain streams in the kth class is 10 per cent and the rate of interest is 4 per cent. Then if a given company had an expected income of 1,000 and if it were financed entirely by common stock we know from Proposition I that the market value of its stock would be 10,000. Assume now that the managers of the firm discover an investment opportunity which will require an outlay of 100 and which is expected to yield 8 per cent. At first sight this might appear to be a profitable opportunity since the expected return is double the interest cost. If, however, the management borrows the necessary 100 at 4 per cent, the total expected income of the company rises to 1,008 and the market value of the firm to 10,080. But the firm now will have 100 of bonds in its capital structure so that, paradoxically, the market value of the stock must actually be reduced from 10,000 to 9,980 as a consequence of this apparently profitable investment. Or, to put it another way, the gains from being able to tap cheap, borrowed funds are more than offset for the stockholders by the market's discounting of the stock for the added leverage assumed. . . . Thus an investment financed by common stock is advantageous to the current stockholders if and only if its yield exceeds the capitalization rate ρ_k.

Once again a numerical example may help to illustrate the result and make it clear why the relevant cut-off rate is ρ_k and not the current yield on common stock, i. Suppose that ρ_k is 10 per cent, r is 4 per cent, that the original expected income of our company is 1,000 and that management has the opportunity of investing 100 having an expected yield of 12 per cent. If the original capital structure is 50 per cent debt and 50 per cent equity, and 1,000 shares of stock are initially outstanding, then, by Proposition I, the market value of the common stock must be 5,000 or 5 per share. Furthermore, since the interest bill is $.04 \times 5,000 = 200$, the yield on common stock is $800/5,000 = 16$ per cent. It may then appear that financing the additional investment of 100 by issuing 20 shares to outsiders at 5 per share would dilute the equity of the original owners since the 100 promises to yield 12 per cent whereas the common stock is currently yielding 16 per cent. Actually, however, the income of the company would rise to 1,012; the value of the firm to 10,120; and the value of the common stock to 5,120. Since there are now 1,020 shares, each would be worth 5.02 and the wealth of the original stockholders would thus have been increased. What has happened is that the dilution in expected earnings per share (from .80 to .796) has been more than offset, in its effect upon the market price of the shares, by the decrease in leverage. . . .

B. Proposition III and Financial Planning by Firms

Misinterpretation of the scope of Proposition III can be avoided by remembering that this Proposition tells us only that the type of instrument used to finance an investment is irrelevant to the question of whether or not the investment is worth while. This does not mean that the owners (or the managers) have no grounds whatever for preferring one financing plan to another; or that there are no other policy or technical issues in finance at the level of the firm.

That grounds for preferring one type of financial structure to another will still exist within the framework of our model can readily be seen for the case of common-stock financing. In general, except for something like a widely publicized oil-strike, we would expect the market to place very heavy weight on current and recent past earnings in forming expectations as to future returns. Hence, if the owners of a firm discovered a major investment opportunity which they felt would yield much more than ρ_k, they might well prefer not to finance it via common stock at the then ruling price, because this price may fail to capitalize the new venture. A better course would be a pre-emptive issue of stock (and in this connection it should be remembered that stockholders are free to borrow and buy). Another possiblity would be to finance the project initially with debt. Once the project had reflected itself in increased actual earnings, the debt could be retired either with an equity issue at much better prices or through retained earnings. Still another possibility along the same lines might be to combine the two steps by means of a convertible debenture or preferred stock, perhaps with a progressively declining conversion rate. Even such a double-stage financing plan may possibly be regarded as yielding too large a share to outsiders since the new stockholders are, in effect, being given an interest in any similar opportunities the firm may discover in the future. If there is a reasonable prospect that even larger opportunities may arise in the near future and if there is some danger that borrowing now would preclude more borrowing later, the owners might find their interests best protected by splitting off the current opportunity into a separate subsidiary with independent financing. Clearly the problems involved in making the crucial estimates and in planning the optimal financial strategy are by no means trivial, even though they should have no bearing on the basic decision to invest (as long as $\rho^* \geqq \rho_k$).

Another reason why the alternatives in financial plans may not be a matter of indifference arises from the fact that managers are concerned with more than simply furthering the interest of the owners. Such other objectives of the management — which need not be necessarily in conflict with those of the owners — are much more likely to be served by some types of financing arrangements than others. In many forms of borrowing agreements, for example, creditors are able to stipulate terms which the current management may regard as infringing on its prerogatives or restricting its freedom to maneuver. The creditors might even be able to insist on having a direct voice in the formation of policy. To the extent, therefore, that financial policies have these implications for the management of the firm, something like the utility approach described in the introductory section becomes relevant to financial (as opposed to investment) decision-making. It is, however, the utility functions of the managers per se and not of the owners that are now involved.

Leverage, Risk of Ruin and the Cost of Capital*

Nevins D. Baxter

When account is taken of the deductibility of interest payments from corporate-tax liabilities, Modigliani and Miller conclude that the use of borrowed funds reduces the cost of capital to the corporation. Solomon has suggested that "the Modigliani-Miller proposition amended to take the tax deductibility of interest into account would postulate that . . . the recipe for optimal leverage . . . is that companies ought to be financed 99.9 per cent with pure debt!" Such a conclusion, however, has little intuitive appeal because of the risks normally associated with servicing and refinancing outstanding debt. And we know that in the real world it is impossible to obtain debt financing unless creditors believe that there is a sufficient equity cushion. Once the "acceptable" amount of leverage has been passed, the rate of interest on debt will begin to rise and may cause the cost of capital for the overlevered firm to increase.

The purpose of the present paper is to explain, in the context of the Modigliani and Miller discussion, how excessive leverage can be expected to raise the cost of capital to the firm. It is argued that when account is taken of "risk of ruin," a rising average cost of capital is perfectly consistent with rational arbitrage operations. Allowing for the possibility of bankruptcy is tantamount to relaxing the assumption that the anticipated stream of operating earnings is independent of capital structure. In the first section the influence of the risk of ruin is examined analytically; the second section brings empirical evidence to bear on the actual effect of extreme leverage on the cost of capital of the firm.

At the outset, consider two firms (A and B) with earnings streams identical with respect to both expected values and quality (variance). Both firms are financed solely by equity. Firm B now issues some long-term debt, retiring an equivalent amount (market value) of equity. According to Modigliani and Miller, the before-tax net operating earnings stream will remain unchanged, and if the cost of capital is greater for the levered firm (i.e., the market value of stocks and bonds is smaller), an opportunity for profitable arbitrage

*Source: 22 J. Fin. 395–403 (1967), reprinted with permission. Nevins D. Baxter is professor of finance at the University of Pennsylvania.

exists. Investors sell shares in the pure equity firm (*A*) and purchase stocks and bonds in the levered company (*B*) thereby obtaining an earnings stream identical in quality to that of the unlevered firm, while increasing expected return.

As the debt-equity ratio of the levered firm rises, the interest rate on debt likely also will begin to rise (though at first perhaps very slowly). Profitable arbitrage is still possible, however, and it is incorrect to conclude that the capitalization rate on equity must decline to keep the overall cost of capital constant. Since the cost of capital is the weighted average of the cost of debt and equity, the overall cost of capital can remain constant while the costs of both components are rising. Such a situation will occur as heavier reliance is placed on the cheaper source, which will always be debt. Ignoring for the moment considerations of the risk of ruin, arbitrage operations, which will assure a constant overall cost of capital, will be profitable as long as the interest rate on debt is less than the rate at which the equity of the unlevered firm is capitalized. And interest rates above this level cannot exist!*

The apparent conclusion of this analysis is that arbitrage will assure that leverage cannot raise the average cost of capital, although the existence of corporate taxes will allow leverage to reduce the cost of capital. Yet there does exist a very real force which reconciles this conclusion with the intuitive notion that firms cannot be financed almost exclusively by debt. As the reliance on debt expands, the profitability of the arbitrage operation may become illusory. While it is perfectly possible to make an *expected* profit by selling the pure equity firm and buying a mixture of debt and equity in the levered firm, there also may be a substantial risk involved. This risk results from the fact that the unlevered firm can experience changes in earnings, but a succession of bad years may throw firm *B* into receivership. The streams of net operating earnings were assumed identical in amounts and quality for both firms *before* firm *B* swapped some of its equity for debt. But it may not be realistic to assume that the earnings streams continue to be identical after *B* has levered itself. The reason is that the risk of ruin becomes very real as leverage increases and cannot be nullified by arbitrage.

To illustrate, consider that identical firms *A* and *B* have expected earnings of $10,000 per year. Earnings are rectangularly distributed, with all values from $5,000 to $15,000 equiprobable. As long as fixed interest claims on outstanding debt do not exceed $5,000, leverage will be "tolerable" in the sense that profitable arbitrage can take

*[This assumes all of the debt is of a single class. In a highly levered firm, a small amount of subordinated debt could easily require a higher rate than the equity of a comparable unlevered firm—Eds.]

place to hold the cost of capital constant. If fixed debt service rose to $6,000, however, with a very high dependence on debt, there would be a 10 per cent chance that the firm would be unable to meet its interest obligations out of current earnings. A few bad years in a row would substantially increase the probability that firm B will declare bankruptcy since it might not be able to borrow to meet its interest obligations because of its state of "financial embarrassment."

What exactly are the implications of such a declaration of bankruptcy by firm B? In particular, how does the possibility of such an event affect the cost of capital of the levered firm relative to that of the pure-equity firm?

If bankruptcy (insolvency) occurs, the debt holders can force the firm into receivership and attempt to gain control of the corporation. If such a transition could occur without in any way disrupting the activities of the business firm — its revenues or its costs — there would be little presumption that the value of the firm (or the cost of capital) would be influenced by the risk of ruin. To be sure, management changes would occur which might alter the fortunes of the firm, but in the main, the total worth of firm B could not differ significantly from that of firm A. If, on the other hand, bankruptcy involves substantial administrative expenses and other costs, and causes a significant decline in the sales and earnings of the firm in receivership, the total value of the levered firm can be expected to be less than that of the all-equity company. Bankruptcy is a more likely event in the case of firm B, and the associated costs lead to a higher probability of extreme variations in B's income stream. This increases the variance of the expected earnings for the levered firm and reduces the overall value of that firm. Arbitrage operations which are necessary to bring the cost of capital of firms A and B into line need not occur because equity in firm A may well be more desirable (less risky) than a combination of debt and equity in levered-firm B. Excessive leverage can thus lead to an increased overall cost of capital.

It therefore remains an empirical question as to whether the risk of ruin raises the cost of capital for highly-levered firms. A demonstration that there are significant "administrative" costs to bankruptcy and that financial embarrassment is likely . . . to have an adverse effect on net operating earnings can be considered as evidence that capital structure does matter. . . .

The process of reorganizing a corporation involves a court-appointed trustee who investigates the causes of financial trouble, assists in operating the firm while it is in receivership, and submits a plan of reorganization to the court. The reorganization invariably involves the raising of new capital from currently-interested parties (equity and debt holders) or from the public in the form of trustee certificates. These certificates are senior to outstanding debt (and thus bear "reasonable" interest rates); therefore their issue can be extremely risky and costly to existing security holders. In the case of industrial companies the court will authorize such certificates only where it believes that such new capital will eventually increase the returns of the company's old creditors and owners (though its judgment may turn out to be incorrect), but in the case of utilities and railroads where the public interest requires the continuance of operations by the bankrupt company, such securities will be authorized even at the expense of the best interests of old security holders. This is a very real cost of reorganization.

There are also direct costs of bankruptcy proceedings in the form of administrative expenses (trustee's fees, legal fees, referee's fees), and in the time lost by executives in litigation. Maximum fees of trustees are established by federal law: legal fees are subject to approval by the court. As a percentage of realizations these costs decline with the dollar value of the assets realized. Unfortunately, detailed figures are available only for personal bankruptcy proceedings but they will give an order of magnitude. In 1965, 25.7 per cent of realizations went for "administrative expenses" on an average realization of $5,227. On realizations in excess of $50,000 (average of $152,000) this percentage fell to 19.9 per cent. For corporate cases, which are typically larger, the administrative costs may average a somewhat smaller percentage of realizations but are still far from insignificant. In short, there is evidence for Burtchett's statement that "a receivership is an expensive luxury in management."

Perhaps the most important cost of bankruptcy proceedings is the negative effect that financial embarrassment may have on the stream of net operating earnings of the business firm. The firm may find it very difficult to obtain trade credit, customers may question its reliability and permanence as a source of supply and may choose to deal elsewhere. Questionable financial condition may be equivalent to negative publicity about the integrity of the firm. Such will certainly be the case for a bank or other financial institution but may hold to a lesser extent for industrial companies.

Of course, it is extremely difficult to separate the proportion of the decline in sales and earnings experienced by a firm in receivership which is attributable to the state of bankruptcy from that associated with the factors that forced bankruptcy in the first place. In other words, the bankruptcy rolls are not filled with otherwise-healthy firms which had too much debt and suffered a random run of bad years. Rather, they are typically firms whose sales and earnings are suffering and it is therefore difficult to isolate the incremental suffering attributable to bankruptcy. . . .

It has been argued above that the risks associated with excessive leverage will likely increase the cost of capital of the firm. A high degree of leverage increases the probability of bankruptcy and therefore increases the riskiness of the overall earnings stream. Since there appear to be very real costs associated with bankruptcy, other things equal, excess leverage can reduce the total value of the firm.

The effect of the risk of ruin is not likely to be linear with the reliance on debt. When leverage is very low, an increase in the reliance on debt is not likely to exert a significant effect on the probability of bankruptcy. When there is considerable debt in the capital structure, however, any increase in leverage is likely to have a much greater effect on the cost of capital. The risk of ruin thus becomes increasingly important as the degree of financial leverage increases. Therefore, the interest rate on debt will rise only very slowly, if at all, with leverage, when reliance on debt is low, but the interest rate may begin to rise very sharply, as the capital structure becomes more risky.

Moreover, the ability of the business firm to "tolerate" leverage will depend on the variance of net operating earnings. Since businesses with relatively stable income streams (such as utilities) are less subject to the possibility of ruin, they may find it desirable to rely relatively heavily on debt financing. Firms with risky income streams, on the other hand, are less able to assume fixed charges in the form of debt interest and may well find that the average cost of capital begins to increase with leverage even when reliance on debt is moderate.

The existence of corporate tax, which treats interest as a deductible expense, suggests that leverage tends to reduce the cost of capital to a firm. This paper has shown how the risk of ruin serves to counteract this influence. When reliance on debt is small, the tax effect is likely to dominate, but as leverage increases the risk of ruin becomes more important. Therefore, the sum of these influences may well lead us to the conclusion that when the restrictive assumptions of Modigliani and Miller are relaxed in accordance with existing institutions, the result is the traditional cost of capital curve, declining at low amounts of debt but rising where leverage becomes substantial.

Debt and Taxes*

Merton H. Miller

. . . [I]n our first joint paper of nearly twenty years ago . . . [Franco Modigliani and I tried] to bring to bear on problems of corporate finance some of the standard tools of economics, especially the analysis of competitive market equilibrium. Prior to that time, the academic discussion in finance was focused primarily on the empirical issue of what the market *really* capitalized. Did the market capitalize a firm's dividends or its earnings or some weighted combination of the two? Did it capitalize net earnings or net operating earnings or something in between? The answers to these questions and to related questions about the behavior of interest rates were supposed to provide a basis for choosing an optimal capital structure for the firm in a framework analogous to the economist's model of discriminating monopsony.

We came at the problem from the other direction by first trying to establish the propositions about valuation implied by the economist's basic working assumptions of rational behavior and perfect markets. And we were able to prove that when the full range of opportunities available to firms and investors under such conditions are taken into account, the following simple principle would apply: in equilibrium, the market value of any firm must be independent of its capital structure.

The arbitrage proof of this proposition can now be found in virtually every textbook in finance, followed almost invariably, however, by a warning to the student against taking it seriously. Some dismiss it with the statement that firms and investors can't or don't behave that way. . . . Others object that the invariance proposition was derived for a world with no taxes, and that world, alas, is not ours. In our world, they point out, the value of the firm can be increased by the use of debt since interest payments can be deducted from taxable corporate income. To reap more of these gains, however, the stockholders must incur increasing risks of bankruptcy and the costs, direct and indirect, of falling into that unhappy state. They conclude that the balancing of these bankruptcy costs against the tax gains of debt finance gives rise to an optimal capital structure, just as the traditional view has always maintained, though for somewhat different reasons.

It is this new and currently fashionable version of the optimal

*Source: 32 J. Fin. 261–275 (1977), reprinted with permission. Merton H. Miller is Brown Professor of Banking and Finance, Graduate School of Business, University of Chicago.

capital structure that I propose to challenge here. I will argue that even in a world in which interest payments are fully deductible in computing corporate income taxes, the value of the firm, in equilibrium will still be independent of its capital structure.

Let me first explain where I think the new optimum capital structure model goes wrong. It is not that I believe there to be no deadweight costs attaching to the use of debt finance. Bankruptcy costs and agency costs do indeed exist as was dutifully noted at several points in the original 1958 article. It is just that these costs, by any sensible reckoning, seem disproportionately small relative to the tax savings they are supposedly balancing.

The tax savings, after all, are conventionally taken as being on the order of 50 cents for each dollar of permanent debt issued. The figure one usually hears as an estimate of bankruptcy costs is 20 percent of the value of the estate; and if this were the true order of magnitude for such costs, they would have to be taken very seriously indeed as a possible counterweight. But when that figure is traced back to its source in the paper by Baxter (and the subsequent and seemingly confirmatory studies of Stanley and Girth and Van Horne), it turns out to refer mainly to the bankruptcies of individuals, with a sprinkling of small businesses, mostly proprietorships and typically undergoing liquidation rather than reorganization. The only study I know that deals with the costs of bankruptcy and reorganization for large, publicly-held corporations is that of Jerold Warner. Warner tabulated the direct costs of bankruptcy and reorganization for a sample of 11 railroads that filed petitions in bankruptcy under Section 77 of the Bankruptcy Act between 1930 and 1955. He found that the eventual cumulated direct costs of bankruptcy—and keep in mind that most of these railroads were in bankruptcy and running up these expenses for over 10 years!—averaged 5.3 percent of the market value of the firm's securities as of the end of the month in which the railroad filed the petition. There was a strong inverse size effect, moreover. For the largest road, the costs were 1.7 percent.

And remember that these are the *ex post*, upper-bound cost ratios, whereas, of course, the *expected* costs of bankruptcy are the relevant ones when the firm's capital structure decisions are being made. On that score, Warner finds, for example, that the direct costs of bankruptcy averaged only about 1 percent of the value of the firm 7 years before the petition was filed; and when he makes a reasonable allowance for the probability of bankruptcy actually occurring, he comes up with an estimate of the expected cost of bankruptcy that is, of course, much smaller yet.

Warner's data cover only the *direct* costs of reorganization in bankruptcy. The deadweight costs of rescaling claims might perhaps loom larger if measures were available of the indirect costs, such as the diversion of the time and energies of management from tasks of greater productivity or the reluctance of customers and suppliers to enter into long-term commitments. But why speculate about the size of these costs? Surely we can assume that if the direct and indirect deadweight costs of the ordinary loan contract began to eat up significant portions of the tax savings, other forms of debt contracts with lower deadweight costs would be used instead.

An obvious case in point is the income bond. Interest payments on such bonds need be paid in any year only if earned; and if earned and paid are fully deductible in computing corporate income tax. But if not earned and not paid in any year, the bondholders have no right to foreclose. The interest payments typically cumulate for a short period of time—usually two to three years—and then are added to the principal. Income bonds, in sum, are securities that appear to have all the supposed tax advantages of debt, without the bankruptcy cost disadvantages. Yet, except for a brief flurry in the early 1960's, such bonds are rarely issued.

The conventional wisdom attributes this dearth to the unsavory connotations that surround such bonds. They were developed originally in the course of the railroad bankruptcies in the 19th century and they are presumed to be still associated with that dismal process in the minds of potential buyers. As an investment banker once put it to me: "They have the smell of death about them." Perhaps so. But the obvious retort is that bit of ancient Roman wisdom: *pecunia non olet* (money has no odor). If the stakes were as high as the conventional analysis of the tax subsidy to debt seems to suggest, then ingenious security salesmen, investment bankers or tax advisers would surely long since have found ways to overcome investor repugnance to income bonds.

In sum, the great emphasis on bankruptcy costs in recent discussions of optimal capital structure policy seems to me to have been misplaced. For big businesses, at least (and particularly for such conspicuously low-levered ones as I.B.M. or Kodak), the supposed trade-off between tax gains and bankruptcy costs looks suspiciously like the recipe for the fabled horse-and-rabbit stew—one horse and one rabbit.

Problems arise also on the other side of the trade-off. If the optimal capital structure were simply a matter of balancing tax advantages against bankruptcy costs, why have observed capital structures shown so little change over time?

When I looked into the matter in 1960 under the auspices of the Commission on Money and Credit, I found, among other things, that the debt/asset ratio of the typical nonfinancial corporation in the 1950's was little different from that of the 1920's despite the fact that tax rates had quintupled — from 10 and 11 percent in the 1920's to 52 percent in the 1950's. Such rise as did occur, moreover, seemed to be mainly a substitution of debt for preferred stock, rather than of debt for common stock. The year-to-year variations in debt ratios reflected primarily the cyclical movements of the economy. During expansions debt ratios tended to fall, partly because the lag of dividends behind earnings built up internally generated equity; and partly because the ratio of equity to debt in new financings tended to rise when the stock market was booming. . . .

. . . Thus, when the returns for the first half of the 1970's are finally in, we are likely to be facing the same paradox we did in the 1950's — corporate debt ratios only marginally higher than those of the 1920's despite enormously higher tax rates.

Actually, the cognitive dissonance is worse now than it was then. In the 1950's it was still possible to entertain the notion that the seeming failure of corporations to reap the tax advantages of debt financing might simply be a lag in adjustment. As corporate finance officers and their investment bankers sharpened their pencils, the tax savings they discovered would eventually wear down aversions to debt on the part of any others in the Boardroom still in a state of shock from the Great Depression. But hope can no longer be expected from that quarter. A disequilibrium that has lasted 30 years and shows no signs of disappearing is too hard for any economist to accept. And since failure to close the gap cannot convincingly be attributed to the bankruptcy costs or agency costs of debt financing, there would seem to be only one way left to turn: the tax advantages of debt financing must be substantially less than the conventional wisdom suggests. . . .

When the personal income tax is taken into account along with the corporation income tax, the gain from leverage, G_L, for the stockholders in a firm holding real assets can be shown to be given by the following expression:

$$G_L = \left[1 - \frac{(1 - \tau_C)(1 - \tau_{PS})}{1 - \tau_{PB}} \right] B_L$$

where τ_C is the corporate tax rate, τ_{PS} is the personal income tax rate applicable to income from common stock, τ_{PB} is the personal income tax rate applicable to income from bonds and B_L is the market value of the levered firm's debt. For simplicity at this stage of the argument, all the taxes are assumed to be proportional; and to maintain continuity with the earlier M M papers, the expression is given in its "perpetuity" form.

Note that when all tax rates are set equal to zero, the expression does indeed reduce to the standard M M no-tax result of $G_L = 0$. And when the personal income tax rate on income from bonds is the same as that on income from shares — a special case of which, of course, is when there is assumed to be no personal income tax at all — then the gain from leverage is the familiar $\tau_C B_L$. But when the tax rate on income from shares is less than the tax on income from bonds, then the gain from leverage will be less than $\tau_C B_L$. In fact, for a wide range of values for τ_C, τ_{PS} and τ_{PB}, the gain from leverage vanishes entirely or even turns negative!

Let me assure you that this result is no mere sleight-of-hand due to hidden trick assumptions. The gain evaporates or turns into a loss because investors hold securities for the "consumption possibilities" they generate and hence will evaluate them in terms of their yields net of all tax drains. If, therefore, the personal tax on income from common stocks is less than that on income from bonds, then the *before-tax* return on taxable bonds has to be high enough, other things equal, to offset this tax handicap. Otherwise, no taxable investor would want to hold bonds. Thus, while it is still true that the owners of a levered corporation have the advantage of deducting their interest payments to bondholders in computing their corporate income tax, these interest payments have already been "grossed up," so to speak, by any differential in the taxes that the bondholders will have to pay on their interest income. The advantage of deductibility at the one level thus merely serves to offset the disadvantages of includability at the other. When the rates happen to satisfy the equation $(1 - \tau_{PB}) = (1 - \tau_C)(1 - \tau_{PS})$, the offset is one-for-one and the owners of the corporation reap no gain whatever from their use of tax-deductible debt rather than equity capital.

But we can say more than this. Any situation in which the owners of corporations could increase their wealth by substituting debt for equity (or vice versa) would be incompatible with market equilibrium. Their attempts to exploit these opportunities would lead, in a world with progressive income taxes, to changes in the yields on stocks and bonds and in their ownership patterns. These changes, in turn, restore the equilibrium and remove the incentives to issue more debt, even without invoking bankruptcy costs or lending costs as a *deus ex machina*.

Taxes and Market Equilibrium

Like so many other propositions in financial economics this, too, is "obvious once you think of it." Let me belabor the obvious a bit, however, by a simple graphical example that will serve, I hope, both to illustrate the mechanism that brings the equilibrium about and to highlight some of the implications of that equilibrium.

Suppose, for simplicity that the personal tax rate on income from stock were zero (and we'll see later that this may be a less outrageous simplification than it looks). And suppose further, again strictly for simplicity of presentation, that all bonds are riskless and that there are no transaction costs, flotation costs or surveillance costs involved in their issuance. Then in such a world, the equilibrium of the market for bonds would be that pictured in Figure [13]. The quantity of bonds outstanding is measured along the horizontal axis and the rate of interest along the vertical. The demand for bonds by the investing public is given by the upward sloping curve labeled $r_d(B)$. (Yes, it *is* a demand curve even though it slopes up.) Its intercept is at r_0 which measures the equilibrium rate of interest on fully tax-exempt bonds (such as those of state and local governments). The flat stretch of the curve immediately to the right represents the demand for fully taxable corporate bonds by fully tax-exempt individuals and organizations. Clearly, these investors would be the sole holders of corporate bonds if the market interest rate on corporate debts were only r_0. Any taxable

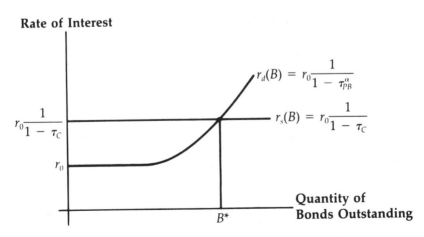

Figure 13
Equilibrium in the Market for Bonds

Source: Miller, Figure 1.

investor who wanted to hold bonds in his or her portfolio would find it preferable to buy tax-exempt bonds.

To entice these taxable investors into the market for corporate bonds, the rate of interest on such bonds has to be high enough to compensate for the taxes on interest income under the personal income tax. More precisely, for an individual whose marginal rate of personal income tax on interest income is τ_{PB}^{α}, the "demand rate of interest" on taxable corporate bonds would be the rate on tax exempts grossed up by the marginal tax rate, i.e., $r_0(1/(1 - \tau_{PB}^{\alpha}))$. Since the personal income tax is progressive, the demand interest rate has to keep rising to pull in investors in higher and higher tax brackets, thus giving the continuous, upward sloping curve pictured.

The intersection of this demand curve with the horizontal straight line through the point $r_0/1 - \tau_C$, i.e., the tax-exempt rate grossed up by the corporate tax rate, determines the market equilibrium. If corporations were to offer a quantity of bonds greater than B^*, interest rates would be driven above $r_0/1 - \tau_C$ and some levered firms would find leverage to be a losing proposition. If the volume were below B^*, interest rates would be lower than $r_0/1 - \tau_C$ and some unlevered firms would find it advantageous to resort to borrowing.

The market equilibrium defined by the intersection of the two curves will have the following property. There will be an equilibrium level of aggregate corporate debt, B^*, and hence an equilibrium debt-equity ratio for the corporate sector as a whole. *But there would be no optimum debt ratio for any individual firm.* Companies following a no-leverage or low leverage strategy (like I.B.M. or Kodak) would find a market among investors in the high tax brackets; those opting for a high leverage strategy (like the electric utilities) would find the natural clientele for their securities at the other end of the scale. But one clientele is as good as the other. And in this important sense it would still be true that the value of any firm, in equilibrium, would be independent of its capital structure, despite the deductibility of interest payments in computing corporate income taxes.

One advantage of graphical illustration is that it makes it so easy to see the answer to the following inevitable question: If the stockholders of levered corporations don't reap the benefits of the tax gains from leverage, who does? Professors of finance, of course — though only indirectly and only after cutting in their colleagues in other departments. As Figure [13] shows, universities and other tax exempt organizations, as well as individuals in low tax brackets (widows and orphans?) benefit from what might be called a "bondholders' surplus." Market interest rates have to be grossed up to pay the taxes of the marginal bondholder, whose tax rate in equilibrium will be equal to the corporate rate. Note that this can cut both ways, however. Low bracket individuals (and corporations) have to *pay* the corporate tax, in effect, when they want to borrow.

An equilibrium of the kind pictured in Figure [13] does not require, of course, that the effective personal tax rate on income from shares of the marginal holder be literally zero, but only that it be substantially less than his or her rate on income from bonds. As a practical matter, however, the assumption that the effective rate at the margin is close to zero may not be so wide of the mark. Keep in mind that a "clientele effect" is also at work in the market for shares. The high dividend paying stocks will be preferred by tax exempt organizations and low income investors; those stocks yielding more of their return in the form of capital gains will gravitate to the taxpayers in the upper brackets. The tax rate on such gains is certainly greater than zero, in principle. But holders need pay no taxes on their gains until realized and only a small fraction of accumulated gains are, in fact, realized and taxed in any year. Taxes on capital gains can not only be deferred at the option of the holder—and remember that by conventional folk wisdom, 10 years of tax deferral is almost as good as exemption—but until the recent Tax Reform Act of 1976, could be avoided altogether if held until death, thanks to the rules permitting transfer of the decedent's tax basis to his or her heirs.

To the extent that the effective tax rate on income from shares is greater than zero, the horizontal line defining the equilibrium interest rate will be above that pictured in Figure [13]. In the limiting case where the tax concessions (intended or unintended) made to income from shares were either nonexistent or so small that $(1 - \tau_C)(1 - \tau_{PS})$ implied a value for τ_{PB}^a greater than the top bracket of the personal income tax, then no interior market equilibrium would be possible. Common stock would indeed be a dominated security from the purely financial point of view, exactly as the standard micro model of the tax effect suggests. Common stock could continue to exist only by virtue of special attributes it might possess that could not be duplicated with bonds or with other forms of business organization, such as co-ops.

The analysis underlying Figure [13] can be extended to allow for risky borrowing, but there are complications. What makes things difficult is not simply a matter of risk *per se*. Default risk can be accommodated in Figure [13] merely by reinterpreting all the before-tax interest rates as risk-adjusted or certainty-equivalent rates. The trouble is, rather, that bonds of companies in default will not, in general, yield the issuing stockholders their full tax shield. Unless the firm has past profits against which its current losses can be carried back, or unless it can escape the vigilance of the I.R.S. and unload the corporate corpse on a taxable firm, some of the interest deduction goes to waste. To entice firms to issue risky bonds, therefore, the risk-adjusted supply-rate would have to be less than $r_0(1/(1 - \tau_C))$, and presumably the more so the greater the likelihood of default.

An essentially similar effect will be produced by the bankruptcy costs discussed earlier. And this will imply, among other things, that the full burden of the bankruptcy costs or lending costs is not necessarily borne by the debtors as is frequently supposed. Part of the costs are shifted to the bond buyers in the form of lower risk-adjusted rates of interest in equilibrium.

A model of the kind in Figure [13] could, in principle, clear up most of the puzzles and anomalies discussed . . . above — the seeming disparity between the tax gains of debt and the costs of bankruptcy particularly for large low-levered corporations; the lack of widespread market interest in income bonds; and especially the failure of the average corporate debt ratio to rise substantially in response to the enormous increase in tax rates since the 1920's (because these increases in rates in the late 1930's as well as subsequent decreases and reincreases have generally moved both the corporate and individual rate schedules in the same direction). The model could also account as well for other of the stylized facts of corporate finance such as the oft-remarked dramatic transition of the bond market from an individual to an institution-dominated market in the late 1930's and early 1940's. On the other hand, many questions clearly still remain to be answered. What about cross-sectional variations in debt ratios, for example — a subject on which surprisingly little work has yet been done? Can they be explained convincingly by the market equilibrium model presented here or some variant of it? Or do the variations observed reflect some systematic part of the equilibrating process that escapes the kind of aggregate market models discussed here? What about the distribution of stocks and bonds among investors? Does ownership sort out in terms of tax status as sharply as emphasized here? Or does the need for diversification swamp the tax differences and thereby throw the main burden of the equilibration onto other factors, such as agency costs?

On Financial Contracting: An Analysis of Bond Covenants*

Clifford W. Smith, Jr. and Jerold B. Warner

In this paper, we examine how debt contracts are written to control the bondholder-stockholder conflict. We investigate the vari-

*Source: 7 J. Fin. Econ. 117–161 (1979), reprinted with permission. Clifford W. Smith, Jr., and Jerold B. Warner are assistant professors at the Graduate School of Management, University of Rochester.

ous kinds of bond covenants which are included in actual debt contracts. A bond covenant is a provision, such as a limitation on the payment of dividends, which restricts the firm from engaging in specified actions after the bonds are sold.

Our description of the specific provisions in debt contracts is based primarily on an American Bar Foundation compendium entitled Commentaries on Indentures. This volume contains both the standardized provisions which are included in the debt contract (the "boilerplates") and a practitioner-oriented discussion of their use.

Sources of the Bondholder-Stockholder Conflict

Corporations are "legal fictions which serve as a nexus for a set of contracting relationships among individuals." To focus on the contract between the bondholders and the corporation, we assume that costs of enforcing other contracts are zero. For example, we assume that contracts between stockholders and managers costlessly induce managers to act as if they own all the firm's equity.

The corporation has an indefinite life and the set of contracts which comprise the corporation evolves over time: as the firm's investment opportunity set changes decisions are made about the real activities in which the firm engages and the financial contracts the firm sells. With risky bonds outstanding, management, acting in the stockholders' interest, has incentives to design the firm's operating characteristics and financial structure in ways which benefit stockholders to the detriment of bondholders. Because investment, financing, and dividend policies are endogenous, there are four major sources of conflict which arise between bondholders and stockholders:

Dividend payment. If a firm issues bonds and the bonds are priced assuming the firm will maintain its dividend policy, the value of the bonds is reduced by raising the dividend rate and financing the increase by reducing investment. At the limit, if the firm sells all its assets and pays a liquidating dividend to the stockholders, the bondholders are left with worthless claims.

Claim dilution. If the firm sells bonds, and the bonds are priced assuming that no additional debt will be issued, the value of the bondholders' claims is reduced by issuing additional debt of the same or higher priority.

Asset substitution. If a firm sells bonds for the stated purpose of engaging in low variance projects and the bonds are valued at prices commensurate with that low risk, the value of the stockholders' equity rises and the value of the bondholders' claim is reduced by substituting projects which increase the firm's variance rate.[4]

Underinvestment.   Myers suggests that a substantial portion of the value of the firm is composed of intangible assets in the form of future investment opportunities. A firm with outstanding bonds can have incentives to reject projects which have a positive net present value if the benefit from accepting the project accrues to the bondholders.

The bondholder-stockholder conflict is of course recognized by capital market participants. Rational bondholders recognize the incentives faced by the stockholders. They understand that after the bonds are issued, any action which increases the wealth of the stockholders will be taken. In pricing the bond issue, bondholders make estimates of the behavior of the stockholders, given the investment, financing, and dividend policies available to the stockholders. The price which bondholders pay for the issue will be lower to reflect the possibility of subsequent wealth transfers to stockholders. . . .

Control of the Bondholder-Stockholder Conflict: The Competing Hypotheses

There seems to be general agreement within the finance profession that the bondholder-stockholder relationship entails conflict and that the prices in security markets behave as if all securityholders form rational expectations about the stockholders' behavior after the bonds are issued. However, there is disagreement about whether the total value of the firm is influenced by the way in which the bondholder-stockholder conflict is controlled. There are two competing hypotheses. We call them the Irrelevance Hypothesis and the Costly Contracting Hypothesis.

The Irrelevance Hypothesis

The Irrelevance Hypothesis is that the manner of controlling the bondholder-stockholder conflict does not change the value of the firm.

---

4. The mere exchange of low-risk assets for high-risk assets does not alter the value of the firm if both assets have the same net present values. However, stockholders will have incentives to purchase projects with negative net present values if the increase in the firm's variance rate from accepting those projects is sufficiently large. Even though such projects reduce the total value of the firm, the value of the equity rises.

Irrelevance under a fixed investment policy.   In the Modigliani/ Miller (1958) or Fama/Miller (1972) models the firm's investment policy is assumed fixed. As long as the firm's total net cash flows are fixed, the value of the firm will not be changed by the existence or non-existence of protective covenants; with fixed cash flows, any gain which covenants give bondholders is a loss to stockholders, and vice versa. Covenants merely alter the distribution of a set of payoffs which is fixed to the firm's claimholders as a whole, and the choice of specific financial contracts is irrelevant to the value of the firm.

Irrelevance when investment policy is not fixed.   Dividend payout, asset substitution, and underinvestment all represent potential opportunities for wealth transfer to stockholders. When these opportunities are available, the firm's investment policy cannot be regarded as fixed because it is likely to be altered by the presence of risky debt. The total value of the firm could be reduced if stockholders engage in actions which maximize the value of their own claims, but not the total value of the firm. However, even if investment policy cannot be regarded as fixed, mechanisms other than covenants exist which could be sufficient to induce the firm's stockholders to choose a firm-value-maximizing production/investment policy

The forces exerted by external markets could induce the stockholders to maximize the value of the firm. Long suggests that the firm will accept all projects with a positive net present value if recapitalization is costless. Fama argues that if takeovers are costless, the firm's owners always have an incentive to maximize the value of the firm. Additionally, ongoing firms have other incentives to follow a value-maximizing policy. Cases can be constructed in which a firm with a long history of deviating from such a policy in order to maximize only shareholder wealth will be worth less than it would have, had a value-maximizing policy been followed and expected to continue.

Ownership of the firm's claims could be structured in a way which controls the stockholders' incentive to follow a strategy which does not maximize the total value of the firm. Galai/Masulis suggest that if all investors hold equal proportions of both the firm's debt and the firm's equity issues, wealth redistributions among claimholders leave all investors indifferent. In such a case, bondholder-stockholder conflict arising over investment policy is costlessly controlled, and, even with risky debt, the stockholders will still follow a firm-value-maximizing strategy.

Thus, even when the firm's investment policy is not fixed, under the Irrelevance Hypothesis the stockholders' behavior is not altered by the presence of the bondholder-stockholder conflict. The influence of external markets or the possibility of restructuring the firm's claims implies that the choice of financial contracts is irrelevant to the value of the firm.

The Costly Contracting Hypothesis

The Costly Contracting Hypothesis is that control of the bondholder-stockholder conflict through financial contracts can increase the value of the firm. Like the Irrelevance Hypothesis, the Costly Contracting Hypothesis recognizes the influence which external markets and the possibility of recapitalization exert on the firm's choice of investment policy. However, this hypothesis presupposes that those factors, while controlling to some extent the bondholder-stockholder conflict, are insufficient to induce the stockholders to maximize the value of the firm rather than maximizing the value of the equity. . . .

Financial contracting is assumed to be costly. However, bond covenants, even if they involve costs, can increase the value of the firm at the time bonds are issued by reducing the opportunity loss which results when stockholders of a levered firm follow a policy which does not maximize the value of the firm. Furthermore, in the case of the claim dilution problem (which involves only a wealth transfer), if covenants lower the costs which bondholders incur in monitoring stockholders, the cost-reducing benefits of the covenants accrue to the firm's owners. With such covenants, the firm is worth more at the time the bonds are issued.

Under the Costly Contracting Hypothesis, there is a unique optimal set of financial contracts which maximizes the value of the firm. Note, however, that the bondholder-stockholder conflict would be resolved and its associated costs driven to zero without bond covenants if the firm never issued any risky debt. But for the firm to follow such a policy is costly if it is optimal to have risky debt in the firm's capital structure. Thus, the Costly Contracting Hypothesis presupposes that there are benefits associated with the inclusion of risky debt. . . .

Evidence Provided by an Examination of Bond Covenants

. . . Debt covenants are a persistent phenomenon. They have been included in debt contracts for hundreds of years, and over time the corporate debt contract which contains them has evolved into "undoubtedly the most involved financial document that has been devised." The covenants discussed in Commentaries are representative of the covenants found in actual practice. . . .

It seems reasonable that the covenants discussed in Commentaries have not arisen merely by chance; rather, they take their current form and have survived because they represent a contractual solution which is efficient from the standpoint of the firm. As Alchian indicates, "success (survival) accompanies relative superiority"; and "whenever successful enterprises are observed, the elements common to those observed successes will be associated with success and copied by others in their pursuit of profits or success." Hence the Commentaries represents a powerful piece of evidence on efficient forms of the financial contract. . . .

Overview of the Paper

Observed debt covenants are discussed in section 2. To facilitate the discussion, observed covenants are grouped into four categories: production/investment covenants, divided covenants, financing covenants, and bonding covenants. We use a common format for the discussion of each covenant; a particular type of covenant is first described, and its impact then analyzed.

Covenants which directly restrict the shareholders' choice of production/investment policy, are discussed in section 2.1. These covenants impose restrictions on the firm's holdings of financial investments, on the disposition of assets, and on the firm's merger activity. The observed constraints place few specific limitations on the firm's choice of investment policy. However, it is important to realize that, because of the cash flow identity, investment, dividend, and financing policy are not independent; they must be determined simultaneously. Thus, covenants which restrict dividend and financing policy also restrict investment policy.

Bond covenants which directly restrict the payment of dividends are considered in section 2.2. The dividend restriction does not take the form of a constant dollar limitation. Instead, the maximum allowable dividend payment is a function of both accounting earnings and the proceeds from the sale of new equity. The analysis suggests that the dividend covenant places an implicit constraint on the investment policy of the firm and provides the stockholders with incentives to follow a firm-value-maximizing production/investment policy.

Financing policy covenants are discussed in section 2.3. These covenants restrict not only the issuance of senior debt, but the issuance of debt of any priority. In addition, the firm's right to incur other fixed obligations such as leases is restricted. These restrictions appear to reduce the underinvestment incentives discussed by Myers. In section 2.4, convertibility, callability, and sinking fund provisions are also examined. These provisions appear to specify payoffs to bondholders in a way which also controls bondholder-stockholder conflict.

In section 2.5, we analyze covenants which specify bonding activities — expenditures made by the firm which control the bond-holder-stockholder conflict. These bonding activities include the provision of audited financial statements, the specification of accounting techniques, the required purchase of insurance, and the periodic provision of a statement, signed by the firm's officers, indicating compliance with the covenants.

Just as the covenants described in section 2 are persistent phenomena, so are the institutions for enforcing these contractual restrictions. The enforcement of bond covenants within the existing institutional arrangements is the subject of section 3. The Trust Indenture Act of 1939 restricts the provisions of the debt contract for public issues in a way which makes the enforcement of tightly restrictive covenants very expensive. Another enforcement cost emanates from the legal liability which bondholders incur when they exercise control over the firm. Default remedies which are available to the firm, and their associated costs, are also discussed.

Our conclusions are presented in section 4. . . . [The detailed examination of bond provisions in sections 2 and 3 is omitted.]

Conclusions

The Role of Bond Covenants

We have examined the specific provisions which are included in corporate debt contracts. Since covenants are a persistent phenomena, we can therefore assume that these provisions are efficient from the standpoint of the firm's owners, and thus we can draw inferences about the role of these contractual forms in the firm's capital structure.

Observed debt covenants reduce the costs associated with the conflict of interest between bondholders and stockholders; the ingenuity with which debt contracts are written indicates the strong economic incentives for the firm's owners to lower the agency costs which can result from having risky debt in the firm's capital structure.

The existence of standardized debt contracts such as those found in Commentaries suggests that the out-of-pocket costs of drafting observed bond contracts are small indeed. However, the direct and opportunity costs of complying with the contractual restrictions appear to be substantial. We have presented no evidence on the precise dollar magnitudes, and we emphasize that a particular covenant included in a given debt contract will not impose opportunity costs with probability one. But our analysis indicates that observed bond covenants involve expected costs which are large enough to help account for the variation in debt contracts across firms. This is consistent with the Costly Contracting Hypothesis. On the other hand, it is inconsistent with the Irrelevance Hypothesis, which predicts that total resources expenditures on control of the bondholder-stockholder conflict will be negligible.

Our analysis also sheds some light on the relative costs of the alternative types of restrictions which can be written into the debt contract. We conclude that production/investment policy is very expensive to monitor. Stockholder use (or misuse) of production/investment policy frequently involves not some explicit act, but the failure to take a certain action (e.g., failure to accept a positive net present value project). It is expensive even to ascertain when the firm's production/investment policy is not optimal, since such a determination depends on magnitudes which are difficult to observe. The high monitoring costs which would be associated with restrictive production/investment covenants, including the potential legal costs associated with bondholder control, dictate that few production/investment decisions will be contractually proscribed. For the firm's owners to go very far in directly restricting the firm's production/investment policy would be inefficient.

On the other hand, we conclude that dividend policy and financing policy involve lower monitoring costs. Stockholder use of these policies to "hurt" bondholders involves acts (e.g., the sale of a large bond issue) which are readily observable. Because they are cheaper to monitor, it is efficient to restrict production/investment policy by writing dividend and financing policy covenants in a way which helps assure that stockholders will act to maximize the value of the firm.

Implications for Capital Structure

With more fixed claims in the capital structure, the benefits to the stockholders from asset substitution, claim dilution, underinvestment, and dividend payout increase; with higher benefits, the stockholders will expend more real resources "getting around" any particular set of contractual constraints. This, in turn, will increase the benefits of increased tightness of the covenants. Accordingly, the costs associated with the bondholder-stockholder conflict rise with the firm's debt/equity ratio. Simply limiting the debt in the capital structure is an efficient mechanism for controlling this conflict. Because of this, the costs associated with writing and enforcing covenants influence the level of debt the firm chooses.

Since observed debt covenants involve real costs, there must be some benefit in having debt in the firm's capital structure; otherwise, the bondholder-stockholder conflict can be costlessly eliminated by not issuing debt. Hence our evidence indicates not only that there is an optimal form of the debt contract, but an optimal *amount* of debt as well. The benefits from issuing risky debt are not well understood, and even though the costs we have discussed in this paper provide a lower bound on their magnitude, our analysis has not permitted us to distinguish between alternative explanations of the benefits: (1) information asymmetries and signalling, (2) taxes, (3) agency costs of equity financing, (4) differential transactions and flotation costs, and (5) unbundling of risk bearing and capital ownership.

The Rights of Creditors of Affiliated Corporations*

Richard A. Posner

[Introductory Note]

[A fundamental attribute of the corporation, as distinct from other types of firm, is the limited liability of the owners for the debts (contract or tort) of the corporation. Their liability is limited to their investment: if the corporation's assets are insufficient to satisfy the debt, the creditor cannot obtain satisfaction out of the personal assets of the shareholders.

The principle of limited liability has seemed to many commentators on corporation law a windfall to shareholders, especially where the shareholder is another corporation rather than a natural person. This point of view is forcefully argued in Jonathan M. Landers, "A Unified Approach to Parent, Subsidiary, and Affiliate Questions in Bankruptcy," 42 U. Chi. L. Rev. 589 (1975). He discusses three interrelated issues in limited liability of affiliated corporations: equitable subordination, piercing the corporate veil, and consolidation of affiliated bankrupt firms. The first relates to the propriety in a bankruptcy proceeding involving a subsidiary or affiliated corporation of

* *Source:* 43 U. Chi. L. Rev. 499–526 (1976), reprinted with permission; copyright © 1976, the University of Chicago. Richard A. Posner is Freeman Professor of Law, University of Chicago.

subordinating the claims of the parent or related corporation against the bankrupt's assets to the claims of other creditors. The second involves a direct effort by creditors of the bankrupt affiliate to reach the parent's assets. The third relates to the case where several affiliated corporations are bankrupt and the creditors of one are contending for a pooling of the assets of the several corporations.

Landers argues that the law has failed to recognize the fact that a group of affiliated corporations will be managed as if they were one: i.e., decisions for each corporation will be made in order to maximize the profits of, not the separate entity, but the ultimate owners. The separate incorporation of divisions of the common enterprise will reflect tax or other financial considerations unrelated to the operating characteristics of the enterprise. But the law mistakenly treats the affiliated group as if it were composed of genuinely independent entities. This treatment hurts creditors because the owners of the group of affiliates may decide for reasons related to the profitability of the entire group to maintain a low capitalization of one corporation, and the creditors of that corporation will thereby incur greater risk than if the law treated the entire group's assets as available to pay the claims of creditors of any of the constituent corporations. Landers concludes that "Through low capitalization requirements and the uncertain prospect of veil piercing, the law has, to a large extent, placed the cost of promoting new businesses on the creditors of the corporation and, through them, on the public as a whole." 42 U. Chi. L. Rev. at 593.

Further, Landers finds that as a matter of history limited liability was never intended to apply in the case where the shareholder claiming limited liability is itself another corporation, for even if limited liability were rejected in such a case no individual shareholder would be at risk for more than his original investment. Landers in consequence recommends that in general the assets of one affiliated corporation should be available to creditors of another in bankruptcy situations, whether through equitable subordination, piercing the corporate veil, or consolidating related bankrupts. However, where creditors of one corporation have relied specifically on its credit, only to find that creditors of an affiliated corporation are seeking to reach the assets to which the first group of creditors is looking for repayment, the reasonable expectations of the first group should be protected.

Landers' position is criticized in the Posner selection that follows.]

Mr. A. Smith wants to borrow $1 million to invest in a mining venture together with $2 million of his own money. He wants the loan for only a year since by the end of the year it will be apparent whether the venture has succeeded; if it has, he would then want to obtain longer-term financing. Since Smith is a man of means, if he gives his personal note to the lender the latter would regard a one-year loan of $1 million as riskless and would offer Smith the riskless short-term interest rate, say six percent. But Smith is reluctant to stake more than $2 million on the outcome of the mining venture. He proposes to the lender a different arrangement, whereby the lender will agree to look for repayment of the loan exclusively to the assets of the mining venture, if any exist, a year hence. Under this arrangement, Smith will be able to limit his liability to his investment in the venture.

The lender estimates that there is an 80 percent probability that the venture will be sufficiently successful to enable repayment of the loan and interest on the due date, and a 20 percent probability that the venture will fail so badly that there will be insufficient assets to repay even a part of the loan. On these assumptions* the solution to the lender's problem is purely mechanical; he must calculate the amount, payable at the end of a year, that when multiplied by 80 percent (the probability that payment will in fact be made) will equal $1,060,000, the repayment he would have received at the end of the year had he made the riskless loan. That amount is $1,325,000. Accordingly, the lender will charge Smith 32.5 percent interest for the loan if Smith's obligation to repay is limited to the assets of the venture. At this rate of interest the lender is indifferent as between the riskless and the risky loan.

This example illustrates the fundamental point that the interest rate on a loan is payment not only for renting capital but also for the risk that the borrower will fail to return it. It may be wondered why the borrower might want to shift a part of the risk of business failure to the lender, given that he must compensate him for bearing added risk. There are two reasons why the lender might be the superior risk bearer. First, the lender may be in a better position than the borrower to appraise the risk. Compare the positions of the individual shareholder in a publicly held corporation and the banks that lend the corporation its working capital. It may be easier and hence cheaper for the bank to appraise the risk of a default and the resulting liability than it would be for the shareholder, who may know little or nothing about the business in which he has invested. Second, the borrower may be risk averse and the lender less so (or risk neutral, or even risk preferring). Thus, unlimited liability would discourage investment in business ventures by individuals who

*[and assuming the lender is risk neutral, an assumption relaxed below—Eds.]

wanted to make small, passive investments in such ventures. It would also discourage even substantial entrepreneurial investments by risk-averse individuals — and most individuals are risk averse.

A borrower could in principle negotiate with the lender for an express limited-liability provision. The more usual course, however, is to incorporate and have the corporation borrow the money. The basic principle of corporation law is that the shareholders of a corporation are not personally liable for the corporation's debts unless they agree to assume such liability. Corporate borrowing therefore automatically limits the borrower's liability to his investment in the corporation. The fact that the law permits Smith to limit his liability by conducting his mining venture in the corporate form does not imply, however, that the law is somehow tilted against creditors or enables venturers to externalize the risks of business failure, as Landers argues. Although incorporation permits Smith to shift a part of the risk of failure to the lender, there is no externality; the lender is fully compensated by the higher interest rate that the corporation must pay by virtue of enjoying limited liability. Moreover, the lender is free to insist as a condition of making the loan that Smith guarantee the debts of the corporation personally or that he consent to including in the loan agreement other provisions that will limit the lender's risk — though any reduction in the risk will reduce the interest rate the lender can charge since a portion of that rate is, as we have seen, compensation to the lender for agreeing to bear a part of the risk of the venture.

There is an instructive parallel here to a fundamental principle of bankruptcy law: the discharge of the bankrupt from his debts. This principle, which was originally developed for the protection of business rather than individual bankrupts, enables the venturer to limit his risk of loss to his current assets; he is not forced to hazard his entire earning capacity on the venture. Incorporation performs the same function of encouraging investment by enabling the risk averse to limit their risk of loss to their investment.

Far from externalizing the risks of business ventures, the principle of limited liability in corporation law facilitates a form of transaction advantageous to both investors and creditors; in its absence the supply of investment and the demand for credit might be much smaller than they are. Landers overlooks this essential point because he is unsure of the basis for limited liability.

In discussing the reciprocal relationship of risk and interest rates, I have concentrated on the risk of default that is anticipated when the loan is first made. During the period that the loan is outstanding, however, the risk of default may change. To the extent that the change can be foreseen, it will be reflected in the interest rate negotiated at the outset. To the extent that it cannot be foreseen, the lender may seek to protect himself by offering an amortized loan (which is repaid continuously rather than in a single payment at the end of the term), even if the assets available to repay the loan are not expected to depreciate physically. Since the balance outstanding on the loan declines as a function of time and hence of the probability of unforeseen changes in the risk of default, the lender is protected in part against those changes. Nor is the borrower prejudiced. Should no unforeseen increases in risk materialize, the borrower will be able to negotiate a reduction in the interest rate as the outstanding balance of the loan declines. If the lender refuses to renegotiate the interest rate, the borrower can replace the loan at a lower rate from another lender; if there is a penalty in the loan agreement for prepayment, the borrower was presumably compensated for agreeing to it and cannot complain.

The parties will find it difficult, however, to adjust the interest rate or other terms of the loan to reflect the possibility of the borrower's deliberately increasing the lender's risk. After the interest rate has been agreed upon and the loan agreement signed, the borrower may increase the risk of defaulting on the loan by, for example, obtaining additional loans not subordinated to the first or transferring assets to its shareholders or others without adequate consideration. In effect the borrower has unilaterally reduced the interest rate he is paying for the loan. That rate was negotiated with reference to a lower anticipated level of risk than has come to pass. Given the actual level of risk, the borrower is being allowed to borrow money at less than its true cost.

To protect himself against such dangers the lender may insist that the borrower agree to limit his total indebtedness or the amount of dividends payable during the term of the loan, where "dividend" is broadly defined to include any disposition of corporate assets for less than full market value. Or the lender may insist on some minimum capitalization, impose other restrictions, or require collateral. Alternatively he may decide to forego protection and demand a higher interest rate. It may be difficult, however, to quantify the probability that the borrower will deliberately attempt to increase the riskiness of the loan.

Although the analysis to this point has focused on the explicit loan, it also applies to extensions of credit in other forms. For example, the merchant who does not insist on payment in cash and the employee who is not paid until the end of the week are creditors, and their estimation of the risk of default will determine the amount of credit extended, the length of time for which it is extended, and the interest rate (which, of course, need not be stated separately from the sale price or wage rate). The major difference between the trade creditor and the financial creditor is that the latter, because he is a specialist in credit and because the amount of credit that he extends to each creditor is apt to be larger, is much more likely to negotiate the terms of credit explicitly. This means, as we are about to see, that the provisions of corporation law will have a greater impact on credit transactions with trade creditors than on those with financial creditors.

An important implication of the foregoing analysis is that the specific doctrines of corporation law should not be expected, in general, to have a profound impact on the credit system or to alter the balance of advantage between debtor and creditor. If corporation law did not provide for limited shareholder liability, then in situations where the parties desired to limit that liability in exchange for a higher interest rate the loan agreement would contain an express provision limiting liability. Conversely, under existing law a firm asked to lend money to a corporation in which it lacks confidence can insist as a condition of making the loan that the shareholders agree to guarantee repayment personally, of course, the interest rate will be lower than it would have been without such a guarantee.

Similarly, if the rules of corporation law limiting the payment of dividends to the amount of "earned surplus" shown on the corporation's books effectively protect creditors against attempts by firms to increase the risk of default after the loan has been made, well and good. But if corporation laws were amended to drop all limitations on the payment of dividends, the major consequence would be that those creditors who wanted dividend limitations would have to ask that they be written into the loan agreement.

There are, however, exceptions to the proposition that corporation law does not affect the allocation of resources. One is the involuntary extension of credit. A pedestrian is struck by a moving van in circumstances making the moving company liable to him for a tort. Pre-existing negotiations, explicit or implicit, between the parties with respect to the moving company's ability to make good on the pedestrian's claim are simply not feasible. Since the parties have no opportunity to transact around the provisions of corporation law, the provisions governing limited liability may alter the relative position of debtor and creditor.

A more common exception occurs where, although the context is one of voluntary transacting, the costs of explicitly negotiating the question of extent of liability are high in relation to the stakes involved. The slight probability that an employee will be seriously injured on the job, when multiplied by the probability that the employer will have insufficient assets to satisfy his claim for workmen's compensation, may be too small to warrant inclusion of an express term in the employment contract to cover that contingency. In this case, too, whatever term is implied as a matter of corporate or bankruptcy law will control the parties' relations even if it is contrary to what the parties would have negotiated in a world of zero transaction costs. But there is an important difference: the wage rate can adjust to compensate the worker for the risk of nonpayment of any compensation claim that he may some day have against his employer. Such compensation for bearing an added risk of nonpayment is precluded in the case where the parties have no contractual or potentially contractual relationship at all—the usual situation in an accident between strangers.

These exceptions to one side, the primary utility of corporation law lies in providing a set of standard, implied contract terms, for example, governing credit, so that business firms do not have to stipulate these terms anew every time they transact, although they could do so if necessary. To the extent that the terms implied by corporation law accurately reflect the normal desires of transacting parties, they reduce the cost of transactions. The criterion of an efficient corporation law is therefore whether the terms do in fact reflect commercial realities, so that transacting parties are generally content with them. A corporation law that is out of step with those realities, and so induces contracting parties to draft waivers of the contract terms supplied by the law, is inefficient because it imposes unnecessary transaction costs.

Thus a corporation law is inefficient if it fails to provide standard implied contract terms that afford creditors the sorts of protections against default that they would normally insist upon in an express negotiation. Such a law can be criticized for creating avoidable costs of explicit negotiation. In some cases it can also be criticized for leading creditors to forego desired protective provisions and to settle instead for a higher interest rate as a second-best alternative to the desired protection.

Landers' criticisms, however, are of an entirely different nature. His complaint against a corporation or bankruptcy law that fails to give creditors adequate protection against default is that it shifts the costs of entrepreneurship from shareholders to creditors. Except in the special case of the tort creditor, this is a serious overstatement. At the worst, such a law may lead to somewhat higher interest rates as compensation for the absence of protective provisions that would reduce the risk of default; more probably it will lead simply to lengthier credit agreements. Transacting parties will negotiate explicitly the inclusion of protective provisions that a proper corporation law would read automatically into the credit transaction. The additional transaction costs, to the extent that they are borne in the first instance by the lender, will be passed on in whole or part to the borrower in the form of a (slightly) higher interest rate, thereby reducing the amount of credit extended, presumably also slightly. But this will be the only allocative effect of a corporation law that fails to give the creditors the protections they would normally demand. And observe that such a law hurts borrowers as well as lenders, by raising interest rates.

Let us take a closer look at the types of protection that creditors would normally insist upon and that would therefore be found in an efficient corporation or bankruptcy statute. It is convenient to divide the sources of risk faced by the creditor into two types along the lines of the earlier analysis. The first is the risk of default based on circumstances known or anticipated when the loan is made. The creditor's interest is not necessarily in minimizing this risk; since it is compensated risk any measures taken to reduce it will also reduce the interest rate. The creditor's interest lies rather in forming an accurate idea of the risk, for otherwise he cannot determine what interest rate to charge. Assessment of the risk of default requires accurate information about the existing and expected assets and liabilities of the borrowing corporation and of anyone else who may be liable for the corporation's debts, insofar as those assets and liabilities effect the creditor's ability to obtain repayment. Coping with this risk presents the problem of *information*. Measures that increase the creditor's costs of information are prima facie undesirable. A good example of such a measure would be misrepresentation by the borrower of his solvency.

The second source of risk to the creditor is the possibility that the corporation will take steps to increase the riskiness of the loan after the terms have been set. The problem of coping with this risk is the problem of *supervision;* the creditor must supervise or regulate the corporation's disposition of its assets to the extent necessary to prevent any deliberate attempts to reduce the assets available to repay the loan. Dividend limitations are an illustration of the supervision type of credit term.

Obtaining information and supervising a corporation's internal affairs are costly undertakings. Economizing on these costs is one objective, social as well as private, of the provisions in a credit instrument. The first question to ask about any existing or proposed creditor's right under corporation or other laws is whether it actually reduces the creditor's information or supervision costs. It is often a difficult question to answer, because of differences in the costs of information and supervision to financial, trade, and nonbusiness creditors, because of the debtor's ability to increase those costs by various acts and omissions, and because of differences in the nature of the collateral put up by different debtors (e.g., land versus inventory).

The analysis, moreover, cannot stop with a consideration of the creditor's costs. The goal is to minimize not just the administrative costs of the credit transaction but its total social costs. Even if a rule abrogating the limited liability of corporate shareholders would lower the costs of credit administration by reducing the risk of defaulting on a loan and thereby decreasing the optimal level of expenditures on supervision and information, it would probably be an uneconomical rule because it would prevent a type of risk shifting (from shareholders to creditors) that is apparently highly efficient, judging by its prevalence. To the extent that — paradoxical as it may seem — risk can often be borne more cheaply by creditors than by shareholders, a rule that prevented the shifting of risk from the latter to the former would impose costs in undesired risk that might be much greater than the savings in reduced costs of credit administration. Similarly, a rule that forbade any payment of dividends to corporate shareholders would reduce supervision costs by increasing the assets available for the payment of creditors' claims, but it would also reduce the attractiveness of owning stock to those investors who do not consider appreciation a perfect substitute for periodic income. It would probably not be an optimal rule considering all the relevant costs and benefits of corporate activity.

The ultimate objective of the credit process is to minimize the overall social costs of capital through a complex allocation of costs, including the disutility of risk, between borrower and lender. Measures that minimize the risk borne by the creditor will lower interest rates both directly and by reducing the creditor's optimum expenditure on obtaining information and supervising the debtor's business. But beyond a certain point the cost to the investors of the added risk they are made to bear may well exceed the reduction in interest rates. It is of no benefit to a corporation to be able to borrow at six percent on condition that its shareholders personally guarantee repayment of the loan, if the expected earnings of the corporation are insufficient to compensate the shareholders for giving such a guarantee. An efficient corporation law is not one that maximizes creditor protection on the one hand or corporate freedom on the other, but one that mediates between these goals in a fashion that minimizes the costs of raising money for investment.

Landers is interested in the special case of the creditor of a corporation wholly owned by, or otherwise 100 percent affiliated with, another corporation. To understand this case it is necessary to consider how it might come about that one corporation was owned by or in common with another corporation. Landers' implicit explanation is that an entrepreneur will decide, typically in order to avoid taxes or limit other liabilities, to divide a unitary enterprise — a single business in economic terms — into a series of formally separate but commonly owned and controlled corporations. Under this view of how corporate affiliation arises, the separate corporate status of the different parts of the enterprise is indeed fictional (whether it is harmful is a separate question). But the view is seriously incomplete.

To begin with, often a group of affiliated corporations is not a single enterprise at all. Even before the vogue of the "conglomerate," there were many highly diversified enterprises, comprising a number of distinct businesses, often separately incorporated and related only in the integration of a few headquarters functions such as legal counseling and securities issuance. How might the common ownership of seemingly unrelated businesses come about? There are a number of possibilities. First, there may be managerial or financial economies (the businesses aren't really unrelated). Second, the owners may be trying to reduce risk through diversification. Third, an enterprise may decide to expand internally (through a separate corporation) into an unrelated line of business because it perceives opportunities for greater profits than its shareholders could earn if the funds employed in entering the new line were instead distributed to the shareholders as dividends. A related point is that a firm which is not well managed is an attractive target for a takeover bid, normally by another corporation rather than by an individual or a group of individuals. The bidder may not be in the same or even in a related line of business. It may instead be a specialist in identifying undervalued firms. But the takeover bid is only the most dramatic illustration of the operation of the market for corporate assets. The existence of such a market implies that corporations are frequently in the market for other corporations, sometimes in different lines of business.

Where a commonly controlled pool of capital is employed in a number of different lines of business, it is not at all obvious that the owners of the pool should be treated differently from other venturers. It is especially doubtful in the case of "lateral piercing," which Landers appears to regard as indistinguishable in principle from piercing the subsidiary's corporate veil to reach the parent's assets. Suppose that individuals who in the aggregate own 100 percent of X Corporation's stock create a new corporation, Y, to engage in an unrelated business. X and Y are affiliates, and Landers I take it would like the creditors of Y to be able to reach the assets of X. But why should a group of investors be treated differently by the law just because they own a corporation engaged in an unrelated business? And if they should *not* be treated differently, then why, if X, acting as an agent of its shareholders, forms Y in order to engage in an unrelated business, should X's liabilities (and therefore those of its shareholders) be greater than those borne by other entrants into Y's market?

Landers' implicit answer is that X may take steps to increase the risks borne by creditors of Y. X may, for example, cast its equity investment in Y in the form of a loan, thus reducing the assets available to satisfy claims of Y's genuine creditors, without disclosure to those creditors. But the same danger is present in the case of two corporations owned by the same individuals. Indeed, it is present in the case of an unaffiliated corporation. There is a conflict of interest between the personal shareholder and the creditor as well as between the corporate shareholder and the creditor; in both cases management has an incentive to try to shift uncompensated risk to the creditor. Is the danger greater when the shareholder is a corporation? Probably it is greatest in the closely held corporation whether the dominant shareholder is an individual or a corporation. Arguably, therefore, if a shareholder that is a corporation should not be permitted to hide behind limited liability when the subsidiary corporation is unable to pay a creditor's claims, neither should the shareholder who is an individual be permitted to invoke limited liability when the corporation in which he owns stock is unable to satisfy the corporation's debts. The logic of Landers' arguments would seem to require the abolition of limited liability across the board.

To this it may be objected that there is a greater social interest in according limited liability to personal shareholders than to corporations, in order to make investment in enterprises attractive to individuals who would be deterred from investing by the prospect of potentially unlimited personal liability for the debts of the enterprise. . . . Making a parent liable for the subsidiary's debts will not result in unlimited personal liability for the parent's shareholders, whereas making a personal shareholder liable for corporate debts would have this effect.

However, the implication of this point — which is that unlimited corporate-shareholder liability would have a less dampening effect on individual investment than unlimited personal-shareholder liability — is applicable primarily to the large publicly held corporation, where, as we shall see, the objections to limited liability in the affiliation context are weak. The investor in the large corporation is ordinarily in a position to minimize the risk that is transmitted to him through the ventures undertaken and liabilities incurred by a corporation in which he owns stock simply by holding a diversified portfolio of corporate securities. Unlimited corporate-shareholder liability would threaten such an investor far less than unlimited personal-shareholder liability. But the investor in a small corporation frequently does not enjoy the same opportunities for diversification. He cannot protect himself against the consequences of unlimited liability of corporate shareholders as effectively as the investor in the large corporation. . . .

Landers' only reason why the case for limited liability is weaker for corporate than for personal shareholders is that affiliated corporations, even if engaged in totally unrelated lines of business, will be managed differently from independent firms because the owners will seek to maximize the profits of the enterprise as a whole rather than the profits of any individual corporation. This argument is unconvincing. Normally the profits of the group will be maximized by maximizing the profits of each constituent corporation. Indeed, if the corporations are engaged in truly unrelated lines of business, the profits of each will be completely independent.

It is true that the common owner can take measures that conceal or distort the relative profitability of his different enterprises, as by allocating capital among them at arbitrary interest rates. But it is not true . . . that owners invariably or typically adopt such measures. For one thing, such measures are costly because they reduce the information available to the common owner about the efficiency with which his various corporations are being managed. The costs rise rapidly with the size of the overall enterprise. That is why large corporations typically treat their major divisions and subsidiaries as "profit centers," which are expected to conduct themselves as if they were independent firms. For similar reasons, divisional managers are compensated on the basis of the profitability of the subsidiary or division rather than of the enterprise as a whole.

Even when the activities of affiliated corporations are closely related — when they produce substitute or complementary goods — normally each corporation will be operated as a separate profit center in order to assure that the profits of the group will be maximized. It is only in the exceptional case that maximizing the profits of a group of related corporations will involve different behavior from what could be expected of separately owned corporations. To be sure, where there are genuine cost savings from common ownership, as in some cases where the affiliated corporations operate at successive stages in the production of a good, the two corporations will be managed differently from separately owned corporations in the same line of business in the sense that their operations will be integrated in a way independent corporations' are not. But that would not mean that either corporation was, in any sense relevant to the reasonable expectations of creditors, something other than a bonafide profit-maximizing firm. Rather, each corporation would simply be more profitable than its nonintegrated competitors because its costs were lower. It would be perverse to penalize such a corporation for its superior efficiency by withdrawing the privilege of limited liability enjoyed by its nonintegrated competitors. Moreover, in this case as well, the common owner has a strong incentive to avoid intercorporate transfers that, by distorting the profitability of each corporation, make it more difficult for the common owner to evaluate their performance. That is why the price at which one division of a vertically integrated firm will "sell" its output to another division is normally the market price for the good in question (less any savings in cost attributable to making an intrafirm transfer compared to a market transaction), rather than an arbitrary transfer price designed artificially to enhance the profits of one division at the expense of the other.

The important difference between a group of affiliates engaged in related businesses and one engaged in a number of unrelated businesses is not that the conduct of corporations in the first group will differ from that of nonaffiliated corporations in the same businesses, but that the creditor dealing with a group of affiliates in related businesses is more likely to be misled into thinking that he is dealing with a single corporation. The mere possibility of deception in some affiliation cases does not in logic justify disregarding the corporate form in *all* such cases. Deception is rather one of the factors to be considered in applying a rule of creditor protection properly based on the creditor's information costs. Such a rule will be described later in this paper.

In sum, Landers' "single enterprise" approach exaggerates the degree to which we can expect affiliated corporations to be operated differently from separately owned corporations. A more reasonable presumption, especially in the case of large publicly owned firms, is that whether a corporation is owned by individuals or by another corporation will in general not affect the way in which the corporation is managed, and so in general should not be a matter of concern to creditors. It may be true that the social interest in limited liability is somewhat attenuated in the case where the shareholder is a large publicly held corporation. But that is scarcely a strong argument for abrogating the limited liability of corporations owned by such shareholders, given that affiliates managed by a large publicly held corporation are not likely to be managed differently from how they would be managed if they were independent firms. The danger of abuse of the corporate form is greater in the case of the small business, where operation of the constituent corporations as separate profit centers is less necessary to assure efficient management. But an offsetting factor is that individual investors' interest in the limited liability of corporate affiliates approaches, in the context of small business, their interest in preserving the limited liability of unaffiliated corporations. . . .

. . . I have already suggested that a role of indiscriminate piercing would often impose unacceptable risks on the personal owners of a small corporation that owned or was otherwise affiliated with the corporation whose veil was pierced. Risk, however, is only one factor to be considered. Another is the creditor's information and supervision costs. Landers believes those costs would be lower under a rule allowing the subsidiary's creditors to pierce the corporate veil. I disagree.

Take the case of unrelated businesses — the parent is engaged in the production of steel, the subsidiary in the production of cornflakes. The costs of supervision to a creditor of the subsidiary may be smaller if he knows that he can pierce the corporate veil and reach the parent's assets; he need not worry that the parent might strip the subsidiary of the assets necessary to satisfy creditors' claims. But the creditor's information costs may now be greater. Evaluating the risk that he will not be repaid will now require an investigation of the creditworthiness of the parent. The creditor unable to pierce the corporate veil would normally forego such an investigation.

More important, a complete analysis of the effect of piercing the corporate veil on information and supervision costs must consider the creditors of the parent as well as those of the subsidiary. If piercing the veil is allowed, the parent's creditors are exposed to an additional risk — that the parent's assets may be diverted to satisfy the claims of the subsidiary's creditors. To determine the parent's creditworthiness, therefore, prospective creditors of the parent must also investigate the subsidiary's creditworthiness. Acquiring the necessary information will become even more complicated if we allow not only the subsidiary's creditors to reach the assets of the parent, but the parent's creditors to reach the assets of the subsidiary, an extension implicit in the unitary-enterprise approach proposed by Landers.

The basic point, however, is a simpler one: there is no basis for believing that a general rule permitting the piercing of the corporate veil in order to reach the assets of an affiliated corporation would minimize the costs of credit transactions, and therefore result in lower interest rates at any given level of risk, even if it did not impose unacceptable risks on the personal owners of affiliated corporations. Stated otherwise, it has not been established that a general rule allowing the piercing of the corporate veil in the case of affiliated corporations would approximate the normal desires of the transacting parties.

Landers' proposal to subordinate a parent's loan to a subsidiary to the claims of the subsidiary's independent creditors is also objectionable, but mainly on different grounds. Like veil piercing, the prospect of subordination would increase the risk of nonpayment to the parent and thereby induce the parent's creditors to take account of that prospect in appraising the parent's creditworthiness. This might in turn lead those creditors to investigate the subsidiary's creditworthiness more carefully than if the parent were merely another creditor of the subsidiary. But the extent and therefore cost of the additional credit inquiry would be less than in the veil-piercing case since the potential liability of the parent would be limited to the amount of the loan.

In effect, Landers is proposing that the only kind of investment that a corporation may make in an affiliated corporation is an equity investment. This is less objectionable than the piercing rule from the standpoint of burdening creditors of the parent, but it is independently objectionable as undermining the overall efficiency of the investment process. Parent corporations are sometimes the most efficient lenders to their affiliates because the enterprise relationship may enable the parent to evaluate the risk of a default at a lower cost than an outsider would have to incur. A rule that placed heavier liabilities on a parent lender than on an outsider lender might thus distort the comparative advantages of these two sources of credit.

The proposed rule is a dubious one even from the excessively narrow standpoint of protecting creditors of the affiliate receiving the loan. The parent may extend credit to its subsidiary on terms more advantageous to the latter than an independent creditor would offer because the parent fears that its own creditworthiness would suffer if the subsidiary became insolvent. The availability of such loans thus reduces the risk that the subsidiary will in fact default. If the parent is not allowed to make a "real" loan to a subsidiary — if in effect the only permitted method of rescue is a contribution of equity capital — the added risks of this method of rescue may deter the parent from trying to salvage the subsidiary. If so, the creditors of the subsidiary will be hurt. There is, to be sure, another side to the coin. The parent may make the loan merely to conceal the subsidiary's precarious state and thereby attract new creditors who, but for the loan, would have been warned away by slow payment or other symptoms of financial distress that the loan may mask. But this possibility indicates only that parent-subsidiary lending is susceptible of abuse, and not that creditors in general would be benefited by a rule of automatic subordination of the parent's loan to the rights of independent creditors.

In the case of consolidation in bankruptcy of affiliated corporations, Landers recognizes that the interests of two groups of creditors are in conflict. . . . Landers urges consolidation as the general rule but would recognize an exception where the creditors of one of the corporations have specifically relied on the corporate separateness of the borrower. The recognition of this exception is inconsistent with Landers's treatment of the veil-piercing case. The problem of reliance on the corporate form arises in the context of attempts to pierce the corporate veil as well as in the consolidation context. Landers assumes it away in the former context by expressly confining his discussion to cases where the parent's assets are so great that it cannot be made insolvent by having to answer for the debts of its subsidiaries. He reasons that in such cases the parent's creditors cannot be harmed by a change in law that would reduce the risks borne by the subsidiary's creditors relative to those borne by the parent's creditors. But this reasoning is unsound. It erroneously treats solvency and insolvency as dichotomous states. As stressed [above] the interest rate on a loan is determined by the estimated risk of default and that estimate will always fall somewhere in between zero and 100 percent; it will not be zero *or* 100 percent. Since anything that increases the estimated risk will lead a creditor to insist on a higher interest rate, creditors will not be indifferent to changes in law that increase the risk of a default, even though, ex post, the default does not materialize. Ex ante they will incur costs to ascertain the change in the risk of default brought about by an expansion in the rights of competing creditors. To assume that the parent corporation will still be solvent after being made liable for the debts of a subsidiary is to assume away the principal policy issue concerning piercing the veil — its impact on the costs of credit.

   . . . Limited liability can be abused but the law should focus on the abuses and preserve the principle. To this end, it is first necessary to make a distinction between the involuntary (normally tort) creditor and the voluntary creditor. In a series of cases in New York, the courts have wrestled with the problem of the taxi company that incorporates each taxicab separately in order to limit its tort liability to accident victims. In terms of the analysis in this paper, the separate incorporation of the taxicabs increases the risk that the taxi company will default on its tort obligations. If this were a negotiated obligation the creditor-victim would charge a higher interest rate to reflect the increased risk, but it is not, negotiations between the taxi company and the accident victims before the accident being infeasible. The result of separate incorporation is therefore to externalize the costs of taxi service. But although this result is socially inefficient, the analysis cannot stop here. Permitting the corporate veil to be pierced would create an inefficiency of another sort: investment in taxi service would be discouraged because investors would be unable to limit their liability, and the information costs of creditors of affiliated corporations (or for that matter of creditors of noncorporate shareholders) would be increased. To be sure, the enterprise could insure itself against tort liability. But this would not be a satisfactory alternative to limited liability. The managers might fail to take out adequate insurance; the insurance company might for a variety of reasons refuse or be unable to pay a tort judgment against the insured (the insurance company might for example become insolvent); the particular tort might be excluded from the coverage of the insurance policy. An alternative would be to preserve limited liability but require every company engaged in dangerous activity to post a bond equal to the highest reasonable estimate of the probable extent of its tort liability. Shareholders would be protected; accident costs would be internalized; and the information costs of the creditors of the affiliated corporations would be minimized.

The other and more important case in which piercing the corporate veil may be warranted is where separate incorporation is misleading to creditors. In this case pooling the assets of the affiliated corporations for purposes of meeting creditors' claims would reduce the creditors' information and regulation costs. If corporations are permitted to represent that they have greater assets to pay creditors than they actually have, the result will be to increase the costs that creditors must incur to ascertain the true creditworthiness of the corporations with which they deal. Misrepresentation is a way of increasing a creditor's information costs, and the added costs are wasted from a social standpoint to the extent that the misrepresentation could be prevented at lower cost by an appropriate sanction against it.

Suppose for example that a bank holding company establishes a subsidiary to invest in real estate. The holding company gives the subsidiary a name confusingly similar to that of the holding company's banking subsidiary, and the real estate corporation leases office space in the bank so that its offices appear to be bank offices. Unsophisticated creditors extend generous terms to the real estate subsidiary on the reasonable belief that they are dealing with the bank itself. In these circumstances it would seem appropriate to "estop" (i.e., forbid) the bank holding company — or even the bank itself — to deny that it is the entity to which the creditors have extended credit. To protect the legal separateness of affiliated corporations in this case would lead creditors as a class to invest a socially excessive amount of resources in determining the true corporate status of the entity to which they were asked to extend credit.

In general, a corporation's creditors should be allowed to reach a shareholder's assets when the shareholder, whether an individual or another corporation, has represented to the creditor that those assets are in fact available to satisfy any claim that the creditor may assert against the debtor corporation. Misrepresentation is a familiar and widely used concept in the law, with strong intuitive appeal, and its use in the present context is firmly grounded in the economics of credit and information. Moreover, it is the dominant approach in fact used by the courts in deciding whether to pierce the corporate veil. True, they often describe the criterion for piercing as whether the debtor corporation is merely an "agent," "alter ego," or "instrumentality" of the shareholder, which as Landers points out is a confusing test. A careful reading of these decisions suggests, however, that in applying the "agent-alter ego-instrumentality" test the courts commonly ask whether the parent engaged in conduct or made representations likely to deceive the creditor into thinking that the debtor had more assets than it really had or that the parent was the real debtor. And some courts have explicitly adopted a misrepresentation rationale for determining whether to pierce the corporate veil. . . .

The misrepresentation approach can also be used to answer the other two specific questions discussed by Landers — subordination of the parent's loans and consolidation of bankrupt affiliates. Although a rule of automatic subordination would be inappropriate , a creditor should be permitted to show that the parent's loan misled him regarding the amount of assets the corporation had available for repayment of his loan. He may have reasonably believed that the corporation had the usual equity capitalization for a corporation of its size and line of business. If these reasonable expectations were defeated because the parent supplied capital to the corporation in the form of a loan rather than equity, the parent should be estopped to deny that the loan is actually a part of the subsidiary's equity capital. Similarly, consolidation of bankrupt affiliates should be permitted where the creditor of one of the affiliates reasonably relied on an appearance of greater capitalization than in fact existed.

In all cases in which estoppel is successfully invoked some competing group of creditors will be disadvantaged whose expectations may have been just as reasonable as those of the creditors invoking estoppel. But to the extent that enforcing the estoppel or misrepresentation principle will discourage borrowers from using the corporate form to mislead creditors, creditors in general will benefit — as will society since the costs of credit transactions will be lower, and hence interest rates will be lower for any given level of risk.

The suggested approach deals automatically with the problem especially troubling to Landers of the entrepreneur who, in order to avoid creditor and other claims, divides a truly unitary business into a number of separate corporations. Insofar as creditors are misled by the proliferation of affiliated corporations, the misrepresentation principle affords them a remedy. If they are not misled, the proliferation of corporations is harmless and should be ignored.

NOTES AND QUESTIONS

1. Modigliani and Miller were not the first to believe that the market value of the firm (that is, the total value of all its debt and equity claims) was not dependent on the proportions of the different securities it issued, but they were the first to undertake a rigorous demonstration. Their "arbitrage" proof, based on the ability of investors to achieve any desired degree of leverage in their own holdings regardless of the actions of the firm, made use of a number of assumptions, but subsequent theoretical papers, in particular by Joseph Stiglitz, have shown that the only assumption logically necessary to the proof is that of perfect and complete capital markets. See, e.g., Stiglitz, On the Irrelevance of Corporate Financial Policy, 64 Am. Econ. Rev. 851 (1974).

2. A simple numerical example of Modigliani and Miller's arbitrage argument is presented in Richard A. Posner, Economic Analysis of Law 322–24 (2d ed. 1977):

> . . . Consider a hypothetical firm that has 1 million shares of common stock outstanding, no debt, and an annual net operating income of $3 million expected to continue at that level. Since the value of a firm is the present discounted value of its expected income, the value of our hypothetical firm will be some multiple of $3 million (what determines the multiple?). Suppose the multiple is 10. Then the firm will be worth $30 million, and the price of a share of stock in the firm will be $30, the earnings per share $3, and price-earnings ratio 10. Now suppose the firm borrows $15 million at 6 percent interest and uses the proceeds of the loan to buy back one half of the outstanding shares of its common stock, which it then retires. The operating net income is unchanged but there is now an interest expense of $900,000, which reduces the shareholders' earnings to $2.1 million—or $4.20 per share, since the number of shares has been reduced from 1 million to 500,000. If the price-earnings ratio is unchanged, each share of stock will be worth $42 and the aggregate shareholders' equity will be $21 million. The value of the firm will therefore be $36 million ($21 million equity plus $15 million debt). It seems that the change in the debt-equity ratio has created a new value of $6 million.
>
> But something must be wrong. The net assets of the firm were worth $30 million originally because they generated net operating income of $3 million a year. Nothing has happened to make those assets more productive; they still generate $3 million in annual income. Why

would a purchaser now pay $36 million for the assets? The answer is that he would not.

The fallacy in the hypothetical is the assumption that the price-earnings ratio is unaffected by the amount of debt in the firm's capital structure. We know the addition of leverage increases the risk to the shareholder. Formerly, if one year the firm's net operating income declined by one-half, the shareholder's return also declined by one-half. Now, should the firm's net operating income decline from $3 million to $1.5 million, the earnings of the shareholder will decline from $4.20 per share to $1.20 per share (a fall of more than 70 percent), because the firm's interest expense is fixed. Since most investors are risk averse, the price-earnings ratio of the stock will be lower than before the addition of leverage. Indeed, since the value of the firm's assets is unaffected by how the firm chooses to arrange its capital structure, we would expect the firm's price-earning ratio to fall to 7.14, for this is the ratio at which the value of the firm is unchanged from before.

There is no reason to expect the purchaser of a firm to pay a premium because its capital structure contains leverage, even if he prefers a high-risk investment with a high expected return. He can create his preferred debt-equity ratio by purchasing some of the stock with borrowed money. Or he can pair his purchase with investments in highly levered or otherwise highly risky firms.

3. The following figure depicts the relationship between the overall market value of the firm (V, which is equal to the sum of the current market value of its bonds or debt (B) and of its stock (S)) and

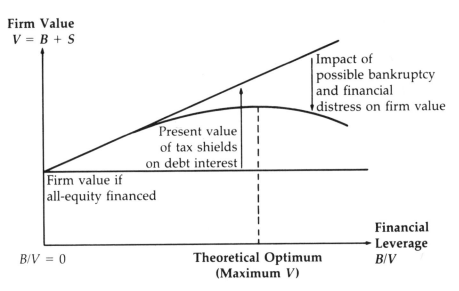

Figure 14
Impact of Financial Leverage on Firm Value

Source: Myers, Figure 1, with permission.

its degree of leverage (B/V), when the M & M logic is combined with tax and bankruptcy effects. It is taken from S. Myers, Modern Developments in Financial Management 128 (1976).

4. Are bankruptcy costs large enough to play the role attributed to them by Baxter and a number of subsequent authors? R. Haugen and L. Senbet, in The Insignificance of Bankruptcy Costs to the Theory of Optimal Capital Structure, 33 J. Fin. 383 (1978), argue that they cannot be a major factor since they can be avoided by, and hence cannot exceed the costs of, an informal reorganization through the capital market. That is, either stockholders or bondholders could buy out the other group (or a third party could buy out both) and thereby avoid bankruptcy altogether; in a rational world, there will be no resort to bankruptcy unless its costs are less than the (relatively low?) transactions costs of such a capital market reorganization.

5. The analysis of tax effects in Miller's article is carried much further in an enlightening but complex paper by Roger Gordon and Burton Malkiel of Princeton: Taxation and Corporation Finance (rev. Nov. 1979).

6. Another explanation for the issuance of debt—or at least secured debt—is that it reduces the value of possible future claims by judgment creditors and tax collectors, to the benefit of present equity holders. See J. Scott, Bankruptcy, Secured Debt, and Optimal Capital Structure, 32 J. Fin. 1 (1977). But this argument too is of limited import, since it should not apply to claims arising out of voluntary customer relationships; see Smith and Warner's Comment, 34 J. Fin. 247 (1979).

7. See Jonathan M. Landers, Another Word on Parents, Subsidiaries and Affiliates in Bankruptcy, 43 U. Chi. L. Rev. 527 (1976), for a reply to Posner's criticisms of his position.

8. An "externality" is a term in economics which refers to a cost or benefit of an activity which the parties engaged in the activity do not take into account in their decisions. An example would be the cost in dirty laundry of a factory's smoke. The factory and its customers will not take account of that cost in deciding on the price and quantity of the factory's output. In his classic article, The Problem of Social Cost, 3 J. Law & Econ. 1 (1960), Ronald H. Coase showed that this result depends on the presence of high transaction costs. If it is feasible for the owner of the laundry to contract with the factory, the externality will be internalized. If, for example, the laundry owner would be willing to pay $10 to the factory to reduce its production of smoke, that $10 becomes a cost (an opportunity cost) to the factory of its present level of pollution. By polluting at this level, it foregoes the $10 receipt which it would otherwise obtain. Thus, even if we

assume that the factory is not legally liable for smoke damage, if a transaction with the victim would be feasible, then the cost of the damage will be internalized to (i.e., be taken into account in the decisions of) the factory and its customers.

Professor Landers' suggestion that, "Through low capitalization requirements and the uncertain prospect of veil piercing, the law has, to a large extent, placed the cost of promoting new businesses on the creditors of the corporation and, through them, on the public as a whole," appears to ignore the Coase Theorem. The creditors are in a contractual relationship with the corporation to which they have extended credit. Given this relationship, it is difficult to see how the corporation could externalize some of its costs to creditors. If, through proliferation of affiliates or whatever, the corporation increases the risk of default, and hence the costs of credit, the creditors will charge a higher interest rate, and the effort at externalization will be defeated.

The externality argument has real bite with respect to the torts of the corporation committed against persons or firms that are not in a contractual relationship with the corporation and where the costs of creating such a relationship would be prohibitive. Consider a corporation that owns trucks which occasionally are involved in accidents injuring third parties who are themselves without fault. If through undercapitalization or other means the corporation is able to insulate itself from liability for the full costs of those accidents to the victims, it is indeed placing accident costs that belong on it on third parties who cannot, as in our hypothetical smoke case, feasibly transact with the corporation. What is the economic argument against piercing the veil in this circumstance?

9. Notice the emphasis in Posner's paper on corporation law as a standard-form contract—here between the corporation and its creditors rather than between the corporation and its shareholders. Does this theory of corporation law imply that transaction costs are significant after all in the case of credit agreements? Is this implication consistent with the Coase Theorem?

10. Related to the last question, is there a reason to distinguish, so far as incorporating creditor-protection provisions in corporation law is concerned, between the trade creditor (i.e., a supplier who does not sell on a strictly cash basis) and the financial creditor (a bank or other lending institution, or the bondholders of the corporation)? Are the relevant transaction costs significantly different between these two groups?

11. For further analysis of the economics of creditor protection in the context of limited liability and affiliated corporations, see Fischer Black, Merton H. Miller and Richard A. Posner, An Ap-

proach to the Regulation of Bank Holding Companies, 51 J. Bus. 379 (1978). And for a lucid, nontechnical discussion of the economics of credit, with references to the technical literature, see Thomas H. Jackson and Anthony T. Kronman, Secured Financing and Priorities among Creditors, 88 Yale L.J. 1143 (1979).

Chapter 9

Dividend Policy

A controversy somewhat analogous to that of the firm's opti-mal capital structure exists with regard to the effects of a firm's dividend policy. The return to investors in common stocks is com-posed of two ingredients: the dividends received and the change in the price of the shares owned. Does it matter to investors whether a firm which earned $X a share proceeds to retain those earnings in the business or pay out some fraction as dividends? Leaving out consideration of personal income taxes for the moment, does the payment of a dividend simply reduce the value of a share by the same amount? Or does the investor set greater store by the divi-dend dollar in hand than on the one left behind in the share price bush? The view one takes of such matters has direct relevance to such legal doctrines as those bearing on the right of stockholders to bring actions against the board of directors to compel the payment of dividends.

The traditional view is expressed succinctly in Graham, Dodd and Cottle, Security Analysis 480–81 (4th ed. 1962):

> . . . For the vast majority of common stocks the dividend record and prospects have always been the most important factor controlling investment quality and value. The success of the typical concern has been measured by its ability to pay liberal and steadily increasing dividends on its capital. In the majority of cases the price of common stocks has been influenced more markedly by the dividend rate than by the reported earnings. In other words, distributed earnings have had a greater weight in determining market prices than have retained and reinvested earnings. The "outside," or noncontrolling, stock-holders of any company can reap benefits from their investment in only two ways—through dividends and through an increase in the market value of their shares. Since the market value in most cases has depended primarily upon the dividend rate, the latter could be held responsible for nearly all the gains ultimately realized by investors.
>
> This predominant role of dividends has found full reflection in a generally accepted theory of investment value which states that a

common stock is worth the sum of all the dividends expected to be paid on it in the future, each discounted to its present worth.

Because (1) dividends play a dominant role in the market price of the typical common stock and (2) the discounted value of near dividends is higher than the present worth of distant dividends, of two companies with the same earning power and in the same general position in an industry, that one paying the larger dividend will almost always sell at a higher price. Or, similarly, when a company raises its dividend, the price of its shares will also rise, even though there is no accompanying increase in earning power.

See also Gordon, Dividends, Earnings and Stock Prices, 41 Rev. Econ. & Stat. 99 (1959).

If investors and stock prices are much more influenced by dividends than (for example) earnings, it behooves management to be rather careful about cutting dividends or establishing levels that may be difficult to maintain. In a study of corporate dividend practices, John Lintner of Harvard found that companies tended to establish an average target pay-out ratio of around 50–60% of earnings and to adjust to earnings changes in a "smoothing" process over several years; Lintner, Distribution of Income of Corporations Among Dividends, Retained Earnings, and Taxes, 46 Am. Econ. Rev. 96 (1956).

On the theoretical level, Miller and Modigliani again asserted an irrelevance theorem: so long as the firm's investment decisions are determined by the profitability of investment opportunities and not dictated by any one source of financing, such as retained earnings, it doesn't matter what dividend policy the firm chooses to follow. Their paper is the first selection in this chapter.

The M & M analysis did more than challenge the view that a generous dividend policy would enhance stock value. When one leaves the theoretical world of perfect capital markets and introduces a personal income tax structure that differentiates between the treatment of dividends (fully taxable, beyond the $200 exclusion, at progressive rates) and capital gains (taxable only when realized and at favorable rates as compared to ordinary income such as dividends), what is the effect on corporate dividend strategy? Would most stockholders be advantaged if the firm retained its earnings, so that they incurred tax liability only when and if they chose to sell part of their holdings at a better price? If that were the case, a generous dividend policy would be costly to stockholders and *depress* stock value — the opposite of the traditional view.

These sharply contrasting interpretations of the results of any given dividend policy have given rise to a number of empirical investigations. Part of the problem in this research is distinguishing the effects of yield differences from those of risk differences, when comparing share prices and returns of companies following different dividend policies. This is a central concern in the next paper, by Fischer Black and Myron Scholes.

Instead of confirming either the view that dividend payments help a stock's market price or the view that they hurt it, Black and Scholes' research could not detect any effect at all—which is *not* what the M & M irrelevance proposition would seem to imply for a real world in which capital gains are given preferential treatment relative to dividends. Where does that leave our understanding of the relevance of dividends to stock prices? Fischer Black sums up the dilemma in our concluding selection.

*Dividend Policy, Growth, and the Valuation of Shares**

Merton H. Miller and Franco Modigliani

The effect of a firm's dividend policy on the current price of its shares is a matter of considerable importance, not only to the corporate officials who must set the policy, but to investors planning portfolios and to economists seeking to understand and appraise the functioning of the capital markets. Do companies with generous distribution policies consistently sell at a premium over those with niggardly payouts? Is the reverse ever true? If so, under what conditions? Is there an optimum payout ratio or range of ratios that maximizes the current worth of the shares? . . .

I. Effect of Dividend Policy with Perfect Markets, Rational Behavior, and Perfect Certainty

The meaning of the basic assumptions. Although the terms "perfect markets," "rational behavior," and "perfect certainty" are widely used throughout economic theory, it may be helpful to start by spelling out the precise meaning of these assumptions in the present context.

1. In "perfect capital markets," no buyer or seller (or issuer) of securities is large enough for his transactions to have an appreciable impact on the then ruling price. All traders have equal and costless access to information about the ruling price and about all other relevant characteristics of shares (to be detailed specifically later). No brokerage fees, transfer taxes, or other transaction costs are incurred

---

Source: 34 J. Bus. 411–433 (1961), reprinted with permission.

when securities are bought, sold, or issued, and there are no tax differentials either between distributed and undistributed profits or between dividends and capital gains.

2. "Rational behavior" means that investors always prefer more wealth to less and are indifferent as to whether a given increment to their wealth takes the form of cash payments or an increase in the market value of their holdings of shares.

3. "Perfect certainty" implies complete assurance on the part of every investor as to the future investment program and the future profits of every corporation. Because of this assurance, there is, among other things, no need to distinguish between stocks and bonds as sources of funds at this stage of the analysis. We can, therefore, proceed as if there were only a single type of financial instrument which, for convenience, we shall refer to as shares of stock.

The fundamental principle of valuation. Under these assumptions the valuation of all shares would be governed by the following fundamental principle: the price of each share must be such that the rate of return (dividends plus capital gains per dollar invested) on every share will be the same throughout the market over any given interval of time. . . . Otherwise, holders of low-return (high-priced) shares could increase their terminal wealth by selling these shares and investing the proceeds in shares offering a higher rate of return. This process would tend to drive down the prices of the low-return shares and drive up the prices of high-return shares until the differential in rates of return had been eliminated.

The effect of dividend policy. . . . If the firm raises its dividend in [time period] *t*, given its investment decision, will the increase in the cash payments to the current holders be more or less than enough to offset their lower share of the terminal value? Which is the better strategy for the firm in financing the investment: to reduce dividends and rely on retained earnings or to raise dividends but float more new shares?

In our ideal world at least these and related questions can be simply and immediately answered: the two dividend effects must always exactly cancel out so that the payout policy to be followed in *t* will have *no* effect on the price at *t*. . . . Thus, we may conclude that given a firm's investment policy, the dividend payout policy it chooses to follow will affect neither the current price of its shares nor the total return to its shareholders.

Like many other propositions in economics, the irrelevance of dividend policy, given investment policy, is "obvious, once you think of it." It is, after all, merely one more instance of the general principle that there are no "financial illusions" in a rational and perfect economic environment. Values there are determined solely by "real" considerations—in this case the earning power of the firm's assets and its investment policy—and not by how the fruits of the earning power are "packaged" for distribution.

Obvious as the proposition may be, however, one finds few references to it in the extensive literature on the problem. . . .

A major source of these and related misunderstandings of the role of the dividend policy has been the fruitless concern and controversy over what investors "really" capitalize when they buy shares. We say fruitless because as we shall now proceed to show, it is actually possible to derive from the basic principle of valuation (1) not merely one, but several valuation formulas each starting from one of the "classical" views of what is being capitalized by investors. Though differing somewhat in outward appearance, the various formulas can be shown to be equivalent in all essential respects including, of course, their implication that dividend policy is irrelevant. . . .

II. What Does the Market "Really" Capitalize?

In the literature on valuation one can find at least the following four more or less distinct approaches to the valuation of shares: (1) the discounted cash flow approach; (2) the current earnings plus future investment opportunities approach; (3) the stream of dividends approach; and (4) the stream of earnings approach. . . .

The discounted cash flow approach. Consider now the so-called discounted cash flow approach familiar in discussions of capital budgeting. There, in valuing any specific machine we discount at the market rate of interest the stream of cash receipts generated by the machine; plus any scrap or terminal value of the machine; and minus the stream of cash outlays for direct labor, materials, repairs, and capital additions. The same approach, of course, can also be applied to the firm as a whole which may be thought of in this context as simply a large, composite machine. . . . [T]he discounted cash flow approach is thus seen to be an implication of the valuation principle for perfect markets given by equation (1) [omitted].

The investment opportunities approach. Consider next the approach to valuation which would seem most natural from the standpoint of an investor proposing to buy out and operate some already-going concern. In estimating how much it would be worthwhile to pay for the privilege of operating the firm, the amount of dividends to be paid is clearly not relevant, since the new owner can, within wide limits, make the future dividend stream whatever he pleases. For him the worth of the enterprise, as such, will depend only on: (a) the "normal" rate of return he can earn by investing his capital in securities (i.e., the market rate of return); (b) the earning power of the physical assets currently held by the firm; and (c) the opportunities, if any, that the firm offers for making additional investments in real assets that will yield more than the "normal" (market) rate of return. The latter opportunities, frequently termed the "good will" of the business, may arise, in practice, from any of a number of circumstances (ranging all the way from special locational advantages to patents or other monopolistic advantages). . . .

. . . As can readily be seen, a corporation does not become a "growth stock" with a high price-earnings ratio merely because its assets and earnings are growing over time. . . . The essence of "growth," in short, is not expansion, but the existence of opportunities to invest significant quantities of funds at higher than "normal" rates of return. . . .

The stream of dividends approach. From the earnings and earnings opportunities approach we turn next to the dividend approach, which has, for some reason, been by far the most popular one in the literature of valuation. This approach too, properly formulated, is an entirely valid one though, of course, not the only valid approach as its more enthusiastic proponents frequently suggest. It does, however, have the disadvantage in contrast with previous approaches of obscuring the role of dividend policy. In particular, uncritical use of the dividend approach has often led to the unwarranted inference that, since the investor is buying dividends and since dividend policy affects the amount of dividends, then dividend policy must also affect the current price.

Properly formulated, the dividend approach defines the current worth of a share as the discounted value of the stream of dividends to be paid on the share in perpetuity. . . .

. . .An increase in current dividends, given the firm's investment policy, must necessarily reduce the terminal value of existing shares because part of the future dividend stream that would otherwise have accrued to the existing shares must be diverted to attract the outside capital from which, in effect, the higher current dividends are paid. . . . Consequently the market value of the dividends diverted to the outsiders, which is both the value of their contribution and the reduction in terminal value of the existing shares, must always be precisely the same as the increase in current dividends.

The stream of earnings approach. Contrary to widely held views, it is also possible to develop a meaningful and consistent approach to valuation running in terms of the stream of earnings generated by the corporation rather than of the dividend distributions actually made to the shareholders. Unfortunately, it is also extremely easy to mistate or misinterpret the earnings approach as would be the case if the value of the firm were to be defined as simply the discounted sum of future total earnings. The trouble with such a definition is not, as is often suggested, that it overlooks the fact that the corporation is a separate entity and that these profits cannot freely be withdrawn by the shareholders; but rather that it neglects the fact that additional capital must be acquired at some cost to maintain the future earnings stream at its specified level. . . . [The authors' proofs that all four approaches yield consistent valuation formulas have been omitted.]

IV. The Effects of Dividend Policy Under Uncertainty

Uncertainty and the general theory of valuation. In turning now from the ideal world of certainty to one of uncertainty our first step, alas, must be to jettison the fundamental valuation principle as given [above]. . . .

All this is not to say, of course, that there are insuperable difficulties in the way of developing a testable theory of rational market valuation under uncertainty. On the contrary, our investigations of the problem to date have convinced us that it is indeed possible to construct such a theory — though the construction, as can well be imagined, is a fairly complex and space-consuming task. Fortunately, however, this task need not be undertaken in this paper which is concerned primarily with the effects of dividend policy on market valuation. For even without a full-fledged theory of what *does* determine market value under uncertainty we can show that dividend policy at least is *not* one of the determinants. . . .

The irrelevance of dividend policy despite uncertainty. In Section I we were able to show that, given a firm's investment policy, its dividend policy was irrelevant to its current market valuation. We shall now show that this fundamental conclusion need not be modified merely because of the presence of uncertainty about the future course of profits, investment, or dividends (assuming again, as we have throughout, that investment policy can be regarded as separable from dividend policy). . . . [proof omitted.]

The informational content of dividends. To conclude our discussion of dividend policy under uncertainty, we might take note briefly of a common confusion about the meaning of the irrelevance proposition occasioned by the fact that in the real world a change in the dividend rate is often followed by a change in the market price (sometimes spectacularly so). Such a phenomenon would not be incompatible with irrelevance to the extent that it was merely a reflection of what might be called the "informational content" of dividends, an attribute of particular dividend payments hitherto excluded by assumption from the discussion and proofs. That is, where a firm has adopted a policy of dividend stabilization with a long-established and generally appreciated "target payout ratio," investors are likely to (and have good reason to) interpret a change in the dividend rate as a change in management's views of future profit prospects for the firm. The dividend change, in other words, provides the occasion for the price change though not its cause, the price still being solely a reflection of future earnings and growth opportunities. In any particular instance, of course, the investors might well be mistaken in placing this interpretation on the dividend change, since the management might really only be changing its payout target or possibly even attempting to "manipulate" the price. But this would involve no particular conflict with the irrelevance proposition, unless, of course, the price changes in such cases were not reversed when the unfolding of events had made clear the true nature of the situation.

V. Dividend Policy and Market Imperfections

To complete the analysis of dividend policy, the logical next step would presumably be to abandon the assumption of perfect capital markets. This is, however, a good deal easier to say than to do principally because there is no unique set of circumstances that constitutes "imperfection." We can describe not one but a multitude of possible departures from strict perfection, singly and in combinations. Clearly, to attempt to pursue the implications of each of these would only serve to add inordinately to an already overlong discussion. We shall instead, therefore, limit ourselves in this concluding section to a few brief and general observations about imperfect markets that we hope may prove helpful to those taking up the task of extending the theory of valuation in this direction.

First, it is important to keep in mind that from the standpoint of dividend policy, what counts is not imperfection per se but only imperfection that might lead an investor to have a systematic preference as between a dollar of current dividends and a dollar of current capital gains. Where no such systematic preference is produced, we can subsume the imperfection in the (random) error term always carried along when applying propositions derived from ideal models to real-world events.

Second, even where we do find imperfections that bias individual preferences — such as the existence of brokerage fees which tend to make young "accumulators" prefer low-payout shares and retired persons lean toward "income stocks" — such imperfections are at best only necessary but not sufficient conditions for certain payout policies to command a permanent premium in the market. If, for example, the frequency distribution of corporate payout ratios happened to correspond exactly with the distribution of investor preferences for payout ratios, then the existence of these preferences would clearly lead ultimately to a situation whose implications were different in no fundamental respect from the perfect market case. Each corporation would tend to attract to itself a "clientele" consisting of those preferring its particular payout ratio, but one clientele would be entirely as good as another in terms of the valuation it would imply for the firm. Nor, of course, is it necessary for the distributions to match exactly for this result to occur. Even if there were a "shortage" of some particular payout ratio, investors would still normally have the option of achieving their particular saving objectives without paying a premium for the stocks in short supply simply by buying appropriately weighted combinations of the more plentiful payout ratios. In fact, given the great range of corporate payout ratios known to be available, this process would fail to eliminate permanent premiums and discounts only if the distribution of investor preferences were heavily concentrated at either of the extreme ends of payout scale.

Of all the many market imperfections that might be detailed, the only one that would seem to be even remotely capable of producing such a concentration is the substantial advantage accorded to capital gains as compared with dividends under the personal income tax. Strong as this tax push toward capital gains may be for high-income individuals, however, it should be remenbered that a substantial (and growing) fraction of total shares outstanding is currently held by investors for whom there is either no tax differential (charitable and educational institutions, foundations, pension trusts, and low-income retired individuals) or where the tax advantage is, if anything, in favor of dividends (casualty insurance companies and taxable corporations generally). Hence, again, the "clientele effect" will be at work. Furthermore, except for taxable individuals in the very top brackets, the required difference in before-tax yields to produce equal after-tax yields is not particularly striking, at least for moderate variations in the composition of returns. All this is not to say, of course, that differences in yields (market values) caused by differences in payout policies should be ignored by managements or investors merely because they may be relatively small. But it may help to keep investigators from being too surprised if it turns out to be hard to measure or even to detect any premium for low-payout shares on the basis of standard statistical techniques.

Finally, we may note that since the tax differential in favor of capital gains is undoubtedly the major *systematic* imperfection in the market, one clearly cannot invoke "imperfections" to account for the difference between our irrelevance proposition and the standard view as to the role of dividend policy found in the literature of finance. For the standard view is not that low-payout companies command a premium; but that, in general, they will sell at a discount! . . .

The Effects of Dividend Yield and Dividend Policy on Common Stock Prices and Returns*

Fischer Black and Myron Scholes

1. Introduction

. . .Let us assume that a corporation can always choose any dividend policy it wants without changing its investment policy, because it has other sources and uses of funds that are good substitutes for dividends. If corporations are generally aware of the demands of some investors for high dividend yields, and the demands of other investors for low dividend yields, then they will adjust their dividend policies to supply the levels of yield that are most in demand at any particualr time. As a result, the supply of shares at each level of yield will come to match the demand for shares at that level of yield, and investors as a group will be happy with the available range of yields. After equilibrium is reached, no corporation will be able to affect its share price by changing its dividend policy. We call this the "supply effect."

In other words, if a corporation could increase its share price by increasing (or decreasing) its payout ratio, then many corporations would do so, which would saturate the demand for higher (or lower) dividend yields, and would bring about an equilibrium in which marginal changes in a corporation's dividend policy would have no effect on the price of its stock. This will be true even if we take into account all kinds of "institutional factors" such as differential taxes on income and capital gains, differential costs of personal and corporate sale of stock, and trust instruments that allow only

*Source: J. Fin. Econ. 1-22 (1974), reprinted with permission. Fischer Black and Myron Scholes are professors of finance at M.I.T. and the University of Chicago respectively.

the dividends from common stock held in trust to be distributed to the income beneficiary.

In fact, there are some classes of investors that might logically prefer high dividend yields, other things being equal, and other classes of investors that might logically prefer low dividend yields. In the first group are (a) corporations, because they generally pay higher taxes on realized capital gains than on dividend income, (b) certain trust funds in which one beneficiary receives the dividend income and the other receives the capital gains, (c) endowment funds from which only the dividend and interest income may be spent, and (d) investors who are spending from wealth and who find it cheaper and easier to receive dividends than to sell or borrow against their shares. In the second class are principally investors who pay higher taxes if they receive dividends than if they receive an equivalent increase in capital gains. In addition, there is a large group of investors who are tax exempt, and who have no reason to prefer dividends to capital gains, and who may therefore be indifferent to the dividend yield of the shares they hold.

If other things could be held equal, we would expect to find the first group of investors holding common stocks with relatively high dividend yields; and the second group holding common stocks with relatively low dividend yields. The third group would tend to hold both kinds of common stocks. But other things cannot be held equal. We will show that it is not possible to construct a high yield portfolio and a low yield portfolio whose returns are perfectly correlated. So it is not possible to give an investor a choice between two portfolios whose returns are perfectly correlated, where one has a high yield and the other has a low yield. There are systematic differences between high yield and low yield stocks, as we will show later in the paper, that ensure that an investor who concentrates his portfolio in high yield stocks (or low yield stocks) will hold a portfolio that is not as well diversified as a portfolio that could be constructed containing both high and low yield stocks. We call this the "diversification effect."

If the tax effect, the supply effect, and the diversification effect were the principal factors affecting the returns on stocks with different levels of dividend yield, we would expect to find a moderate preference for dividends on the part of some investors, a moderate aversion to dividends on the part of other investors, and an attempt by corporations to choose dividend policies that satisfy the aggregate demand for high and low yield stocks.

Nevertheless, the number of companies with generous dividend policies would appear from casual observation to be far greater than the number of investors who have logical reasons for preferring dividends to capital gains. If these factors were the only important ones, and if both corporations and investors acted rationally, we would expect to find a far larger number of companies paying a small dividend or no dividend at all, to satisfy the demands of the large number of investors who prefer capital gains to dividends for tax reasons. From this point of view, it seems that either corporations or investors are not acting rationally. Either investors are demanding dividends in spite of the cost in terms of higher taxes, or corporations are failing to reduce their dividends, even when this would increase the price of their shares because of increased demand by tax-paying investors.

Some might argue that the Internal Revenue Service won't allow corporations to reduce their dividends in many cases, and that these corporations appear to act foolishly only because they are prevented from cutting their dividends. But the laws that forbid "unreasonable" accumulation of capital in a corporation are easy to circumvent for its retained earnings. If it has no way to invest its income in new plants and the like, it can usually invest some in buying back its own common stock, and it can invest large amounts in buying other businesses, in whole or in part. And a company that is periodically issuing new securities to raise capital will certainly have no trouble with the IRS if it reduces its dividend; it can simply issue fewer securities to balance the increase in its retained earnings.

There is another factor, that we call the "uncertainty effect," that may help explain why investors and corporations act the way they do. As we will attempt to show in this paper, it is not possible to demonstrate, using the best available empirical methods, that the returns on high yield securities are different from the returns on low yield securities either before taxes or after taxes. A taxable investor who concentrates his portfolio in low yield stocks may have no way of knowing whether he is increasing or decreasing his expected after-tax return by so doing. The evidence we will present is perfectly consistent with the hypothesis that low yield stocks have lower expected after-tax returns, even for an investor in a 70% tax bracket, than high yield stocks. Such an investor does know, however, that concentrating his portfolio in low yield stocks is likely to increase its risk by reducing its level of diversification, and is likely to involve increased transaction costs, because he will have to replace stocks of companies that experience large increases in yield. The uncertainty in the effects of dividend yield on stock returns is so great that the taxable investor holding a "market portfolio" does not even know that it would improve his expected return to eliminate just the one highest yield stock from his portfolio. In this situation, he may well decide to adopt a simple portfolio strategy that does not take dividend yield into account at all. Similarly, a tax exempt investor has no way of knowing how to shift the dividend yield of his portfolio to increase its expected return. In the light of the probable costs in terms of loss of diversification and higher turnover, he may decide to ignore dividend yield entirely.

If investors act as if dividend yield is not important in constructing their portfolios (because they don't know how to take it into account), then changes in dividend yield will not affect their portfolio decisions. A change in the yield of a stock, whether caused by changes in the dividend or changes in the price of the stock, will not cause investors to change their decisions to buy, hold, or sell the stock. Thus there will be no mechanism by which changes in a corporation's dividend policy can influence the price of its stock. A corporation may then ignore the effects of its dividend policy on its stock price.

Even if there is some "true" effect of dividend policy on stock price, the evidence presented below suggests that we have no way of knowing what that effect is. The evidence is consistent with the hypothesis that increasing the dividend increases the stock price, and it is consistent with the opposite hypothesis that increasing the dividend reduces the stock price. Given the great uncertainty about the direction and magnitude of the effects of its dividend policy on its stock price, the corporation may decide to ignore the effects of dividend policy on its stock price. It may, for example, decide to reduce its dividend whenever it needs money for promising new investment projects, without worrying that the dividend reduction will cause a drop in its stock price.

It is possible, of course, that a decrease in a corporation's dividend will cause a temporary fall in the stock price, because of the "information effect" of changes in dividends. The market may tend to interpret a cut in the dividend as a signal that the directors of the corporation expect troubled times ahead. If the troubled times do not materialize, the effect will only be temporary. And this sort of effect can be minimized if the directors make it clear that they are cutting the dividend to provide funds for investment rather than to prevent financial difficulties during a period of reduced earnings.

Thus the "uncertainty effect" can be stated as follows. Investors are ignorant of the direction and magnitude of the effects of dividend yield on portfolio returns, either before or after taxes, so they may decide to ignore yield in making portfolio decisions. Corporations are ignorant of the direction and magnitude of the permanent effects of dividend yield on stock prices, so they may decide to ignore any such effects in making decisions on the financial policies of the corporation.

2.   A New Methodology

. . .We being by noting that there are two ways to state any hypothesis about dividend policy. We can state the effect in terms of the price of the company's shares, or in terms of the expected return on the company's shares, where return is defined as including both capital gains and dividends. For example, if we believe that increasing a company's dividend will increase the price of its shares, then we can say this in either of two ways:

(a) increasing the dividend will increase the price of a company's shares.

(b) Increasing the dividend will reduce the expected return on a company's shares.

While most previous work has been aimed at testing the hypothesis in form (a), we have tested it in form (b).

In addition to restating the hypothesis about dividend policy in form (b), we have made use of an expanded form of the capital asset pricing model.* The original capital asset pricing model says that the expected return on any security should be a linear function of its 'β', as follows:

$$E(\tilde{R}_i) = R + [E(\tilde{R}_m) - R]\beta_i, \tag{1}$$

where the symbols are defined as

$E(\tilde{R}_i)$ = the expected return on security i,

$E(\tilde{R}_m)$ = the expected return on the market portfolio,

R = the riskless short term interest rate,

β_i = the covariance between $\tilde{R}_i$ and $\tilde{R}_m$, divided by the variance of $\tilde{R}_m$.

. . .We would like to find out whether eq. (1) holds equally for stocks at all levels of dividend yield. If we find that high yield stocks tend to have higher expected returns than eq. (1) predicts, then we would like to know whether this is due to the effects of the dividend yield itself or the effects of some other factor that is correlated with dividend yield. For example, it might be that high yield stocks tend to be low risk stocks, so that any tendency we find for high yield stocks to have higher expected returns than eq. (1) predicts might be simply a reflection of a tendency for low risk stocks to have higher

*[The reader may wish to consult the article by G. William Schwert in Chapter 6 of this volume for a review of capital market theory and the terms of this analysis — Eds.]

expected returns than eq. (1) predicts. Since we believe that there is a relation between dividend yield and risk, our tests are designed to sort out these two possibilities.

3.   Creating Efficient and Unbiased Tests

Let us suppose that dividend yield is related to expected return on stocks, and that the relationship is linear. Then we can rewrite eq. (1) as follows:

$$E(\tilde{R}_i) = R + [E(\tilde{R}_m) - R]\beta_i + \gamma_1(\delta_i - \delta_m)/\delta_m, \qquad (2)$$

where δ_i stands for the dividend yield on stock i, and δ_m stands for the dividend yield on the market. We would like to develop efficient and unbiased estimators for the constant γ_1. If γ_1 turns out to be significantly different from zero, then we will have evidence that dividend policy matters; while if γ_1 turns out to be insignificantly different from zero, we will have evidence that dividend policy may not matter. . . .

We used monthly data on dividends, prices, and returns for every common stock listed on the New York Stock Exchange at any time in the period January 1926 to March 1966. The information was compiled by the Center for Research in Security Prices of the University of Chicago; a detailed description of the file is given in Fisher and Lorie (1964). Prior to 1950, we used yields on 90-120 day dealer commercial paper as given in the Federal Reserve Bulletin, for our interest rates. From 1950 on, we used the yields on one month finance paper given in Salomon Brothers & Hutzler's "An analytical record of yields and yield spreads." . . .

5.   Empirical Results

. . . [W]e see that for the entire period and for every subperiod, the estimate of γ_1 is insignificantly different from zero. This means that the expected returns on high yield securities are not significantly different from the expected returns on low yield securities, other things equal. Since the return on the portfolio estimator for γ_1 is equal to the difference between the return on a well-diversified high yield portfolio and the return on a well-diversified low yield portfolio, it means that even highly diversified portfolios at different levels of yield do not have significant differences in mean return.

Since γ_1 is not significantly different from zero for the whole period or for any of the subperiods we looked at, we cannot say either that high yield stocks tend to have higher returns than low yield stocks or that high yield stocks tend to have lower returns than low yield stocks. The value of γ_1 is approximately 1% per year, and that is nowhere near the level that would make it statistically significant. Thus the data are consistent with true values of γ_1 that are very different in economic terms. The true value of γ_1 might easily be − 1% per year, which would mean that high yield stocks have lower expected returns than low yield stocks of equal risk. This would be consistent with a preference for dividends on the part of investors. Or the true value of γ_1 might easily be 3% per year, which would be consistent with great aversion for dividends on the part of investors because of their tax disadvantages or for other reasons. In other words, we cannot reject any of a number of very different hypotheses that have been proposed. Since this analysis was designed to give the most efficient test of these hypotheses, it follows that the investor has little to go on in deciding how to take yield into account in making his investment decisions. He doesn't even know whether high yield stocks have higher or lower expected returns than low yield stocks with the same risk. So it might make sense for him simply to ignore yield in making his investment decisions. . . .

6.   Dividend Policy and Stock Prices

We have been unable to show that differences in dividend yield lead to differences in stock returns. This implies that we are unable to show that dividend policy affects stock prices. If an increase in a company's dividend tended to increase the price of its stock, then we would expect to find high yield stocks selling at high prices and offering low returns. The only circumstance under which this reasoning would not hold would be if the increase in the payout ratio increased the price of the stock so much that its yield actually fell. In this case, we would expect to find that high yield stocks tend to have lower payout ratios than low yield stocks.

To test for this possibility, we constructed a new data file. . . The results . . . indicate that high yield portfolios do, in fact, have high payout ratios, and that increasing a company's payout ratio does not increase the price of its stock so much that its yield is decreased.

Thus the results we obtained for dividend yields carry over to payout ratios as well. Stocks with high payout ratios do not have returns that are significantly different from the returns on stocks with low payout ratios. The portfolio estimator for a "payout ratio" factor is taken to be the same as the portfolio estimator for the "dividend yield" factor. We are simply thinking of dividend yield as an instrumental variable for payout ratio, so the portfolios constructed to have different levels of dividend yield are thought of as portfolios constructed to have different levels of payout ratio. . . .

7.   Portfolio Strategy for an Investor

Our evidence does not allow us to show significant differences between the returns on high yield stocks and the returns on low yield stocks. In our analysis, we measured the returns without taking into account any taxes that the investor might pay on dividends or realized capital gains. Thus the analysis has direct implications for the tax-exempt investor. It implies that a tax-exempt investor may not gain significantly by emphasizing high yield stocks over low yield stocks, other things being equal.

Furthermore, we used a rather elaborate procedure for separating high yield stocks from low yield stocks, while holding other factors constant. Using our procedure, one could shift a portfolio toward higher yield stocks or lower yield stocks without increasing its risk very much. But using more informal methods, an investor would have a tendency to increase the risk of a portfolio substantially while trying to change its yield, because he would make his portfolio less well diversified.

So there are two reasons why a tax-exempt investor might not pay attention to dividends in trying to maximize his expected return for a given level of risk. First, dividend yield does not have a consistent impact on expected return, so increasing the average yield of a portfolio will cause it to have higher returns in some periods, but lower returns in other periods. And second, attempts to maximize or minimize the yield in a portfolio are likely to lead to a badly diversified portfolio, so that the expected return on the portfolio, given its level of risk, will be lower than it might be with a better diversified portfolio.

It turns out that the same is true of an investor in a high tax bracket. . . .

Thus even an investor in a high tax bracket can ignore yield in maximizing the expected return on his portfolio for a given level of risk. If he tries to emphasize stocks with low yields, he will find that he does not consistently improve his after-tax returns. In some periods, his after-tax returns will be higher, while in other periods, his after-tax returns will be lower. But unless he is very careful, he will find that he increases the risk of his portfolio significantly, by causing it to be less well diversified. So he is likely to reduce the expected return on his portfolio for a given level of risk.

It is true that if an investor knew exactly how dividends affect common stock yields, and if the cost of maintaining a portfolio with a given dividend yield were zero, it would be advantageous for him to take the yield effect into account when constructing his portfolio. If the known yield effect were small, and the loss of diversification incurred by emphasizing high or low yield stocks were large, then he might shift his portfolio only slightly in the direction of higher or lower yield. But the yield effect would always cause him to make some shift in his portfolio.

However, the direction and magnitude of the yield effect are not known, and there is no prior reason for believing that it should have a certain direction and magnitude. There appear to be many investors who prefer dividends to capital gains, possibly for reasons other than maximizing the expected after-tax returns on their portfolios. There are many other investors who prefer capital gains, for tax reasons. And there are many investors who ignore dividend yield in making investment decisions. So there is neither theoretical nor empirical justification for choosing any specific non-zero value for the mean of the yield factor.

The evidence in this paper does not imply that an investor in any tax bracket should take yield into account in choosing his portfolio strategy. An investor who is trying to maximize his expected after-tax return for a given level of risk may ignore dividends and concentrate instead on improving his portfolio diversification. It is much more likely that he can reduce his risk by improving his diversification than that he can increase his expected return by emphasizing stocks with a given level of dividend yield.

8.   Dividend Policy for a Corporation

Perhaps the most important implications of these findings are for corporate dividend policy. We have found that a corporation that increases its dividend can expect that this will have no definite effect on its stock price. The price may change temporarily in response to a change in the dividend, because the market may believe that the change indicates something about the probable future course of earnings. If it becomes clear that the change was not made because of any change in estimated future earnings, this temporary effect should disappear.

Thus a corporation may want to choose its dividend policy under the assumption that changes in dividend policy will have no permanent effect on its stock price. If it has a continuing need for a new capital, then a reduction in its dividend would be a very inexpensive way of providing that capital. If it believes that the tax disadvantages of dividends outweigh in its shareholders' minds any reasons they may have for preferring dividends, then it can do the majority a favor by reducing its dividends.

The Dividend Puzzle*

Fischer Black

Why do corporations pay dividends?

Why do investors pay attention to dividends?

Perhaps the answers to these questions are obvious. Perhaps dividends represent the return to the investor who puts his money at risk in the corporation. Perhaps corporations pay dividends to reward existing shareholders and to encourage others to buy new issues of common stock at high prices. Perhaps investors pay attention to dividends because only through dividends or the prospect of dividends do they receive a return on their investment or the chance to sell their shares at a higher price in the future.

Or perhaps the answers are not so obvious. Perhaps a corporation that pays no dividends is demonstrating confidence that it has attractive investment opportunities that might be missed if it paid dividends. If it makes these investments, it may increase the value of the shares by more than the amount of the lost dividends. If that happens, its shareholders may be doubly better off. They end up with capital appreciation greater than the dividends they missed out on, and they find they are taxed at lower effective rates on capital appreciation than on dividends.

In fact, I claim that the answers to these questions are not obvious at all. The harder we look at the dividend picture, the more it seems like a puzzle, with pieces that just don't fit together.

The Miller-Modigliani Theorem

Suppose you are offered the following choice. You may have $2 today, and a 50-50 chance of $54 or $50 tomorrow. Or you may have nothing today, and a 50-50 chance of $56 or $52 tomorrow. Would you prefer one of these gambles to the other?

*Source: 2 J. Portfolio Man. 5–8 (1976), reprinted with permission.

Probably you would not. Ignoring such factors as the cost of holding the $2 and one day's interest on $2, you would be indifferent between these two gambles.

The choice between a common stock that pays a dividend and a stock that pays no dividend is similar, at least if we ignore such things as transaction costs and taxes. The price of the dividend-paying stock drops on the ex-dividend date by about the amount of the dividend. The dividend just drops the whole range of possible stock prices by that amount. The investor who gets a $2 dividend finds himself with shares worth about $2 less than they would have been worth if the dividend hadn't been paid, in all possible circumstances.

This, in essence, is the Miller-Modigliani theorem. It says that the dividends a corporation pays do not affect the value of its shares or the returns to investors, because the higher the dividend, the less the investor receives in capital appreciation, no matter how the corporation's business decisions turn out.

When we say this, we are assuming that the dividend paid does not influence the corporation's business decisions. Paying the dividend either reduces the amount of cash equivalents held by the corporation, or increases the amount of money raised by issuing securities.

If a Firm Pays No Dividends

If this theorem is correct, then a firm that pays a regular dividend equal to about half of its normal earnings will be worth the same as an otherwise similar firm that pays no dividends and will never pay any dividends. Can that be true? How can a firm that will never pay dividends be worth anything at all?

Actually, there are many ways for the stockholders of a firm to take cash out without receiving dividends. The most obvious is that the firm can buy back some of its shares. This has the advantage that most investors are not taxed as heavily on shares sold as they are on dividends received.

If the firm is closely held, it can give money to its shareholders by giving them jobs at inflated salaries, or by ordering goods from other firms owned by the shareholders at inflated prices.

If the firm is not closely held, then another firm or individual can make a tender offer which will have the effect of making it closely held. Then the same methods for taking cash out of the firm can be used.

Under the assumptions of the Modigliani-Miller theorem, a firm has value even if it pays no dividends. Indeed, it has the same value it would have if it paid dividends.

Taxes

In a world where dividends are taxed more heavily (for most investors) than capital gains, and where capital gains are not taxed until realized, a corporation that pays no dividends will be more attractive to taxable individual investors than a similar corporation that pays dividends. This will tend to increase the price of the non-dividend-paying corporation's stock. Many corporations will be tempted to eliminate dividend payments.

Of course, corporate investors are taxed more heavily on realized capital gains than on dividends. And tax-exempt investors are taxed on neither. But it is hard to believe that these groups have enough impact on the market to outweigh the effects of taxable individuals.

Also, the IRS has a special tax that it likes to apply to companies that retain earnings to avoid the personal taxation of dividends. But there are many ways to avoid this tax. A corporation that is making investments in its business usually doesn't have to pay the tax, especially if it is issuing securities to help pay for these investments.

If a corporation insists on paying out cash, it is better off replacing some of its common stock with bonds. A shareholder who keeps his proportionate share of the new securities will receive taxable interest but at least the interest will be deductible to the corporation. Dividends are not deductible.

With taxes, investors and corporations are no longer indifferent to the level of dividends. They prefer smaller dividends or no dividends at all.

Transaction Costs

An investor who holds a non-dividend-paying stock will generally sell some of his shares if he needs to raise cash. In some circumstances, he can borrow against his shares. Either of these transactions can be costly, especially if small amounts of money are involved. So an investor might want to have dividend income instead.

But this argument doesn't have much substance. If investors are concerned about transaction costs, the corporation that pays no dividends can arrange for automatic share repurchase plans much like the automatic dividend reinvestment plans that now exist. A shareholder would keep his stock in trust, and the trustee would periodically sell shares back to the corporation, including fractional shares if necessary. The shareholder could even choose the amounts he wants to receive and the timing of the payments. An automated system would probably cost about as much as a system for paying dividends.

If the IRS objected to the corporation's buying back its own shares, then the trustee could simply sell blocks of shares on the open market. Again, the cost would be low.

Thus transaction costs don't tell us much about why corporations pay dividends.

What Do Dividend Changes Tell Us?

The managers of most corporations have a tendency to give out good news quickly, but to give out bad news slowly. Thus investors are somewhat suspicious of what the managers have to say.

Dividend policy, though, may say things the managers don't say explicitly. For one reason or another, managers and directors do not like to cut the dividend. So they will raise the dividend only if they feel the company's prospects are good enough to support the higher dividend for some time. And they will cut the dividend only if they think the prospects for a quick recovery are poor.

This means that dividend changes, or the fact that the dividend doesn't change, may tell investors more about what the managers really think than they can find out from other sources. Assuming that the managers' forecasts are somewhat reliable, dividend policy conveys information.

Thus the announcement of a dividend cut often leads to a drop in the company's stock price. And the announcement of a dividend increase often leads to an increase in the company's stock price. These stock price changes are permanent if the company in fact does as badly, or as well, as the dividend changes indicated.

If the dividend changes are not due to forecasts of the company's prospects, then any stock price changes that occur will normally be temporary. If a corporation eliminates its dividend because it wants to save taxes for its shareholders, then the stock price might decline at first. But it would eventually go back to the level it would have had if the dividend had not been cut, or higher.

Thus the fact that dividend changes often tell us things about the corporations making them does not explain why corporations pay dividends.

How To Hurt the Creditors

When a company has debt outstanding, the indenture will almost always limit the dividends the company can pay. And for good reason. There is no easier way for a company to escape the burden of a debt than to pay out all of its assets in the form of a dividend, and leave the creditors holding an empty shell.

While this is an extreme example, any increase in the dividend that is not offset by an increase in external financing will hurt the company's creditors. A dollar paid out in dividends is a dollar that is not available to the creditors if trouble develops.

If an increase in the dividend will hurt the creditors, then a cut in the dividend will help the creditors. Since the firm is only worth so much, what helps the creditors will hurt the stockholders. The stockholders would certainly rather have $2 in dividends than $2 invested in assets that may end up in the hands of the creditors. Perhaps we have finally found a reason why firms pay dividends.

Alas, this explanation doesn't go very far. In many cases, the changes in the values of the stock and bonds caused by a change in dividend policy would be so small they would not be detectable. And if the effects are large, the company can negotiate with the creditors. If the company agrees not to pay any dividends at all, the creditors would presumably agree to give better terms on the company's credit. This would eliminate the negative effects of cutting the dividend on the position of the stockholders relative to the creditors.

Dividends as a Source of Capital

A company that pays dividends might instead have invested the money in its operations. This is especially true when the company goes to the markets frequently for new capital. Cutting the dividend, if there are no special reasons for paying dividends, has to be one of the lowest cost sources of funds available to the company.

The underwriting cost of a new debt or equity issue is normally several percent of the amount of money raised. There are no comparable costs for money raised by cutting the dividend.

Perhaps a company that has no profitable investments projects and that is not raising money externally should keep its dividend. If the dividend is cut, the managers may lose the money through unwise investment projects. In these special cases, there may be a reason to keep the dividend. But surely these cases are relatively rare.

In the typical case, the fact that cutting the dividend is a low cost way to raise money is another reason to expect corporations not to pay dividends. So why do they continue?

Do Investors Demand Dividends?

It is possible that many, many individual investors believe that stocks that don't pay dividends should not be held, or should be held only at prices lower than the prices of similar stocks that do pay dividends. This belief is not rational, so far as I can tell. But it may be there nonetheless.

Add these investors to the trustees who believe it is not prudent to hold stocks that pay no dividends, and to the corporations that have tax reasons for preferring dividend-paying stocks, and you may have a substantial part of the market. More important, you may have a part of the market that strongly influences the pricing of corporate shares. Perhaps the best evidence of this is the dominance of this view in investment advisory publications.

On the other hand, investors also seem acutely aware of the tax consequences of dividends. Investors in high tax brackets seem to hold low dividend stocks, and investors in low tax brackets seem to hold high dividend stocks.

Furthermore, the best empirical tests that I can think of are unable to show whether investors who prefer dividends or investors who avoid dividends have a stronger effect on the pricing of securities.

If investors do demand dividends, then corporations should not eliminate all dividends. But it is difficult or impossible to tell whether investors demand dividends or not. So it is hard for a corporation to decide whether to eliminate its dividends or not.

Portfolio Implications

Corporations can't tell what dividend policy to choose, because they don't know how many irrational investors there are. But perhaps a rational investor can choose a dividend policy for his portfolio that will maximize his after-tax expected return for a given level of risk. Perhaps a taxable investor, especially one who is in a high tax bracket, should emphasize low dividend stocks. And perhaps a tax-exempt investor should emphasize high dividend stocks.

One problem with this strategy is that an investor who emphasizes a certain kind of stock in his portfolio is likely to end up with a less well-diversified portfolio than he would otherwise have. So he will probably increase the risk of his portfolio.

The other problem is that we can't tell if or how much an investor will increase his expected return by doing this. If investors demanding dividends dominate the market, then high dividend stocks will have low expected returns. Even tax-exempt investors, if they are rational, should buy low dividend stocks.

On the other hand, it seems that rational investors in high brackets will do better in low dividend stocks no matter who dominates the market. But how much should they emphasize low dividend stocks? At what point will the loss of diversification offset the increase in expected return?

It is even conceivable that investors overemphasize tax factors, and bid low dividend stocks up so high that they are unattractive even for investors in the highest brackets.

Thus the portfolio implications of the theory are no clearer than its implications for corporate dividend policy.

What should the individual investor do about dividends in his portfolio? We don't know.

What should the corporation do about dividend policy? We don't know.

NOTES AND QUESTIONS

1. Efforts to put at least some of the pieces of the dividend puzzle into place continue. On the theoretical level, M. Miller and M. Scholes of the University of Chicago suggested that certain features of the current tax law can be used to eliminate most of the tax penalty on dividends as compared to capital gains; Miller and Scholes, Dividends and Taxes, 6 J. Fin. Econ. 333 (1978). Their explanation, however, does not seem to fit the actual borrowing behavior of most individual investors of the period prior to the 1969 tax law changes.

Others have suggested that sustained dividends serve as a reliable (if expensive) signal of management's expectations as to the firm's future income. S. Ross, The Determination of Financial Structures: The Incentive Signalling Approach, 8 Bell J. Econ. 23 (1977); S. Bhattacharya, Imperfect Information, Dividend Policy, and 'The Bird in the Hand' Fallacy, 10 Bell J. Econ. 259 (1979).

M. Feldstein and J. Green have argued in a recent paper that if shareholders in different tax brackets desire portfolio diversification, firms will maximize the value of their shares by adopting some positive level of dividend payout. M. Feldstein and J. Green, Why Do Companies Pay Dividends? NBER Working Paper 413 (Dec. 1979).

2. A recent paper by Robert Litzenberger of Stanford and Krishna Ramaswamy of the Bell Labs, The Effect of Personal Taxes and Dividends on Capital Asset Prices: Theory and Empirical Evidence, forthcoming in the Journal of Financial Economics, tries to attack the empirical problem with more sensitive econometric techniques. They conclude:

> The results indicate that, unlike prior studies, there is a strong positive relationship between before-tax expected returns and dividend yields of common stocks. The coefficient of the dividend yield variable was positive, less than unity and significantly different from zero. The data indicates that for every dollar increase in return in the form of dividends, investors require an additional 23 cents in before-tax return. There was no noticeable trend in the coefficient over time. . . .
>
> Evidence was also presented for a clientele effect: that is, that stockholders in higher tax brackets choose stocks with low yields, and vice versa. Further work is needed to derive a model that implies the existence of such clienteles and to test its implications.

Thus Litzenberger and Ramaswamy find that, even if there are different clienteles among investors for different payout policies, on balance dividend payments are costly for a company and disadvantageous for its stockholders. The opposite conclusion, that investors have a net preference for receiving their return in the form of cash dividends, was reached by S. Bar-Josef and R. Kolodny, Dividend Policy and Capital Market Theory, 58 Rev. Econ. & Stat. 181 (1976), and by a case study reported by J. Long, The Market Valuation of Cash Dividends, 6 J. Fin. Econ. 235 (1978).

3. Given the foregoing state of theory and research, is there any basis for a court to concern itself, in the interest of shareholder protection, with the dividend payment policy of a publicly traded company? Of a closely held, untraded company?

Part IV

Federal Securities Regulation: Protection of New Investors

Chapter 10

The Economic Basis for Disclosure Requirements

As Brealey pointed out, stock prices and returns reflect an assessment of the earnings prospects and risk associated with the issuing company and its operations. If there were very limited data available to investors about a company, that would increase the uncertainty of such an assessment and thus increase the risk discount applied to the estimated future earnings and dividends of the company — thereby lowering the present value of its shares and raising its cost of capital. A company has incentives, therefore, to provide information about itself to purchasers of its securities, and to find ways (as through CPA audits) to assure investors of the reliability of that information.

Why, then, is there any need to have a statute and an administrative agency imposing a system of mandated disclosure, in accordance with an elaborate set of forms? Long before there was any SEC, issuers supplied potential purchasers with a "prospectus" of information, though not in the highly standardized format with which we are now familiar. If it was false or misleading in its statements, there were state fraud laws; if it was inadequate in its coverage, there were incentives to supply investors with the desired additional information or suffer the added discount for added uncertainty (and any negative inferences from the omission). The investor, after all, always has the simple option of not investing in a company that does not disclose the information he deems relevant. If some purchasers want turquoise cars, manufacturers have ample reason to try to learn that desire and meet it; no statute is needed. Does that hold equally true for the quantum of disclosure desired by purchasers of securities? These are the issues addressed by William Beaver, in the first selection in this chapter. Beaver also develops the implications for securities regulation of the portfolio theory and efficient market hypothesis discussed in Chapter 6.

If one assumes the justification for, or accepts the continuing existence of, a system of government-mandated disclosure in the securities field, that brings up the next question — just what is the information that has to be disclosed, and why? What determines the contents of the famous Form S-1? Does the SEC have a theory of how investors *do* determine securities' prices? Of how they *should?* Is that theory supported by research evidence? By anything? One perspective on these questions is given by Homer Kripke in the second paper. The Kripke selection illustrates the ways in which modern finance theory is beginning to affect the legal analysis of securities-law issues.

*The Nature of Mandated Disclosure**

William H. Beaver

When the Securities Act of 1933 was enacted, Congress felt that a mandated disclosure system was needed to protect the public against fraud in the sale of securities. The Securities Exchange Act of 1934 adopted a year later continued to reflect this philosophy . . . .

The current mandated disclosure system consists of a series of highly technical documents which are filed with the SEC and reside in its archives. Many investors, the intended beneficiaries of the Securities Acts, usually do not read and, in the case of 10-K, 10-Q and 8-K filings under the 1934 Act, do not usually even receive copies of these filings. There is an implicit reliance on the functioning of the professional investment community in order to justify the current system as an effective mechanism for disclosure. Moreover, this community often relies on investment information that is more comprehensive and in some cases more timely than that contained in the mandated filings. Under these conditions, the question arises concerning the role of the SEC and its mandated disclosure system in the entire framework. Why is it desirable to have a portion of that disclosure system contain a mandated set of disclosures?

There have been two common forms of justification for the desirability of disclosure regulation.

Source: Report of the Advisory Committee on Corporate Disclosure to the SEC, 95th Cong., 1st Sess. 618-656 (House Comm. Print 95-29 1977), reprinted with permission. William H. Beaver is professor of accounting at Stanford's Graduate School of Business.

The first approach consists of citing a litany of perceived abuses. Several questions can be raised in connection with such an approach. Were the actions in question in fact "abuses?" What one person might label "manipulation" another might label "arbitrage." In particular, what harm was inflicted as a result of such actions? Was inadequate disclosure a contributing factor to the abuses? In other words, will mandating disclosure of some form deter or reduce such activities? What was the frequency of abuses relative to some measure of total activity? This is potentially important because mandated disclosure tends to be imposed on broad classes of corporations, not merely those who committed the perceived abuse.

However, more fundamentally, the point is that perfection is unattainable. Any corporate disclosure system, even one with a mandated portion, will incur some frequency of abuse. It is not clear that there has been a decline in the frequency of abuse over the 44 years since the inception of the Acts, and in the presence of increased regulation of corporate disclosure. Moreover, it is as inappropriate to judge a disclosure system solely on the basis of its perceived abuses as it would be to judge the merits of a public agency, such as the SEC, solely on the basis of its perceived worst regulations. The central issue is whether there is some flaw in the private sector forces that would lead to the conclusion that governmental regulation is a more desirable solution.

A second approach is to define the objectives of the corporate disclosure system and by implication the role of mandated disclosure. For example, "informed, rational investment decisions" is one frequently cited objective. However, again the central issue is why is governmental regulation necessary or desirable to achieve this objective?

Rationale for Disclosure Regulation

This section will attempt to develop a framework for the consideration of issues regarding disclosure regulation. In order to do so, the nature of economic problems and the purpose of government with respect to those problems will be briefly discussed.

Economic issues fall into two major categories: issues of efficiency and issues of equity. The first category is concerned with the most efficient means of achieving some specified result, where movement to a more efficient solution could in principle result in everyone in the economy being in a more preferred position (or at least as preferred a position) with no one being in a less preferred position (often called a Pareto-optimal solution). The second category deals with the choice among efficient solutions, where each solution will leave some individuals better off but others worse off. Issues as to how wealth should be distributed among individuals in the economy would be one example of an issue of equity. The government becomes involved in both types of issues. However, the rationale for governmental intervention can vary considerably depending upon the type of issue involved. Therefore it is imperative to state the extent to which the rationale for disclosure regulation rests on efficiency or equity considerations.

In general, the government has a variety of means available to deal with these issues, including the enforcement of private contracts, the definition and enforcement of property rights, taxation, regulation, and direct ownership. The Securities Acts provide two primary methods by which the flow of information to investors is effected. First are the general anti-fraud provisions; the second is the power to explicitly mandate corporate disclosure via the SEC filings and annual reports to shareholders.

With respect to the first method, the Securities Acts provide that it is unlawful to make a false or misleading statement or to omit a material fact in connection with the sale of a security. Laws against fraud are commonplace in the sale of a variety of commodities and they reflect concern over the pervasive problem that the quality of the product or service being sold is uncertain. Moreover, often one party to the transaction may naturally be in a position of superior information regarding the quality. Under anti-fraud provisions, certain parties to the transaction face the prospect of civil or criminal penalties when and if the quality of the commodity is eventually discovered and their behavior is deemed "fraudulent."

While the deterrence of fraud via legal liability is fairly commonplace, the presence of a regulatory mechanism that explicitly mandates the nature of what must be disclosed is a rather special feature of securities' regulations. For example, neither federal nor state laws require filing a prospectus when an individual sells a home, even though the seller is in a potentially superior position with respect to information regarding the quality of the home.

The [next] subsection deals with arguments that potentially provide a rationale for disclosure regulation, which by implication asserts that reliance solely on the anti-fraud provisions is inadequate. The arguments fall into three major categories. (1) Corporation disclosures induce externalities and therefore have aspects of a public good. (2) Left unregulated, market forces would lead to an asymmetrical or uneven possession of information among investors. (3) Corporate management has incentives to suppress unfavorable information.

Corporate Disclosure Externalities

An externality exists when the actions of one party have effects on other parties, who are not charged (or compensated) via the price mechanism. While in principle it would be possible to conceive of an elaborate price system that would charge or compensate the third parties for these effects, it may be undesirable to do so because it is too costly or simply infeasible.

However, without some form of collective action, the party undertaking the action has no incentive to internalize the effects on third parties, and it may lead to an inefficiency. For example, in the classic public good analysis with positive external effects on third parties, there will be an underproduction of the public good in the absence of a collective action that incorporates the third parties, who benefit from the public good but do not participate in the decision to produce or pay for it. For this reason, these third parties are often referred to as "free riders." In this situation, the private incentives are less than the social incentives to produce the public good.

In the disclosure context, two examples are frequently offered. Externalities could occur when information about the productive opportunities of one firm convey information about the productive opportunities of other firms. Shareholders in the disclosing firm pay the costs of disclosure but shareholders in the other firms do not, even though they are affected by the disclosure. For example, disclosure by a firm about its success (or lack thereof) with respect to some product development may provide information to other firms about their chances of success in similar product developments. In fact, it might even obviate their having to expend resources on product developments. Thus the familiar objection to disclosure on grounds of competitive disadvantage is one form of externality. In this setting there will be a lack of incentive to fully disclose because of the benefits of disclosure to other firms for which the disclosing firm is not being compensated.

The second example deals with positive external effects on prospective shareholders. Investors demand information in order to assess the risks and rewards (i.e., the array of potential future cash flows) associated with alternative portfolios of securities. In making consumption and investment decisions, the investor finds information about a security useful whether or not that particular security ultimately is one of the securities in the portfolio chosen by the investor. The process of selecting the "best" portfolio inherently involves a consideration of investment alternatives (i.e., alternative portfolios). Therefore information on securities in these alternative portfolios may be valuable at the decision making stage, even though after-the-fact some of those securities may not be included in the portfolio chosen. In this setting, current shareholders bear the costs of disclosure, yet prospective shareholders share in the benefits of disclosure (i.e., they are free riders). If the prospective shareholders neither participate in the decision to disclose nor share in bearing the costs, there will tend to be less disclosure than there would be under a collective agreement which included them. They would be willing to pay for additional disclosure such that everyone (both current and prospective shareholders) would be in a more preferred position (i.e., a more efficient solution would be attained).

There are a number of additional issues to be introduced in considering an externality or public good approach to disclosure regulation.

First, what is the materiality of the externality or public good aspects to corporate disclosure? Currently, little empirical evidence exists to assess the importance of potential externalities.

Second, issues of cost must be introduced. These include the direct costs of disclosure, the indirect costs of disclosure, and the costs of regulation. The direct costs of disclosure include the costs of the production, certification, dissemination, processing, and interpretation of disclosures. These costs are borne by the corporations and the analyst community and ultimately by investors. The indirect costs include the adverse effects of disclosure on competitive advantage (e.g., creating a disincentive to innovate or invest in product development) and legal liability, which may induce an inefficient bearing of risk by management and auditors, among others. The costs of regulation include the costs involved in the development, compliance, enforcement, and litigation of disclosure regulations. These costs are borne by taxpayers and by shareholders (and perhaps indirectly by consumers and employees).

Third, there are issues related to the information demanded by the regulatory agency in order to develop and monitor the regulations. In the context of disclosure regulation, the SEC attempts to determine the amount and nature of corporate disclosure that would take place, absent the inefficiencies induced by the externalities. In the case where the prospective shareholders are free riders, this involves an attempt to determine their demand for information. In general, investor demand for information will be influenced by the wealth, risk preferences, and beliefs of investors, which is a nontrivial demand for information by the regulatory agency. Economic analyses which show the attainment of a more efficient solution via governmental regulation typically assume perfect knowledge on the part of the regulatory body, which is obviously an unrealistic assumption. Where it is too costly or simply infeasible to obtain the desired information, implementation error by the regulatory agency due to imperfect information may occur.

For example, individuals may not have incentives to honestly reveal their preference for corporate disclosure. They may understate or overstate the desirability of additional disclosure depending on the extent to which they perceive their indication of preference will be used as a basis to assess their share of the costs. A clear illustration is provided when there is no attempt to include the free riders in sharing in the costs of disclosures. In other words, suppose some groups are invited to participate in the process that determines the quantity and nature of corporate disclosure but are not invited to share in bearing the costs of those additional disclosures (e.g., financial analysts). In this situation, the result may be excessive disclosure, rather than inadequate disclosure as suggested by the standard public good analysis. Issues of efficiency and equity are raised by such a process.

Fourth, there are issues that relate to the incentives of the regulatory agency itself. The economics of regulation offers two primary views of regulatory behavior. The first is the "public interest" view, which states that regulatory behavior is directed toward furthering the public interest. This view implicitly assumes the incentives of regulators are aligned so as to further the public interest and that the concept of public interest is well-defined. The second view is known as the "capture theory" and states that the prime beneficiaries of regulation are not the public (or investors, in the case of the Securities Acts) but rather those being regulated. This has led critics of the Securities Acts, such as Stigler, to argue that the primary beneficiaries of the Acts are various members in the professional investment industry rather than investors at large.

Fifth, there is the issue of alternatives to governmental regulation, such as private sector collective agreements. For example, many goods with externalities are dealt with in the private sector. Newspapers and television are two examples. The issue of whether to deal with the problem collectively in the private or public sector revolves around the issue of relative costs of the alternative approaches. It is generally felt that the government has a comparative advantage in dealing with certain types of collective agreements. In particular, where it would be extremely costly or infeasible to preclude free riders or where it would be extremely costly or infeasible to attempt to charge them, it is intuitively felt the comparative advantage favors governmental action.

Uneven Possession of Information Among Investors

A second major argument for disclosure regulation is that, left unregulated, market forces would lead to an uneven possession of information among investors. Selective disclosure is one example. In other words, the result would be a continuum of informed investors ranging from well informed to ill informed. It is further argued that such asymmetry of access to information is inherently unfair and violates the meaning of "fair" disclosure under the Securities Acts. Hence the basis of the argument is typically one of equity rather than efficiency. Simply stated, it is only fair that the less informed be protected from the more informed.

Recent economic analysis of the demand for privately held information suggests that considerable incentives exist to expend efforts searching for and obtaining nonpublicly available information for trading purposes. Studies described elsewhere in the Report document the existence of a large informal information network, where information flows from management to the analysts. However, the unfairness of such a process is not self-evident.

Presumably, the analysts pass along the benefits of the information search to their clients, either directly or indirectly. In this sense, the clients of analysts become more informed investors. However, they pay for the analysts' services either directly or indirectly. As long as the services are available to anyone willing to pay for them, there is no obvious way in which harm is occurring. At the margin, investors will purchase analysts' services to that point where investors are indifferent between being more informed or less informed, given the costs of becoming more informed. In other words, the expected benefits of being more informed (e.g., in the form of expected superior returns due to better information) are equal to (or offset by) the costs incurred to obtain the additional information. A common argument is that some investors cannot afford to purchase the services of analysts. However, the existence of financial intermediaries makes the force of this argument unclear. Moreover, it ignores several alternatives open to relatively less informed investors. One such alternative is to partially insulate themselves from more informed traders via buy-and-hold strategies and index funds. Also the actions of the more informed may signal their information to the less informed and as a result prices may partially (in the limit, fully) reflect the information.

The purchase of analysts' information can be viewed as the decision to purchase a higher quality product (in this case, superior information). In general, quality differences exist with respect to any commodity, and usually it is not thought to be unfair when one consumer chooses to purchase a higher quality product while another chooses a lower quality item. The purchase of automobiles is one example, but illustrations could be provided for almost any commodity.

While selective disclosure is commonly cast as an equity issue, there are grounds for considering it on the basis of efficiency. For example, Hirshleifer argues that the social value is zero to the acquisition of private information for trading purposes. If there were no costs to forming private-sector collective agreements, investors would agree among themselves not to privately seek information. Everyone would gain in that society would no longer incur the costs of private search for information, whose sole purpose is to redistribute wealth among investors via trading on superior information. In other words, the trading gains in the form of superior returns due to privately held information net out to zero across all investors. It is a zero-sum game in that every investor with superior returns is offset by other investors with inferior returns. However, to the extent that such search causes investors to incur real costs, it is not a zero-sum game but these costs constitute dead weight losses to investors as a whole. Investors would be better off to avoid such costs.

However reaching and enforcing such a collective agreement might be extremely costly or simply infeasible. In the absence of effective enforcement, the agreement would rapidly deteriorate, because there would always be a private incentive to cheat on the agreement. Therefore the SEC may have a comparative advantage in effectively eliminating private search for information. It could be accomplished by either or both of its two major means of regulation. (1) It could preempt private search by mandating the disclosure of the item in public filings or annual reports. (2) It could impose sufficient legal liabiity on transmittal of information from management to analysts such that information flows would be deterred (or in the limit eliminated).

This poses a dilemma. This argument suggests there will be a tendency for an excessive amount of information, as analysts and others privately search for information and disseminate it. However, this is the converse of the public good argument which implies an inadequate amount of disclosure. There are opposing forces operating. In one case the private incentives for disclosure fall short, while in the second case the private incentives are excessive. To the extent the former exists, it might be desirable to permit a certain amount of private search to compensate for the otherwise inadequate incentives to publicly disclose. However, permitting too much will lead to the inefficiencies described above.

Management Incentives to Disclose

A third major argument for disclosure regulation is that management has incentives to suppress unfavorable information. While there may be a general awareness of this potential among investors, investors would not know specifically the nature or materiality of the suppressed information. As a result, investors will be unable to distinguish quality differences among stocks to the same extent they would under fuller disclosure. Hence, security prices will not fully reflect quality differences among stocks and there will be uncertainty regarding the quality of each stock. There may be a tendency for lower quality stocks to be selling at a higher price than would prevail under fuller disclosure and conversely for the higher quality stocks. This can lead to a phenomenon known as adverse selection, where the managements of poorer quality stocks have greater incentives to offer additional shares for sale than the managements of higher quality stocks.

Firms will tend to respond to this problem in a number of ways. (1) Higher quality firms will attempt to signal their higher quality by undertaking actions that would be irrational unless they were in fact of higher quality. The effectiveness of this signaling behavior will be influenced by the extent to which the lower quality firms can imitate the signaling behavior. Moreover, signaling may be a costly activity with no rewards beyond those of signaling. (2) Managements will offer to have their disclosure system monitored and certified by an independent party, leading to a demand for auditing services. (3) Managements may offer warranties to shareholders whereby they will incur penalties if it is eventually discovered that unfavorable information was suppressed. In fact, managements' willingness to be audited and to offer warranties can be signals in themselves. Obviously both auditing services and warranty contracts are not costless. One of the most important costs in the warranty is that management may end up bearing more risk than that associated with failure to disclose.

After-the-fact it may be difficult to disentangle the deterioration in the stock price that was due to correcting inadequate disclosure as opposed to other unfavorable events. As a result, management may become an insurer for events in addition to those induced by management's disclosure policy. This may lead to an inefficient sharing of risks, relative to that that would attain if there were no uncertainty about the quality of the stocks. The costs may be prohibitive that such warranties would not be offered.

The anti-fraud provisions can be viewed as requiring firms to provide disclosure warranties to investors, where presumably the legal liability is sufficient to offset the incentives of management to suppress unfavorable information. The argument for governmental intervention as opposed to private sector contracting would be that the SEC has a comparative (cost) advantage in achieving the same result. However, while this argument forms a basis for anti-fraud statutes, it is not clear why a mandated disclosure system is desirable. In other words, why is reliance upon anti-fraud statutes deemed to be inadequate? . . .

. . . Recent security price research in the areas of portfolio theory and efficient markets provides a framework within which to view the investor demand for information. These areas represent an important part of what is currently known about the investment decision and the environment within which that decision is made.

Portfolio Theory

Portfolio theory characterizes the investment decision as a trade-off between expected return and risk (i.e., as measured by the extent to which the actual return may differ from the expected return). Each portfolio of securities offers the investor a given combination of risk and expected return. Given the risk attitudes of the investor, the best portfolio is one that is the most preferred combination of risk and expected return. There are two immediate implications of portfolio theory for corporate disclosure. (1) Each individual security cannot be viewed in isolation but must be evaluated in the context of its membership in a portfolio consisting of other securities. The individual security is irrelevant, *except* insofar as it contributes to the overall risk and expected return of the portfolio. (2) The investor is concerned with *risk* as well as expected return (sometimes referred to as performance). Hence, corporate disclosure is concerned with the assessment of risk as well as the assessment of performance.

However, portfolio theory distinguishes between two types of risk. The first type is called unsystematic or diversifiable risk, because it can be virtually eliminated by diversification. The second type is called systematic or nondiversifiable risk, because it cannot be eliminated via diversification. The basis for this distinction rests on the view that two types of events affect the price of a security. There are economy-wide events, such as changes in anticipated inflation and interest rates, which affect the fortunes (and hence prices) of all securities with varying sensitivity. However, there are other events whose implications are largely firm-specific, such as changes in management, contract awards, and litigation. Unsystematic events by their very nature tend to be uncorrelated among firms at any point in time. To the extent that prices reflect only unsystematic or firm-specific events, returns among securities would be uncorrelated, and risk of the portfolio of such securities could be driven to zero via diversification across securities. However, to the extent that prices vary due to systematic events, security returns would be perfectly correlated, and diversification would not reduce the risk. Portfolio theory states that each security's return is subject to both types of risk. However, at the portfolio level only the systematic risk prevails, because the unsystematic risk has been diversified away. The investor is unnecessarily incurring unsystematic risk by failing to diversify. Therefore, there is a basic presumption in favor of diversification, unless the investor has some justification for choosing to remain undiversified. One reason for doing so would be superior information.

Investor Demand for Firm-Specific Information

Portfolio theory stresses the importance of diversification in the reduction of much of the risk associated with holding a single security. It is unrealistic to believe that investors hold only one security (e.g., the one being described in a registration statement). In fact, investors have the opportunity to purchase well diversified portfolios through financial intermediaries. The recent trend toward index funds is but one manifestation of the realization of the desirability of diversification. If the investor holds a well diversified portfolio, how, if at all, does this alter the way disclosure is viewed? It has been argued that diversification may substantially reduce the investor's demand for firm-specific information. The investor is concerned with firm-specific information only insofar as it is useful in assessing the portfolio attributes. While the investor may have considerable uncertainty about the risks and rewards associated with any one security, this uncertainty is considerably reduced at the portfolio level because of the effects of diversification. For example, while there may be considerable uncertainty as to the riskiness of any one security, typically the riskiness of the portfolio can be assessed with much greater confidence. In other words, an overestimate of the risk of one security will tend to be offset by an underestimation of the risk of another security. The effects of diversification are potentially powerful, and the benefits from incremental improvements in the precision of firm-specific information may be minimal.

In another context, suppose the investor is concerned that the security being purchased is mispriced, relative to the price at which it would sell if additional disclosures were available. From the point of view of the additional disclosure, some of the securities will be overpriced but some will be underpriced. A diversified portfolio will likely contain some of each and their effects will tend to be offsetting. Hence, the net effects of additional disclosure may differ considerably from the effects analyzed on a security-by-security basis.

This is not to suggest that portfolio theory implies that additional disclosure is valueless, but only that it can alter the way in which disclosure issues are viewed. There are a number of obvious additional considerations. (1) Many investors may choose to remain relatively undiversified, even though they have the opportunity to do so. These investors, for one reason or another, perceive that the disadvantages of diversification outweigh the advantages. The SEC faces a social choice question of to what extent to impose disclosure requirements on companies (and hence impose costs on all investors) in order to accommodate investors who have chosen not to diversify. (2) Not all investors may have access to a given item (i.e., a problem of selective disclosure). (3) Management may use nondisclosure to obtain greater compensation than otherwise would be the case. (4) There may be effects on resource allocation that are ignored when the investor setting is narrowly viewed.

Efficient Security Markets

A securities market is said to be *efficient* with respect to some defined information if the security prices in that market "fully reflect" that information. The term, "fully reflect," is not a precise term. Operationally, if prices fully reflect a given set of information, then investors are playing a "fair game" with respect to that information. This means that all trading strategies based on that information will yield only the normal, expected return, commensurate with the risk involved.

A more precise definition is that the market is efficient with respect to a given piece of information if prices act *as if* everyone possessed that information and were able to interpret its implications for security prices. For example, several empirical studies have examined market efficiency with respect to changes in accounting methods. To say the market is efficient with respect to changes in accounting methods is to say that the stock prices behave as if all investors had knowledge of the change in method and knew how to interpret it.

The term, *market efficiency*, is unfortunate in some respects, because it may convey normative or value-laden connotations which have nothing to do with the concept itself. The concept of market efficiency refers to a relationship between stock prices and some defined information set. It is not to be confused with other uses of the term, *efficiency*, such as those which refer to how resources are allocated in the economy. It can also be misleading to use the term, *market efficiency*, without also specifying the information set. For example, to say simply that the market is efficient is an incomplete statement unless the intended implication is that the market is efficient with respect to any or all information. However, such an implication usually is not intended. Typically, when market efficiency is used in an unqualified manner, it is intended to imply that the market is efficient with respect to publicly available data, since most of the empirical research has been concerned with market efficiency of this form. Three major forms of market efficiency have been delineated: (1) weak form efficiency, which refers to market efficiency with respect to past security prices, (2) semi-strong form efficiency, which defines market efficiency with respect to publicly available information, and (3) strong form efficiency, which is concerned with market efficiency with respect to all information, including inside information.

There are several potential implications of market efficiency with respect to publicly available data. (1) Disclosure may still be a substantive issue. Merely because prices fully reflect publicly available information does not imply that prices necessarily reflect nonpublicly available information. (2) Once disclosure is provided, the method of formatting is unlikely to have an impact on stock prices. (3) Given the large, active private sector information system, many items may be reflected in prices even though they are not reported in annual reports, SEC filings, or any publicly available document. Moreover, any one type of data may have a number of substitutes which can provide similar information. Therefore, before proceeding to mandate any given item, it would be appropriate to consider if that item would be a material addition given the other data effectively being disseminated to the investment community and reflected in prices.

There is one nonimplication of the efficient market that deserves explicit recognition. Merely because prices reflect a broad information set does not preclude or presume the desirability of mandated disclosures. With respect to certain types of information, there still may be inadequate private incentives to gather and disseminate such data. Moreover, even if it is being disseminated via the private sector system, it may be deemed more efficient (i.e., less costly) to have it disseminated via public disclosure by the corporation rather than via the private search activities for the reasons discussed earlier. . . .

Concluding Remarks

Empirical research . . . may be useful in dealing with some aspects of mandated disclosure. If the particular item is being mandated because it is expected to add to the information used by the market, it seems reasonable to expect the disclosure of such data to impact on stock prices. If no stock price reaction is observed, then the question must be asked—what are the effects, if any, of requiring disclosure of that item? For example, one effect could be a lower cost to investors via mandating disclosure rather than relying on the private sector's informal information network.

In other words, it is virtually inconceivable that the SEC would not be able to find some disclosures that would have a price effect. . . . However, this is not the issue. Merely because the private sector has chosen not to disseminate a given item cannot be taken as prima facie evidence that the incentives to disclose are inadequate. It may be that the "benefits" of disclosure of that item are perceived to be not commensurate with the costs, such that disclosure is not worthwhile. The crucial issue is how to distinguish nondisclosure on the basis of perceived insufficient benefits from nondisclosure due to some inadequacy in the market system.

Similarly, the observation that the current system incurs a certain level of abuse is a slim basis on which to justify the desirability of mandated disclosure. Other issues must be considered. (1) To what extent, if any, would abuse be reduced by mandating additional disclosure? (2) What are the additional costs associated with mandated disclosure? (3) Are there alternative methods of dealing with the problem that might be more effective and/or less costly? Reliance on anti-fraud statutes and private sector collective agreements are two possibilities. In any event, no system, even a mandated one, is likely to drive the level of abuse to zero nor is it likely such a result would be desirable, even if it were feasible, because of the costs of achieving that result. Implementation error caused by a lack of evidence on investors' demand for information and/or biases induced by reliance on vested interests must also be considered.

Currently, there is little or no evidence that bears on these questions. As a result, the desirability of a mandated disclosure system is still an open issue. However, the issues raised here provide a framework within which to structure future research by the Commission and others. Elsewhere I have called for an increased reporting by the SEC as to the intended and actual effects of disclosure regulations. This proposal was based on the notion that the SEC, as a public agency, has a stewardship responsibility at least as great as any corporation and hence has a commensurate reporting responsibility.

While it is premature to conclude that such a proposal is clearly desirable, it is not unreasonable to suggest that an effort be made, at least on an experimental basis. Such efforts may provide some evidence on the fundamental issue of the desirability of a public agency that has been regulating disclosure for over forty years.

Can the SEC Make Disclosure Policy Meaningful?*

Homer Kripke

If one looks at the history of the SEC's control of the securities disclosure process, two unarticulated assumptions stand out: First, that until recent changes of administration, it was based on the principle that the past foretells the future reasonably well; that is, disclosure may be backward-oriented, dealing with "facts" (by which a spokesman for the SEC point of view meant events in the past), and that this will be a reasonable basis for prediction of the future which determines security values. Second (in keeping with the foregoing but having an independent existence of its own), the standard accounting model, based on reporting the past on a historical cost basis, reasonably corresponds with reality, and the net income figure thus produced is useful for determining securities values. . . .

A Historical Note

At the beginning of my search, I was aware of course, that the Securities Act of 1933 made extensive borrowings from the English Companies Act of 1929, and I wanted to see what the borrowing had been as to accounting.

Professor Harold Edey of the London School of Economics has written extensively on the history of accounting in the United Kingdom. He has shown that the formulation of rules in the United Kingdom in the 1920s—and, indeed, up until the last few years— had nothing to do with the needs of investors. Instead, it arose out of some 19th century legal requirements of the courts (which would now seem naive to us) for distinguishing working capital from fixed capital.

Thus, when the SEC statutes borrowed this accounting as the

*Source: 2 J. Portfolio Man. 32–45 (1976); also 31 Bus. Law. 293 (1975). Reprinted with permission. Homer Kripke is Rohrlich Professor of Law at New York University School of Law.

basis for disclosure to investors, its theoretical foundations left a great deal to be desired. In the legislative history of the Securities Act, one finds that there is almost nothing in the Hearings or the Reports as to the substance of the disclosure that was to be made. Most of the legislative history deals with the scope of exemptions and the scope of liability, but not the substance of disclosure. The only witness who testified to the latter point to any extent was Robert E. Healy, then the Chief Counsel to the Federal Trade Commission. He had conducted the famous 95-volume study of the history of public utility holding companies before and after the great 1929 crash, and saw one fixed point—that anything that was *not* original cost *was* original sin. When he became one of the first members of the Securities and Exchange Commission, he took that position strongly. I think because he knew most about the subject and felt most strongly about it, his opinion carried the Commission. I was on the SEC staff at the time and involved in the decision, when after some years of case-by-case decision, the SEC became firm on the point that historical cost was the required basis of accounting. Healy's strong views influenced two whole generations of the Commission's Chief Accountants, until the retirement of Andrew Barr in 1972.

The practicing profession accepted this position, partly, no doubt, in principle, but also partly because that position fitted neatly in their minds with the needs of objectivity and conservatism, especially in the face of the statutory liabilities under the securities legislation. But it left American accounting with the asset values irrelevant and "net worth" meaningless, without a theory to explain itself.

That theory was supplied by the Paton and Littleton book, which was the first integrated statement of the theory that accounting is a process of matching costs and revenues to the reporting periods to which they relate. The practicing accountants fixed on that theory and on the word "costs" in that formulation, to say that "costs" meant "historical costs," and that this is the underlying principle of accounting. They have purported to find the solution to all kinds of accounting problems in achieving what they call a better matching. Professor Paton, when he saw the inflation, soon repudiated that position, emphasizing asset value rather than historical cost. But the literal reading of the matching formulation has prevailed. . . .

Accounting and the Economic Concept of Income

Accounting is sometimes thought of and taught as a branch of economics. Actually, however, it had very little contact with economics as it arose as a bookkeeping device for merchants. But today there can be no doubt that we can get some insights into the fundamentals of accounting concepts of income by comparing them with the concepts of economics, and we must question the significance of terms like "income" if they cannot be related to the same terms as used in economics.

Sir John Hicks, Professor of Political Economy at Oxford University, promulgated the economic definition of periodic income which is most widely used as a basis of comparison with accounting — the amount which can be spent during a period while leaving oneself as well off as before. There are many complications and subtleties in the Hicks approach. But it translates quite readily into the concept that income is the difference between the net worth set forth in a balance sheet at the beginning and net worth set forth in a balance sheet at the end of an accounting period, with, of course, adjustments for distributions and capital contributions. This concept of income — the difference between the net worths in successive balance sheets — happens to have had strong antecedents in accounting history, but not recently after the emphasis shifted to an income statement based on matching costs and revenues. The problem is how one determines the value of assets in determining net worth. Despite the current emphasis on the income statement rather than the balance sheet, accounting is still ultimately a problem of valuing the assets shown on the balance sheet that have not yet been treated as expenses and passed through the income statement.

To this question economics gives the answer that one does not value the individual assets, but values the worth of the enterprise by calculating the present worth of net future cash flows. The trouble with this is that estimates of net future cash flow are constantly changing, and are subjective. Likewise, the appropriate discount rate factored into the computation both to reflect the estimated time value of money and also to reflect risk is also subjective. Thus, on this approach, subjective changes in future estimates affect changes in net worth. Accountants and economists have struggled a long time to get past that difficulty. I think it is certain that under modern conditions, American accountants are never going to undertake to determine and record enterprise value.

The first reason is the direct Securities Act liability imposed on accountants, which will surely keep them from undertaking any such valuation. The second reason that accountants are never going to determine enterprise value is the point made by Jack Treynor: the Hicks formula requires that in order to determine income you must first determine value, but if you have value, you have no need to search for income. Thus, the Hicks formulation is simply not an operational concept of income for accountants.

We still have a question: Is there anything that the Hicks concept can teach us for the balance sheet? If we cannot undertake to record enterprise value in the balance sheet, is there an intermediate position between enterprise value and historical cost? We could abandon the attempt to determine goodwill, which is the added factor of enterprise value beyond the worth of individual assets, but we could nevertheless try to determine current values of specific assets. If we weigh this possibility, we can see that periodic recognition of current values of individual assets would eliminate many of the current problems in the recognition and realization of increases in asset values. Revaluation periodically without regard to the current rules on realization of revenues would eliminate a large part of the matching process which delayed recognition of revenues makes necessary. It would provide for basing depreciation on current values, and thus solve one of the acute current problems of overstatement of income that has recently been confronting us so sharply.

The great obstacle to the consideration of any kind of fair value accounting has been, quite rightly, the accountants' fear of taking on a risk of liability under the Securities Act if they undertook a valuation process for assets. Professor Morton Backer, in the book which he recently published for the Financial Executives Research Foundation, has proposed a solution to the valuation problem. He recognizes the need for certainty and objectivity and suggests that we should not determine current values for specific assets by appraisal methods, but simply by establishing a series of price index numbers for the respective types of fixed assets involved. He reaches the conclusion that perhaps 70 or 80 index numbers for particular types of machinery and other fixed assets would accomplish this purpose. One would get a very close approximation to current values of fixed assets, with the understanding that if the reporting company could prove to the accountants that that was not the right answer and the latter were willing to certify a different answer, then the company could use that different answer.

If we approach valuation on this basis, the standard to be applied would be in most cases the replacement cost of the remaining services of the present asset. An asset is essentially a resource which enables us to avoid a future cash outflow, that is, negative cash flow. We can avoid it because we already command the resource and do not have to spend money to get it in the future. On that basis, the cost of replacing the services would seem to be the value of the asset. . . .

A part of the foreseeable cash flow for continuing businesses is the problem of replacing these assets some time. That will involve a future cash outflow. In order to avoid tremendous lumpiness of our reporting, we ought to start to amortize the cost of replacing these assets when they wear out on an annuity method. Thus, one gets an expense charge not to depreciate the present asset, but a NIFO charge (Next-In, First-Out), the annual provision necessary to build up for replacement of the future asset. The focus shifts to the replacement of the present by the future asset.

Because the cash flow approach is so important, I believe the SEC has been wrong in its fulminations against cash flow accounting, especially since many sophisticated investors who know what they are doing make substantial investments in real estate on a straight cash flow basis, ignoring conventional earnings. Professor Lawson of the University of Manchester Business School in England . . . has built up a substantial body of writing to the effect that modern accrual accounting overstates the true income of a corporation. It constantly shows as undistributed earnings amounts that are necessarily already invested in additional working capital as a corporation grows and because of endemic inflation. Those funds are not in fact available for reinvestment and are not in any useful sense current earnings of the corporation, because they were expenditures necessary to achieve the reported sales growth. He has built up a considerable theory from several points of view, arguing for a total cash flow basis of accounting, except for the annuity provision, to replace fixed assets in the future. . . .

The Goals of Accounting

Where does all this leave us as to the goals of financial accounting? Basically, I think we have to orient accounting to the events of the year, and not to the accruals that even out income. As Professor Hawkins points out, accrual accounting has offered many opportunities for managing income to create a level and moderately increasing picture of improvement. The FASB [Financial Accounting Standards Board] tendencies seem to be to eliminate these possibilities to the extent possible. A great deal more emphasis should be placed on cash flows. Because the cash flows will change from year to year and can vary depending on investment in receivables and in inventory, one has to look at a substantial series of annual statements rather than an individual statement to get a clear picture of it.

There turns out to be an incongruity in my suggestions for the balance sheet and those for the income statement. On the big item of fixed assets, approaching it from a balance sheet point of view I concluded that what we should be looking for is the replacement cost of existing fixed assets. In approaching the problem from an income or cash flow point of view, what we should be looking for is future replacement cost of the present assets when they have to be replaced. These are not the same thing. How can we reconcile them? How can we make the financial statements articulate? . . . Let us not worry about the articulation of the balance sheet and the income statement. Let them tell us different things. At the present time we waste two statements by having them both tell us the same thing — the balance sheets showing a change in net worth, and the income statement tracing how the change in net worth occurred.

Finally, one comes away from the study of accounting with a picture that the Securities Acts have put too much emphasis on accounting as the conveyor of all financial information. Ultimately, value is in the future. It is determined by future expectations. We will never get the accountants to undertake the job of giving us future expectations, except in narrow matters like like of depreciable assets or collectibility of receivables. The overall look into the future must come from someone else.

The question is whether that look into the future can come from SEC documents or must come from some other source. So in the first instance, modern portfolio theory points not to the accountant, but to the portfolio manager to offer the investor the benefits of diversification and purposive selection of a risk level for his investments.

Portfolio Theory: Diversification and Beta

Reading the economic literature against the Securities Act mythology that the lay investor is going to make an informed investment decision if given all the material facts, we run immediately into the fact that disclosure under the Securities Acts deals with each single company, separately. Any specific statements about the reporting company's competitors or its place in the industry would be looked upon by the SEC's examiners with great concern; but *comparison* of availabilities, investments, expected returns, and risks is the heart of securities selection realistically, despite the mythology.

Modern portfolio theory emphasizes that much of the risk of individual securities can be eliminated by appropriate diversification, and that it does not take too large a number of securities to achieve a good diversification. In fact, it is contended that the market provides a return only for taking the risks of the market, and not for taking the risks of individual securities that can be almost eliminated by appropriate diversification.

Portfolio theory teaches that investments should be appraised not by the particular security, but by the overall portfolio and its overall risks. The suitability of a particular investment should be considered not on its individual merits alone, but on its contribution to the diversification and the risk of the total portfolio. There is no reflection of that kind of thinking in the securities legislation to date.

The economists have also proposed a measure of risk of a security in terms of the risk of not realizing the expected return on the investment (dividends plus appreciation). It is known as the Beta coefficient. . . .

This does not mean that I think there ought to be an item in the registration forms requiring the computation of the Beta coefficient of a company. But this seems to me to be an illustration of how economics could be brought into securities disclosure—a very simple thing could be done. We now waste half a page in every prospectus with a table showing the highs and lows of the security's market value for each quarter over two years. That table is completely meaningless, among other reasons because it does not show continuity between quarters or what was happening at the same time to the general market. If the same space were used to print a graph showing the market range of the security superimposed on a graph of the market range of a broad-based market index, one could see the essence of the Beta coefficient and reach one's own conclusions.

Beyond the portfolio manager is the question of the financial analyst. Here the economists unanimously reject technical analysis, i.e., "chartism," and also produce a strong argument against the usefulness of the financial analyst in helping the investor to determine enterprise value, and hence, ultimately, future market prices, by fundamental analysis.

The Efficient Market Hypothesis

The efficient market hypothesis suggests that information circulates rapidly, and market prices adjust rapidly to the information. One conclusion is that the material disclosed in SEC documents is not information, in the sense that it is new, at the time the document comes out. Another conclusion proposed is that the average lay investor cannot, and even the professionals competing against each other cannot, by fundamental analysis, find under-valued securities sufficiently often to cover the cost of research and the transaction costs. This is emphasized by another proposition: the likelihood that tomorrow's price will be higher or lower is already reflected in today's price—e.g., if you think that oil tool stocks are going up because of increased oil exploration, others have also had the same thought, and they have already bid the price up to a consensus value representing today's discounted present value of the future's fair value. Thus, many economists conclude that on average for the individual, nothing makes sense except a "buy and hold" strategy on a diversified portfolio. Obviously, that is not the theory underlying the Securities Acts, with their emphasis on individual securities and the thesis that the individual investor can make informed judgments after reading the prospectus. . . .

Yet it is curious that it is only because there are a sufficient number of disbelievers who search actively for information and trade thereon that the market is made efficient. Given the strong elements of disbelief and contrary conduct, we cannot basically fault the SEC for continuing along the course of individual security disclosure, although it would seem that the continuous disclosure process of the Securities Exchange Act of 1934 makes a great deal more sense than the convulsive effort involved in the spasmodic disclosure of the 1933 Act. One ends up here with the strong impression that the goals of the disclosure system are not realistic, but that there is sufficient lack of unanimity on the question to preclude a clear conclusion of disapproval. . . .

There is another aspect of the efficient market hypothesis. With the market at its lowest levels, two successive chairmen of the SEC and other Commissioners were worrying in public addresses about how they could help get the public back into the market. In the light of the uncertainties of the current world and the questions as to the advantages of trading—one must ask, "Is this a function of the SEC? Cui bono? Does the SEC's brokerage constituency outweigh its public constituency?"

Of course, there have been studies indicating that historically common stocks on average have done better than bonds, and that in general on average over the long-term common stocks have provided a return (dividends plus appreciation) of about 9% per annum, while bond interest rates have been typically less. Can anyone predict with any confidence that the historic long-term relationships will reassert themselves and again validate the comparison? If not, should it be the SEC's function to encourage the public back into the market?

The Random Walk

The efficient market hypothesis also tells us that prices react so rapidly to new information that there is no consistent progression of prices as the information circulates, but that prices follow a random walk: i.e., past movements of prices do not foretell the direction of future movements. This conclusion is buttressed by studies of the factors that affect stock prices: Past earnings do not foretell future earnings. There are no growth stocks except with the benefit of hindsight. If you think you have a growth stock and expect continuation of the present growth rate, you are likely to be disappointed. The basic conclusion is that looking to the past is not a very sure way of seeing the future, and that the SEC's past almost exclusive emphasis on the past leaves us bereft of an adequate guide to the future where value will be determined.

This is not to say that the empirical studies are remarkably encouraging on the accuracy of projections of earnings. But the worst that can be said is that the projections may be better and are no worse than naive extrapolations from the data from the past which the SEC requires to be furnished to us in abundance. The SEC waited far too long in moving in the direction of permitting projections, and its present proposals are bogged down in rigidity. As an SEC administrative judge said: " . . . a company's own . . . projections which are of manifest importance to investment judgment fall nevertheless in the category of material information though subject to future judgment or reconsideration." It is high time that the SEC give up its distrust of the common sense of the investor (which belies all of its rhetoric about disclosure) and permit projections to reach him in Commission documents.

The Security Valuation Model

Economists are divided between two basic views as to the relationship of earnings to cash dividends in the valuation of securities. A view associated with Professors Miller and Modigliani is to the effect that earnings are all-important, and that dividends are unimportant because earnings retained in the business will earn at least as fruitfully for the company as they could in the hands of the stockholder and will increase the future dividends flow and exit value upon sale. Thus, the present net worth will be the same. While this view was originally worked out technically on the assumption of a tax-free world, it is asserted that the conclusion remains valid even in the real taxable world.

On the other hand, a view associated with John Burr Williams and Myron Gordon argues that dividend and dividend policy are important theoretically. Practically, their view seems to be supported by the market's seeming valuation of dividend-paying stocks higher than it does stocks with comparable earnings that are paying little or no dividends. . . .

The point in this group of disputes is that the SEC need not decide the issues between disputing economists in order to provide for effective disclosure. All that would be necessary would be for the SEC to permit a management to disclose its intentions with respect to dividend payout as an amount or percentage of earnings, and similarly to disclose its target concerning debt as a percentage of total capitalization, if it has one. This kind of disclosure has been precluded by a stultifying staff view that any statement of dividend policy is an impermissible optimistic forecast, a view that is in my mind inexcusably extreme when the dividend policy is a conservative percentage of the earnings of a stable company. Yet as late as October, 1974 (even after the Commission had announced its intention to permit projections under certain circumstances), the Commission abandoned a proposal to require a statement of dividend policy in annual reports, " . . . because this type of disclosure may, in part, involve future orientated [sic] information, which is not presently required to be disclosed in filings with the Commission, and may result in meaningless 'boiler-plate statements.' "

Seeing into the Future

Although the research evidence on the accuracy of projections is not encouraging, this seems to me not to be the point. That investors pay attention to projections is conceded. The time has come to end the SEC's excessive preoccupation with verifiable data for which it cannot be criticized, to assume that the investor who is supposed to make an "informed investment judgment" can exercise a common sense skepticism toward non-verifiable information, and to relax the rigidity of the disclosure process.

It has been frequently asserted that the public tends to believe that all printed figures are "written on stone" and therefore accurate, even though unverifiable. It is submitted that there is no reason to fear this. The SEC has always made two fundamental mistakes about the investor public. On the one hand, it has believed that the public could handle highly technical disclosure of accounting and other matters to an extent which belies its own calls for simplification in writing. The writer has argued to the contrary that the concept that the lay public can understand a technical prospectus is a myth. The SEC has more recently countered with the concept of differential disclosure, i.e., full technical disclosure for the professional and a simplified version for the layman.

On the other hand, the SEC has always improperly denigrated the common sense of the public. The businessman who every day has to view with a skeptical eye the exaggerated advertising claims for a product and who has seen his expectations in the stock market disappointed time and time again is unlikely to take without appropriate skepticism the forecasts of management or his broker if they are too optimistic.

There will doubtless be instances in which the freedom to forecast will be abused and in which the resulting liabilities will provide the public no adequate remedy after the fact. However, it is not apparent that Securities Act disclosure as practiced to date has prevented the public either from losses or from outright frauds. As we move into the future of constant technological change and vast national and international shortages and strains, we have no choice but to experiment with disclosure with a forward look instead of marching backward into the future.

The SEC with new Commissioners and a new Chief Accountant is slowly recognizing this point of view and is beginning to depart from the hard concept that only the past is factual, and is requiring disclosures oriented to the future. Thus in its registration Guide 22, it requires management discussion of the five-year earnings summary, with express disclosure of factors which might make the past not a reliable guide to the future. In Accounting Series Release No. 166, it calls for disclosure of unusual risks of the business, clearly a forward-looking concept. In its alternate proposals on interim financial statements, it invites disclosure of major uncertainties of the business, another forward-looking concept.

Of course, the big forward-looking step is its proposal on projections, but it is marred by its rigidity. After 40 years during which the SEC was wrong in its prohibition of projections in filed documents, as it now gingerly admits, neither it nor the persons filing the documents is in a position to be sure what the appropriate limits and procedures of projections should be, and the Commission is wrong to come up with so rigid a proposal . . . . *

Conclusion

If the SEC really expects that the documents which are produced under its command will be the guide to securities investment decisions, it has to change its emphasis from the past and from threats of liability, by providing broader safe harbors by rule and encouraging efforts to present guides to the future — the sensitivities

*[Most of the rigidities referred to by Professor Kripke were eliminated from Rule 175, the safe harbor rule for projections, as finally adopted. See 17 C.F.R. §230.175; Rel No. 33-6084 (June 25, 1979) — Eds.]

I have mentioned, forecasts, opinions, what Carl Schneider has called "soft information." On the other hand, it may be that . . . the SEC has never really believed its rhetoric and has never believed that its documents could be the basis for securities decisions, and it has merely been trying to give us a solid objective collection of past information, leaving it to the investor and the analyst to look to the future.

In that case, filed documents are not going to be the basis on which investment decisions are made. Then we all have to ask ourselves whether the enormous amount of time and expense and effort of lawyers and accountants and the best minds in Wall Street to produce these documents under great pressure is justified, if all that is created in the long-run is a free government-compelled hand-out competing with Standard and Poor's yellow sheets. That, I think, is the big challenge on which the SEC sometime has to make up its collective mind.

NOTES AND QUESTIONS

1. Among the mandatory disclosure rationales mentioned by Beaver is the proposition that, while management is likely to be the cheapest producer of information about the firm, it has incentives to suppress or delay unfavorable information, which may lead others to expend resources on the same task. This point, along with some of the other arguments for required disclosure, is further developed in N. Gonedes, N. Dopuch and S. Penman, Disclosure Rules, Information-Production and Capital Market Equilibrium: The Case of Forecast Disclosure Rules, 14 J. Accounting Res. 89 (1976):

> Another argument that can be advanced in support of forecast disclosure involves a possible reduction in the extent to which efforts are duplicated. Suppose that agents external to the firm allocate resources to the kinds of information-production activities leading to forecasts. The "duplication" argument would essentially state that it is more efficient to have one entity, and in particular management, produce and distribute forecasts than to have many agents produce forecasts on the same terms of trade. This argument, as reasonable as it seems, is based upon several critical implicit assumptions, two of which are considered below.
>
> In order to assert that there really is wasteful and completely avoidable duplication, it must be that the forecasts being produced are perfect substitutes, so that all agents could use any of the forecasts (including managements' forecasts) just as they would their own. Loosely speaking, the information content of one forecast in this situation is the same as that of any other forecast. This appears to be a very

strong assumption, especially if the forecasts are based upon different models. A priori, it would seem that the forecasts produced by different models represent competing or rival products. This may be the case when, for example, the "quality" of managements' forecasts is not viewed as being the same as that of other forecasts. Such a viewpoint might be motivated by the incentives and opportunities that managements might have for issuing "distorted" forecasts. If different forecasts are viewed as competing products, then each may provide an important contribution, in terms of information content . . . . The main point that we wish to emphasize is that different forecasts may not be perfect substitutes and, thus, the "duplication" argument seems less forceful than it did at first glance.

2. Kripke suggests a number of respects in which he thinks the SEC has erred, and required information of dubious worth or excluded information of genuine value to investors. But if we return to the perspective of the previous selection, the fundamental question is: as to what sorts of information is government-required disclosure needed to supplement that information which companies would in any event be induced to provide to investors? Many commentators have pointed out that a large part of the contents of prospectuses, proxy statements and '34 Act filings is at best "stale" information, previously released or anticipated and long since impounded in the market price of traded securities. What is "new" information, that without the federal mandate would not have been disclosed anyway in connection with the transaction now taking place? And how much of that "new" information is of significant value to investors in making their assessments of the future?

3. During the last decade, an increasing number of accounting studies have tried to explore those questions through empirical research. Studies have been made of the impact on stock prices of the release of annual reports, quarterly earnings announcements and other financial data. Accounts of some of this research may be found in B. Lev, Financial Statement Analysis: A New Approach 226-44 (1974), G. Foster, Financial Statement Analysis 332-82 (1978), and J. Cox, Financial Information, Accounting and the Law (1980) 184–185, 272–275, 727–730.

4. A particularly interesting recent controversy has centered on efforts to determine whether the SEC's adoption of "line of business" reporting requirements provided investors with any information of value. In 1969 the SEC decided, over strong industry opposition based on its high costs, to make companies show not only the sales revenue but also the profitability of each material line of business in which they were engaged. Using the market model technique, Professors Bertrand Horwitz and Richard Kolodny, then of the School of Management, State University of New York, Binghamton, undertook

to measure the effect, if any, of the new required disclosure on the market risk (*beta*) and security prices of the affected firms. They concluded:

> The null hypothesis that the required disclosure had no effect on the risk and return of securities close to the time of its reporting could not be rejected at the 0.05 level in any of the tests. Thus the authors' results provide no evidence in support of the universally accepted contention that the SEC required disclosure furnished investors with valuable information.

B. Horowitz and R. Kolodny, Line of Business Reporting and Security Prices: An Analysis of an SEC Disclosure Rule, 8 Bell J. Econ. 234, 247 (1977).

The Horowitz-Kolodny research design was criticized, and a decline in market beta for affected firms was detected, in a Comment by Richard Simonds and Daniel Collins, 9 Bell J. Econ. 646 (1978). See also the Rejoinder by Horwitz and Kolodny, 9 Bell. J. Econ. 659 (1978), and an expanded study by Collins and Simonds, SEC Line-of-Business Disclosure and Market Risk Adjustments, 17 J. Accounting Res. 352 (1979).

5. If one accepts the propostion that SEC prospectuses and proxy statements provide simply one of many channels of information, and by no means always the most timely or valuable, flowing into the market to be reflected promptly in stock prices, should liability for a market transaction be founded on a "material omission" in that single document, if it can be shown that the omitted information was previously and widely disclosed by other means? To what end do lawyers and accountants and management expensively labor to make such documents so comprehensive a compendium of all possible "material" information about the company and the transaction that the resulting tomes are actually read by very few stockholders or purchasers? The answer, of course, is to try to avoid legal liability if, for usually quite unrelated reasons, the stock price should decline. Are these liability rules, such as Section 11 of the '33 Act and the private causes of action being developed under Section 14 of the '34 Act, sound? Could they be made so if the courts gave greater attention to a realistic assessment of damage causation and measurement?

6. The reaction of the SEC's Advisory Committee on Corporate Disclosure to the sorts of questions considered in this chapter was relatively untroubled:

> The Committee considered the significant studies concerning the functioning of securities markets, theories concerning capital asset pricing and portfolio organization and belief in some quarters that

market forces may adequately provide sufficient reliable firm-oriented information, and determined that the basics of the present system should be continued and that major change in the federal securities laws or their administration is not needed. The Committee concluded, with some dissent, that:

(1) The "efficient market hypothesis" — which asserts that the current price of a security reflects all publicly available information — even if valid, does not negate the necessity of a mandatory disclosure system. This theory is concerned with how the market reacts to disclosed information and is silent as to the optimum amount of information required or whether that optimum should be achieved on a mandatory or voluntary basis;

(2) Market forces alone are insufficient to cause all material information to be disclosed;

(3) Commission-filed documents often confirm information available from other sources. The Commission's filing requirements, while often not a source of new information to investors, assure that information disclosed by publicly held companies through many means is reliable and is broadly accessible by the public.

Report of the Advisory Committee on Corporate Disclosure to the SEC, 95th Cong., 1st Sess. D-5 (House Comm. Print 95-29 1977).

7. For the last decade, Professor Louis Loss of Harvard Law School and the American Law Institute have labored to bring clarity and order, at least from the lawyer's perspective, to the complicated field of securities regulation. The result is the proposed Federal Securities Code, which may soon be receiving serious consideration by Congress. For a discussion of the (quite limited) extent to which the Code addresses the issues of this chapter, see the symposium in 33 U. Miami L. Rev. 1425-1549 (1979).

Chapter 11

Assessments of the SEC's Performance

Whatever the rationale for precisely what the SEC was doing, for the first thirty years of its existence the Commission received general approbation from the academic community as a model regulatory agency — effective and untainted by corruption, with high employee morale and a reputation for expertise. Partly for these reasons, there was little in the way of systematic criticism, or even examination, of its performance. The first attempt at a comprehensive evaluation of the consequences of the SEC's disclosure regulations, particularly as they affected the sale of the new issues, came in a 1964 paper by George Stigler, in response to the SEC's release of its Report of the Special Study of the Securities Markets (1963). Among other things, Stigler's article contained an attempt to measure empirically whether investors in new stock issues had benefited from the institution of disclosure requirements.

The Stigler study drew a prompt, and heated, rebuttal from Irwin Friend and Edward Herman. Friend and Herman attacked both the accuracy of some of Stigler's data and, more importantly, the interpretations to be placed on his findings. The exchange went through several rounds, and illustrates both the value and the difficulties of empirical research.

The next major effort at an appraisal of SEC regulation was undertaken by George Benston. Benston's 1973 article sought in a number of ways to measure the effects of the formal reporting requirements imposed on listed companies by the '34 Act; in particular, he used the new finance techniques to see if the institution in 1934 of required disclosure of sales data was of value to investors. Once again Irwin Friend, this time with Randolph Westerfield, came to the defense of the SEC and its requirements. Their exchange is excerpted in the second group of papers in this chapter.

1. THE STIGLER STUDY

Public Regulation of the Securities Market*

George J. Stigler

It is doubtful whether any other type of public regulation of economic activity has been so widely admired as the regulation of the securities markets by the Securities and Exchange Commission. The purpose of this regulation is to increase the portion of truth in the world and to prevent or punish fraud, and who can defend ignorance or fraud? The Commission has led a scandal-free life as federal regulatory bodies go. It has been essentially a "technical" body, and has enjoyed the friendship, or at least avoided the enmity, of both political parties . . . .

The regulation of the securities markets is therefore an appropriately antiseptic area in which to see how public policy is formed. Here we should be able to observe past policy appraised, and new policy defended, on an intellectually respectable level, if ever it is. . . .

The paramount goal of the regulations in the security markets is to protect the innocent (but avaricious) investor. A partial test of the effects of the S.E.C. on investors' fortunes will help to answer the question of whether testing a policy's effectiveness is an academic scruple or a genuine need. . . .

The basic test is simplicity itself: how did investors fare before and after the S.E.C. was given control over the registration of new issues? We take all the new issues of industrial stocks with a value exceeding $2.5 million in 1923–28, and exceeding $5 million in 1949–55, and measure the values of these issues (compared to their offering price) in five subsequent years. It is obviously improper to credit or blame the S.E.C. for the absolute differences between the periods in investors' fortunes, but if we measure stock prices relative to the market average, we shall have eliminated most of the effects of general market conditions. The price ratios (p_t/p_o) for each time span are divided by the ratio of the market average for the same period. Thus if from 1926 to 1928 a common stock rose from $20 to $30, the price ratio is 150 (per cent) or an increase of 50 per cent but, relative

*Source: Reprinted by permission of The University of Chicago Press, from 37 J. Bus. 117-142 (1964). George J. Stigler is Walgreen Professor of Economics at the University of Chicago.

to the market, which rose by 68.5 per cent over this two-year period, the new issue fell 12 per cent.

The prices of common and preferred stocks were first analyzed to determine whether they varied with size of issue after one, three, or five years. In each case there was no systematic or statistically significant variation of price with size of issue. The elusiveness of quotations on small issues makes it difficult to answer this question for issues smaller than the minimum size of our samples ($2.5 million in the 1920's, $5 million in the 1950's). One small sample was made of fifteen issues in 1923 of $500 thousand to $1 million for which quotations were available, and this was compared with the twenty-two larger issues of the same year. The differences were sufficient to leave open the question of the representativeness of our findings for smaller issues.

The annual averages of the quotations (relative to market) are given for common stocks in Table [16]. In both periods it was an unwise man who bought new issues of common stock: he lost about

Table 16
New Stock Prices Relative to Market Averages, Common Stocks
(Issue Year = 100)

	Year After Issue				
	1	2	3	4	5
Pre-S.E.C.					
1923	92.7	85.0	77.8	62.1	67.0
1924	98.0	76.3	69.1	65.9	51.0
1925	85.0	66.9	54.8	42.2	33.0
1926	90.2	81.8	77.1	62.6	66.9
1927	84.7	69.1	60.1	72.6	103.4
1928	71.6	50.4	40.8	45.0	57.0
Average	81.9	65.1	56.2	52.8	58.5
Standard deviation	43.7	46.7	43.7	48.5	65.1
No. of issues	84	87	88	85	84
Post-S.E.C.:					
1949	93.3	88.1	86.7	86.9	64.9
1950	84.3	76.0	53.0	57.8	46.9
1951	83.6	78.7	76.3	80.4	74.5
1952	87.7	74.3	70.7	70.4	69.8
1953	88.1	79.2	75.4	70.4	93.6
1954	53.2	48.7	56.4	48.1	42.4
1955	71.8	64.9	82.3	77.8	83.4
Average	81.6	73.3	72.6	71.9	69.6
Standard deviation	23.9	27.7	31.0	30.9	38.9
No. of issues	47	47	47	47	47

Source: Stigler, Table 1.

one-fifth of his investment in the first year relative to the market, and another fifth in the years that followed. The data reveal no risk aversion.

The averages for the two periods reveal no difference in values after one year, and no significant difference after two years, but a significant difference in the third and fourth, but not fifth, years. The ambiguity in this pattern arises chiefly because the issues of 1928 did quite poorly, and the number of issues in this year was relatively large — one-third of all issues of the 1920's were made in 1928. It may well be that these enterprises did not have sufficient time to become well launched before the beginning of the Great Depression. With an unweighted average of the various years, there would be no significant difference between the averages in the 1920's and the 1950's.

The proper period over which to "hold" a new stock in these comparisons is difficult to specify: presumably it is equal to the average period the purchasers held the new issues. With speculative new issues one would expect the one-year period to be much the most relevant, for thereafter the information provided by this year of experience would become an important determinant of the investor's behavior.

These comparisons suggest that the investors in common stocks in the 1950's did little better than in the 1920's, indeed clearly no better if they held the securities only one or two years. This comparison is incomplete in that dividends are omitted from our reckoning, although this is probably a minor omission and may well work in favor of the 1920's.

The variance of the price ratios, however, was much larger in the 1920's than in the later period: in every year the difference between periods was significant at the 1 per cent level, and in four years at the 0.1 per cent level. This is a most puzzling finding: the simple-minded interpretation is that the S.E.C. has succeeded in eliminating both unusually good and unusually bad new issues! This is difficult to believe as a matter of either intent or accident. A more plausible explanation lies in the fact that many more new companies used the market in the 1920's than in the 1950's — from one viewpoint a major effect of the S.E.C. was to exclude new companies. . . .

These studies suggest that the S.E.C. registration requirements had no important effect on the quality of new securities sold to the public. A fuller statistical study — extending to lower sizes of issues and dividend records — should serve to confirm or qualify this conclusion, but it is improbable that the qualification will be large, simply because the issues here included account for most of the dollar volume of industrial stocks issued in these periods. Our study is not exhaustive in another sense: we could investigate the changing industrial composition of new issues and other possible sources of differences in the market performance of new issues in the two periods.

But these admissions of the possibility of closer analysis can be made after any empirical study. They do not affect our two main conclusions: (1) it is possible to study the effects of public policies, and not merely to assume that they exist and are beneficial, and (2) grave doubts exist whether if account is taken of costs of regulation, the S.E.C. has saved the purchasers of new issues one dollar.

The S.E.C. Through a Glass Darkly*

Irwin Friend and Edward S. Herman

Our over-all reaction to Stigler's paper is that it represents a triumph of ideology over scholarship. Stigler is so convinced that the Report, the S.E.C., and government regulation of securities markets are unsound that any evidence to the contrary is either overlooked or explained away. . . .

Stigler of course is aware of the fact that since the advent of the S.E.C. the stockmarket has had no debacle corresponding to that in the early 1930's, but he apparently feels that he has adequately covered this point by his statement, "It is obviously improper to credit or blame the S.E.C. for the absolute differences between the periods in investors' fortunes." In fact, he does not find it necessary even to mention the 1929–32 experience, during which the stock market declined by 85 per cent. In the absence of evidence to the contrary, we can only assume that he would have shown similar forbearance if the stockmarket debacle had occurred after the advent of the S.E.C.

We shall show, however, that Stigler's complete disregard of the well-known changes since the 1920's in the stock market as a whole (including *outstanding* issues as well as *all* types of new issues), and of the scope and objectives of the securities legislation, constitutes a serious deficiency in his argument. This deficiency may significantly bias his results for new issues as well as invalidate his more general

*Source: Reprinted by permission of the University of Chicago Press, from 37 J. Bus. 382-405 (1964). Irwin Friend is Hopkinson Professor of Finance and Economics at the University of Pennsylvania. Edward S. Herman is also a professor of finance at the University of Pennsylvania.

denial of any positive relation between securities legislation and investor welfare. Moreover, we shall also demonstrate that, even if the
methodology and data Stigler uses to compare the pre-S.E.C. and
post-S.E.C. performance of new stock issues are valid, he has misin-
terpreted his own statistical results which, contrary to his conclusion,
indicate relatively better performance in the post-S.E.C. period. Finally, we shall show that a more careful reworking of his data in
conjunction with supplementary information which we have compiled seems to point fairly conclusively to superior performance of
new issues relative to outstanding issues in the post-S.E.C. period as
compared with the earlier years.

It should be pointed out that Stigler's test of the effect of the
S.E.C. on new stock issues envolves two basic assumptions that he
does not explicitly mention: first, that the market for *outstanding*
stock issues is not affected by the S.E.C.; and second, that any
differences in the relation of the markets for new and outstanding
issues in the two periods are mainly a reflection of the S.E.C. influence on new issues. The deficiencies in both assumptions are obvious, but it is still of some interest to follow through the logic of
Stigler's test. However, before we do so, we should note that a more
convincing test of the S.E.C.'s accomplishments in the markets for
both new and outstanding issues than the one Stigler proposes, and
chides the Special Study group for not carrying out, is provided in
the Pecora hearings and the Report, with their documentation of the
massive securities abuses of the earlier period and the much health-
ier post-S.E.C. experience. . . .

Stigler neglects to point out what virtually every student of finance recognizes: that the market for outstanding securities — which
is, of course, many times greater than that for new issues — has
been radically changed by securities legislation and regulation since
the 1920's. Though it is not possible to take a census of stock-market
pools, bucket-shop operations, misuse of insider information, and
other types of manipulation and fraud, which frequently relied on
misinformation and the absence of full disclosure, there is little
doubt that such activities were widespread in the pre-S.E.C. period,
involved vast sums of money, and are much less prevalent today.

In the earlier period, enormous losses were absorbed by the
public in excessively leveraged, highly speculative, and frequently
manipulated new issues of public utility holding companies, investment companies, and foreign bonds, each of which was frequently
sold under disclosure conditions bordering on fraud. It is undoubtedly true that a substantial part of the blame for such losses lies
elsewhere; but inadequate and deliberately misleading information,
and widespread violations of fiduciary responsibilities by corporate

insiders, were integral parts of the pre-S.E.C. environment of the securities business. They are entitled to an important though un-measurable share of responsibility. Stigler entirely ignores these ma-jor disaster areas in his test of S.E.C. regulation, which seriously biases his results against the S.E.C.

The Pecora investigation was also able to catalogue 107 issues on the New York Stock Exchange and seventy-one issues on the New York Curb in which members of these exchanges participated in pools in 1929, and the evidence, though incomplete, is complete enough. Though many (but by no means all) manipulative and fraud-ulent activities may have been illegal under common law before the federal securities legislation administered by the S.E.C. was enacted, it was not possible to enforce the law effectively. We doubt that any person reasonably well acquainted with the evolution of stock-mar-ket practices between the pre- and post-S.E.C. periods could lament or underrate the success of the new legislation in eradicating many of these weaknesses in our capital markets. . . .

Although Stigler's "test of previous regulation" involves an at-tempt to measure the effects of the registration requirement on in-vestor welfare, he offers no serious discussion of the purposes or background of this requirement, or how the achievement of its ob-jectives might be expected to manifest itself. This is understandable perhaps, in view of the fact that his article is essentially an attack on the provision of information to prospective investors (albeit under government sponsorship). Stigler states facetiously in the first para-graph of his article, "The purpose of this regulation is to increase the portion of truth in the world and to prevent or punish fraud, and who can defend ignorance or fraud?" Who indeed? Certainly if they *are* defended, it would have to be done somewhat obliquely.

A direct attack on disclosure would also be awkward in light of the emphasis commonly placed on *knowledge* as a highly important ingredient and condition of efficient markets by theorists and advo-cates of free-market organization (ordinarily including Stigler). It is true that they are also generally opposed to government intervention in market processes. However, given the importance of adequate information for the proper functioning of markets and the massive evidence of widespread deficiencies in the provision of information relating to new security issues in the pre-S.E.C. period, it seems to us that the limited regulation brought into play by the Securities Act of 1933 is far more consistent with free-market principles than an im-plicit defense of the imperfectly competitive conditions in securities markets which preceded it. By omitting any discussion of the pur-poses of the Securities Act, Stigler is able to ignore the pre-S.E.C. background, as well as the sticky question of why economic information is highly beneficent when privately generated but of dubious value when required by law and regulatory authority. . . .

The consequences of Stigler's failure to explore the disclosure purpose of the registration requirement are nowhere better evidenced than in his discussions of the "puzzling finding" that the variance of the price ratios of a sample of new security issues was much larger in the 1920's than in the post-S.E.C. years examined. He comments that

> . . . the simple-minded interpretation is that the S.E.C. has succeeded in eliminating both unusually good and unusually bad new issues! . . . A more plausible explanation lies in the fact that many more new companies used the market in the 1920's than in the 1950's — from one viewpoint a major effect of the S.E.C. was to exclude new companies.

Entirely ignoring the wide prevalence of manipulative activities in the pre-S.E.C. securities market, Stigler does not even mention the reduction of such activities as a possible factor influencing the "puzzling" behavior of the variances of pre- and post-S.E.C. price ratios. More important, he fails to suggest the possibility that the "elimination" of issues by the S.E.C. was a result of improved disclosure of the degree of risk and a consequent greater reluctance by investors to buy risky new issues. The reduction in the variance of the price ratios is precisely what we might expect if disclosure requirements were effective. The finding is "puzzling" only if the logical implications of a successful disclosure policy are not admitted to consideration! What makes this treatment by Stigler particularly striking is the extent to which it contradicts his earlier work, in which "price dispersion is a manifestation — and, indeed, it is a measure — of ignorance in the market." . . .

In this section we consider Stigler's test results, and his interpretation of these findings — which we find to be unsupported by his own evidence. We take Stigler's methods and findings as given and evaluate them largely on the basis of his own framework. In the succeeding section we examine the numerous deficiencies in his data and methods, and indicate the effects of making the more vital corrections.

Common-stock findings. Stigler discusses, first, his findings on average prices relative to issue prices, adjusted for changes in the market as a whole, for a sample of new common-stock issues of the years 1923–28 and 1949–55, for each of the five years after issue date. Examining his Table [16], we see that in four of the five years after issue date the annual average of deflated price relatives was higher in the post-S.E.C. period; in the remaining year it was equal; and in two of the five years the superiority of the post-S.E.C. performance was sufficiently large to be statistically significant. Stigler summarizes these findings as follows:

> The averages for the two periods reveal no difference in values after one year, and no significant difference after two years, but a significant difference in the third and fourth, but not fifth, years. The ambiguity in this pattern arises chiefly because the issues of 1928 did quite poorly.

It will be noted that Stigler fails to state the *direction* of the differences; or that *all* the differences, significant or not, are favorable to the post-S.E.C. period. Nor does he indicate in what sense there is an "ambiguity" in the pattern — certainly there is no such ambiguity as would result if the average in even *one* of the five years had shown superior result for the pre-S.E.C. period. The attempt to explain away the results by the poor performance of the 1928 issues is simply to question the validity of his own test. He does not point out that the poor performance of the 1954 issues was a result of one spectacular flop in a total sample of four issues. If that single issue were eliminated, and it should be anyway because it is included contrary to Stigler's own criteria, each of the five years after issue date would show higher averages for the post-S.E.C. period, and thus one minor "ambiguity" would be eliminated.

Following his summary of findings on common-stock averages, Stigler concludes, "These comparisons suggest that the investors in common stocks in the 1950's did little better than in the 1920's, indeed clearly no better if they held the securities only one or two years." It should be noted, first, that "clearly no better" if held two years is a misreading of his own figures, which show a two-year average of 73.3 for the post-S.E.C. period and 65.1 for the earlier period. Second, "little better" is hardly a summary phrase meeting "academic standards of accuracy," when the post-S.E.C. figures are measurably better in four of five years, significantly better in two years, and inferior in none of the five years. Third, Stigler generalizes about investor performance in "common stocks" without regard to the restricted coverage of his partial test and without consideration of the implications of his own findings on variance differences between the two periods.

Fourth, Stigler overemphasizes the importance of the first-year results, the only year for which his uncorrected figures do not show a measurably superior average performance for the post-S.E.C. years. We consider the longer time spans more important tests of investor results than the one-year period, which is the perspective more appropriate to professionals and speculators (as opposed to the bulk of public investors). In addition, there is probably an upward bias in Stigler's first-year values for the pre-S.E.C. period, a consequence of the numerous manipulative pools in the late twenties which were frequently active in the first year after the public sale of a new issue. Thus, of his thirty-three common-stock issues of 1928, a minimum of seven were subjects of pool operations in the year 1929. The one-year stock price performance of these seven is well above the average for the 33 issues; thus there would appear to be a strong possibility that Stigler derives support for his argument against required disclosure from private cartel arrangements operative in the pre-S.E.C. period.

Having dealt with the differences in common-stock averages, Stigler turns to a comparison of the variances of the price ratios of common stocks in the pre- and post-S.E.C. periods. He acknowledges that the variance "was much larger in the 1920's than in the later period." From the standpoint of the stated objective of Stigler's inquiry — "how did investors fare before and after the S.E.C." — this would appear to constitute a major vindication of the S.E.C. entirely consistent with theoretical expectations of the effects of improved information and a reduction of manipulative activity. In dealing with the differences in post- and pre-S.E.C. averages, Stigler attempted to draw conclusions as to the implications of his findings for investor welfare. In connection with the variance differences, he fails to relate his findings to his original question. Instead, he "explains" the phenomenon in terms of the effects of the S.E.C. on the number of new companies floating new issues. Briefly, his test not pointing to a satisfactory outcome, Stigler omits any conclusion as to the implications of reduced variance for investor welfare and rejects his own test as unsatisfactory. . . .

In order to ascertain fully the nature and validity of Stigler's data and methods, we attempted to reproduce his common-stock results for four of his twelve years, two pre-S.E.C. (1923 and 1928) and two post-S.E.C. (1949 and 1955). The corrections called for by this effort were so numerous and one-sided that a recomputation of his Table [16] on the basis of these four years alone resulted in a significant alteration of the test results. We have also extended his test of the performance of large common-stock issues to the years 1958 and 1959 (first half). In addition, we have examined the price performance of pre- and post-S.E.C. small issues. These further tests again confirmed the superiority of post-S.E.C. performance.

Errors in data. Our examination of Stigler's common stock data for 1923, 1928, 1949, and 1955 uncovered two major classes of errors (a) inappropriate inclusions and exclusions of common-stock issues, and (b) a listing of prices as "N.A." (not available) when such prices were in fact obtainable. . . . The effects of these corrections are presented in tabular form in Appendix 1[omitted]. They may be summarized as follows.

a) The pre-S.E.C. averages are reduced in four of the five years after issue, with an average reduction of 1.7 percentage points per year. The post-S.E.C. averages were raised by these corrections in every year, and by an average of 3.1 percentage points per year.

b) The pre-S.E.C. standard deviations are reduced moderately (an average of 0.7 percentage points per year); the post-S.E.C. standard deviations are reduced more substantially (an average of 2.1 percentage points per year).

c) The decrease in the pre-S.E.C. average for the first year and the post-S.E.C. first-year increase now establish a gap favorable to the post-S.E.C. experience (79.2, pre-S.E.C.; 83.8, post-S.E.C.). Thus, on a corrected basis, Stigler's averages show a post-S.E.C. superiority in each of the five years after issue.

d) The changes in the fifth year reduce the pre-S.E.C. average from 58.5 to 53.8 and increase the post-S.E.C. average from 69.6 to 73.2. This 19.4 per cent difference in fifth-year deflated averages is so large that it now proves to be statistically significant (at the 5 per cent level). Thus all of Stigler's "ambiguities" disappear when his own test is applied in greater conformity with his stated criteria.

Comment*

George J. Stigler

I confess to some disappointment with my critics. I had thought they would have commended me, perhaps fulsomely, for my central arguments: (1) public policies should be evaluated on the basis of their effects; and (2) it is possible (witness my study of registration of new issues) to ascertain these effects, at least approximately. The critics say my numbers support the conclusion opposite to that which I draw from them: be it so, and a source of chagrin to me. Then they should have been all the more grateful for my having given the first quantitative evidence in thirty years that the review of new stock issues by the S.E.C. is worth the while.

Alas, they display little gratitude. The Friend-Herman piece, in fact, displays instead what must be described as acerbity, and I feel that I owe them an apology for inadvertently fraying their regulatory nerves. . . .

*Source: 37 J. Bus. 414-422 (1964). Reprinted by permission of the University of Chicago Press.

. . . The issue is precisely that of the use of "scientific method" versus "common sense." Either we present explicit hypotheses and test them by the developing techniques of the social sciences, or we rely upon the a priori case for protecting investors plus the scandals revealed by a Pecora, or the a priori case for letting men conduct their own affairs plus the counterscandals revealed by some new counter-Pecora. (Does anyone doubt that a microscopic review of the Commission's history would reveal some shocking episodes?) One can question how much evidence is needed to act—I shall say something about this later—but my general position is surely the only defensible one: indeed it is simply the standard case for scientific method addressed to policy formulation. Only this method will sift out plausible error, and only this method will lead cumulatively to greater precision of knowledge.

The registration procedure of the S.E.C. seeks to provide information relevant to the purchase of the registered issues. I sought to measure the importance of the information so provided by the outcome of the purchase of new issues, as compared with that of the purchase of the portfolio comprising the Standard and Poor Index. I chose to price the new issues annually for a five-year period.

The choice of the time periods was intuitive: *immediately* after a new issue is floated, its price has not changed enough as a rule to reveal the outcome of purchase; *long after* the flotation the price is dominated by events which took place after the purchase. Clearly this intuitive argument, though plausible, gives no explicit guidance: the right period to study could be six months or six years.

At any date after the individual purchases a new issue, he has three types of information on which to act: (1) the information available through private channels at the time of flotation, which would include information on the industry as well as on the firm; (2) the information provided only because it is demanded by S.E.C. requirements; (3) information which appears subsequent to the flotation. In practice the distinction between types (1) and (2) would often be hard to draw: the S.E.C. supporter will claim all the improvements over time in type (1) information are due to his agency; the more detached scholar will study the improvements in information which came before 1934, and in areas not subject to regulation. If the distinction is feasible, we could make a direct test of the S.E.C. registration procedure by analyzing stock prices to determine the influence of the S.E.C.-dictated information. In fact, unless such tests can be made, there is no objective way of deciding which kinds and amounts of information to require in a registration statement.

To return to our problem of the period of possible effect of the disclosures in the registration statement, I now believe that the annual time intervals I employed should be approximately halved. Consider the purchase of the stock of a new company: its preflotation history will be brief and meager, and the prospects at flotation time will be completely submerged by the results of the next two years of operation. Or consider an established enterprise: its preflotation history is lengthy and substantial, so the disclosures in the prospectus must report chiefly very recent changes, which again are confirmed or refuted by the events of the next year or two. Friend and Herman favor a five-year period as more appropriate to investors, in contrast to speculators—I am always amazed by the kinds of stocks widows and orphans buy. I have not been able to devise a suitable procedure for measuring the period, and the reader must make his own choice.

One other major problem of interpretation of the evidence requires comment. I deliberately carried the analysis of the 1920's up to the threshold of the greatest stock-market crash in our history. I now consider this an inappropriately severe test of the new issues market in the absence of an S.E.C., and for the following reason. A new company is vulnerable to a major depression, just as a new swimmer cannot fight a strong current, but with experience and reserves the company gradually builds up resistance even to major depressions. A test which ignores this fact (and related facts for older companies) is biased in favor of the period in which no major depression occurred. Of course if the S.E.C. were responsible for the disappearance of major depressions, such periods should be included in the test, but I refuse to believe that Friend and Herman are more than 5 per cent serious in their claims in this direction.

This argument finds substantial support in the data. The 1932 common-stock prices relative to issue price, by age of company are shown in Table [17]. Thus the issues of new companies fell in price to one-half or one-third of the level of older companies. Accordingly, I omit 1928 from subsequent textual discussion, but in footnotes give data including this year.

One final point of interpretation: Since the comparison with established securities serves to eliminate extraneous influences, the new and established securities should be comparable. Thus common-stock flotations should be compared with established common stocks—and in a more precise study perhaps even standardized for industry composition. . . .

And now for the evidence. Before we turn to it I wish to thank Friend and Herman for reviewing our data. They discovered a considerable number of errors, and we have carried the review further and discovered others. The revised data are described in [Table 19]. A number of oversights and differences of judgment are inevitable

Table 17
1932 Common-Stock Prices Relative to Issue Price, by Age of Company

Age of Company Time of Issue	No. of Issues	Average Ratio of 1932 Price to Issue Year Price
1927 issues:		
Under three years	2	0.33
Three years or more	7	0.62
1928 issues:		
Under three years	13	0.07
Three years or more	10	0.18

Source: Stigler, Table 1.

in this kind of work, but I must apologize to readers and critics for the considerable number of avoidable mistakes in the original lists.

The results for common stocks are given in Table [18]. The differences are not statistically significant in any year. If the first two years are decisive, as I believe, there simply is no difference; if Friend and Herman's preference for the fifth year is accepted, things are hardly different. . . .

The variances of the price relatives continue to be larger in the earlier period than in the post-S.E.C. period. Unfortunately we do not have corresponding variances for established securities so it is not possible to deduce that there has been a differential change in new issues' prices. I would conjecture that the "calibrated" variance has declined, and primarily because of the exclusion of new companies by the registration requirements. The Friend-Herman insistence that the reduction in variance is a strong positive achievement of the S.E.C. is esoteric: a zero variance would mean that all buyers of new issues would fare the same, but they could fare very badly or very well. . . .

My earlier conclusion was that the S.E.C. review procedures

Table 18
Average of Common-Stocks Relative to Market (Issue Year = 100)

Period	Years After Issue				
	1	2	3	4	5
1923–27	89.9	77.9	72.5	66.2	70.7
1949–55	87.9	79.1	78.4	77.7	74.9

Source: Stigler, Table 2.

had not significantly improved the market performance of new issues relative to outstanding issues. The data revisions and the new analysis do not call for amendment of this conclusion. . . .

I had little to say about public policy in the securities markets, because I felt that the information to formulate intelligent policy was inadequate — and my knowledge of what is available is inadequate also. I did remark on the cartel on commission rates on the exchanges, where competition would serve traditional purposes, and upon the meagerness of the results of the S.E.C. review of prospectuses for new issues. To such remarks the reply is made: Where is the evidence for my proposals? This raises the problem of policy, which I shall discuss briefly in a more general way.

Public policy should serve proper goals, and do so efficiently — this is a statement of the problem. To solve the problem by definition is simply impossible. Yet the critics wish to do so. They ask: How can any man of good will (and a little economic knowledge) oppose the demands for disclosure of information? The plain fact is that information costs money, and no society is rich enough to get all the available information. So, the problem is one of how much information should be collected. The plain fact is that information can be obtained through various systems of organization. We can have the S.E.C. demand it, or we can make issuers responsible for misstatements, or we can trust the CPA's, or we can create guarantees (insurance), or we can use a dozen other systems. The questions of which procedure is most efficient is one to be answered by analysis, not to be answered by a God-given corollary of the Exchange Acts of 1934 or 1964. I cannot really believe my critics when they hint that extremism in the demand for facts is no vice.

The functions of the S.E.C. are presently based upon a grossly inadequate knowledge of their costs and effects. Does that mean that we should abolish the S.E.C.? Not necessarily, for our knowledge of the pre-S.E.C. market is also grossly inadequate, and we cannot assert that some deficiencies in that earlier market may not have been remedied. There is no proper substitute for the research necessary to relate ends and means.

We shall often (and sometimes correctly) feel the need to act before the lethargical scholars and misdirected *Special Studies* have performed the needed work. The only defensible solution is to use our general economic theory, which, for all its deficiencies, is our most tested and reliable instrument for relating policies to effects. It was on this basis that I proposed that we restore much more competition to the securities markets. I know of no other responsible procedure for making policy recommendations.

Table 19
New Stock Prices Relative to Market Averages — Common Stocks
(Issue Year = 100)

Period	Year After Issue				
	1	2	3	4	5
Pre-S.E.C.:					
1923	90.4	81.5	76.4	63.7	73.6
1924	104.1	81.8	77.2	74.5	59.7
1925	87.2	72.6	61.1	51.2	43.3
1926	88.4	83.2	84.8	64.8	67.2
1927	89.7	76.4	72.7	91.6	127.9
1928	63.6	51.9	40.7	37.9	45.0
1923–27 average	89.9	77.9	72.5	66.2	70.7
Standard deviation	38.8	45.6	44.4	56.3	80.6
Number of issues	44	46	47	47	47
1923–28 average	80.9	69.2	62.1	56.9	62.3
Standard deviation	43.1	50.0	48.5	52.8	73.9
Number of issues	67	69	70	70	70
Post-S.E.C.:					
1949	92.6	92.1	90.8	90.1	70.4
1950	102.8	90.6	61.3	68.3	60.9
1951	89.9	83.9	83.0	86.7	79.8
1952	91.6	75.9	72.9	72.2	73.2
1953	91.1	86.6	86.5	81.1	86.7
1954	67.8	61.9	69.0	55.5	51.8
1955	74.5	68.9	89.6	87.2	94.2
1949–55 average	87.9	79.1	78.4	77.7	74.9
Standard deviation	21.2	25.1	27.7	27.6	36.0
Number of issues	46	46	46	46	46

Source: Stigler, Table A1.

Professor Stigler on Securities Regulation: A Further Comment*

Irwin Friend and Edward S. Herman

Stigler now claims that it is more appropriate to compare 1949–55 with 1923–27 rather than with his earlier choice of 1923–28; . . . and that his former use of a five-year period after issue date as the relevant time span for assessing the performance of new issues should be approximately halved (though here he permits the reader to make his own choice). Purely coincidentally, of course, these changes all appear to lend support to his thesis. However, we shall not only show that these changes are dubious, but that even with these revisions the evidence is still strongly in favor of superior new issue performance in the post-S.E.C. period. . . .

Turning now to his new results comparing the relative price experience of selected new common stock issues in the pre-S.E.C. and post-S.E.C. periods, he states that in the 1923–27 versus 1949–55 test the "differences are not statistically significant in any year." He neglects to point out that the post-S.E.C. price performance is superior in four of the five years and inferior in only one (the first year). The differences in the first and second years are quite small but range from 6 to 17 per cent in the other years. Nor does he even mention our earlier caveat and evidence that in view of extensive price pegging and the numerous manipulative pools in the late 1920's, which might be expected to be particularly active in the first year after the public sale of a new issue, "there would appear to be a strong possibility that Stigler derives support for his argument against required disclosure from private cartel arrangements in the pre-S.E.C. period." Stigler mentions in a footnote that, with the revised data, "If 1928 is retained [in the earlier period], the difference is significant at less than the 10 per cent level only in the third and fourth years, when the post-S.E.C. period was superior." He does not indicate that with this inclusion the post-S.E.C. price experience is now superior (by from 9 to 37 per cent a year) in all of the five years. . . .

Stigler objects to our position that the reduction in the variance of the price ratios from the pre-S.E.C. to the post-S.E.C. periods was, from the investor viewpoint, a positive achievement of the S.E.C. He states that "a zero variance would mean that all buyers of new issues would fare the same, but they could fare very badly or very well." If this is to be taken seriously, it seems to imply either

*Source: 38 J. Bus. 106–110 (1965), reprinted with permission.

that investors have no risk aversion or that the variance measure used has no relevance to risk. Surely, either view represents a novel and seemingly implausible position which Stigler makes no attempt to justify.

2.   THE BENSTON STUDY

Required Disclosure and the Stock Market: An Evaluation of the Securities Exchange Act of 1934*

George J. Benston

I.   The Disclosure Requirements of the Securities Exchange Act of 1934

The '34 Act requires that a corporation whose stock is traded on a registered stock exchange or who registered a stock issue:

a) file detailed balance sheets, income statements, and supporting substatements (form 10K) within 120 days after the close of its fiscal year;

b) file a much less detailed semiannual report (form 9K) within 45 days after the first half of the fiscal year;

c) file a "current report" (form 8K) 10 days after the end of any month in which certain "significant" events occurred (such as a change of control of the corporation, material legal proceedings undertaken, material change of securities outstanding, and revaluation of assets).

In 1964, the disclosure requirements were extended to almost all corporations with at least 500 stockholders or $1 million in assets. (Exceptions are regulated companies whose statements were prescribed, such as banks and insurance companies). Thus, all but the smallest corporations now are covered by the Act.

Section 13(b) of the '34 Act (and section 19(a) of the '33 Act) gives the SEC the power to prescribe the form and content of the financial statements filed under the Act. In general, the SEC has followed generally accepted accounting procedures, although it has

---

Source: 63 Am. Econ. Rev. 132–155 (1973), reprinted with permission. George Benston is professor of accounting, economics and finance at the University of Rochester.

influenced these procedures by insisting that assets not be revalued upward, goodwill be amortized rapidly, and other "conservative" biases be reinforced. In this regard, the SEC has not followed the "disclosure rather than approval" philosophy of the Securities Exchange Act. This policy was established by Accounting Series Release No. 4 in 1938, which states that

> . . . where financial statements filed . . . are prepared in accordance with accounting principles for which there is no substantial authoritative support, such financial statements will be presumed to be misleading or inaccurate *despite disclosures* contained in the certificate of the accountant or in footnotes to the statements provided the matters involved are material. (italics added.)

Whether disclosure, as defined and required by the SEC, has been meaningful and beneficial, is the question asked here — not whether disclosure, as such, is good or bad.

II. The Rationale Underlying the Legislation

It would seem that any argument against disclosure is equivalent to an argument for secrecy. But such is not the case. Prior to the passage of the Securities Exchange Act, corporations could disclose what they wished to their current and potential stockholders and, if they were listed on the New York Stock Exchange (NYSE), American, Chicago (Midwest), or other regional exchanges, had to submit balance sheets and income statements to the Exchange. For the year ended December 31, 1933, all NYSE corporations were audited by CPA firms, all listed current assets and liabilities in their balance sheets, 62 percent gave their sales, 54 percent the cost of goods sold, and 93 percent disclosed the amount of depreciation expense. These percentages had been increasing fairly steadily prior to 1933, although there was little change after 1928. One could argue (as did the NYSE), that the legislation was not needed.

One could also argue that the disclosure policy followed by corporations in the absence of legislation is in the best interests of their stockholders. If management believed that the marginal revenue to the stockholders as a group from disclosure would exceed the marginal cost of preparing and supplying the information, they would disclose their financial and other data. The marginal revenue might include the savings to stockholders of not having to gather the data privately, the reduced cost of capital to the firm if prospective stockholders' uncertainty about the firm were reduced, improvement in the marketability of the firms' shares if investors desired financial information, etc. The marginal costs of disclosure might include the cost of preparing and distributing the statements, the costs incurred in informing competitors, suppliers, customers, and government officials, and the cost of misinforming stockholders when accounting statements report economic events incorrectly or inadequately (as when all research and development and advertising expenditures are charged to expense currently).

However, management might not issue financial statements (or might issue incomplete statements) if they underestimate the value of these statements to their current or potential investors, mismanage the corporation, intend to defraud investors, or if there are positive externalities in the efficient allocation of resources when all (or most) companies disclose financial data. Thus, one cannot immediately dismiss the argument that there is need for required disclosure solely by reference to the invisible hand of the market. Rather the question must be examined with respect to the rationale upon which the Securities Exchange Act of 1934 is based.

Underlying the disclosure requirements of the '34 Act is the belief that required disclosure of financial data is necessary for the fair and efficient operation of capital markets. The SEC's 1969 Wheat Report (and most other writings on the subject) view disclosure as necessary to 1) prevent financial manipulation and 2) provide investors and speculators with enough information to enable them to arrive at their own rational decisions. (Wheat Report, p. 10.) Perhaps even more important is the concept of "fairness," the belief that all investors, big and small, insiders and outsiders, should have equal access to relevant information. Whether these objectives can be achieved, a priori, by disclosure of financial data, and if they can, whether or not the evidence supports or rejects the hypothesis that they were, is considered in the balance of the paper. . . .

III. Fraud and Manipulation

Fraud and manipulation may be of two different types with respect to disclosure. Published statements may contain false or misleading data or desired data may not be published at all but may be released in the form of news stories, rumors, etc., to manipulate the public's expectations and so affect stock prices. These are discussed in turn.

It is very difficult to determine whether the '34 Act prevented the publication of fraudulent or misleading financial statements or even whether such fraud existed to any greater extent before or after the passage of the Act. In a situation of personal fraud by self-dealing or simple defalcation, required disclosure is of little value. Certified Public Accountants insist that they do not audit explicitly for fraud nor does the SEC ask them to do this, although I believe a good case could be made for this requirement. With respect to fraudulently prepared financial statements, I have reviewed such evidence as exists in another article. A search of the available literature, including the Senate and House hearings on the proposed securities legislation, fails to reveal much evidence of fraud in the preparation or dissemination of financial statements prior to 1934. . . .

The lack of evidence on fraudulent financial statements does not imply that published financial statements were or were not misleading. Prior to the passage of the Securities Act, it was very difficult for third parties, such as prospective stockholders, to sue accounting firms for negligently prepared financial statements. The courts held, under the rule of privity, that these reports were prepared for management only.

However, accountants were (and still are) liable for fraud " . . . if their audit has been so negligent as to justify a finding that they had no genuine belief in its adequacy for this again is fraud." (See Ultramares Corp. v. Touche, Niven and Co. [225 N.Y. 185, 174 N.E. 488]) The Securities Act changed accountants' liability dramatically, and now an investor may sue an accountant if, having relied on false or misleading statements, he "shall have purchased or sold a security at a price which was affected by such statement" (Section 18). It is important to note that the accountant must prove that the investor's loss was not a consequence of the financial statements rather than that the investor prove that he actually was misled by or even saw the statements.

In contrast to the lawmakers' expectations, an important consequence of this change in the law and of the SEC's administration of the Acts appears to be that financial statements are more misleading than they were. The considerable liability of accountants under Section 18 has contributed to accountants following conservative, often worthless practice, since it is difficult to sue them successfully for preparing misleading statements if they follow traditional procedures. In addition, the SEC has insisted on historically based accounting, discouraging price level and other revaluation of assets and liabilities, refusing to permit publication of sales and income projections and other valuable economic data, etc. Thus published financial statements are more misleading than they otherwise might have been. Although accountants might not have made much progress in reporting the economic position and progress of corporations had there been no Securities Act, there is no empirical or a priori basis for an assertion that the '34 Act has had a net positive effect on the publication of fraudulent or misleading financial statements. . . .

IV. Information and Rational Decisions of Investors and Speculators

The second rationale for the disclosure requirements is to allow "investors [to] make a realistic appraisal of the merits of securities and thus exercise an informed judgment in determining whether to purchase them." This rationale is based on a belief that the data required by the SEC are "information." That is, the financial statements must provide data about a corporation that affect investors' expectations about its future prospects and relative riskiness and that were not previously known, such that the information was completely discounted and impounded in the market price of the securities before the time of disclosure.

There is serious question whether the financial data approved by the SEC can provide the investor with information. The SEC does not allow current market valuation of assets, estimates of future sales or projection of the effects of discoveries, favorable regulatory rulings, public acceptance of new products and other economic events. . . . In requiring the filing of financial statements, the SEC is caught in a choice between speed and accuracy (in the sense of reporting to the letter of the formal and informal regulations), a choice which is resolved in favor of accuracy. As is noted above, the annual reports (10K) need not be filed with the SEC until 120 days after the close of a corporation's fiscal year. Whether the statements that have been filed are meaningful to investors and sufficiently timely to be of value is, of course, an empirical question, to which I now turn.

A. The Information Content of Published Financial Data — Financial Statements and Stock Prices

If the SEC's disclosure requirements are meaningful, the statements they require should contain information, and thus investors' expectations about a corporation's earnings and prospects, riskiness, relationship to other firms, etc., should be affected by the information. Since numerous studies show that the market adjusts rapidly to new information, the effect, if any, of previously unexpected data published in the financial reports of a corporation should be reflected in changes in its stock prices in the period when these unexpected financial data become publicly available. Other factors also may occur during the same period and must be accounted for. Principal among these are changes in general market conditions, changes in expected dividend payments (which often are announced at the same time that earnings data are announced), and changes specific to the corporation's industry. . . .

The regressions reveal that, except for the sales definition of financial data, none of the financial data variables in any of the expectations forms has a greater than minimal economic relationship to changes in stock prices, although the coefficients estimated are statistically significant. On the average, a 100 percent unexpected increase (or decrease) in the rate of change of income is associated with a 2 percent increase (or decrease) in the rate of change of stock prices in the month of announcement. Similar regressions were computed for the month when earnings were announced (which usually is a month before the SEC receives them), and similar results were found. The findings are not very dependent on the form of the expectations model used, although the naive model, where last year's rate of change is expected this year (a sort of "no-expectations" model), performed the best. This finding is contrary to the SEC's requirement that companies provide comparative data for several past years. Thus, I conclude that this evidence is not consistent with the underlying assumption of the legislation, that the financial data made public are timely or relevant, on average. . . .

. . . Thus the research . . . [by others shows] that financial statement data seem to reflect the economic situation of corporations but either are completely discounted by the market before they are published or do not predict the economic future. In either case, the data are not useful to investors at the time the SEC requires disclosure.

B. Returns to Sophisticated Users of Financial Data

It may be that the studies cited above approach a complicated problem in too simple a way. It often is claimed that the detailed reports required by the SEC are more useful to trained analysts than to the ordinary stockholder. The analyst then passes on his information to his clients or, in any event, trades on the information, thereby bringing its effects to the market. No doubt information about firms does get to the market. But does it get there by means of the financial reports required by the SEC?

One way to answer these questions is to examine whether well-trained analysts out-perform the market. I am aware of two studies that test directly the ability of security analysts to use published financial data. John G. Cragg and Burton Malkiel recorded predictions made by five investment firms of the earnings of 185 corporations whose stock is widely held. In particular, they compared the earnings' growth rate forecast by the analysts with the actual growth rates. They report that " . . . the remarkable conclusion of the present study is that the careful estimates of security analysts participating in our survey, the bases of which are not limited to public information, perform little better than the past growth rates" [the naive predictor, that the future will be like the past]. The second study, by Lyn Pankoff and Robert Virgil, was a controlled, laboratory study. They allowed security analysts to "buy" financial statements of companies in whose stock they can invest. The data are actual data and the stock prices are those that actually prevailed for the stocks whose identity they disguised. While their study is not yet complete, Pankoff and Virgil found that analysts who use financial data (or any other data) do not do as well as they could have had they followed a "naive" buy and hold strategy.

Several indirect tests of the ability of trained analysts to use financial data publicly can be derived from studies of the performance of mutual funds and research departments of brokerage houses. F. E. Brown and Douglas Vickers, William Sharpe, and Michael Jensen studied the performance of mutual funds compared to that of random selections of securities with similar risk characteristics. They used different techniques and all came to the same conclusion. Mutual funds do not earn for their investors a higher rate of return than would have been earned had the investors held a similarly diversified market portfolio, gross of research costs. Nor is the record of the research departments of brokerage houses any better. A study by R. E. Diefenback of the market performance of stocks whose purchase or sale was recommended by twenty-four institutional research services found that their recommendations, if followed, would have yielded returns equivalent to those earned by investments in the Standard and Poor's (S and P) 425 Index. Thus, even mutual fund and brokerage house research department analysts do not benefit from detailed analysis of SEC reports, among other data.

Even though the evidence reviewed does indicate that the financial reports required by the SEC, when made available, have almost no information content, this does not prove that the required disclosure is not valuable to investors. One might argue that the statements provide a confirmation of data previously released. Because investors know that a corporation's sales, operating expenses, extraordinary gains and losses, assets and liabilities will be reported, they may have some assurance that the preliminary reports, press releases, etc., are not prevarications. Thus when the financial statements are made public the data they contain are fully anticipated. But had it not been for the SEC's disclosure requirements, such a state of affairs might not exist. It is to this consideration that I turn next.

V. An Empirical Analysis of the Effect of the '34 Act on NYSE Securities

When the Securities Exchange Act was enacted in June 1934, the United States was in the midst of the Great Depression. Hence, it is difficult to separate the effect of the legislation on the stock market from other economic events, and the effect of the disclosure requirements of the Act from its other provisions. In addition, it is necessary to determine when the legislation affected the stock market, since it might have been anticipated such that, when passed, its impact already had been discounted.

Fortunately, the data and the particular legislative history of the '34 Act allow an unusual opportunity to test the effect of legislation. Hearings on the '34 Act did not begin until February 1934, nor was there much belief before this date by most observers that such legislation would be enacted. Prior to this time, it was not considered part of the President's legislative "package." Nevertheless, the bill was signed by President Roosevelt in June 1934 and took effect that year, although full compliance did not occur within the year. Therefore, I have considered the period of adjustment to include February 1934 through June 1935. Thus there is a relatively short and distinct period over which the effect of the legislation may be measured.

The effect of the disclosure provisions of the Act may be tested by examining its differential effect on the securities of corporations that were and were not affected by the legislation. At the time of the passage of the Securities Exchange Act of 1934, about 70 percent of stock exchange transactions were made on the NYSE, 13 percent on the American (Curb) Exchange, 1.6 percent on the Chicago (Midwest) Stock Exchange, and the balance on nineteen other regional exchanges. The three principal exchanges, at least (the others didn't reply to my inquiries), had similar rules that required listed companies to send certified income statements and balance sheets to stockholders in advance of the annual meeting. The principal reporting requirement imposed by the '34 Act, in addition to the filing of detailed forms, was the required disclosure of sales. Of the 508 corporations whose stock was traded on the NYSE in 1934, 193 (38 percent) did not disclose their sales. Since sales are considered very important information by analysts, and the study reported above (Benston (1968)) found sales the only relatively important accounting number, these corporations are considered as those most likely to be affected by the disclosure requirements of the '34 Act.

Thus two samples of NYSE corporations can be distinguished: the 314 (62 percent) "disclosure" corporations and 193 (38 percent) "nondisclosure" corporations (with respect to sales). These data allow a fairly comprehensive test of the law, since the '34 Act applied (until 1965) only to corporations whose stock is traded on registered exchanges, and most of these corporations were listed on the NYSE in 1934. If disclosure of the sales data required by the '34 Act were meaningful to investors, these effects should be observed in the market returns of the securities affected in the period after the law was effective. As was discussed above in greater detail, if the data disclosed are information, investors would alter their previous estimates of the relative value and/or riskiness of the firms. . . .

Five hypotheses about the effectiveness of required disclosure can be tested with observations for the periods before and after disclosure and for the adjustment period following immediately after required disclosure.

1) Managers avoided disclosure to hide their poor performance . . .
2) Managers did not disclose because they did not realize the value of the information to investors . . .
3) Required disclosure imposes a cost on corporations without compensating benefits to stockholders . . .
4) Required disclosure results in benefits to the market as a whole because investors would prefer stocks on registered exchanges to alternative investments, such as over-the-counter stocks or real estate. However, some costs are imposed on those firms that would not otherwise have disclosed . . .
5) Required disclosure did not impose sufficient costs or benefits to be measured . . .

. . . Of course there could be costs to firms not traded at the time (such as the cost of newly registering with the SEC) or costs or benefits too small to be measured by the model. . . .

In summary, the tests indicate that the disclosure requirements of the '34 Act had a somewhat lesser effect on the securities of corporations that did not previously disclose sales as compared with those that did. This finding is inconsistent with hypothesis 1) and casts doubt on hypothesis 2). . . .

Two basic conclusions can be derived from these data. First, there appears to be somewhat less variance of the residuals of both groups during the months of the adjustment period of February 1934 through June 1935 compared to the following and preceding months. These data indicate that by the time the initial hearings on the Securities Act of 1934 were begun, the impact of the Great Depression on the revaluation of individual shares was largely spent. Second, there is little difference in the behavior of the average residuals of the nondisclosure compared with the disclosure groups. The plots (not presented) show that their residuals behaved almost the same over time, with differences between the two groups being far overshadowed by differences between time periods. . . .

From these data and the data reported above, I conclude that the '34 Act did not contribute to a reduction in the variance of returns from securities traded on the NYSE, as measured by the . . . covariance-variance ratio of security j to the market as a whole and the standard deviations of the residual returns on securities . . .

Considering the evidence presented above, I must conclude that the data are consistent only with the hypothesis (5), that the disclosure provisions of the '34 Act were of no apparent value to investors. . . .

VII. Investor's Confidence in the Market — Risk and Fairness

A major reason for enactment (and continuance) of the disclosure provisions of the '34 Act was the belief that disclosure was necessary to restore the confidence of investors in the stock market. It is obvious that depressions and the reduction of stock values (either with a "crash" or gradually over a relatively short period) reduce investor confidence and that such events have occurred before and since the passage of the '34 Act and were little affected by it. Therefore, a more meaningful (and charitable) definition of "investor confidence" might be related to the riskiness of returns from securities and to the concept of fairness, that all investors should' have equal access to financial information about a company whose shares they own or contemplate buying. Each of these somewhat related concepts is considered in turn.

A reduction of the riskiness of returns, *ceteris paribus*, is considered a benefit because this would reduce the cost of capital to firms and increase investors' confidence in the market. Both assertions are based on the belief that investors are risk averse. (Speculators may prefer risk, but they are considered by legislators to be a nonpreferred group.) Of course, disclosure, as such, cannot reduce the inherent riskiness of corporations except where disclosure reduces or prevents the risk of fraud. However, disclosure might reduce the risk to the investor of not knowing about significant events (such as a large loss, lawsuit, discovery, etc.) and/or diversifiable risk by reducing the residual variance of security returns (as is discussed above in Section V).

The evidence presented above indicates that disclosure as required by the '34 Act did not reduce fraud, nor did corporations who disclosed their sales fare better in the depression than those who didn't. The data on the variance of the securities of disclosure firms compared to that of nondisclosure firms, discussed above, indicates that the '34 Act did not have the desired effect on risk (as measured herein). The percentages of large residuals (outlyers) also provide evidence on the effectiveness of the '34 Act in reducing the risk of large, presumably unanticipated stock movements. The percentage of outlyers in the pre-SEC period was about the same for the disclosure and the nondisclosure firms. However, in the post-SEC period, there were relatively fewer mean $\pm 1\sigma$ outlyers for the disclosure group but more mean $\pm 2\sigma$ outlyers for the nondisclosure group. . . .

The concept of fairness is difficult to define operationally. The belief that all investors should have equal access to financial information about a company whose shares they own or contemplate purchasing is perhaps the most important concept, politically, that supports the federal disclosure requirements. While some writers, such as Henry Manne, have argued that investors and the economy are served better when insiders are allowed to profit from information before it is disclosed, legislators argue that all current and potential owners of a corporation have an equal right to information without regard to cost. But since any information must be available to someone before it is known to all, this is a nonoperational concept in its extreme form. And, insofar as the SEC's disclosure requirements require the publication of useless or untimely data (as seems to be the case), the '34 Act has not served its purpose.

Nevertheless, the stock market could be considered "fair" if the prices of securities at any point in time are unbiased estimators of their intrinsic values, at least with respect to the financial data which corporations must disclose under the '34 Act. Then whenever an investor decides to buy or sell or hold a security, he can be assured that the market price has discounted completely the financial information. The average investor need not worry about discovering some important financial information about which he is unaware. He will just as often find himself buying or selling a security that is "overvalued" as "undervalued." In this event, the market would be "efficient" in what Fama calls the semi-strong form of the martingale hypothesis.

Fama reviews the theory and evidence on efficient capital markets and concludes that " . . . for the purposes of most investors the efficient markets model seems a good first (and second) approximation to reality. In short, the evidence in support of the efficient markets model is extensive, and (somewhat uniquely in economics) contradictory evidence is sparse." But this evidence is based on data from years after enactment of the '34 Act. The Act may have altered the way in which information gets to the market and the speed with which it is dispersed such that a previously inefficient market became efficient.

The data presented above, that the disclosure required by the '34 Act had no measurable effect on the residual market prices of companies that did and did not disclose their sales, are consistent with the hypothesis that the market was efficient before the legislation was enacted, at least with respect to the financial data. In addition, runs tests on the signs of price changes before 1934 of the securities of the disclosure and nondisclosure corporations revealed that the price changes of both groups confirmed to a random walk. The results of this weaker test of the efficient markets hypothesis is consistent with the belief that the '34 Act did not make the stock market a "fairer game" for investors. . . .

The conclusion of this study, then, must be that the disclosure requirements of the Securities Exchange Act of 1934 had no measurable positive effect on the securities traded on the NYSE. There appears to have been little basis for the legislation and no evidence that it was needed or desirable. Certainly there is doubt that more required disclosure is warranted.

Required Disclosure and the Stock Market*

Irwin Friend and Randolph Westerfield

In his recent article in this *Review*, George Benston concludes that empirical analysis provides no support for the belief that the disclosure and related provisions of the Securities and Exchange Act of 1934 were either needed or desirable. Since Benston considers disclosure the basic reason for enactment of the 1934 Act, he is highly dubious about the usefulness of this legislation. We shall indicate that the conclusions he draws from his analysis seem faulty. . . .

Benston . . . classifies 508 NYSE stocks in the predisclosure period into two groups, one consisting of 193 stocks which did not disclose their sales versus 314 which did. Benston uses his earlier study to justify the selection of sales, maintaining it indicates that sales was the only relatively important accounting number. However, net income would seem to be the more theoretically relevant variable and in fact is the more consistently significant in its effect on price according to his earlier test, even though the estimated elasticity of price with respect to income was considerably smaller than with respect to sales.

*Source: 65 Am. Econ. Rev. 467–472 (1975), reprinted with permission. Randolph Westerfield is associate professor of finance at the University of Pennsylvania.

It is interesting therefore that (with one possible exception) all of the 193 stocks which did not disclose sales did disclose net income as well as balance sheet and other financial data, so that Benston's second set of tests does not distinguish between nondisclosure and disclosure firms but between less and more disclosure firms that trade on the New York Stock Exchange. Moreover, this type of test tells us nothing about the relative quality of disclosure for both groups of firms before and after the 1934 Act, so that with relatively moderate differences in the quantity of financial data disclosed for these two groups, changes in the quality of disclosure which are likely to affect both disclosure and nondisclosure firms similarly may well be much more important.

To distinguish between the relative performance of nondisclosure and disclosure firms after the 1934 Act, Benston estimates *beta* coefficients, residuals from the market model, and the variance of these residuals for individual stocks in both groups of firms before and after the Act. There is no evidence from the *beta* coefficients that the nondisclosure firms were adjudged relatively less risky in the post-Securities and Exchange Commission (SEC) period. This is the only substantive evidence supporting Benston's position. However, even this evidence seems weak to us, because of the question of the difference between the two groups in the degree of nondisclosure. Moreover, there are several external studies showing that current accounting data can be used to make at least as good and possibly superior forecasts of future asset risk (as measured by *beta*) than forecasts dependent only on historically estimated asset risks (see William Beaver, Paul Kettler and Myron Scholes, and Richardson Pettit and Westerfield (1972)). The accounting data which turn out to be useful for this purpose are balance sheet and income account items other than sales.

Before leaving this discussion of the impact of the 1934 Act on stock *betas*, we should point out that of the three ways the Act might be expected to affect the level and variability of stock prices — through effects on expected return, *beta* coefficients, and residual variability — *beta* coefficients, which measure the covariability of returns on a stock with those on the market, would be expected to be affected least. We have indicated that Benston's analysis suggests that the 1934 Act did improve estimates of expected return. We turn now to its apparent impact on residual variability.

The residuals from the market model in this second set of tests, derived from regressions for each stock fitted to the entire pre-SEC and post-SEC periods covered, seem to indicate that both disclosure and nondisclosure firms performed better in the post-SEC than in the pre-SEC periods in the sense that residual risks were reduced for both groups of firms. The algebraic and absolute means of these residuals were computed for disclosure and nondisclosure firms separately for each of four pre-SEC periods, for an "adjustment period" (representing the estimated time between congressional action on the bill and "full compliance"), and for three post-SEC periods. The absolute means of these residuals, which seem more meaningful than the algebraic means, exhibit a steady increase throughout the pre-SEC periods both for disclosure and nondisclosure firms, turn downward in the adjustment period and then continue at the lower level thereafter, with a lower absolute mean in the post-SEC than in the pre-SEC period.

The pattern of the algebraic means is also revealing. In the four periods before the transition period there is no significant difference between disclosure and nondisclosure firms, although in each period the difference is negative. However, in the first period after the transition period, July 1935–June 1937, the difference between the algebraic means of the residual terms for the disclosure and nondisclosure firms becomes positive and is greater than the differences observed in the other periods. In the subsequent two periods the residuals become negative. Thus, in only one period are the differences in residuals positive. Moreover, this difference appears in the first period after the disclosure legislation (which is the critical period if adjustments and revaluations take place quickly) and does not support Benston's conclusion that the 1934 Act had no effect on stock market prices. In contrast, the results tend to support the hypothesis that managers avoided disclosure to hide their poor performance. The mean of the standard deviations of residuals is also lower in the post-SEC period for both groups of firms.

Thus Benston's conclusion that " . . . the '34 Act did not contribute to a reduction in the variance of returns . . . as measured by . . . the standard deviations of the residual returns on securities . . ." may be questioned from his own results. It may also be questioned on the basis of a more comprehensive analysis carried out elsewhere which regresses on time the standard deviation of residuals (of the capital asset pricing line) from a series of cross-section relationships of portfolio monthly return and risk for twenty-one periods of twenty-four months each from July 1926 through June 1968. This study finds a statistically significant downward time trend in these residuals. This analysis avoids many of the problems affecting the Benston analysis. . . .

Benston's last argument relating to the impact of the 1934 Act on fairness is similarly flawed because he draws no distinction between efficiency and fairness in the stock market. While his definition of fairness is not clear, it would appear from his reference to Eugene

Fama's "semi-strong form of the martingale hypothesis" that Benston considers a market fair in which corporate insiders make large profits at the expense of other investors so long as this is accomplished quickly.

In fact, none of his tests is relevant to the fairness of the market as between corporate or market insiders and public investors. Yet corporate investors who have access to inside corporate information and stock exchange specialists who have access to inside market data are the only two groups in the market who apparently receive above average returns in the market (see Friend and John de Cani, and Fama). It is our strong impression, based on a reading of congressional reports, scholarly studies, newspaper articles, and many discussions with professionals in the market, that the ability to take advantage of inside information and the relative profitability of corporate insiders and specialists in the pre-SEC period were much greater than in the post-SEC period. Clearly this would not be reflected in Benston's analysis, which does not distinguish between the experience of insiders and outsiders.

Benston's analysis is relevant (though deficient) to whether disclosure improved certain types of market efficiency, but not to whether disclosure improved fairness as between insiders and the public. . . .

Required Disclosure and the Stock Market: Rejoinder*

George J. Benston

Irwin Friend and Randolph Westerfield's (F-W) comment on my article is appreciated. . . . For the reader's convenience, the order of their presentation is followed and the most succinct expression of their criticism, wherever possible, is quoted for reference. . . .

6. " . . . net income would seem to be the more theoretically relevant variable [than sales]. . . . " It should be noted that virtually all companies who were affected by the 1934 Act reported net income. Sales was the principal important datum not generally disclosed before the Act and therefore whose disclosure was mandated, de facto, by the Act.

7. " . . . changes in the quality of disclosure which are likely to affect both disclosure and nondisclosure firms similarly may well be much more important." Granted. Unfortunately, neither F-W nor anyone else, to my knowledge, has defined "quality of disclosure"

*Source: 65 Am. Econ. Rev. 473–477 (1975), reprinted with permission.

operationally or offered any evidence of greater quality after than before passage of the 1934 Act. . . .

11. "We have indicated that Benston's analysis suggests that the 1934 Act did improve estimates of expected return." I have been unable to detect where in their comment F-W so indicate. Indeed, F-W do not question the key finding that the residuals (which measure changes in the returns on securities) over the adjustment period are initially the same for companies whose financial reporting were and were not affected by the Act. . . .

16. " . . . Benston considers a market fair in which corporate insiders make large profits at the expense of other investors so long as this is accomplished quickly." I never said this, though given profitable insider trading (which regulation apparently has not eliminated; see Jeffrey Jaffe), it would be better if whatever information the insiders had was impounded in the market price of shares as quickly as possible. The sooner the information is reflected in the prices, the sooner the price at which outsiders buy and sell is "fair." In any event, I know of no reasoning or evidence that supports the assertion that the amount of insider profits or the probability of their occurrence is affected by required disclosure of corporate financial statements.

17. "It is our strong impression, based on reading of . . . [cited material] that . . . [insider profits] in the pre-SEC period were much greater than in the post-SEC period." I have reviewed most of the cited materials and have found no more than anecdotes and assertions. Since specific page references were not provided by F-W, I was unable to check my memory. Apparently we both have formed very different impressions based upon roughly the same "evidence." However, to my knowledge there have been no empirical tests performed which have measured the extent of the insider trading profits in the pre- and post-SEC period. Until these measurements occur, F-W and I merely hold different subjective opinions.

NOTES AND QUESTIONS

1. Neither Stigler nor Friend and Herman make use of the capital asset pricing model and efficient market theory, which at that time (1964) was just being developed. Viewed in the light of that theory, however, it is apparent that they all assumed that the pre-SEC portfolio and the post-SEC portfolio of new issues had the same degree of sensitivity to market price changes, and indeed that their riskiness was identical to that of the overall market — in technical

terms, that they had a beta coefficient of 1.0. This is what is implied by their direct comparison of index numbers based on the movement of new issue prices relative to the movement of market averages. To the extent that their implicit assumption was incorrect, the price relatives on which they based their conclusions would be inaccurate. Empirical studies indicate that the beta of new issues is considerably higher than 1.0; see R. Ibbotson, Price Performance of Common Stock New Issues, 2 J. Fin. Econ. 235 (1975).

2. Did either Stigler or Friend and Herman adequately specify the theory underlying their interpretations of the findings of the study? Their measure of the success of SEC securities regulation is an increase in returns to investors in new issues, which under the capital asset pricing model would imply an *increase* in the market risk of the portfolio of new issues. Why would one expect the mandatory disclosure of information, by hypothesis of value to investors, to lead to an increase in either the mean or the variance of estimates of the market risk of new issues?

3. Even if the disclosure requirements of the SEC for new issues benefited investors to a discernible degree, the costs of disclosure also have to be taken into account. *If* the SEC requirements constitute a more efficient collective method of supplying to the market information whose value exceeds its costs, there is a net social gain; in effect, the aggregate transactions costs of the public capital market have been lowered — to the benefit of issuers, not investors. In that case, the recourse to that market should be facilitated and the role of public financings should increase. Can that hypothesis be tested empirically?

4. If Benston's conclusions are correct, and the reporting requirements created by the Securities Exchange Act of 1934 did not generate additional information of value to investors, did they work to the benefit of some other group? For example, did the provisions of the '34 Act "restore public confidence" in the securities markets, to quote a familiar refrain from SEC releases, and thereby increase trading volume and the profitability of brokerage firms? If so, that should increase the value of the (fixed) number of seats on the New York Stock Exchange. A time series study of the behavior of stock exchange seat prices showed an unexpected *fall* of about 50% immediately following the February 1934 introduction of the Act in Congress. G.W. Schwert, Public Regulation of National Securities Exchanges: A Test of the Capture Hypothesis, 8 Bell J. Econ. 128-50 (1977).

If neither investors nor exchange member firms benefited from the '34 Act, what accounts for its passage? Clearly further examination of these studies, or of the theory of regulation, is needed. See

R. Posner, Theories of Economic Regulation, 5 Bell J. Econ. & Man. Sci. 335–58 (1974).

5. As these articles indicate, a demonstration of the benefits of mandated disclosure has proved considerably more elusive than might have been supposed. Has the time come for the Commission to start displaying an active interest in encouraging such research, both externally from academic sources and internally from its recently created Directorate of Economic and Policy Research and an awareness of the conclusions being reached? Each individual study has its limitations of technique and interpretation, however, so it takes an accumulation of findings pointing in the same direction to be at all convincing. Has that accumulation reached sufficient dimensions that the SEC should no longer proceed on the assumption, cast in the form of an unsupported finding, that the (unevaluated) benefits of some additional disclosure requirement always outweigh its (unevaluated) costs?

Index